# DIPLOMAT IN KHAKI

*Frank Ross McCoy in France, 1919. (Courtesy National Archives)*

# DIPLOMAT IN KHAKI

Major General Frank Ross McCoy and
American Foreign Policy, 1898–1949

A. J. BACEVICH

University Press of Kansas

Published by the University Press of Kansas (Lawrence, Kansas 66045), which was organized by the Kansas Board of Regents and is operated and funded by Emporia State University, Fort Hays State University, Kansas State University, Pittsburg State University, the University of Kansas, and Wichita State University

Library of Congress Cataloging-in-Publication Data

Bacevich, A. J.
    Diplomat in khaki: Major General Frank Ross McCoy and American
foreign policy, 1898–1949 / A. J. Bacevich.
        p.    cm.—(Modern war studies)
    Bibliography: p.
    Includes index.
    ISBN 0-7006-0401-4 (alk. paper)
    1. McCoy, Frank Ross 1874–1954. 2. Diplomats—United States—
Biography. 3. Generals—United States—Biography 4. United
States. Army—Biography. 5. United States—Foreign relations—20th
century.  I. Series.
E478.M456B33  1989
327.73'0092—dc20                                        89-5749
[B]                                               CIP

British Library Cataloguing in Publication Data is available.

Printed in the United States of America
10  9  8  7  6  5  4  3  2  1

The paper used in this publication meets the minimum requirements of the American National Standard for Permanence of Paper for Printed Library Materials Z39.48-1984.

To Nancy

# Contents

# Preface

According to the standard view, the United States Army before World War II occupied only a peripheral place in American life. Scholars have tended to dismiss American soldiers before 1941 as enjoying neither influence nor popularity. Apart from intermittent emergencies, political authorities in Washington before that time seldom showed interest in military affairs or in the army as an institution. The nation's military posture—measured by the beggarly state of the regular establishment surviving between periodic military adventures—stemmed in part from the geographic invulnerability of the United States. The absence of any credible threat to American security made an army of European scale unnecessary. Yet historians advancing this interpretation regularly cite two other influences on American military policy. The first concerned the way Americans have traditionally viewed the use of force, a view springing from a long-standing tendency to see war and peace as distinct and wholly separate phenomena. A corollary of this notion was that only war legitimized the use of force in international politics; once war ended, force became impermissible. One historian summarized American thinking about force this way: "In the night of war the soldier by 'victory' restored the peace which the statesman had somehow lost. With the dawn of peace, the soldier marched back to his barracks, and the statesman resumed the direction of affairs. There was little in this view for politics in time of war and very little for force in time of peace."

The second influence, related to the first, was the idea that military and democratic values were antithetical and that a large standing army constituted a threat to liberty. This alleged antagonism enforced upon soldiers an isolation from the mainstream of American life. Generations of scholars have accepted popular antimilitarism and the soldier's consequent estrangement from society as cardinal determinants of American military history. This notion of alienation defined and stunted the study of American civil-military relations, reducing it to an extended debate as to the effects of the military's supposed isolation.[1]

Recently, historians have begun challenging this interpretation. Pioneering studies by Richard D. Challener, John Morgan Gates, Peter Karsten, Richard H. Kohn, Paul A. C. Koistinen, Jack C. Lane, and others have enlarged our understanding of the military's role in American life. These writers do not constitute a coherent "revisionist school." Yet they question whether American views about the utility of force were quite so naive as they are often portrayed, and they reject the assumption of a military establishment divorced from society. They have sought to redefine the tenor of relations between soldiers and civilians and to integrate the military into the overall fabric of American history. Cumulatively, their efforts make it impossible any longer for Americans to see themselves as a uniquely unwarlike people with a military heritage composed of long intervals of peace interrupted only by occasional outbursts of crusading idealism.[2]

This study employs biography as a vehicle to explore further some of the issues raised by these revisionists. Its twofold aim is to examine the relationship between American military and political elites and to assess the army's contribution to American foreign policy during the half-century following the Spanish-American War. Its subject, Maj. Gen. Frank Ross McCoy, was an army officer whose extraordinarily diverse career spanned the nine administrations from William McKinley to Harry S Truman. A leader of proven skill and courage in battle, McCoy did not march back to his barracks when war ended. In the absence of declared war, he played a recurring role in the ceaseless conflict of international politics, first as an aide or junior assistant and later as an advocate or principal in his own right. Adept at the noncoercive methods of diplomacy, he also understood the utility of force to achieve policy objectives even in peacetime.

This book focuses on the periods of McCoy's life that fall between wars. As a result, it departs from the tendency of conventional military biography to stress combat episodes in which the subject figures prominently. One consideration shaping this narrative was my desire to show how McCoy's close connections with men such as Leonard Wood, Theodore Roosevelt, and Henry L. Stimson enabled him to enjoy a long and fruitful career as an agent of American diplomacy. Of course, when deploying as an expeditionary force to Cuba in 1898 or to France during World War I, the army in which McCoy served was functioning as a political instrument, a fact overlooked by those who insist on seeing American wars as righteous crusades. For the purposes of this study, however, McCoy's participation in those wars is less important than his role in peacetime missions to Latin America or the Far East. For there, too, and with much greater frequency, the army served as an instrument of the national purpose.

I alone am responsible for any errors of fact or interpretation contained herein. Many others have contributed to the preparation of this work, however, and deserve credit for whatever merit it may possess. I would be remiss if I failed to express my appreciation for their assistance and support. My earliest debt is to Col. Paul Miles, who first brought Frank McCoy to my attention. At the United States Military Academy where I began this book, Brig. Gen. Thomas E. Griess and Brig. Gen. Roy K. Flint, at that time the head and deputy head respectively of the Department of History, provided sympathetic interest that enabled me to devote my summers at West Point to research and writing. Richard D. Challener and Arthur S. Link both read the manuscript at an early stage, providing valuable guidance and direction. Col. James L. Abrahamson carefully read each chapter as it was drafted, provided gentle criticism where necessary, and offered encouragement throughout. I learned much from him, of a scholarly nature and otherwise, and will always cherish our association. Deborah Bittle and Myrna Watkins typed different versions of the manuscript and saved me from innumerable errors. The staff at the University Press of Kansas provided the right mix of advice along with sympathetic understanding of the sort needed by an author whose daily endeavors involve the American army's present-day concerns rather than its past.

Jenny, Amy, Andy, and Kate generously permitted "the mole" to work at his desk for long hours without discernible purpose. Their frequent queries as to whether or not the final chapter had yet been completed provided a useful spur to bring things to a close. My greatest debt, however, is to my wife, Nancy. In this, as in all other endeavors, her patience, confidence, and affection sustained me.

A. J. Bacevich
Wellesley, Massachusetts

# 1

# The Road to Kettle Hill

At an early age, the boy learned to revere those dedicated to serving their country. He also acquired an unshakable faith, typical of his time, in his country's greatness, as evidenced by its indisputable economic, political, and racial superiority. He attributed that superiority in no small measure to the efforts of those great leaders who appeared at critical moments to guide the nation to its destiny. As a graduating senior in June 1892, he summed up these conclusions of his boyhood in an address to his high school class. Love of liberty had always been a peculiarly Anglo-Saxon trait, he told his schoolmates, adding expansively that even "two thousand years ago our ancestors worshipped freedom and [had been] ready to fight to the death" for it. For centuries, Englishmen had kept alive the fire of liberty. After the discovery of the New World, colonization "fanned [it] into an unquenchable flame." This transplanting of English values across the Atlantic had profound consequences. From it emerged a new society: a people with an air of freedom that generated "an intense and persistent energy, distinctly American"; an economy "fifty years ahead of Europe in progressiveness" yet still "advancing at a rate which no other has ever equalled"; and a political system that shone as "the World's Charter of Liberty." Such achievments, however, had not come cheaply. They owed their existence to the sacrifices of the "great and noble men" who had led the country and to those citizens who served it in time of need.[1]

Such windy patriotism, of course, has long typified American commencement-day oratory. But for Frank Ross McCoy, the sentiments expressed were heartfelt. They reflected the ideals distilled from his youth. More important, they summarized beliefs that were representative of his generation. These beliefs sustained McCoy throughout a long career in which he played a noteworthy role in twentieth-century America's attempt to graft its values onto an unreceptive world. They carried him into the councils of the "great and noble men" of his own day whose views often paralleled his own. Such ideals would not always serve the young man or the United States well, but to both they imparted a sense of confidence and direction that withstood decades of erosion.

McCoy's heritage befitted such beliefs. For generations after his great-great-grandfather Thomas had emigrated from Scotland to central Pennsylvania in the eighteenth century, his family prospered as prominent residents of the Juniata Valley west of Harrisburg. The McCoys had early established a tradition of patriotic service: Thomas's five sons fought in the War for Independence, with William, great-grandfather of Frank, being captured while a member of the Seventh Pennsylvania Regiment. William's son, John, served with the militia during the War of 1812, and his grandson, Thomas Franklin McCoy, twice interrupted a successful legal practice for military service, first campaigning in Mexico with Winfield S. Scott as an officer of the Eleventh U.S. Infantry (Juniata Guards) and later returning to uniform in 1861. Beginning the Civil War as a lieutenant colonel and his state's deputy quartermaster, Thomas McCoy rose to the rank of brevet brigadier general, commanding the 107th Pennsylvania Volunteers.

After the war, General McCoy returned to Lewistown, Pennsylvania, and married Margaret Eleanor Ross. On October 29, 1874, Mrs. McCoy gave birth to the couple's first child, Frank Ross. The boy's early years in Lewistown were uneventful. He suffered through the usual childhood diseases—scarlet fever, diphtheria, and pneumonia—and although small, pursued the usual childhood games with élan. An unexceptional student, Frank possessed a lively curiosity that made him an avid reader. His relations with his parents, especially his mother, and with his younger sisters and brother were warm and affectionate. The McCoys raised their children to be responsible citizens and devout Presbyterians. But to a young boy thrilling to the military exploits of his forebears, patriotism and service were the values that suffused his childhood. Mexican colors captured at Chapultepec and the sword worn by his father as a heroic regimental commander were displayed prominently in the house, reminding him of the family's martial tradition. It is hardly surprising, then, that the high school graduate of 1892 had already decided upon a military career of his own by seeking entrance to the U.S. Military Academy.[2]

Gaining admission to West Point proved to be no easy task. Although McCoy received an appointment from Congressman Thad Mahon of Pennsylvania's Eighteenth District, the prospective cadet still had to pass a rigorous entrance examination. To qualify, he had first to meet the academy's exacting physical standards. McCoy's first attempt to do so ended in dismal failure. The army surgeons who examined the slight, 120-pound candidate classified him as flat-chested, nervous, and suffering from irregular "heart-action" indicating "probable valvular trouble." In short, McCoy was unfit for military service. Undaunted, he traveled to Highland Falls, New York, outside the academy's main gate, and there enrolled in Braden's Preparatory School to cram for the entrance exam and undergo a medical reexamination. His persistence paid off. By the summer of 1893, he had overcome both hurdles and on June 21 joined the Corps of Cadets as a member of the class of 1897.[3]

Faithfully adhering to the regimen that Sylvanus Thayer had devised in the 1820s, West Point had achieved renown as a school of engineering as much as of military science. Yet the academy that Frank McCoy entered in 1893 had stagnated. Once it reached the zenith of its prestige during the Civil War, its leaders—above all, the powerful Academic Board—became increasingly reluctant to tamper with the system credited with securing the institution's past success. At a time when American higher education was undergoing far-reaching modernization, West Point, once a center of academic innovation, stood still. Failing to keep pace with the latest developments in the sciences and engineering or to broaden its curriculum to include the humanities, it succumbed to mediocrity.[4]

The Academic Board rationalized the institution's educational shortcomings, claiming that the curriculum was designed, in the words of one member, "not at all for its utility," but "chiefly because of its value in mental discipline and development." Thayer's latter-day disciples viewed the academy's purpose as character building rather than education. According to Prof. Charles W. Larned, West Point's scholastic inferiority mattered little because as "a school of character" its genius remained undiminished. Larned and his colleagues believed that the key to character development lay in isolating their charges from the civilian world's harmful "atmosphere of commercialism" while immersing them in an environment of hard work, high standards, and integrity. Above all, the cadets learned to respect authority: "The entire existence of the Cadet is one of subordination," observed Larned. The faculty's contribution to this process was not to teach but to train, employing methods that were frankly coercive. The goal was a system of virtually total control, requiring of the cadets "a rigid accountability for every moment of their time and every voluntary action." Those who survived this ordeal to receive their commissions would have acquired the soldierly attributes of obedience, self-discipline, courage, and honor while being "free from the bias of either political or commercial interest." They would have become something distinct from the average American.[5]

McCoy's encounter with such grim high purpose probably did him little harm and may even have provided occasional benefit. Yet in thoroughness and intensity, the overall experience fell short of Professor Larned's intentions. As his later career would amply demonstrate, McCoy did master the military virtues somewhere along the line. Whether he did so as a result of attending the academy, or despite it, is difficult to say. He had come to West Point, after all, already professing a commitment to those values that Larned strove so mightily

*McCoy as a cadet, U.S. Military Academy, class of 1897. (Courtesy U.S. Military Academy Archives)*

to inculcate. McCoy wanted to be a good soldier—honorable, loyal, and brave. While still at home, he had acquired the rudiments of obedience and self-discipline. At most, the military academy may have reinforced certain traits that already characterized McCoy and most others who sought admission.

Character building aside, McCoy did his best to enjoy West Point. Years later, he complained of the academy's narrow education and its narrow point of view. But throughout four years as a cadet, he avoided academic trouble, remaining comfortably near the middle of his class. Poor in mathematics and engineering, he fared better, though not brilliantly, in foreign languages and the single history course offered. He devoted much of his time to books unrelated to schoolwork. Despite his small size, McCoy earned his varsity "A" as a baseball outfielder and catcher. He participated in other extracurricular activities and earned a reputation for being socially adept. (The caption of his *Howitzer* yearbook portrait reads: "I am the very pink of courtesy.") He also displayed the sort of mild rebelliousness guaranteed to win the regard of his peers. In the summer of 1893, for example, he organized his fellow plebes into a short-lived movement to subvert the "obsolete and effete" fourth-class system that made West Point's first year particularly excruciating. Such exploits helped him garner an impressive total of 356 demerits over the course of four years. His most recurrent delinquency was tardiness—he was reported late or absent 106 times—but other offenses ranged from smiling in ranks and yelling in the latrine to "allowing members of [his] company to sit on tents and crow in a ridiculous manner" while at summer camp. Yet McCoy's relations with the tactical department remained cordial enough for him to be named a cadet company commander as a first classman.[6]

Perhaps the high point of McCoy's cadet career occurred in August 1893 when Chicago feted the Corps of Cadets for ten days at the Columbian Exposition. At the fair, according to one newspaper, the cadets availed themselves of "breakfasts without number, flirtations by the score, dinners that test the liver, hops and receptions at the rate of three a night, concerts, and bathing in the lake." According to another account, "acres of people . . . jammed, pushed, and mauled themselves in a wild effort to see the West Point cadets" at evening parade. "The

*A thrilling moment for a young West Pointer: the Corps of Cadets on evening parade at the Columbian Exposition, August 1893. (Courtesy Library of Congress)*

crowd was simply beyond human ken." The Corps of Cadets, concluded another reporter, "attract[ed] more attention from world's fair visitors than any other exhibit."[7] The experience made a lasting impression on McCoy. "Never," he reported to his parents, "has a body of young men been treated in such a royal manner." "Nearly every concern there from the 'Ferris Wheel' to the Beduin [sic] and Java Villages had special performances for us. . . . At such times they always treated us to refreshments and I think I have eaten something from every nation on the globe. . . . One would think," he added, "that the 'Corps of Cadets' were the only people around."[8]

Despite the supposed unpopularity of American soldiers, and despite the physical and intellectual isolation that Larned and his colleagues believed to be the hallmarks of the West Point experience, the young cadet who carefully preserved his newspaper clippings of the fair had gained an inkling of the ambiguity with which his countrymen viewed the military. He had listened to Americans cheering that special group of soldiers to which he belonged, celebrating its members as exemplary representatives of the nation. Perhaps as a result, the crabbed perception, common among many soldiers, that popular hostility inevitably left the army ignored and unappreciated would never persuade McCoy. Nor would he accept the usual corollary: that such sentiments perforce confined military men exclusively to that narrow role defined by their specific area of expertise. The fair gave McCoy a glimpse of the potential for a military elite to assert for itself a broader part in national life. It was the most important lesson he was to take from his years as a cadet.

McCoy survived West Point, finishing thirty-fourth in a class of sixty-seven. Notwithstanding his frail appearance—the doctor performing his graduation physical pronounced him sickly and emaciated—he was commissioned a second lieutenant of cavalry in June 1897. Two months later, he reported to his first station: Fort Meade, South Dakota, home of the Eighth U.S. Cavalry. At that desolate post, McCoy might have remained indefinitely, his enthusiasm and ambition waning in the face of the tedium of garrison life. Within a year, however, war intervened to save him from that fate and to set him off on an adventure that ultimately changed the place of the United States in the world as well as the army's place in America.[9]

From his distant vantage point at Fort Meade, McCoy followed the course of the Cuban imbroglio that progressively threatened to involve the United States. More than a bit of a jingo, he applauded the gradual toughening of the American position toward Spain, confident that such a policy would have "a salutary effect on the greasers." Once American toughness culminated in war in April 1898, McCoy's only interest was to get into the fight. He requested and received an immediate posting to the Tenth U.S. Cavalry. As one of the army's two black cavalry regiments, the unit was generally considered an inferior assignment for an officer, despite the superb record of the Buffalo Soldiers. In this instance, however, racial fastidiousness was less important than the fact that the War Department had slated the Tenth Cavalry to participate in the liberation of Cuba.[10]

McCoy joined his new unit at Camp Thomas, Georgia, on May 9 and was assigned to Troop A, commanded by Capt. William H. Beck. The young lieutenant found his regiment engaged in a crash program of training raw recruits who were steadily trickling in to fill the unit to its wartime strength. Sweltering in heavy woolen uniforms brought from their home station in Montana, the regiment's veterans were still better off than the new arrivals, who showed up with only the clothes on their backs and thus had to be furloughed home to retrieve the underclothing that the army could not provide. Less than a week after McCoy arrived, the entire unit interrupted its routine to entrain for Lakeland, Florida. Here, as at Camp Thomas, shortages of equipment and experienced leaders, the lack of a well-defined training program, and the hostility of local whites all hampered efforts to prepare for combat. Yet within a month, the regiment moved again, this time leaving its horses behind as it traveled to Tampa, headquarters of the U.S. expeditionary forces. Arriving without rations— the owner of a local restaurant refused to serve the regiment because "to have colored men eat in her dining room would ruin her business"—McCoy's unit immediately crowded onto the steamer *Leona,* moored in Tampa Bay. Here the men waited, confined to ship and provided only with combat rations of canned beef, canned beans, and hardtack.[11]

After seven cramped, scorching days in the harbor, the Tenth Cavalry set sail with the rest of General William Shafter's Fifth Corps. Although it gave the impatient cavalrymen a psychological boost, putting to sea neither eased the fetid conditions between decks nor improved the quality of rations. Indeed, conditions grew worse: After several days at sea, the *Leona*'s supply of water became brackish and scarcely drinkable. Finally, on June 20, the convoy bearing Shafter's force of 16,000 soldiers completed its voyage around the eastern tip of Cuba and arrived off Santiago, the principal American objective. While McCoy recovered from a bout of seasickness, the high command debated its next step. After two days of hesitation, Shafter decided to avoid storming Santiago's well-fortified heights. Instead he would put ashore at Daiquiri, 18 miles to the east.[12]

The American command managed this landing—to the extent that it was managed at all—according to what Theodore Roosevelt called the go-as-you-please principle. Because the bay at Daiquiri could not accommodate the expedition's transports, makeshift landing craft, towed by steam launches and supported by fire from a squadron of warships, delivered the army ashore. Two troopers of the Tenth Cavalry who drowned when their boat capsized in the surf became the campaign's first casualties. Horses and mules, McCoy recalled, were simply dumped into the sea and expected to make their own way ashore. Fortunately, the entire operation was unopposed, and by late afternoon McCoy's regiment had established itself on the beach in comparative safety.[13]

The following morning, while the bulk of the American force was still coming ashore, McCoy's troop joined other elements assembling to form Maj. Gen. Joseph Wheeler's Cavalry Division. This organization was not as imposing as its name suggested. Although cavalry, its troopers did not have horses, and despite the six different regiments that comprised the fighting strength of the division, its rolls numbered fewer than 2,700 officers and men. Furthermore, the division's various units had never trained together under Wheeler's control. Even so, dawn on June 23 found this composite force optimistically setting out on a reconnaissance in the direction of Santiago.

Jungle so thick that McCoy "could not see the sky overhead" slowed the Americans' advance. Yet, however halting, the movement sufficed to intimidate the Spanish forces, who fell back toward Santiago. On the morning of June 24, the Americans stumbled onto a 1,500-man rear guard at La Guasimas, a steep, well-fortified hill, thereby precipitating the campaign's first real fight. Although badly outnumbered, two squadrons of regulars, one each from the First and Tenth Cavalry, supported by the Rough Riders of the First Volunteer Cavalry, attempted a coordinated assault. In thick vegetation and under heavy fire, the attack by the inexperienced Americans soon dissolved into a disorganized melee. As the Tenth Cavalry's regimental historian proudly noted, however, "the men needed no leading," and they carried the position, inflicting heavy casualties on the defenders. Although one Buffalo Soldier was killed and several others were wounded, success boosted the spirits of those who had been distressed by the handling of the campaign thus far. An elated McCoy bragged to his parents of "driving the Dagoes" from the field and proudly gave credit to his troops: "The men did nobly, even the Rough Riders were as cool and brave as the regulars, and our discipline was perfect."[14]

Pushing on toward Santiago, the Tenth Cavalry reached Sevilla, 8 miles east of the city, on June 26 and bivouacked there for four days. The mismanagement that characterized the entire campaign made the pause an unpleasant one. Baggage left on the *Leona* was lost. Rations were virtually inedible and hard to come by at that. Potable water was too scarce to permit the men to wash. In the hope of reducing the risk of fevers, nearby streams were put off limits for bathing. Lacking a brush or comb, McCoy shaved his head, his "bald pate, rocky beard, and hopeful mustache" thereafter presenting an incongruous picture. The large numbers of Cubans pestering the Americans were another irritant. Like many of his compatriots, McCoy developed a low opinion of the people the army had come to liberate, dismissing them as "the most worthless . . . lot of bushwackers extant." Cuban troops under General Demetrio Castillo failed to provide promised support at La Guasimas, yet it seemed to McCoy that they were "all around when there is no fighting," useless to the Americans, "barring helping us eat our rations."[15]

By June 30, the American command had untangled itself sufficiently to resume the offensive. The San Juan heights, a range of hills running generally north to south and shielded on the east by the Aguadores River, controlled the approaches to Santiago. Spanish fortifications on San Juan Hill and Kettle Hill, the dominant features of the range, held the key to the position. Wary of a costly direct assault against these strong points, Shafter planned to launch Brig. Gen. Henry W. Lawton's division against El Caney, 3 miles north of San Juan Hill, pivoting the division to the south once success had been gained and thereby enveloping the main Spanish position. The remainder of Shafter's corps, including the Cavalry Division, would remain east of San Juan Hill and join in the attack once Lawton's force had completed its maneuver.[16]

Shafter's ambitious plan disintegrated at virtually the moment of execution. Stubborn Spanish resistance on July 1 stalled the drive on El Caney. Securing an objective that they had expected to find lightly defended cost the Americans ten hours of fighting and 440 casualties. To prevent the Spanish from reinforcing El Caney and perhaps even repulsing Lawton's attack altogether, Shafter felt compelled to release the remainder of his forces against the main objective. Here again, faulty American staff work resulted in a near debacle. To deploy to their assigned attack positions, the Americans first had to cross Las Guamas creek. But the stretch of creek below Kettle Hill contained only a single ford, reached by way of a narrow, open road that lay within range of Spanish guns. The ill-timed deployment of an American reconnaissance balloon above the road fixed the attention of any Spanish gunners who might not have grasped the importance of the target before them. As successive American units jammed into this natural bottleneck (soon nicknamed the "Bloody Ford"), they suffered heavy casualties and even panic—the Seventy-first New York Infantry simply lay down and refused to go farther. Once across, the men waited, still under fire, as commanders tried to reorganize for the assault. The frustration of such prolonged delay proved to be too much: At 12:30 P.M. and without orders, as McCoy recalled years later, the Buffalo Soldiers, along with the First Cavalry, the Ninth Cavalry, and the Rough Riders, began charging up Kettle Hill. Moving in two ranks, "crawling, running, stumbling . . . up the slope of the hill in the terrific heat, all in the face of a galling fire," the Americans routed the defenders. Nearly half of his regiment's officers became casualties during this sharp fight, but McCoy emerged unscathed. And he had done well. McCoy's "coolness and skillful performance of duty under heavy fire," reported his commander, "could not be surpassed."[17]

The occupation of Kettle Hill by no means ended the action. While consolidating their hold on the crest, the Americans continued to take fire from enemy marksmen who had withdrawn only a short distance. Sensing a counterattack, Captain Beck dispatched McCoy forward with a team of sharpshooters and instructions to "pick off Spanish officers trying to reorganize their troops." McCoy directed his patrol onto the forward slope of the hill, exposing himself to enemy view as he scanned the distance through his field glasses. An alert enemy sniper put an end to the American lieutenant's nonchalance, however, by putting a bullet in his left leg below the knee. McCoy's orderly, Pvt. Daniel Blue, himself already hit in the shoulder, hastily applied a dressing to the wound and dragged the officer to cover behind a tree.

Conscious but unable to move, McCoy watched the continuing American efforts to secure their position. "There was a din of shouting and cursing," he recalled, "as the officers urged their men on. Drivers lashed the mules and horses pulling the heavy guns and wagons. The air was filled with gunpowder smoke and the crash of shells and the whine of bullets." A battery of artillery unlimbering nearby attracted Spanish fire, making McCoy's "pleasant observation post" progressively less tenable. The commander of the First Volunteer Cavalry, Col. Leonard Wood, a military surgeon until the war broke out, saw that McCoy's wound was still bleeding and stopped to apply his own dressing to it and to order the lieutenant's evacuation. "Braced . . . up with his sympathy and interest," McCoy became "a devoted admirer from that moment."[18]

At Wood's direction, McCoy was moved to an aid station at the Bloody Ford. From there, a mule-drawn ambulance hauled him and several others back to the American coastal base at Siboney. While his comrades won the battle of San Juan Hill and the surgeons manning a hastily erected hospital cared for the critically wounded, McCoy lay untended for a full day, except for a tin cup of wine and a plate of slumgullion that he cadged from a passer-by. Eventually, McCoy was moved down to the beach in preparation for further evacuation. A whaleboat carried him out to the S.S. *Iroquois,* pressed into service as a hospital ship, but rough seas complicated the problem of transferring him to the ship. A large wave struck the ship as he was about to be hoisted aboard, dumping McCoy into the Caribbean. "I was picked up by a boat hook," he recalled, "and dragged in like a wet rat." On July 5, he finally reached Key West, Florida, and was hospitalized, by this time expressing "very thankful feelings to our heavenly Father" for having survived. Less than two weeks after going ashore at Daiquiri, "the war was over as far as I was concerned."[19]

# 2

# In Cuba with Wood

*It strikes me . . . as highly romantic,*
*that the pearl of the Antilles that Spain's grandees*
*proved unable to govern, was set on its feet*
*as a nation . . . by an ex-army doctor,*
*a second lieutenant of cavalry, a first lieutenant*
*of infantry . . . and a German-Jew top sergeant.*
HERMANN HAGEDORN TO FRANK ROSS McCOY[1]

With the Santiago campaign at an end, the men of the Tenth Cavalry departed Cuba for a detention camp at Montauk Point, Long Island, where they remained until medical authorities certified them as free from communicable diseases. Following convalescent leave, McCoy rejoined his regiment there in late August 1898. Although still a second lieutenant, he now commanded a succession of cavalry troops as the Tenth Cavalry shuttled from Montauk Point to Huntsville, Alabama, in October and then to Fort Clarke, Texas, in January 1899. His Cuban experiences having whetted his appetite for adventure, McCoy felt impatient at being relegated to garrison life. Excited by reports of an American campaign against Filipino insurgents, he wired a friend at the War Department to arrange a transfer to the Philippines with a cavalry unit "or [in] any other capacity." But no vacancies existed.[2]

In the spring, his prospects brightened when the War Department ordered his regiment back to Cuba. A sizable force had stayed in Cuba after the war to maintain order and provide a visible American presence. Many units assigned to this role encountered difficulty. Volunteers who had enlisted for the glorious war against Spain lacked the discipline and temperament for occupation duty—they wanted only to go home. Even more serious was the malaria and yellow fever that

11

were exacting a terrible toll. The War Department was counting on the regulars who replaced the departing volunteers to improve the quality of the occupation force. Army medical authorities also hoped—as events proved, in vain—that black soldiers would be immune to the tropical diseases felling so many white soldiers. Thus, the end of May found McCoy's Troop A garrisoning the town of Manzanillo, across the Sierra Maestra mountains from Santiago. He confessed to his family that closer and longer acquaintance with the Cuban people only confirmed the low opinion that he had formed so quickly and vigorously in 1898. Overall, however, he found duty with the occupation forces to be to his liking. "After two years of service in the Army," he told his parents, "after trying it in several parts of the country, in post and in the field, and enjoying all of it, I say it with a good deal of satisfaction that I'm satisfied with my lot." He added a single caveat that he was not perfectly satisfied, of course, so long as he was deprived of "so much good experience and excitement in the Phillippines [sic]."[3]

Cuba offered an excitement of its own, though of a different sort than that encountered by army officers assigned to recent Pacific acquisitions of the United States. On December 20, 1899, Maj. Gen. Leonard Wood became military governor in Havana, ending the year-long drift of American policy regarding Cuba. In sharp contrast to the modest goals and passive methods of the previous governor, General John R. Brooke, Wood inaugurated a phase of the American occupation that was ambitious in scope and dynamic in character. Unlike Brooke, Wood entered into his responsibilities with a well-defined vision. General Adna R. Chaffee, for a brief, unhappy time the new governor's chief of staff, observed that Wood was a man "impressed with the idea [that] he has a mission" in Cuba, that he had been "charged with a great transformation." The objective of that mission, in Wood's words, was "the establishment . . . in a Latin military colony . . . of a republic modeled closely upon the lines of our own great Anglo-Saxon republic." Conversion of the ramshackle former Spanish possession into a progressive, efficient society would lay the foundation for a permanent and mutually advantageous Cuban-American partnership, perhaps culminating in outright annexation by the United States.[4]

By all accounts, the conditions existing in Cuba in the early days of the American occupation were appalling. Cuban cities and towns were pestholes. Unable to provide even minimal public services, government had acquired a well-deserved reputation for inefficiency and corruption. According to Wood, the prevalence of old customs and ideas bequeathed by Spain resulted in the "entire destruction of public spirit and interest in good government." Public institutions lay in shambles. Education was without organization and of little value; prisons were so backward as to be simply medieval; medical facilities were found to be hospitals only in name; taxation was inequitable. The courts had long ceased dispensing justice: "There seemed to be an unlimited number of ways of getting a man into prison," reported Wood to the War Department, "but unless rich and influential it was difficult for him to find his way out." Most depressing of all was

*McCoy (fourth from right) as a cavalry subaltern in occupied Cuba, 1899. (Courtesy U.S. Army Military History Institute)*

the treatment accorded those least able to help themselves. The mentally ill were outcasts, with patients locked in cramped boxes that resembled large dog kennels. The young fared no better. Visiting an orphanage, Wood found children "covered with vermin. . . . Their heads were in many instances lousy, and the dormitories were overrun with bedbugs. . . . In passing through the various dormitories many of the beds were opened. The linen was found soiled with excretions, and in many cases the pillows were well stained with dried pus from affected eyes and ears."[5]

Cuba had been too long exploited by Spain and too ravaged by war, Wood believed, to act as the agent of its own salvation. To shed its colonial past and become a suitable partner for the future, Cuba needed help from the United States. In the general's view, the Americans best suited to provide that help were the military forces already on occupation duty. What Cuba needed, he wrote in 1899, was a "government of the people, for the people, and by the people, under American military supervision."[6] Soon after initiating this experiment in what a friendly journalist labeled "benevolent despotism," Wood and Chaffee embarked upon a two-week inspection trip up and down the length of Cuba. Traveling by boat, train, and horseback, Wood sought to assess personally the conditions existing throughout the island. His itinerary included a stop at Manzanillo and a visit to the headquarters of the Tenth Cavalry. As Wood prepared to leave, McCoy was detailed to escort his party as far as its next destination. This second encounter with the man he had last seen amidst the gunfire of Kettle Hill proved to be a turning point in McCoy's life.[7]

*Leonard Wood, foremost among McCoy's mentors. (Courtesy U.S. Army Military History Institute)*

To the disinterested observer, the burly, handsome, energetic Wood was a bundle of contradictions. Yet few who actually knew Wood were capable of appraising him disinterestedly. More than most figures prominent in public life, he inspired the extremes of either intense animosity or enthusiastic devotion. To his detractors, Wood was an arrogant and ambitious martinet, an insubordinate demagogue, all the more suspect for the irregular pattern of his career: educated not at West Point, but at Harvard; trained as a physician at Harvard Medical School; apparently destined for obscurity as an army surgeon until the Spanish-American War and his wartime friendship with Theodore Roosevelt vaulted him to a senior position in the line army. Wood's background and determination to make the most of his suddenly transformed career combined to give him an outlook on the army's role in national affairs that departed substantially from the narrow ethos of the old Indian-fighting army. Yet this outlook captured with striking precision the military requirements of a nation struggling with the implications of its seemingly inevitable rise to great-power status. Thus, within the army's ranks, Wood represented something like the model for a new officer.

Many senior army leaders considered Wood to be an upstart. They either did not comprehend or rejected out of hand his new model of officership. But for young officers of McCoy's generation, Wood represented an approach to military service that possessed enduring appeal. In comparison to more traditional soldiers, Wood's approach was expansive, taking for granted a broader involvement of the army and individual officers in affairs of state. Wood's approach also had an affirmative or creative aspect. He viewed the army not simply as an instrument of destruction, but as an agency of positive political and social change primarily abroad and to a lesser extent at home. The values that Wood espoused struck a responsive chord among officers searching for their place in the new empire they had helped win for the United States. They shared his enormous confidence in the rightness of American values. They were drawn to his idealistic vision of remaking societies rather than merely maintaining order within them. They admired and sought to emulate the personal qualities that he exemplified: rectitude, forthrightness, charisma, breadth of vision, a love of the outdoors, and an insatiable appetite for adventure and strenuous activity. Those who admired Wood tended either to be blind to his faults or to have an enormous capacity to forgive them.

"So often I have been disappointed on close contact with big guns," McCoy told his mother, but not so in this case. Wood was different. The former Rough Rider had already established enviable credentials as a combat leader. Now, however, it was Wood's stature as "a real statesman of high ideals and of great doings" that impressed McCoy. To a subaltern whose view of the occupation derived from patrolling back roads and chasing stray bandits, introduction to the overall dimensions of American aims in Cuba was eye opening. "What a problem this Cuban one is," McCoy wrote. Yet even brief contact with Wood convinced McCoy that the governor could overcome any obstacle: To Wood, "all of the quantities seemed to be a,b,c, [whereas] with most men they would have been x,y,z."[8]

For his part, McCoy made a similarly favorable impression on Wood. Observing the young officer dash into an uncharted river to test its fordability, Chaffee casually expressed interest in having McCoy on his staff. "I am sorry, General," replied Wood. "I have just made up my mind to have him myself." It was the sort of opportunity that an intrepid junior officer could hardly resist. On April 21, 1900, McCoy joined Wood's staff as an aide-de-camp and a member of the intimate circle of subordinates assembled to assist Wood in fulfilling his mission.[9]

As Wood's aide, McCoy accompanied his chief throughout his daily schedule and found his wide-ranging activities invigorating. As he later recalled, "Wood's routine as Military Governor was no routine at all.'' The only predictable element was the intense hour of *jai-alai* with which Wood and McCoy regularly began their day. After breakfast, the governor seldom remained in his office, instead seeking further firsthand information on existing conditions and personally inspecting projects undertaken under American auspices. In McCoy's view, the military government's earlier ineffectiveness resulted from Brooke's insistence upon operating "by system and routine, rather than by personal intervention. He did not visit the hospitals and prisons, and, therefore, he did not know of their awful condition." In contrast, "Wood visited everything everywhere," from the capital to the farthest reaches of rural Cuba, "and saw with his own eyes what had to be done." In short, "Wood's was a personal form of government."[10]

After accompanying his chief on inspection tours through most of the day, McCoy faced an evening of socializing, attending functions sponsored by well-to-do residents of Havana or helping Wood entertain dignitaries from the United States. McCoy enjoyed these encounters with the social elite, although they tested his uncertain mastery of Spanish. "The girls here talk away and we . . . look intelligent when we're groping hard at the beginning of the flow," he told his parents. "But we try to laugh at the proper time."[11]

Besides acting as Wood's aide and personal factotum, McCoy assumed specific responsibility for government finances. A recurring theme of Wood's administration was the progressive centralization of authority wielded by the military governor. McCoy's role as Wood's agent in controlling the government's disbursements and supervising its finances reflected this centralizing tendency. McCoy's financial report for the year 1900, published as part of the military governor's annual report, depicts his contribution to the efficient management of Cuban finances. The effects of Spanish fiscal practices, according to McCoy, were as dismal as the legacy of Spanish rule in general: "At the time of the relinquishment of Spanish sovereignty the [Cuban] treasury was left bare of money, and even many of the records concerning the administration of public moneys were lost." The "vicious" Spanish provisions for compensating public officials—designed, it seemed, to encourage corruption—excited McCoy's particular contempt. Graft became so widespread and pronounced that positions with *no* salaries at all were the most eagerly sought. Essential facilities, such as banks, were all but unknown. Colonial bookkeeping had ranged from sloppy to nonexistent. Standard business practices were widely ignored and, where practiced, were seldom understood or trusted. Among the common people, "a corollary to the hostility to government in general was their lack of confidence in all forms of paper."[12]

Wood's ambitious plans to remake Cuba in the American image demanded prompt eradication of corrupt and careless financial habits. Absent businesslike and efficient means of monitoring the distribution of funds, Wood risked throwing away the government's $20 million annual budget. Proper financial management thus became a precondition for overall success. In McCoy's view—

and doubtless in Wood's as well—"the loose philanthropic methods of the early days of the American occupation" permitted the dubious practices of the Spanish era to survive. Under Brooke, the occupation government's Department of Finance each month provided lump sums to Cuba's six provinces, each of which in turn distributed funds to individual municipalities based on requests prepared by local officials. These *alcaldes,* who in McCoy's eyes had all "the independence and faults of town bosses[,] . . . did not see the necessity of accounting for their expenditures, nor for making them in accordance with the specific allotments." In short, so long as requests for governmental funds were generated by the provinces and disbursed according to the whim of the *alcaldes,* the military governor in Havana could neither determine how occupation funds would be spent nor prevent their misuse.[13]

The controls that McCoy devised corrected this situation by expanding the role of the military governor at the expense of both provincial and local officials. McCoy created eleven fiscal zones, each directly responsible to the Department of Finance in Havana and hence to Wood. The chief of each fiscal zone was charged with transferring funds from the national government to local agencies and jurisdictions, thereby cutting the provinces out of the process altogether. In addition, McCoy stripped the *alcaldes* of their authority for disbursing revenues provided by the military government. Supplanting the *alcaldes* were officers of the U.S. Army, appointed as bonded disbursing officers for public activities such as hospitals, school systems, and penal institutions. Under this system, the *alcalde* received funds to pay his local police force but little else. No longer were lump sums transferred by the Department of Finance to the provinces for distribution to local municipalities. The sums given to disbursing officers were issued as checks for specified projects or activities already approved by Wood, thus reducing the likelihood of funds being diverted to unauthorized uses. And because Wood himself acted as the government's unrestricted approving authority and personally scrutinized the monthly estimates that McCoy assembled from the fiscal zones, the new system assured the military governor for the first time that resources were being used precisely as he intended. As McCoy commented, "With this system it is possible to know the exact purpose for which every cent has been allotted."[14]

Supported by McCoy's reliable system for managing the military government's financial affairs, Wood proceeded with his plan for remaking Cuba. The highhandedness and arrogance with which the general went about his task stirred controversy in his own time, and historians since have debated his underlying aims and the long-term effects of his tenure. Yet few dispute that Wood succeeded in what he set out to do and that the Cuban people benefited from the immediate fruits of that success. A hostile journalist classified the first American intervention as "a model of fine trusteeship." And the historian Philip Foner, otherwise an unrelenting critic of the American presence in Cuba, admitted that Wood's administration had "many important achievements, especially in the areas of sanitation, education, and public works.'' Under Wood, recounts Foner,

> Havana and other cities were modernized; yellow fever was suppressed; the judicial system was overhauled; municipal government reorganized; sanitary campaigns were pushed with vigor; roads were built, harbors dredged, sewers installed, streets paved and telegraph lines strung. Finally, and perhaps most important of all, public education became a reality in Cuba.[15]

From 1899 to 1902, Cuba became a workshop for American progressivism. Wood and his band of military reformers experimented with techniques that civilian progressives later applied to the United States itself. As measured by the desperately needed improvements made to everyday Cuban life, the experiment was a great success. Vastly improved public services, schools, and administrative efficiency improved the quality of Cuban life. As a result, the American occupation of Cuba acquired a humanitarian reputation unique in the annals of imperialism. Yet Wood's brand of progressivism was not as benign as the circumstances existing in Cuba permitted it to appear. Unlike many domestic progressives, Wood did not see reform as a vehicle for preserving—or, in Cuba's case, creating—democracy. Wood cared little about whether Cuban politics were undemocratic or not. What Wood did care about, and could not abide, was that nothing in Cuba worked properly—not the schools, not the hospitals, not the economy, and not the bureaucracy. Finding such chaos intolerable, he set out to provide Cuba with a rational and efficient order. With the local populace too exhausted by war to do anything but acquiesce, Wood enjoyed a remarkably free hand. This situation permitted him to satisfy simultaneously the imperatives of American control, societal efficiency, and the basic needs of the people. The Cuban experience did not show—as Wood's subsequent assignment to the Philippines would—how the army's progressives would react if forced to choose among those imperatives.[16]

From McCoy's perspective, whether the military government's policies did or did not conform to the principles of the embryonic progressive movement mattered little. McCoy viewed Wood's reforms less as a comprehensive plan to determine Cuba's destiny than as a pragmatic, expedient response to a crisis of monumental proportions. The conditions confronting Americans in Cuba were so awful, he later told Hermann Hagedorn, that ''it was no time for a theoretic economy.'' Devastated by war and revolution, Cuba required immediate relief effectively administered. This Wood delivered.[17]

McCoy did recognize that in devising remedies for Cuba and in measuring their effectiveness, the military government drew exclusively on American practices and familiar American standards. Echoing sentiments expressed by his chief, McCoy concluded his financial report for 1900 with assurances that the military government's objectives were being secured ''by the use of American methods and in conformity with American ideals." In McCoy's eyes, Americanization was not a device for fastening U.S. domination on Cuba but was simply the logical medium for ameliorating the conditions that existed in the aftermath of Spain's departure. Although later generations may find such a belief in national superiority smug and unjustified, men of McCoy's upbringing and experience considered it self-evident. Indeed, the officers who staffed the military government would not have known where else to turn for guidance. What other nation could match the achievement of the United States? To McCoy, American success in Cuba only confirmed such predispositions.[18]

At the same time, McCoy sensed that many Cubans disliked their liberators. He knew that many of the original leaders of the Cuban revolution strenuously opposed Wood (they were "jealous"); he heard the charge that American policies "were rapidly wiping out all of the old Spanish customs without regard to the wishes of the people" (though the elimination of diversions such as cockfighting, he claimed, "met with the full approval of all of the educated people"); he recognized that "the great mass of the Cubans don't know or care about the money that has been put into public works, charities, hospitals and schools." Inasmuch as everything had been "shoved down their throats," McCoy "never blamed the Cubans for this apparent lack of appreciation or gratitude." He knew that Cuban pride had been injured "by the way we talk about educating them and cleaning them and their towns." As individuals, thought McCoy, Cubans secretly harbored "that same suspicion that we so often express as to their ability to govern themselves." They resented having the Americans accomplish so swiftly a transformation of Cuba that they believed themselves incapable of accomplishing. Given such a motivation, McCoy refused to take Cuban hostility toward the military government seriously.[19]

McCoy remained with Wood until the occupation ended in May 1902. Indeed, his last official duty symbolized the end of American authority in Cuba. From atop the palace in Havana's Plaza des Armes—residence of the military governor since 1898—McCoy watched civilian officials, American troops, and thousands of Cubans assemble on May 20 for ceremonies marking the establishment of the new island republic. At noon, the harbor fortress of Cabana fired a forty-five gun salute, following which McCoy lowered the American colors for what would supposedly be the last time. "It was a hard thing to do," he reported to his mother, "—and for the General to give me the orders too!—pulling down the Stars and Stripes even in this very honorable manner."[20]

If ending the occupation—a step Wood considered premature—was more than slightly bittersweet for McCoy, his role in the army's first venture in military government profoundly influenced his life. Service in Cuba reinforced McCoy's belief in the superiority of American methods and values and in their relevance for other peoples. More important, McCoy's Cuban experiences provided an invaluable apprenticeship in civil administration, convincing him, as it did Wood's other disciples, that this was a field in which military men should play a leading role. As Maj. Hugh L. Scott, Chaffee's successor as Wood's chief of staff, concluded, "A military government is the only kind fit to cope with such conditions" as existed in Cuba. McCoy agreed wholeheartedly. As governor, Wood addressed "a great many problems which he was confident the military government could settle, but which a political government could never in the world untangle."[21]

As a result of his Cuban service, too, McCoy established himself as an intimate member of Wood's circle, an elite group that continued to expand in size and influence after 1902. Indeed, by the time he boarded the U.S.S. *Brooklyn* in Havana harbor to accompany Wood back to the United States, McCoy had become the general's closest professional confidant and virtually a member of his family. His relationship with Wood—the army's youngest general, a personal friend of Theodore Roosevelt, and a man with connections throughout Washington—all but guaranteed McCoy's career. More important, through his service at Wood's side, McCoy matured professionally. If the youthful subaltern spoiling for a fight had not altogether disappeared, he had certainly broadened his appreciation of the purposes that the army might serve even in peacetime. Wood's imprint on Cuba would fade; his impact on McCoy would endure.

# 3

# Pacifying the Moros

From Havana, Wood's entourage returned directly to Washington. McCoy's patron, while winning nationwide acclaim (in the eyes of some, notoriety) for his Cuban exploits, had also secured his integration into the regular army as a brigadier general. Finding a new assignment suited to the abilities and ambitions of such a controversial soldier presented the War Department and Wood's friend, President Theodore Roosevelt, with no small difficulties. McCoy, now a first lieutenant, and Scott, reduced to his prewar rank of captain, established an office for Wood at 1812 H Street, N.W. "Good Old Scott," as he was known throughout the officer corps, was a durable and steady if unimaginative West Pointer, class of 1876. He was stocky, tending even to stout; wire-rimmed spectacles gave him a bookish appearance that was offset by a long, ragged mustache that recalled his apprenticeship in the cavalry. During his years in the West, Scott won recognition as a master of Indian lore and sign language. In the new American empire, however, such expertise counted for naught. So, despite being senior to Wood in years of service, Scott accepted recurring employment as one of Wood's key subordinates. Standing in Wood's shadow never troubled the modest Scott; indeed, he prospered there and revived his career, his subsequent advancement to high rank surprising and delighting his many affectionate admirers. Despite the gap between them in seniority, McCoy and Scott became fast friends, joined by a mutual admiration for their general.

Having set up Wood's office, McCoy and Scott helped the former military governor assemble his final report while addressing what his official stationery termed "Business Pertaining to the Late Military Government of Cuba." Wood's desultory stay in this official limbo soon received welcome interruption in the form of an invitation to attend the Imperial German Army's autumn maneuvers. The general accepted with alacrity and set out for Europe, with McCoy assigned to follow in the capacity of aide-de-camp. "Good Old Scott" stayed behind to tie up the loose ends.[1] In mid-August, McCoy sailed from New York aboard the S.S. *Potsdam*. His voyage was uneventful but pleasant, due largely to the presence on board of Prof. Albert Bushnell Hart, the noted historian and, in McCoy's view, "the all around man of the ship, . . . starter of games, getter up of concerts, and the talker until further orders." Although the official purpose for McCoy's junket was to observe the German maneuvers, both the young lieutenant and his chief intended to exploit to the utmost a ready-made opportunity to see the rest of Europe. As soon as he arrived in Rotterdam, McCoy "started off at a rapid gait to do the old countries." After touring Holland, he joined General and Mrs. Wood in Paris, at which time the pace immediately quickened to a "fast gallop." Although it was still before daybreak when McCoy reached his hotel in the French capital, he wrote, "before I was out of the tub the Chief was in my room and we started off," visiting the Eiffel Tower, Notre Dame, the Louvre, and Les Invalides in rapid succession. Wood "sees the sights as he works and plays," observed McCoy, "on the run."[2]

As McCoy reported to his mother, both he and Wood realized keenly their ignorance of the fine arts. The spare moments provided by their undemanding three-month itinerary consequently found the two Americans—"determined to absorb all we could in a short time"—tramping through museums and undertaking pilgrimages to European cultural shrines. In addition to Paris and Berlin, their stops included Switzerland, the chief cities of Italy, Monte Carlo, southern France, and Great Britain. Reflecting on the effusive account of his travels that he was sending back to Lewistown, McCoy wondered if some might suspect that he and Wood had engaged in "little of the real soldier business" since leaving the United States. Should that be his family's view, he told his mother, "you are right."[3]

The visit to England, at least, was not entirely without serious purpose. There Wood hoped to assess a British army recently blooded by its experience against the Boers. Because Wood's own accomplishments in Cuba attracted the admiration of the British establishment, the Americans received a cordial welcome. When they arrived in London, a "pile" of invitations awaited. Besides the obligatory call on the American ambassador and a visit to the British training base at Aldershot, Wood and McCoy lunched with King Edward VII at Buckingham Palace and dined with Prime Minister Arthur Balfour; Lord Roberts, the army commander in chief; Lord Kitchener, the commander in chief for India; and General Sir John French.[4]

Despite such flattering attention by English cousins, the centerpiece of the trip remained Germany itself. Arriving in Berlin in early September, the Americans were whisked off to Frankfurt in the private railway car of Prince Henry. The kaiser's brother greeted each of them with a hearty hand-shake and a cigar and commented favorably—and accurately, thought McCoy—"about the great all around resemblance" between the kaiser and the American president. In

Frankfurt, Wood and McCoy attended a review of the Guards Corps and afterward were presented to Wilhelm II and his empress. Riding up to the imperial party in his turn, McCoy "got a handful of a Marshal's baton and the family clasp" from the kaiser, accompanied by a rapid-fire series of questions: "What branch of service do you belong to? Have you been serving in the West? How did you like Cuba?" Other encounters with the imperial family followed their return to Berlin: a "very jolly informal" dinner given by the kaiser exclusively for the American and British observers and a more elaborate affair the following evening for all foreign officers attending the maneuvers. Wood's impressionable young aide found the surroundings, the company, and the conversation dazzling.[5]

With the social amenities out of the way, the real business of the maneuvers began. Throughout the exercise, the Americans accompanied the kaiser and his party as they followed the clash of the Red and Blue forces. For McCoy, Wilhelm himself was part of the show:

> He looked his part . . . , uniformed as a red Hussar and mounted upon a splendid white Arab. There he stood upon a little knoll just as Napoleon used to stand, with his brilliant staff, the heralds and the imperial standard: like a picture of 1806. And we in our plain khaki had a little smile to ourselves as we looked at the Emperor, his officers and army, in one way at least as far behind the times as the picture he made.

Nonetheless, he warned, "you make a bad mistake if you judge the Kaiser and his army by this picture." The precision-drilled German war machine was a formidable sight and made a deep impression. Wood's experience here, McCoy believed, provided the inspiration for the general's preparedness campaign preceding American entry into World War I.[6]

The climax of the maneuvers came on the final day: an exhilarating cavalry charge, 10,000 strong, led by the kaiser himself into the flank of the retreating Blue forces. For McCoy, it was the greatest spectacle of all. He and Wood found themselves wedged between regiments of Black Hussars on one side and Grand Cuirassiers on the other and swept along by yelling, charging cavalry all around. It was a wild, bracing moment: "For four or five miles it was a mad charge over . . . plowed fields into a thick turnip patch, over a ditch and up and over and down a railroad embankment, through an orchard." Whether either American recognized the charge for the anachronism that it was, McCoy did not record.[7]

On November 1, McCoy and Wood departed for home. McCoy's first transatlantic visit and his introduction to many of Europe's leading political and military figures provided yet another episode in the continuing education that he was receiving at Wood's side. The German maneuvers offered the military equivalent of finishing school combined with a grand tour. Little further was needed to cement his position within the American military elite. And what little remained was soon accomplished.

Back in Washington, while Wood awaited a decision on his next assignment, McCoy was detailed as military aide to President Roosevelt, thereby entering the "charmed circle of his friends and playmates." McCoy's White House duties were not taxing. He reported to Roosevelt's office at 9:00 each morning to await the chief executive and, upon his arrival, reviewed with Roosevelt the day's schedule. McCoy also screened the enormous influx of books received at the White House, selecting those of likely interest to the president. McCoy's most important function lay in contributing to Roosevelt's regimen of strenuous exercise. He served as one of the president's riding companions and refereed his notorious fencing matches with Wood (substituting as a combatant when Wood was unavailable). As McCoy wearily remarked, whenever the Rough Rider tired of flailing about with wooden broadswords, "it was jiu jitsu and boxing." Assignment to the White House even in a minor capacity opened the doors of Washington's hostesses for an eligible, well-mannered bachelor. "I'm getting the dining out habit bad," he complained halfheartedly to his mother. "Every night last week there were doings." Thanks to his closeness to both Roosevelt and Wood, McCoy gained the acquaintance of cabinet members and congressmen, forging relationships that would someday pay dividends.[8]

While McCoy was enjoying Washington social life, negotiations for Wood's assignment were finally concluded. Roosevelt and Wood agreed that the latter would become the senior American military official in the Far East, assuming command of the Philippine Division in Manila. But because the current occupant of that position, Maj. Gen. James F. Wade, was not scheduled to rotate for several months, Wood accepted an interim assignment as commander of the Department of Mindanao and governor of the newly created Moro Province. Inevitably, Wood asked McCoy to join him as his personal aide. As always, the younger officer found the prospect of a new assignment exciting: "*Los Moros* are worth handling," he told his mother with misplaced confidence.[9]

To study the handiwork of the world's other imperial powers and perhaps also to compare it to his own efforts as a colonial administrator, Wood decided to tour the principal European possessions in Asia on his way to the Philippines. McCoy's first journey to Asia thus began in Boston on March 28, 1903, when he joined Wood and Scott on board the S.S. *Commonwealth* bound for Gibraltar. The Americans's route took them across southern Europe, from Vienna to Constantinople on the Orient Express, and by sea again through the Suez to the Far East.[10] Something akin to missionary fervor impelled the voyagers toward the challenges awaiting them at their new station. Wood and Scott left their families behind to follow later, so the three officers travelled unencumbered by women or children. One senses that they preferred it that way: Nothing distracted them from preparing for the job to come. During the journey, the comradeship that Cuba inspired assumed quasi-monastic overtones. The long voyage served as a rite of preparation that sharpened their shared sense of

*McCoy as aide to President Theodore Roosevelt. McCoy's admiration for Roosevelt was second only to his devotion to Leonard Wood. (Courtesy U.S. Army Military History Institute)*

purpose. The weeks spent at sea and inspecting European possessions completed the conversion of Wood, Scott, and McCoy into single-minded zealots intolerant of opposition to purposes that were in their eyes unimpeachably worthy. They sailed to the Philippines determined to play a role in a historic undertaking— converting the islands into prosperous bastions of order and Western civilization. Whatever the defects of their vision, never had more genuinely idealistic American soldiers ever set sail for distant shores.

The trip itself reinforced McCoy's confidence in the superiority of Western values and convinced him further of the need for colonial rule of backward peoples. Societies lacking the enlightened guidance of the West elicited McCoy's wholehearted contempt. Constantinople was "the filthiest, most evil-smelling city since Santiago." It had been "500 years since the Turks burst into this beautiful city, burning, destroying, and killing everything that was good, and it looks as though they've been camping out on the ruins ever since." For American khaki imperialists the compulsion to clean up such untidiness was great indeed. "I believe in the crusades," McCoy wrote, "and feel like joining one myself against the Turk and his dogs."[11]

From Turkey, Wood's party proceeded to Egypt. From this point onward, wrote McCoy, "everything has taken new interest; and much . . . may be of use to us in time and occupations to come." As Wood and McCoy took turns reading a biography of General Charles "Chinese" Gordon, their steamer made its way from Egypt to Aden and on to "the writhing mass of Bombay." An extended stay in India provided "a liberal education of the work among two hundred million people." McCoy quickly adopted the prevailing attitudes of the raj. "This punka business is rather worrying at first," he confessed. But with "natives" competing for the privilege of pulling his punka rope to stir up a bit of breeze at a wage of 6 cents per day, he concluded that it must be considered good pay for light work. And, having experienced the "keenest enjoyment of a cold bath poured over you by a naked Hindu," McCoy decided that "it's necessary and I find I'm getting hardened already."[12]

"At first sight everybody in India looks hopeless," he observed. "Millions of heathen coolies squat . . . thick over the face of the earth . . . readier to rot than to keep clean, bound down by caste, and without a ray of hope from their religion." Western rule and Western religion alone provided an optimistic note. "The only decent, clean people east of Suez are the native Christians and the British native soldiers. The British flag stands for a lot more than one knows," he commented, "and where it waves is government, good government of a kind, but it only goes so far. The work of the missionary is the rest." Despite such advances, India remained a daunting challenge. "It's a question of centuries and the British know it, and are ready to wait," McCoy believed. Although the Philippines were a small proposition in comparison, he worried lest Americans become impatient if their Pacific possession were not thoroughly Americanized overnight.[13]

From India, Wood and his companions made their way to the Dutch East Indies. "This green isle," he reported from the residence of the Dutch governor general in Batavia, "seems bright and happy and wholesome." At first, the Americans were put off by the submissiveness of the locals. Observing the way that they "went down on their heels on our approach, squatted . . . in the most servile, sickening way . . . as the almighty white man went by," McCoy reported that "it made us 'sick at the stomach.' " He noted approvingly Wood's hope that the Filipinos "take to the woods occasionally and kill off a few of us, for their rights and manliness [rather] than squat and cringe."[14]

By the time his ten-day visit as a guest of the Dutch ended, however, McCoy's views had changed. He now rated the Dutch system of colonial government as a thoroughly good one, worthy of emulation. The power and energy of the Dutch permeated the entire society. "Their civil service," thought McCoy, "is such as we should build up for our colonies." An inspection of Dutch East Indian troops provided ideas that would come in handy in the Philippines. The key to Dutch success, McCoy believed, was their assumption that "the natives are the simplest of children" and the governor general their father and protector. Having accustomed himself to the servile, cringing behavior of the local people, McCoy concluded that Java was "the richest, greenest, and happiest country we've visited."[15] From Java, Wood and his party proceeded to Singapore. There they dined with the exiled leader of the Philippine insurrection, Emilio Aguinaldo, to whom McCoy and Wood took quite a liking. "He is very much a man," observed McCoy. After Singapore, the three officers visited Hong Kong, stopped briefly at Saigon, and at last, at the end of July 1903, reached Manila.[16]

Viewed from Washington, assuming responsibility for a mere portion of the Philippines after having reconstructed all of Cuba may have seemed a simple task. In many respects, however, Wood's dual responsibilities as military commander of the Department of Mindanao and first civil governor of the Moro Province proved more demanding than anticipated. By far the largest in the Philippines, the province encompassed not only Mindanao, itself larger than Ireland, but also the islands of Basilan and Palawan, and the Sulu Archipelago, a string of several hundred lesser islands. This vast territory consisted largely of rugged mountains and uncharted jungle, penetrated by a few roads and edged by a handful of ramshackle towns. Its habitants numbered about 400,000. Of the total, perhaps 40,000 were Christian Filipinos, 275,000 were Muslims (Moros), and the remainder other non-Christians, for the most part members of primitive hill tribes. The Moros were a fiercely independent people who for centuries frustrated Spanish efforts to establish more than nominal control over the southern Philippines. That independence may also explain the Moros' inability to achieve political unity among themselves. By the time that the United States supplanted Spain, Moro society had evolved into innumerable separate tribes, each controlled by its own chief (variously called *datto, panglima,* or *hadji*) and each inflamed by a warrior tradition that required periodic warfare against believer and nonbeliever alike.[17]

From 1899 to 1903, the American administration tolerated this Moro penchant for fighting, reflecting a policy that avoided any interference with Moro internal economy and political administration. The motive for this apparent disinterest was simple. During that period, American officials were preoccupied with suppressing rebellious Filipino nationalists opposed to American occupation of the islands. In comparison with the Philippine insurrection, the disposition of the Moros was a minor question that the United States could safely defer until able to give it full attention.[18]

Despite the urgency of pacifying the northern islands, the United States took the precaution of establishing at least theoretical claim over Moroland. Toward that end, Brig. Gen. John C. Bates in 1899 initiated negotiations with the Sultan of Sulu, the Moros' powerless titular leader. The resulting Bates Agreement prescribed future relations between the United States and the Moro people. The sultan recognized American sovereignty in exchange for promises to protect the sultan's subjects, to pay him a personal annuity, and to respect his jurisdiction over criminal matters involving only Moros. The United States also pledged that Moro religious customs should be respected and implicitly recognized the Moro practice of slavery. As McCoy later conceded, the Bates Agreement "was in the nature of a *modus vivendi* until a better way of handling the Moro question could be worked out." To the sultan, however, American negotiators made no attempt to indicate its temporary nature.[19]

From the outset, American officers in Mindanao disliked the Bates Agreement, complaining that it restricted their authority. By 1903, with the Philippine insurrection crushed, such complaints gave added weight to the assertion that the time had arrived to gain full control of the southern islands. On June 1, 1903, the Philippine Commission, the central American authority in the islands, acted on this conclusion by combining into one province all areas in which Moros predominated. The commission designated a governor as chief executive of the province and vested legislative authority in a provincial council composed of the governor and his five principal assistants—none of whom in practice would be Moros. In the words of the commission's senior member, William Howard Taft, this provincial government was granted "a very large measure of discretion in dealing with the Moros." The commission did insist that the provincial council preserve "the customs of the Moros, the authority of the dattos, and a system of justice in which Moros should take part." The commission also subdivided the province into five districts—Zamboanga, Lanao, Cotabato, Davao, and Jolo— each with its own administration subordinate to the provincial government. The creation of this elaborate machinery did not mean that the Philippine Commission viewed the Moro problem as susceptible to a strictly administrative solution. Noting that union of the civil and the military power seemed admirably adapted to the Moro Province, the commission directed that there, as nowhere else in the Philippines, the civil governor and military commander were to be one and the same. Indeed, soldiers dominated the civil administration from the provincial to the district and municipal levels.[20]

On August 8, 1903, Theodore Roosevelt nominated his friend Leonard Wood for promotion to major general. Two days earlier, accompanied by McCoy and Scott (now a major), Wood had planted his headquarters at Mindanao's southern tip in the provincial capital of Zamboanga. Driven as always by enormous stores of impatient energy, the new governor quickly immersed himself in his new realm, grasping at the essence of the situation he confronted and establishing his presence at its core. Within a week, he and McCoy were far from Zamboanga, trekking through the interior of the province accompanied by a battalion of infantry. Wood used the expedition to gauge conditions in the province and, through persuasion or intimidation, to elicit pledges of fealty from local chieftains. One of a series of operations mounted in succeeding months, it permitted Wood to refine his pacification strategy while allowing McCoy to develop his own perceptions of the Moro problem.

McCoy, a captain as of August 16, held a low opinion of the Moro. Clothed in garish attire, sporting an arsenal of archaic weaponry, his visage stained with betel nut, the Moro seemed a queer figure, at once eccentric, childlike, and menacing. In McCoy's eyes, the Moros' cultural backwardness threatened to defeat altruistic American efforts to redeem them. Given "their befogged and supersticious [sic] brains," the Moros refused even to avail themselves of the medical services offered by the American military. "You mention Cholera to them and they throw up their hands with a fatalistic gesture. 'God has given and God has taken away.'" Moro polygamy and slavery, their incessant warfare, and a criminal justice system in which "the maximum punishment for murder is [a fine of] 105 dollars" fascinated and appalled McCoy. Describing Moro customs to an acquaintance in the War Department, he observed: "It is hard to realize that we are living in the same century with you law abiding American citizens." And to a friend from Cuban days he wrote: "Over here we are living in the midst of feudalism and slavery, with pirates and bloody murder." Altogether, it was an "opera bouffe performance."[21]

In the early 1900s, the army's long-standing role as a frontier constabulary loomed large in the memory of the officer corps. Not surprisingly, when officers in the Philippines attempted to relate the Moro to something more akin to their own experience, they described him as an oriental equivalent of the American Indian. Indeed, authorities in Washington viewed the Moro in much the same way. Secretary of War Elihu Root's initial guidance concerning the Moro instructed the Philippine Commission to adopt the same course followed by Congress in dealing with "the tribes of our own North American Indians." Soldiers serving in the Philippines found the analogy a persuasive one. Despite limited experience in the West, McCoy himself drew similar comparisons. Within

*Moro chieftain and warriors: primitive, fanatical, and fearless. (Courtesy National Archives)*

two months, he concluded that Americans could best pacify the Moros by adopting the methods used in taming the Indians. The military problem in the province, he wrote on September 25, "is not a hard one. The methods employed are very much the same as in handling the Indians of the Plains"; he added that the Moros were not nearly the fighting men of the Sioux and Cheyenne.[22]

Nearly a half-century after his introduction to the Philippines, McCoy recalled that it had been Rudyard Kipling "who opened up the whole Far East to the men of my time." The remark was a revealing one. A product of Western culture, McCoy thoroughly absorbed the prevailing fin de siècle assumptions of Anglo-Saxon superiority.[23] The racist preconceptions that informed the notion of the white man's burden provided the foundation of American khaki imperialism whether in Cuba or the Far East. Given such ethnocentrism, the American army's attitude toward subject peoples had two faces—one benign and one harsh. For Cuba, too exhausted by war to resist American occupation, military rule provided social uplift and efficient, well-ordered government. If the army's manner in providing these benefits was patronizing, they were still tangible improvements of no little value. In contrast to the Cubans, the Moros in 1903 were unbroken, independent, and disinclined to accept American domination. It remained for them to expose the other face of American military imperialism. The military's easy identification of Moros with Indians provided an early hint of what that face would reveal.

From the outset, Wood found the disorderly qualities of Moro tribal life and their pretensions to autonomy intolerable. In his eyes, order and acceptance of

American dominion were prerequisites to reorganizing Moro society along more efficient lines. Hence, his immediate goal upon assuming office was to overcome the Moros' penchant for looting, piracy, slave raids, and internecine warfare while securing their unqualified recognition of American authority. In his first annual report to the Philippine Commission, Wood defined his mission as one of establishing "order out of the chaos existing among the savage peoples" and bringing the province's "various and diverse elements . . . under a similar form of control."[24] McCoy agreed with Wood on the one language that would fix the Moros' attention: force. McCoy noted that some observers of the Philippine experiment speculated that Americans would become "the most popular white men with Asiatics and may be able to convey to them ideas more acceptably than any other." Personally, however, he believed that the United States would rule only by force. Given the preponderance of American military power, Wood's clique assumed that pacification would be easily achieved. From the American point of view, Moro resistance would be irrational and foolhardy. Even before arriving in Zamboanga, Wood predicted to the president that "one clean-cut lesson will be quite sufficient for them."[25]

But, if the objective of Mindanao's military commander was the straightforward one of imposing order, the aims of the governor of the Moro Province were more ambitious. Confronted with the Moros' peculiarities, American military imperialists embraced what they saw as an obligation to eliminate the uncivilized and reprehensible aspects of Moro culture—the promised restraint of the Bates Agreement notwithstanding. The Moros, fulminated Wood, were religious and moral degenerates. Their laws were "utterly and absolutely undesirable from every standpoint of decency and good government." Given that their native languages were "crude, devoid of literature, and limited in range," Wood could find no object whatever in attempting to preserve them. The Moro practice of slavery attracted especially heated attention. Although engaged in imposing colonial bondage on a people who had long enjoyed de facto autonomy, American soldiers viewed involuntary servitude among the Moros as, in McCoy's words, "beastly and repulsive beyond expression."[26] Predictably, such views led the military to expand its purpose from simple pacification to an experiment in social engineering aimed at elevating the Moro to American standards of behavior. Topping Wood's agenda of essential social reforms was the abolition of slavery.

American officers stationed in Mindanao prior to Wood's arrival backed away from proposals to tamper with Moro slavery. Although they did not approve of the practice, these Americans considered noninterference with the institution of slavery to be the only way to prevent a religious war over the issue. Wood refused to accept such a "largely passive" approach that resulted in "little influence [being] exercised upon the vicious practices of the Moros." He was determined to confront the problem directly. Thus, on September 24, 1903, Wood engineered approval by his legislative council of a measure abolishing slavery. McCoy heartily approved. "The only reason I can give for our Generals permitting slavery so long," he wrote shortly afterward, "is that they didn't . . . see the Moros enough to understand the conditions. . . . It has taken the General just two months to feel sure of the right thing to do, and to do it with life." The likelihood of Moro opposition to the law left McCoy unfazed. "It may cause fighting," he observed, "but better fight hard and often than permit it [slavery] longer."[27]

The abolition of slavery was only a first step. Wood's scheme for uplifting the Moros required the complete abandonment of the approach signified by the Bates Agreement. To gain the authority that he sought, Wood intended to abrogate the agreement. The first major military action of his tenure provided the needed pretext to do so. On November 6, Scott, by now district governor of Jolo, notified Wood that a local chief, Panglima Hassan, was causing mischief near the town of Jolo, most boldly by sniping at American survey teams working in the field. To McCoy, accompanying Wood on an arduous expedition around Lake Lanao in the interior of Mindanao, the tenor of Scott's report suggested a conspiracy to take Jolo by treachery. To Wood, in all probability, the opportunity to teach that one clean-cut lesson appeared to be at hand.[28]

Acting with deliberation, Wood abandoned his trek around Lake Lanao. After assembling several infantry battalions augmented by artillery and cavalry, he landed on Jolo on November 12. According to Scott, Hassan had no intention of running away, so the American forces might have waited a week to attack him. But Wood was eager to press the action and immediately began sweeping the area suspected of harboring Hassan. According to McCoy's account, this resulted in sharp fighting that netted 100 Moro dead within two days. The Americans easily destroyed Hassan's *cotta* (fortress), but the Moro chief himself eluded capture. On November 14, having convinced Wood temporarily to suspend operations, Scott personally tracked down Hassan in the jungle and persuaded him to surrender. "It seemed that the bloody war was finished by the colonel's fine bit of work," wrote McCoy. Later that day, however, Scott carelessly permitted his prisoner to escape, sustaining gunshot wounds to both hands in the process. "The General marched right back" continued McCoy, "captured the cotta where the Colonel had been shot, and swept the big swamp of refuge clean."

> The infantry swept over every part of it and in two days' fighting killed about 300 Moros without the loss of a man. Then Mr. Andung's turn came [another *datto*] and his cotta was taken by a pretty bit of work, with the loss of one man killed and three wounded. *The lesson will do for all time.* In the next few days the troops marched over various parts of the Island and found the most friendly and subdued lot of people on record.[29]

Wood estimated total Moro casualties at 1,000 to 1,200 killed in less than two weeks. Having thus "pacified" Jolo with dispatch, he returned to Zamboanga and immediately drafted his plea for abrogating the Bates Agreement. The Moros failed to keep their half of the bargain, Wood told Taft, citing as proof the recent fighting on Jolo. What began, he wrote, as an armed plot to massacre the garrison and inhabitants of Jolo culminated with an "attack on November 12 of between 2,000 and 3,000 armed Moros upon United States troops." Wood's description of what he called "these acts of treachery and rebellion" was luridly inaccurate. Yet the events on Jolo provided the necessary touch of plausibility to Wood's claim that "serious disorder often amounting to anarchy" would exist so long as the Bates Agreement remained in effect. On March 21, 1904, Wood received his wish. By direction of the president, the United States unilaterally revoked the treaty.[30]

Disavowal of the Bates Agreement, reminiscent of the cavalier American attitude regarding Indian treaties throughout the previous century, symbolized the shift in U.S. policy from accommodation to forcible reconstruction of Moro society. Wood moved quickly to implement this change in policy, so much so that the abrogation of the agreement in March merely indorsed a process that was by then well under way. In addition to outlawing slavery, the legislative council scrapped the Moro legal system in favor of one that conformed to American standards. It severely restricted the use of alcohol and levied a tax—called the *cedula*—of one peso on every adult male in the province. It created a school system in which English was the primary language and for which it published English-language textbooks. The council also launched a program of public works and sought to co-opt selected local leaders by appointing them as "headmen" to serve as the governor's deputies in each tribal ward. All of this the legislative council accomplished while the Bates Agreement remained nominally in effect.[31]

McCoy served on the council from late 1904 through early 1906, first as acting secretary and later as provincial engineer. In the latter capacity, he supervised the province's extensive public works program, with projects ranging from building bridges and roads to constructing schools, government buildings, and harbor facilities. Assessing the council from his perspective, he told his mother that its members operated in perfect harmony. He claimed that "never yet has there been a measure but what went through unanimously." Such unanimity reflected a harmony stemming from Wood's domination of the council and his ability to secure approval of whatever measures he put before it. Both the provincial secretary and the engineer were always army officers, chosen like McCoy for their loyalty to Wood. If ever the council deadlocked on a motion, Wood's vote counted twice. The result guaranteed a majority for Wood at all times, making opposition by the council's three civilians quixotic at best. In practice, moreover, Wood seems to have encountered little difficulty in persuading the council's civilian representatives to defer to his views—the superintendent of education, Najeeb M. Saleeby, being an occasional exception.[32]

Nor was there doubt in Wood's mind as to the ultimate aim of these reforms. His objectives were precisely those that the Philippine Commission had earlier enjoined him to avoid. As the prohibition of slavery showed, Wood intended to recast the Moros's culture into a version compatible with Western standards. McCoy called it "educating them away from . . . customs of which the American mind disapproved." To accomplish this goal, Wood sought to undercut the position of the *datto,* whose authority made him the linchpin of the old tribal system. This objective found expression in Wood's plan to convert the Moros into a nation of yeoman farmers integrated into a cash-crop economy. "Our policy," wrote Wood in Janaury 1904, "is to develop individualism among the people and . . . [to] teach them to stand upon their own feet independent of petty chieftains." Toward that end, Wood intended to distribute to the head of each Moro household 40 acres of land for cultivation. To provide the Moros with models for emulation and to stimulate their ambition for better surroundings, the American governor also hoped to recruit "desirable immigrants" from Europe or the United States.[33]

Wood offered further encouragement to his would-be yeomen by guaranteeing a market for their produce. He created government-supervised commodity exchanges, first in Zamboanga and then elsewhere in the province. McCoy viewed the exchanges as "a great thing." He termed them "the best sort of charity, and really the only kind needed in the Philippines, . . . teaching [the Moros] to help themselves." More than mere social uplift was involved, however. Wood believed that these exchanges would "exert a far-reaching influence in building up trade relations with the Moros and other non-Christian peoples." Or, as Scott commented succinctly, the exchange was "a great educator." By forging ties of self-interest between the Moros and the market economy, loyalty to the larger socioeconomic system would eclipse traditional tribal bonds.[34]

The immediate effect of these attempts to alter their way of life was to stiffen Moro resistance. The Moros would not obligingly abide by the prohibitions against slavery and polygamy; they would refuse to pay taxes, however trivial; and, above all, the *dattos* would not relinquish their privileged position. Thus, the policies of Wood the reform governor added immeasurably to the difficulties of Wood the military commander in maintaining order and respect for American authority. One historian explains this seeming contradiction by suggesting that the tenacity of Moro opposition surprised the Americans who did not "fully grasp . . . that virtually no aspect of Moro culture was unrelated to Islam (or the Moro concept of it)." In other words, the Americans failed to see that their civilizing reforms threatened deeply held beliefs that would permit no compromise.[35]

The evidence nevertheless suggests just the opposite: Americans understood quite well the connection between their reforms, Moro beliefs, and the ensuing violence. The Moros, wrote McCoy in November 1903, believed that the aim of American policy was to Christianize them, "hence most of the trouble." Scott, too, recognized the religious context in which the Moros viewed such requirements as the *cedula,* recalling that "the attempt to collect the tax was regarded by the Moros as an attack upon Islam." Even those who overlooked the religious connotations of Moro resistance conceded its deep-seated character. Wood himself implicitly acknowledged as much. The Moros, hitherto entirely free from restraint, objected to paying the *cedula*, he said, because they saw it as a token of submission to the government—as indeed it was. And Capt. Daniel B. Devore, district governor of Lanao, sensibly observed that the difficulty lay in convincing the Moros "that a government which taxes them without their having a voice in the matter of taxation nor use of the funds is really the best sort of government for them."

Wood's superiors on the Philippine Commission also understood that the reforms threatened the Moro way of life. As Luke E. Wright, Taft's successor as governor general, reported in 1904:

> The new order of things [created by Wood] was distasteful [to the Moros] in every respect. . . . They resented any interference with their customs or habits of life . . . as an unwarranted and offensive intrusion. . . . The promulgation of the law against slavery and the protection of escaped slaves from recapture were regarded by their chiefs and headmen as an unwarranted invasion of their vested rights and was deeply resented.[36]

Rather than failing to appreciate the depth of Moro opposition, the Americans were determined to follow through on their civilizing mission despite that opposition and—as events would show—no matter how great the cost.

As Moro resistance to Wood's policies stiffened, hostilities escalated into a full-fledged guerrilla war, though one largely shielded from public view. American soldiers clashed with Moro fighters over one hundred times during the thirty-two months that Wood served as governor. Like other conflicts rooted in assumptions of the enemy's inherent inferiority, this one grew uglier the longer it endured. American tactics emphasized the use of large, deliberate sweeps designed to flush the Moros out of their jungle hiding places. The Americans succeeded in fixing their opponents, usually within the *cotta* of some rebellious *datto*, and punished the enemy with artillery fire before beginning a final assault. Given the superiority of American firepower, the outcome of such encounters was seldom in doubt.[37]

McCoy frequently accompanied these expeditions, operating with the advance guard in his capacity as intelligence officer of the Department of Mindanao. Describing one such operation into the Taraca Valley near Lake Lanao in April 1904, he explained to his family that "the General's idea was not to slaughter a lot of people, but to thoroughly demoralize the chiefs, and to show them that we could go any place . . . without the slightest hesitation." Wood demanded that each *datto* in the area permit troops to search his *cotta* for weapons. Should a *datto* refuse, Wood shelled his fortress, an effective tactic, said McCoy, because "the Moro cannot stand artillery fire." Afterwards, the *cotta* of the offending chief was put to the torch. Resistance was apparently common; on this operation alone, Wood's troops destroyed over one hundred Moro strongholds.[38]

Typically, the Americans sustained only light casualties. In the Taraca Valley, for example, only two were killed and eight wounded. Moro casualties are more difficult to calculate. Although McCoy never included specific figures in his letters home, the number of Moros killed was undoubtedly great, as a letter in May 1905 suggests. Wood cornered a chief named Peruka Utic and demanded his surrender. When the Moro leader replied from his *cotta* that he would surrender to "no dog of an infidel," Wood battered the fortress for an hour and then assaulted with the Twenty-second Infantry. The American battalion, reported McCoy, "finished the business killing Utic and his whole outfit like mad dogs."[39]

The Moros's persistent refusal to submit even when faced with overwhelming odds exasperated the Americans. "It's harder to keep the people alive than to kill them," McCoy complained at one point. And on the Taraca Valley expedition, Wood observed, "It seems a pity that these people insist upon hostilities which can only result in their destruction." Yet, however stubbornly the Moros might resist, Wood had no intention of relenting. A few days later, he wrote:

> The people of this valley have been so hostile and intractable for generations that I have decided to go thoroughly over the whole valley, destroying all warlike supplies, and dispersing and destroying every hostile force, and also to destroy every cota [*sic*] where there is the slightest resistance. While these measures may appear harsh it is the kindest thing to do.[40]

In short, Wood offered the Moros the alternatives of submission or extermination, a policy that bore fruit most notoriously in the so-called battle of Bud Dajo in March 1906. Although well known, it bears recounting as the best-documented illustration of the consequences of Wood's policies.

Bud Dajo was an extinct volcanic crater on the island of Jolo, several miles from the district capital. With its conical shape, heavily overgrown slopes, and 2,100-foot summit, it was an ideal defensive position. In mid-1905, several hundred Moros congregated at the top of this previously uninhabited mountain, apparently intending to settle there permanently. Scott, the district governor, viewed this development uneasily but promised that, if the Moros behaved themselves and "did not set themselves up . . . as being in defiance of the American government, he would not attack them." In essence, Scott would tolerate the Dajo settlement so long as the Moros did not force his hand.[41]

Amicable relations prevailed until early in 1906 when Scott departed on home leave and Capt. James H. Reeves became acting district governor. American officials began to take a different view of the Moro presence on Dajo. Instances of violence, theft, and arson in the local area were blamed on the Dajo Moros. The Americans were soon attributing a broader significance to the encampment. On March 1, Reeves reported to Capt. George T. Langhorne, the provincial secretary, that the Dajo Moros were boasting "that they have established . . . an impregnable position, and that they are in open defiance of the American authority, and that we . . . cannot force them off the hill and cannot make them obey the laws." By claiming to be "patriots and semi-liberators of the Moro people," he continued, "they had forfeited any right or claim that Colonel Scott had promised them." Reeves saw only one solution: "This thing will continue . . . until we finish the job and these people are whipped." Such a recommendation merely confirmed conclusions already reached by higher authorities. Three weeks earlier, Langhorne told Wood that the Dajo Moros would probably have to be exterminated. Wood agreed. Such a "ridiculous little affair" should be brought to an end. He recommended that "a couple of columns should take the place some night and clean it up."[42]

Convinced that they had unearthed the embers of insurrection, the Americans ruthlessly proceeded to snuff them out. Several battalions under the command of Col. Joseph W. Duncan assembled at the base of Bud Dajo on March 5 and began scaling its sides the next day. Wood at this time was nowhere near the battlefield. Indeed, he was no longer governor of the province, having recently assumed his long-delayed command of the Philippine Division. In the company of his successor as provincial governor, Brig. Gen. Tasker H. Bliss, Wood intended to monitor the action at Dajo by reports cabled to Zamboanga. But when the cable failed, Wood and Bliss, accompanied by McCoy, sailed for Jolo. They arrived at daybreak on March 7, "just in time," wrote McCoy, "to see through our glasses the khaki dots swarming over a cotta silhouetted against the sky." At about this time, Wood was stricken with one of the seizures that plagued him throughout the last twenty years of his life. Despite McCoy's efforts to hold him in the saddle, the general collapsed to the ground. Wood quickly recovered but was obviously in no condition to assume active command. He thus remained merely an observer throughout the action.[43]

Although the Americans secured a foothold on Dajo's crest that day, much fighting remained. "The whole rim of the crater was . . . fortified with cottas and trenches," wrote McCoy. Rather than engage in costly assaults against each separate stronghold, the Americans laboriously dragged several light artillery pieces up the side of the mountain to use in reducing the Moro fortifications, a process that McCoy followed for the next twenty-four hours: "It was most remarkable the fierce dying of the Moros. At every cotta efforts were made to get them to surrender or to send out their women but for an answer a rush of shrieking men and women would come cutting the air and dash amongst the soldiers like mad dogs." The result was predictable: "The hostiles [were] wiped out to a man," McCoy reported. "Only about twenty women and children were saved." Approximately 600 Moros were slaughtered, including a sizable number of women and children. American losses totaled 18 killed and 52 wounded.[44] A brief outcry ensued in the United States when a low-ranking official in Manila leaked reports of the battle to American newspapers. Press accounts stressed the

*The Battle of Bud Dajo, 1906: American soldiers contemplate the results of their victory. (Courtesy National Archives)*

number of noncombatants killed on Bud Dajo, and congressmen—principally Democrats—hastened to demand an explanation.[45]

For two and a half years, Wood's excursions against the Moros had gone virtually unnoticed. Now, ironically, he was called to account for an operation in which he played only a peripheral role. Of necessity, he publicly assumed "entire responsibility for the action of the troops in every particular." But, while admitting that "a considerable number of women and children were killed in the fight," he strenuously denied that "any American soldier [had] wantonly killed" a noncombatant. The fault lay with the tactics used by the Moros: The women "were dressed and armed much like the men and charged with them." As for the children, they were "used by the men as shields while charging troops." In short, the Moros "apparently desired that none be saved."[46]

Writing privately to Roosevelt, Wood did not attempt to blame the Moros for their own massacre. He rejected the notion that the sex or comparative youth of those killed on Dajo mattered. "No part of such an aggregation can be given any protection or consideration from those who are ordered to destroy it. . . . Work of this kind," he told the president, "has its disagreeable side, which is the unavoidable killing of women and children; but it must be done, and disagreeable as it is, there is no way of avoiding it."[47] Roosevelt, Taft, and the Republican party rallied to Wood's defense. Within a month—amazingly, given the lingering presence of other similar atrocities—the issue was forgotten. Wood emerged with his career intact. It was, however, a sour note on which to end his stewardship and one that McCoy—ever the defender of Wood's reputation—in later years was hard pressed to justify.[48]

For McCoy, the high point of his first tour in the Philippines occurred several months prior to Bud Dajo. While Wood was in the United States on medical leave the previous autumn, McCoy conceived and commanded an operation that led to the elimination of the most elusive of all Moro leaders, Datto Ali, thereby emerging for the first time from his mentor's shadow. Ali, a prominent chief who dominated the Cotabato Valley in the Lanao district, was the single most formidable opponent of the American presence in the Moro Province. A shrewd and ruthless fighter, he eluded the Americans longer than any other Moro leader. His talent for survival, however, served to so incite army officers that getting Ali became an obsession, a litmus test of Wood's ability to deny any exception to his authority.

Prior to Wood's arrival, the American authorities who avoided interfering with Moro customs found Ali generally agreeable. Yet, as early as December 1903, McCoy already identified the *datto* as chief among the opponents of the American antislavery law and predicted that "he'll either be in prison or up in arms against us before a great while." Wood sought assurances of Ali's willingness to abide by the rules laid down by the new regime. When Ali refused even to talk, Wood expected to play out the usual sequence of events—an attack on his adversary's *cotta*, to be followed inevitably by submission on the part of any survivors. Ali, however, refused to play the role of compliant victim. In early March 1904, Wood assembled a multibattalion force to take Ali's fortress at Saranaya. Showing unusual caution, Wood shelled the *cotta* for a full twenty-four hours. When the infantry finally assaulted the ruins of the stronghold, they found only a single wounded Moro. The remainder, including Ali, escaped during the night. Gauging the enormous *cotta* to be capable of sheltering 6,000 warriors, McCoy remarked that the evacuation "was the most astonishing piece of work for any but a civilized people." Ali's tactical skills earned grudging respect. The Moro chief, McCoy commented, was "a soldier and a gentleman. . . . I don't blame him for fighting for his 'ancient customs.' "[49]

Two months later, Ali retaliated. In May, he ambushed an infantry company in the Rio Grande Valley and killed fifteen Americans without losing a man. Wood's hastily mounted pursuit again came up empty-handed. As McCoy remarked after a futile two-months' search—during which another American patrol was ambushed—Ali was "still chasing from one end of the valley to the other." Although U.S. troops doggedly clung to his trail, "it's just by accident when they encounter" him.[50] Wood combined his pursuit of Ali with attempts to coax the

Moro leader into surrendering. Ali refused such ploys. As he replied to one proposal on July 14, 1904 (in a letter that McCoy translated): "Which is better for you, to kill me or not? . . . Until I die all the people will not submit to the government, because I will try to kill all the people who are friends of the Americans." Perhaps convinced by Ali's threat, Wood the following day posted a reward of $500 for Ali's capture, dead or alive.[51]

The new year brought no better luck. Ali, however, suspended his attacks on American troops and withdrew to the rugged Cotabato Valley. Yet, if the Moro chief no longer molested the Americans, his determination to remain free was undiminished. He no longer wished to fight, but neither did he intend to surrender—as fruitless negotiations by Saleeby and Halstead Dorey, McCoy's classmate and another member of Wood's circle, showed. Despite Ali's inactivity, the Americans still viewed him as an irritating symbol of Moro resistance. Thus, Langhorne, as acting provincial governor in August 1905, commented, it was necessary "to get entirely rid of a disturbing element like Ali" to guarantee that he would not "be in a position to create further trouble in the future." Langhorne opposed any further bargaining with Ali, arguing that "every concession to an Asiatic . . . is a mistake."[52]

Shortly thereafter the prospects for getting Ali brightened when McCoy extracted a key piece of information from two of Ali's rivals—Datto Piang and Entu Enok. Ali, they revealed, had abandoned his usual hiding place and was now camped along the Malala River near the Gulf of Davao. Brig. Gen. James A. Buchanan, commanding the Department of Mindanao in Wood's absence, decided to mount yet another expedition against the Moro leader. Buchanan's inclination was to do as Wood had done in the past: to march a large force up the Cotabato Valley, sealing off avenues of escape as it advanced. Yet such maneuvers repeatedly failed to surprise Ali because, as McCoy commented, "every movement of troops there was known by him almost at once." McCoy proposed instead to rely on a small body of troops that could move quickly and avoid notice while approaching Ali's hide-out, not by the expected route up the valley but from the rear. On an expedition in late 1904, McCoy explored such an indirect approach into the area, and he believed that he could retrace his route. Impressed with McCoy's alternative, Buchanan not only approved it but appointed the young captain to lead the operation.[53]

On October 16, at the head of a column of 100 American infantrymen, 140 Filipino bearers, and 10 scouts, McCoy went ashore at Digos on the Gulf of Davao. Knowing that success depended on catching Ali unawares, McCoy moved quickly into the interior, pushing his troops to the limit of their endurance. By October 20, the bearers, the scouts, and several Americans were exhausted. Refusing to ease up, McCoy left the lame behind to follow at leisure and with the remaining 77 infantrymen, "stripped of all impedimenta, excepting one day's cooked rations," pushed on. After marching for two more days and nights, the party reached Ali's hide-out before dawn on October 22.[54]

McCoy divided his small force into three groups, deploying them around the clearing that contained Ali's hut. As flanking elements skirted the edges of the clearing to prevent any escape, the center, led by Lt. Philip Remington, burst into the clearing to find Ali and two companions lounging in the doorway. Ali grabbed a rifle and opened fire, killing Pvt. Llewellyn W. Bobb. Remington returned fire and hit the Moro chief. A brief fire fight with other Moros still inside Ali's quarters ensued. The outcome was never in doubt, and soon McCoy sounded a ceasefire. Ali, his son, and ten followers lay dead. Some fifty others, many of them women and children huddled inside the house, were captured. Of these, several had sustained wounds that the Americans treated. McCoy immediately dispatched "messengers to surrounding rancherias [settlements] that since Ali's death the hostile operations in the Rio Grande Valley were over."[55]

From a tactical standpoint, McCoy's operation succeeded brilliantly. Given the enormous—perhaps exaggerated—importance attributed to Ali's elimination, McCoy reaped substantial accolades. Besides official commendations from Buchanan and Wood, there was a cherished letter from the White House that conveyed congratulations "not merely as President but as an old personal friend." McCoy's feat also won him a first heady taste of national publicity. According to an enthusiastic correspondent in *Collier's,* Ali's death marked "the last phase in that war of extermination which the American race has waged for nearly three centuries against, first the red and then the brown race." With Bud Dajo still to come, such a prediction was obviously premature. Still, the momentary importance of McCoy's accomplishment permitted him to stand alone for the first time. As such, this climactic event of his Philippine tour inaugurated a new phase in his career.[56]

# 4

# An Available Agent

Schooled in Cuba, Europe, and the Far East, McCoy had established himself as an able soldier whose competence extended well beyond strictly military matters. Thanks to his highly visible position as Wood's aide, McCoy's reputation reached beyond the army's ranks, bringing him to the attention of civilian officials—most notably the president—who on occasion required the services of a discreet and politically astute military officer. Over the next several years, this reputation earned McCoy a series of assignments in which he functioned as the eyes and ears of officials charged with deciding matters about which they lacked adequate firsthand knowledge.[1]

McCoy's first chance to engage in this new role came while he was still in the Far East. In late 1905, the hero of the Ali expedition took a brief leave in Japan. On his first holiday since arriving in the Philippines, McCoy welcomed the chance to cut loose from all the ties of work and responsibility and to explore the Japanese countryside. That Japan was fresh from its triumph over Russia only added further interest. In Tokyo, McCoy called at the War Ministry, toured Japanese military installations, and dined with the American chargé d'affaires, Francis Huntington Wilson, and with the military attaché, Capt. John J. Pershing—both old acquaintances. In early December, however, a cable from Wood interrupted his vacation; it directed McCoy, without explanation, to Canton. Confidential instructions explaining his mission would await his arrival at the American consulate.[2]

Canton in December 1905 was the lone holdout in a boycott against American goods that since midyear had enveloped the principal cities of China.

Portions of an earlier version of this chapter appeared as "Family Matters: American Civilian and Military Elites in the Progressive Era," *Armed Forces and Society* 8 (Spring 1982): 405–418.

Although in a broad sense the movement reflected China's swelling nationalism, the immediate provocation for the boycott lay elsewhere—specifically, in American exclusionist immigration policies and in the mistreatment of Chinese living in the United States. After lengthy negotiations with a vocal anti-Chinese lobby at home as well as with Chinese officials (who sympathized with but did not sponsor the boycott), the Roosevelt administration partially defused the situation. Only Canton stubbornly persisted. And with the murder of five American missionaries near that city on October 29—the so-called Lienchow Massacre—the president began to contemplate more drastic action. He ordered the army and navy to prepare a punitive expedition against Canton. The soldiers who would actually occupy the offending city would be 5,000 men from Leonard Wood's Philippine Division. Wood himself looked forward to the prospect of action on the Asian mainland. Yet the operations of his force once it embarked for Canton—how it would land; what it would undertake to achieve; how it would sustain itself—were cloudy. To answer such questions, Wood diverted McCoy to China.[3]

McCoy arrived at Shanghai on December 20, two days after antiforeign riots rocked the city, to find "marines and blue jackets patrolling the streets and eleven war-ships lined up on the other side of the bund." He quickly sensed the rapidly awakening national life of China, saw its connection to the boycott, and predicted that the privileges of foreigners, merchant and missionary alike, would be "fussed over and probably fought over sooner or later." Traveling to Canton, he received his instructions from the American consul general, Julius Lay. For the next several days, accompanied by an American naval lieutenant, Clark H. Woodward, McCoy surveyed the city. He analyzed the local terrain, identified obstacles and probable points of occupation, assessed the likelihood of serious opposition to an American landing, and located potential sources of supplies. His work completed, he hastened back to Manila shortly after New Year's to render his report to Wood. To his delight, he arrived to find "the expeditionary force . . . all on board ship awaiting final orders from Washington to proceed."[4] The final orders never arrived. Having ostentatiously waved his big stick, Roosevelt now withheld it. In the early months of 1906, he used less-drastic means to extract a Chinese commitment to end antiforeign agitation. But the proposed strike against Canton that McCoy helped prepare had been no bluff. Although in the end Roosevelt had not deployed the expedition, he told Wood, "I wanted to be sure that if it was needed we would not be unprepared."[5]

In June 1906, McCoy again departed the islands, this time on leave to the United States. Less than a decade out of West Point, he had accumulated about six years of overseas service. However exciting and rewarding, that service had interfered with McCoy's obligations to the family which as first-born son he nominally headed. Although he had always been a faithful correspondent who shared his adventures with his family, he decided that it was time to go home. After an extended visit in Lewistown, however, he fully intended to rejoin Wood. Yet no sooner had McCoy arrived home than Roosevelt got wind of his presence in the United States. The president requested that after his leave the army captain return to the White House as senior military aide. Throughout his career, McCoy treated any presidential request as tantamount to an order. Thus, Roosevelt's action in this instance obliged McCoy to scrap his plan to return to Manila.[6]

Another diplomatic crisis delayed the start of McCoy's White House detail—and abruptly terminated his reunion with his family. Months of simmering unrest in Cuba culminated by mid-1906 in insurrection. Stemming from the disputed elections of December 1905, the troubles reflected the Liberal party's determination to oust from office President Tomás Estrada Palma and his Moderate party, whose dominance the elections reaffirmed. In August 1906, a Constitutional Army raised by Liberal leaders took to the field, vowing to overthrow the government. Citing the provisions of the Platt Amendment, Estrada Palma requested American troops to restore order and support his government. The insurgents also hoped for American intervention, calculating that they would handily win the new elections that they expected the United States to sponsor. Roosevelt at first resisted pressures to interfere. Eventually, however, the danger that persistent disorder posed to American interests and the coaching of Frank Steinhart, Wood's chief clerk during the first intervention and now U.S. consul general in Havana, prodded the president into more direct involvement. In September 1906, in a last-ditch effort to forestall a full-scale American takeover, he decided to send Secretary of War William Howard Taft and Assistant Secretary of State Robert Bacon to negotiate an end to the revolt.[7] Unfortunately, neither of Roosevelt's two envoys could claim more than passing familiarity with the situation. Writing to Secretary of State Elihu Root, Taft confessed that he was so "lacking in knowledge of Cuba" that it was "quite embarrassing" even to undertake the mission. Clearly, these senior officials would require expert advice if they were to succeed.[8]

When it came to practical knowledge of Cuban affairs in American official circles, the U.S. Army at this time enjoyed a near monopoly. Taft and Bacon did not hesitate to exploit that expertise. When Roosevelt subsequently decided to impose direct American control over Cuba, army officers filled key positions throughout the provisional government. Even at the time of the Taft-Bacon mission, when the president still hoped to avoid reoccupation, the military provided information about Cuban politics and personalities and acted as a liaison to the contending armies. Given McCoy's previous Cuban experience, his ready availability, and the regard in which Roosevelt and Taft held him (having known the secretary in the Philippines), the young officer was a logical candidate to assist the mission. It was not too surprising, therefore, when Taft, after conferring with the president at Oyster Bay on September 14, telegraphed McCoy with orders to report without fail to the War Department the following day.[9]

For a junior officer to receive a direct and urgent summons from the secretary of war more than compensated for the disappointment of having a leave cancelled. McCoy responded with his usual alacrity and enthusiasm. Joining the mission in Washington, he accompanied it by train to Tampa on September 16. Along the way, he and Frank S. Cairns, another veteran of the first Cuban occupation attached to the mission, provided Taft and Bacon with a cram course on Cuban politics and the personalities they would encounter. After a brief stopover in Tampa, the party embarked for Havana on the cruiser *Des Moines*.[10]

A twofold problem awaited the mission in Cuba. To avert an American takeover, Taft and Bacon had first to quell internal unrest. Then they had to negotiate a political settlement acceptable to both Liberals and Moderates. Progress had been made toward the first objective even before the mission reached Havana. According to McCoy, each party convinced itself that arrival of the American envoys promised to benefit its own cause. Therefore, a tacit ceasefire took effect as soon as Roosevelt announced the mission. Yet even though actual fighting had stopped, insurgent forces remained in the field, some of them located ominously near Havana. These troops Taft and Bacon hoped to disarm, thereby precluding the possibility of renewed violence. McCoy's first assignment was to arrange a formal truce with Liberal commanders near Havana, a task completed within days of the mission's arrival. With the truce established, Brig. Gen. Frederick Funston began disarming the rebels. McCoy assisted there as well. He and Bacon traveled through rebel lines to confiscate the weapons of General José Rumán Montero's brigade, totaling 174 small arms.[11]

In settling the larger political dispute, the mission enjoyed less success. McCoy personally entertained a low opinion of the entire affair. "In a nut shell," he reported to Wood, "it was a fight between the 'Ins' and 'Outs,' with no principle at stake." Estrada Palma "tried to adopt the Porfirio Díaz scheme of running a Latin-American Republic." Lacking the authority or prestige of the Mexican dictator, however, the Cuban president "relied on the Platt Amendment, with its backing of the United States," to prop up his position.[12] Despite his disdain for Estrada Palma, McCoy believed that the United States should support the Cuban government, using force to crush the insurrection if necessary. In his view, a hard-line approach offered the best hope for ending Cuban political unrest. Taft, who in McCoy's view sought peace at any price, rejected such a course. Still hoping for a compromise, Taft and Bacon consulted with both parties as well as with business leaders not directly connected with politics. Because, as Taft and Bacon noted, McCoy "knew all the public men of the island," the army captain played a key role in deciding who the American envoys should see and in briefing them beforehand on each visitor.[13]

For Estrada Palma's supporters, realization that the Americans had come not to rescue the government but to negotiate with its enemies came as a dreadful disappointment. Many of them thereafter "sulked in their tents," making meaningful discussions impossible. Days of talks in late September produced nothing. McCoy credited the Liberals with being "shrewd enough to be most reasonable" and blamed the Moderates for the lack of progress. "All the time thinkin[g] of their sacred honor and dignity," government spokesmen refused to make concessions. Preferring an American takeover to compromise with the Liberals, Estrada Palma's cabinet brought matters to a head on September 28 by resigning en masse, thereby throwing responsibility for governing Cuba into Taft's spacious lap. With Roosevelt's concurrence, Taft issued a proclamation the next day that established an American provisional government.[14]

Now the thrust of McCoy's responsibilities shifted. The problem became one of rapidly staffing the new government with qualified Americans. Here again, Taft and Bacon turned to McCoy, consulting him on the personnel to be included in the government. Yet the two senior American officials themselves had no intention of remaining in Cuba indefinitely to oversee the new government. Having failed to restore political harmony in Cuba and having reluctantly assumed control to forestall chaos, the Taft-Bacon mission had exhausted its charter. Another novice to Cuban affairs, Charles E. Magoon, succeeded Taft as provisional governor on October 13, permitting the mission to depart.[15]

Magoon appreciated only too well his lack of firsthand experience in Cuba. To provide continuity between Taft's short-lived administration and its successor, the secretary of war ordered McCoy to remain in Havana as the connecting link. Taft told McCoy that his job was to "put [Magoon] in touch with all the people whom you know, and . . . give him the same benefit you extended to me." Although this additional stay was intended to be brief, McCoy made himself so valuable that Magoon repeatedly arranged for his extension. McCoy was soon

*"El capitán Mac Koy" among the belles of Havana during the Taft-Bacon mission, 1906. (Courtesy Library of Congress)*

remarking unhappily that "it begins to look as though I might be with Governor Magoon all winter."[16]

McCoy's unwillingness to remain long in Havana reflected the limited purpose of the provisional government, especially in comparison with that of Wood's regime. The personal qualities that Magoon brought to his job hinted at those limits: However likable, Judge Magoon was a dull bureaucrat who had found shelter in the War Department's Bureau of Insular Affairs since the presidency of William McKinley. He was the last person to look to for imaginative policy or bold action. Although not presuming to criticize Magoon himself, McCoy observed that the governor did not face "the same problem of reorganizing the government and getting results as in the Military Intervention." Magoon's assignment was merely to make peace "between the expectant Liberals and the very disgruntled Moderates." For politicians and their squabbles, McCoy had no use. He warned Roosevelt, Taft, and Magoon in succession regarding "the very bad characters of every one of the leading lights of the Liberal Party," but American officials still acted as if the Liberals represented the people of Cuba. McCoy lamented that for Cuba, "universal suffrage will continue to be the root of all evils."[17]

Brig. Gen. J. Franklin Bell, who stepped down as army chief of staff to command the American troops in Cuba, told McCoy that Magoon could not "expect to find your equal in the Army for the place you are filling. I have repeatedly told him that there are not many McCoys and he must not expect to find them." Notwithstanding such flattery, McCoy remained anxious to leave. As soon as he found a replacement in November, he left Havana for home.[18] McCoy's contributions during this second American occupation of Cuba earned the plaudits of Taft, Bacon, Magoon, and Bell. Unquestionably, participation in the affair enhanced his reputation. Yet, overall, he came away from the experience dissatisfied. Association with powerful officials even on a basis of trust and intimacy no longer turned his head. The purposes for which those officials labored impressed McCoy more than their personal prominence. However great the influence he had exerted as an adviser, McCoy regretted the cramped and timid goals of the cause he had served in Cuba. In comparison to what he had come to expect at Wood's side, the vision of a Taft or Magoon possessed neither scope nor grandeur. In the end, the second American occupation merely involved McCoy in politics without a worthy goal.

Once back in Washington, McCoy rendered a personal report to Elihu Root and to Taft, bringing each up-to-date on conditions in Cuba. He then reported to the White House to assume his much delayed duties as the president's military aide. As so often during his career, McCoy undertook his assignment at a propitious moment. During the era of Theodore Roosevelt, Washington shed its reputation for provincialism. The rising tide of progressivism and the lingering excitement of having recently become an active world power were causing important changes in the nation's capital.[19]

Not least among the legacies of the Spanish-American War was the emergence of a new breed of American public servant. The new frontier established by the victories of 1898 stirred the popular imagination and, by bestowing upon the United States weighty imperial obligations, generated heightened interest in government as a worthwhile career. In one sense, the ensuing migration of able and ambitious young men to Washington merely symbolized the overall shift of the nation's attention from Wall Street, where it had rested throughout the Gilded Age, to the seat of an increasingly powerful federal government. Bored by the prospect of what William Phillips called a "pallid career" in business, sons of the American upper classes—many of whom had impetuously followed Roosevelt up San Juan Hill—now followed the Rough Rider to Washington.[20]

This growing interest in federal service, especially pronounced during TR's tenure in office, reflected the challenging ideals and boundless exuberance of the president himself. Roosevelt, recalled Phillips, "turned men's thoughts from the localities where they lived to the dignity of the nation and our national problems." He fostered "a new conception of what the United States stood for and of the responsibility involved [in] citizenship." Many others could agree with this career diplomat that "it was T.R.'s call to youth which lured me to Washington."[21]

This commitment to national service carried many of Phillips's contemporaries far beyond Washington to posts overseas. Just as domestic affairs in the progressive era increasingly became the realm of the nonpartisan expert, so also diplomacy—long the preserve of political hacks—seemed to require the attention that only a corps of skilled professionals could provide. Thus, in the words of one official of the period, there developed under Roosevelt's tutelage a new generation of diplomatists "with their new American outlook on the world and their vision of a new American position and influence in it. They took charge of the new diplomacy wherein a man could hope to become one day a new kind of proconsul or procurator in some tropical province or tetrarchate." Men such as Phillips, former Rough Rider Henry Prather Fletcher, and Joseph Clark Grew, who first commended himself to TR by shooting a tiger in China, "became the elite or legendary 'inner circle' of the Department of State ... for the next twenty years."[22]

Before Roosevelt's second term ended, an informal expression of this inner circle had appeared in the form of an exclusive bachelors' club. The seat of this club was a stately Washington townhouse at 1718 H Street. Waldo Heinrichs described this establishment—located next to the Metropolitan Club and a short walk from the State Department—as a "club for the social elite of the Diplomatic Service." According to Robert Schulzinger, the club's members—who called themselves "the Family"—wielded so much influence that 1718 became "virtually a second foreign office." For the military historian, this group holds a special interest. Despite its predominantly civilian character, the Family not only included army officers as members but had actually been founded by soldiers in the first place. Indeed, 1718 was the brainchild of Frank McCoy.[23]

When he finally assumed his White House duties in the fall of 1906, McCoy discovered that the demands of his assignment were strenuous and time consuming. In addition to his formal duties, the army captain was among those frequently enlisted by the robust chief executive to trek through Rock Creek Park, take long horseback rides, or engage in any of the combative sports that Roosevelt enjoyed. The Roosevelts even recruited McCoy to act as a companion for their children. The need to secure quarters close to the president soon persuaded McCoy (with two friends from the army general staff, Capt. Sherwood Cheney and Capt. James Logan) to undertake the considerable expense of renting the house at 1718 H Street, two blocks from the White House.[24]

The three bachelors soon made 1718 a popular gathering place for many of the capital's bright young career men. The house became, in the estimation of a frequent female visitor, "the most delightful bachelor quarters in the world." After years of overseas service that thrust him largely into the company of military men, McCoy was delighted to discover how much soldiers shared with their counterparts in the diplomatic service and the federal bureaucracy. Recognizing the inevitability of being posted away from Washington but anxious to sustain 1718 on a permanent footing, the three officers began inviting other congenial spirits to take up residence.[25]

The silk-stocking credentials of the Family's diplomatic members testify to the group's unabashedly elitist character. William Phillips (Harvard, '00) and Willard Straight (Cornell, '01) of Manchuria fame shared backgrounds of social respectability, inherited wealth, and superb education. Other early members and foreign service pioneers such as Basil Miles (Oxford), Leland H. Harrison (Eton and Harvard, '07), and Frederick Sterling (Harvard, '98) fit the same pattern. Eventually, the club's State Department contingent included such notables as Fletcher, Grew, Joseph P. Cotton, James C. Dunn, Francis White, and Norman Armour. The first three career diplomats to serve as undersecretary of state all resided at 1718 at one time or another. Bound by intimate ties, these men regularly corresponded, consulted, and advised one another about professional as well as personal matters. Those at home cultivated the interests of those abroad; the latter, in turn, kept 1718 informed with inside information on the latest overseas developments.

Yet 1718 was more than an extension of the State Department. Family membership, for example, was by no means restricted to foreign service officers and soldiers. By 1914, the group already included men of such varied professional backgrounds as Benjamin Strong, governor of the Federal Reserve Bank of New York; Assistant Secretary of the Treasury Andrew J. Peters; and Arthur Wilson Page, editor of the popular monthly *The World's Work*.[26] Overall, social antecedents and vocations were less significant in uniting Family members than was a common outlook—one that zealously supported an expanded role for the United States in world affairs and saw individual opportunity as concomitant with that expansion. Seventeen-eighteen's habitués recognized the indivisibility of power. The successful projection of American influence overseas required the integration of economic, political, and military resources—the type of mutual support that the Family's international bankers, diplomats, and soldiers regularly provided for one another as individuals.

Like their mentor, these heirs of Roosevelt did not differentiate between service in government or outside of it. What mattered was that Family members were enlistees in a common cause, a status unaffected by any shift in base of operations. In 1909, for instance, when Straight left the State Department for the investment banking firm of J. P. Morgan & Company, he remained a trusted member of the team. Thus, Fletcher's appointment as ambassador to Mexico in early 1916 also carried with it implications of opportunity for Straight, the diplomat-turned-banker. Foreseeing the possibility of American intervention during Fletcher's tenure, "in which case your position will be more interesting than ever before," Straight predicted that "Seventeen Eighteen will surely then be very much in the front as always." Straight expected 1718's Wall Street branch to play an important role in making a success of Fletcher's mission because "J. P. Morgan & Company and their associated groups will be the people upon whom you will have principally to rely." To lay the basis for such cooperation, he urged Fletcher before assuming office to share with Wall Street "the benefit of your advice regarding the South American situation."[27]

The group's influence, although difficult to measure with precision, was by no means negligible. Even before 1920 when Family members occupied the second or third tier of authority, typically as assistant secretaries or their diplomatic equivalent, they enjoyed ready access to the upper echelons and often exercised great latitude when assigned to the field. Strategically placed in government and well connected with higher-ranking officials, the Family worked with persistence and a minimum of publicity to put its own imprint on government policy. So effective were its members that the British scholar Graham Wallas, after visiting 1718, announced the "quite astounding" discovery that the U.S. government was "really run by a little group of young fellows mostly assistant secretaries who really do the work and suggest most of the things to be done to their bosses." A more recent view by William Appleman Williams described Miles, Phillips, and Straight in 1917 as the nucleus of "a tightly knit team . . . unknown to the general public and tucked away safely beyond the reach of even an aroused congressman" that was chiefly responsible for the anti-Bolshevik cast of State Department policy.[28]

The Family's clout, although perhaps not as great as either Williams or Wallas suggested, was especially evident when 1718 rallied to protect the fortunes of fellow members. With the change of administration in 1913, for example,

*Portrait of self-assurance: The Family assembles at 1718 H Street. Top row from left: James Logan and Henry P. Fletcher; second row: William Phillips and George Marvin; third row: Basil Miles and Willard Straight; bottom row: McCoy and an unidentified Family friend. (Courtesy U.S. Army Military History Institute)*

Secretary of State William Jennings Bryan's determination to replace all
Republican diplomatic appointees with "deserving Democrats" jeopardized
Fletcher's position as envoy to Chile. When McCoy picked up rumors in
Washington that Bryan sought Fletcher's post for some "long-haired apostle of
free silver," he immediately alerted Straight in New York. Straight later told
Fletcher that as soon as "we got the news that the wolves were after your job,"
1718 began lobbying in the latter's behalf. Straight arranged for a Family friend,
Daisy Harriman, to call on Secretary Bryan and then went himself to see Col.
Edward M. House. When House offered assurances, Straight cabled Santiago:
"EVERYTHING ALL RIGHT SITTITE [sic] SAY NOTHING PERIOD SILENCE EMPHATI-
CALLY EMPHASIZED." The Family campaign apparently succeeded, for Phillips
soon passed the word from inside the State Department that—in Straight's
words—"although the big noise [Bryan] wants to land your place for a friend, the
President will not stand for it and you'll be retained."[29]

Seventeen-eighteen remained an important part of McCoy's life until it was
finally sold in the 1950s. After 1914, he lived at the house for only short periods.
Yet, in later years, he stayed there whenever his duties took him temporarily to
Washington. Although marriages reduced the number of permanent lodgers at
the house, McCoy made a point of keeping in touch with old Family friends. He
attended their weddings, stood up as godfather at their children's christenings,
shared their vacations, and joined the periodic reunions at 1718. He always
prized the camaraderie that the house signified. Yet, if McCoy appreciated the
Family primarily because of its fellowship, he could not have failed to recognize
how associations formed there would help advance his own career.


McCoy's routine in Washington was not merely social, nor was his relationship
with Roosevelt entirely recreational. Throughout his presidency, the commander
in chief showed a sharp interest in modernizing the armed forces. Roosevelt
found the army, in McCoy's words, "dead on its feet." In order to create a
climate conducive to military reform, the president "stirred up trouble, pacifists
and the old men trying to smother" any departure from tradition. Roosevelt
made himself accessible to innovators such as Wood and the navy's William S.
Sims, whom he discovered "more or less lost among the great mass of mediocre
men of both services." McCoy encouraged the president's interest in military
affairs by funneling impressions and ideas coming to him from the field. Wood in
particular called upon McCoy to reinforce his own ideas to the president.[30]

In the spring of 1908, McCoy interrupted his White House duties to return
again to Cuba at Taft's behest. His new mission grew out of a controversy over an
American public works concession that had become a bone of contention between
local politicians. In June 1906, officials in Cienfuegos, a city suffering from a
chronic water shortage, negotiated a $3 million contract with Hugh J. Reilly, an
American, to construct a new municipal water and sewage system. This initiative

by the Moderate-controlled municipal council drew charges of fraud from the Liberal opposition, including allegations that Reilly had promised to funnel a portion of his profits to Moderate party loyalists. Thus, when control of the council changed hands following the American intervention, the Liberals revoked the contract. Reilly petitioned Magoon for assistance in reinstating the agreement, but the provisional governor rejected his appeal. With greater success, Reilly next appealed to Taft. The secretary of war suggested to Magoon that it would be more equitable as well as more expeditious to modify the Reilly contract in a way that would make it acceptable to officials in Cienfuegos. Still, Magoon hesitated. In a letter to Taft on April 8, 1908, he contended that too much political animosity existed in Cienfuegos to gain acceptance of a contract so laden with partisan feuding. The significance of this otherwise trivial dispute lay in its political implications. In the midst of preparing for elections billed as a prelude to American withdrawal, Magoon warned that "when the campaign gets hot the danger of disturbance will be increased and it is impossible for anyone to predict what will happen or what will cause it." The provisional governor feared that the Cienfuegos problem, if mishandled, might ignite unrest that could delay the American departure.[31]

Reluctant either to overrule Magoon or to ignore Reilly, Taft asked McCoy to obtain a firsthand view. So, by mid-April, Roosevelt's aide was off again for Cuba. After brief stopovers in Havana and Santiago, McCoy reached Cienfuegos, where he spent nearly a week interviewing "the representative men of every class, color, and condition [while] purposely avoiding the politicians and interested parties." Hoping to gauge the political danger by broadly sampling public opinion about the Reilly contract, McCoy in practice gave disproportionate weight to the views of the propertied interests and foreign residents of the city. Still his investigation was a thorough one. Having completed it, he hastened to Washington to submit his report.[32]

McCoy agreed with Magoon that the Cienfuegos dispute revolved around politics rather than principle. "It is simply a bitter factional fight for the control of the City Government," he told Taft. The Liberals feared that restoring the Reilly contract would give the Moderates control of enough jobs to determine the outcome of the approaching elections. On the other hand, McCoy's survey of local opinion indicated that, apart from the politicians themselves, the local populace cared little about jockeying for partisan advantage. Although the people evinced no particular interest in protecting Reilly's investment, few would object if he resumed construction. "The people of Cienfuegos want a water and sewage system," McCoy reported, and they did not especially care who did the work so long as it was done. Concerning Magoon's fear of possible domestic unrest, McCoy offered categorical assurances: "The idea of public disturbance if the Reilly contractors were to proceed with the work was treated as a joke." Conceding the difficulty of forcing the Liberals of Cienfuegos into any direct dealings with Reilly, however, McCoy devised a new approach to break the stalemate—let the provisional government contract with Reilly to do the work. The American authorities in Havana would furnish the funds to complete the Cienfuegos project, thereby skirting partisan sensitivities. After the fact (and long after the election), the municipality could reimburse the central government for its investment.[33]

Reassured that there was little chance of disorder and persuaded by McCoy's suggestions, Taft recommended to Roosevelt that the provisional government negotiate a new contract with Reilly. Roosevelt concurred, as did the municipal government of Cienfuegos itself, promising to reimburse the central government for most of the cost. So this miniature crisis came to a satisfactory end. Magoon's exaggerated fears inflated the problem completely out of proportion. In putting such fears to rest and in solving the main issue, McCoy demonstrated again his competence as a troubleshooter. That his assignment in this instance possessed no military implications whatsoever suggests how far he had travelled on the road to becoming a valued diplomatic operative.[34]

In the spring of 1908, the War Department directed all officers on detached service for longer than four years to return to their regiments. The order applied to the military aide of the president no less than to anyone else. Thus, the end of that year found McCoy far from the White House and his H Street companions at the remote, primitive cavalry garrison of Fort Wingate in eastern New Mexico. A vestige of the Indian-fighting army, Wingate served as the home of Troops I and M of the Third Squadron, Third Cavalry. Prior to McCoy's arrival, the garrison's complement of officers totaled six, none of whom ranked above first lieutenant. McCoy took up residence in an austere adobe structure that he found adequate though "a bit draughty and inconvenient for women in winter," adding by way of sardonic consolation that "as there are only two women on post all is well." Other than trips to inspect national guard units throughout New Mexico, McCoy remained at Fort Wingate for most of the next two years. With little to do but devote himself to the basic military chores of training, housekeeping and caring for horses, men, and equipment, McCoy was soon writing that "the experience I need is coming in chunks." He even asserted that the routine at Wingate provided "the life . . . most to my taste."[35]

McCoy meant what he said. He loved the peculiar joys of troop duty: the intimate contact with soldiers; the freedom provided by the none-too-taxing daily routine; the ample opportunities to ride, hunt, and fish. In his mid-thirties, the captain of cavalry was wiry and fit and exuded a quiet self-confidence. His military career had obliged him perforce to adopt a version of Roosevelt's strenuous life, and he flourished in it. One doubts that the grudging surgeon who pronounced McCoy marginally fit for commissioning out of West Point would have recognized the same specimen a decade later. Only a receding hairline foretold the passing of youth.

That McCoy needed the tour at Fort Wingate to sharpen his skills in practical soldiering is beyond question. Eight years had elapsed since his last assignment to a troop unit. Not unexpectedly, McCoy's commander judged him "somewhat rusty in line duties," although in tribute perhaps to McCoy's more recent experience, he also described him as "one of the most courteous officers I have ever known."[36]

Having completed his requisite tour with troops—and having tasted something of the isolation that military service implied for the average officer—McCoy returned from idyllic exile early in 1911. His mentor, Leonard Wood, had become army chief of staff and summoned McCoy to join him. Assignment to the general staff brought McCoy into contact with Henry L. Stimson, secretary of war in the Taft administration that was now in office. A principled Republican lawyer-statesman just beginning a long career as heir to the mantle of Elihu Root, Stimson admired soldiers and the virtues they represented. Although he never developed a popular following, Stimson's record as a shrewd attorney, patriot, and outspoken advocate in diverse causes earned him respect throughout the elite establishment. The army came to hold him in especially high regard. To officers as far apart in temperament as Leonard Wood and George C. Marshall, Stimson exemplified the ideal of a public servant. Frank McCoy shared that view. Despite the disparity in their positions, he and the secretary were drawn to each other as kindred spirits. From the time that McCoy escorted Wood and Stimson on a relaxed and fondly recorded tour of army posts in the Southwest during the autumn of 1911, he and the secretary became lifelong friends. Of all McCoy's associations with civilian officials, Stimson's would be the one that he cherished most and that would prove most valuable in later years.[37]

While on the general staff, McCoy became an ardent proponent of Wood's crusade for military preparedness. In the years leading up to World War I, the officer corps—its enthusiasm for colonialism spent—began to give increasing attention to the prospect of all-out conflict with another great power. McCoy's own views illustrate this trend. Without abandoning his interest in Asian or Caribbean affairs, his correspondence began to reflect a new emphasis on modernizing the army to improve its capacity for waging war on a massive scale. Having endured the mismanagement of the Santiago campaign, having seen for himself the armies of Europe, and having recently returned from a posting with his own country's fragmented, irrationally deployed forces in the field, McCoy entertained few illusions about the American army's ability to conduct such a war. He understood that other tasks had long preoccupied the army, but with other forward-looking officers, McCoy now wanted his service to fasten its attention on threats previously considered too distant to be taken seriously. As McCoy commented to Felix Frankfurter, then a War Department official: "War is still and must be the real reason for an Army and Navy. It may be a good war or

*Henry L. Stimson as secretary of war in the Taft administration. McCoy became first Stimson's friend and later his confidant and collaborator. (Courtesy Library of Congress)*

a bad war, but the Army must always be ready.''[38] In operational terms, readiness translated into what McCoy characterized as ''effective fighting power'' immediately available and capable of prolonged sustainment. Yet stating the principle was easy; transforming a tradition-bound institution into a responsive instrument for waging wars presented a far more formidable challenge. If McCoy's commitment to this task earned him a place in the army's reform tradition, his contribution in truth was not an especially original one.

Neither as soldier nor as diplomatist did McCoy ever show much evidence of creative thought. A man of his time, he possessed little capacity to see beyond its confines. On the other hand, he was sensitive to the ongoing interplay of ideas in the contemporary United States. And he paid particular attention to those ideas that applied to his own pursuits. Thus, in describing the army that he hoped would come into being, McCoy with other like-minded officers easily—perhaps glibly—evoked the reigning concepts and language of American progressivism. The hallmark of such an army, remarked McCoy, would necessarily be ''constructive efficiency.'' Besides being effective in war, the army needed to be affordable and politically acceptable. Mindful of those requirements, McCoy realized the drawbacks of relying upon a large standing army to provide that fighting power. Economically and politically, the cost of such an establishment would be prohibitive. "As business men and the country's representatives," McCoy thought, military planners should seek alternatives that "will give efficiency with the least cost." McCoy's solution—like Wood's—was to depend upon a mass citizen army, well trained and well led but maintained in reserve until called upon in an emergency.[39]

While on the general staff, McCoy also acted as Wood's spymaster. He assigned, paid, and collected reports from a network of agents in Cuba, Mexico, the Far East, and even California and Hawaii during a period of anti-Japanese agitation. McCoy's value to his clients stemmed from his access to Wood. Intelligence provided to McCoy was funnelled directly to the army's senior leadership. Directives from McCoy reflected the priorities and interests of the army chief of staff himself. McCoy's proximity to Wood enabled him to solve the problems confronting operatives in the field. One agent writing in May 1911, for example, acknowledged receipt of $25,000 and called on McCoy to find out "what Gen[eral] Wood wants in Manchuria. I have got to let my man know as soon as I can." Nor was McCoy's involvement in intelligence strictly administrative. On one occasion, he became a covert agent himself.[40]

By 1912, the Panama Canal, then two years short of completion, had become the focal point of American defense planning. Any threat—however remote—to the security of the canal or American control over the isthmus sent ripples of concern through the War Department. A somewhat improbable threat surfacing during Wood's term as chief of staff was the possibility of a competing European canal along the so-called Atrato route in northern Colombia. Informants in London claimed that a Chilean engineer, Luis Arturo Undurraga, had acquired a concession for "an entirely new and feasible route, over which a canal could be constructed at a fraction of the cost of the Panama Canal." Furthermore, Undurraga was offering to resell his concession, and "certain German bankers were negotiating to purchase it." This hint of German involvement obliged Wood to examine the proposition's feasibility. Various schemes for a canal along the Atrato River had surfaced in the past. Did there exist a route, as Undurraga claimed? Or was this merely an attempt to stampede the United States into purchasing a "concession" whose only value was as a scheme to enrich its current holders? To answer these questions, Wood dispatched McCoy and Sherwood Cheney, McCoy's classmate and a Family member, to investigate.[41]

To act as a guide through the jungles of Colombia, Father Henry Collins, a Catholic missionary familiar with the area, was hired to accompany the Americans. Concerned lest the expedition raise the suspicions of local authorities, Wood proposed that McCoy and Cheney imitate Father Collins and "go disguised as priests, tonsured, robed, and so on." Even more than Colombian officials, Wood saw Indians as a threat. As he noted privately, "They kill everyone who has tried to get across." All in all, the chief of staff anticipated "an extremely dangerous and hazardous trip."[42] Undaunted by Wood's melodramatic fears, McCoy and Cheney made their way absent tonsures and cassocks from New Orleans to Panama and then by tug to Cupica Bay, Colombia, arriving on January 6, 1912. Here, they encountered a Colombian official who was less impressed by their claim to be British subjects on a missionary trip than by their inability to produce any passports. The official ordered them to remain at Cupica until higher authorities cleared them to proceed. He also posted a guard over the American officers to insure their compliance. For two weeks, McCoy and Cheney waited. Their hammocks strung from large trees next to the beach, they swam, fished, loafed, and read the books and magazines that McCoy, with foresight, had packed. Finally, on January 21, with Cheney complaining that they had "generally exhausted the role of Lotus eaters," permission came for them to move on.[43]

The Atrato River flowed generally north-south with its mouth on the Atlantic side of the isthmus at the Gulf of Uraba. Approximately 130 miles up the Atrato, a tributary, the Napipi, sheared off to the west, entering the Pacific at Cupica Bay. The premise of the Undurraga claim was that shipping would navigate each of these streams and easily pass from one to the other—a scheme that on a map appeared at least plausible. But on January 22, as the Americans began moving up the Napipi, they found it virtually unnavigable. Not Indians but nature threatened their mission. Dragging their canoes over rocks, shoals, and fallen trees, looking like the "victims of some fell disease" as a result of attacking insects, the Americans advanced only 40 miles in three exhausting days. Dense undergrowth crowded the small stream, making it difficult to gain any perspective on the surrounding terrain. Although the promoters of the route claimed that nowhere did its height exceed 36 meters above sea level, McCoy and Cheney estimated that they finally crossed the continental divide at an altitude of over 150 meters. After a brief rest at the entrance of the Napipi, the weary officers started down the Atrato. It, too, showed little potential for ocean-going traffic. Blocked by sandbars and silt deposits, the Atrato would require enormous effort to prepare and maintain.[44]

When the officers reached the Gulf of Uraba on February 2, they made no attempt to conceal their relief. Recovering their strength as they returned to the Canal Zone by steamer—"God bless the U[nited] F[ruit] C[ompany]," wrote Cheney, "the only efficient thing in Central America"—the two Americans prepared their report. Emphasizing the difficulty of crossing the divide and the near impassability of the Napipi, they characterized the route as "impractical as compared to that of Panama. [In short,] the government need not be concerned over any scheme for rival canals from this river to the Pacific." With that, worry about the Undurraga concession was put to rest.[45]

McCoy remained on the general staff until the end of Wood's term as its chief in April 1914. He then accompanied Wood to his next assignment as commander of the Eastern Department with headquarters at Governor's Island in New York harbor—a strategic location from which Wood could carry on his preparedness campaign. After several months in New York, however, McCoy and Wood again parted ways. McCoy fell victim to the so-called Manchu law of August 1912, which restricted the time that an officer could spend on detached duty and mandated McCoy's return to his regiment by early 1915.

For McCoy, the years from 1906 to 1914 were eventful ones. With the exception of his interlude at Fort Wingate, he remained close to the center of power. Thanks to his background, reputation, and growing network of influential friends, he received opportunities for service unavailable to most officers. In no single instance had McCoy's role as yet assumed independent significance. Cumulatively, however, his activities in the years preceding the outbreak of World War I suggest the extent to which members of the political elite viewed their military counterparts not as alien to mainstream American society but as valued adjuncts in implementing national policy.

# 5

# Mexico and
# the Approach of War

On March 4, 1913, Woodrow Wilson became president of the United States, ending a decade throughout which McCoy had been personally acquainted with his commander in chief. Although the new president's election was due principally to his record as a reform governor in New Jersey—combined with a fortuitous split in the Republican party—foreign crises time and again wrenched Wilson's attention from domestic concerns to international affairs. The most recurrent of these crises and, in Arthur S. Link's judgment, "the major cause of perplexity, in both domestic and foreign affairs, for the Wilson administration" during its first two years was the Mexican revolution. The president's willingness to use military means to shape his response to that revolution insured that for the American army, too, Mexico would become a great preoccupation. Even in the years from 1915 to 1917, as war across the Atlantic relentlessly drew the United States toward intervention, Mexico remained the focus of immediate concern for soldiers such as McCoy.[1]

Taft, the outgoing president, bequeathed to Wilson a sticky situation. The revolution that had begun in 1911 when Francisco Madero overthrew Mexico's long-time dictator, Porfirio Díaz, had recently entered a new phase. The month before Wilson's inauguration, General Victoriano Huerta, an ambitious and unscrupulous freebooter, had overthrown Madero. Hoping to protect himself from Díaz's fate, the usurper had Madero murdered. When Huerta called upon Taft to recognize his new regime, the outgoing president cautiously deferred the issue to his successor.[2]

After two months of inaction during which he sought the measure of both Huerta and the Mexican revolution, Wilson initiated a policy aimed at eliminating Huerta, whom he considered a vile butcher, and setting the revolution on a path toward constitutional democracy. Over the course of the next year, a campaign of sharp and increasingly direct pressure enabled Wilson to achieve his first aim. In the process, however, the American president alienated the revolutionary leaders who sought to succeed Huerta, all of whom resented Wilson's meddling and none of whom shared his vision of the revolution's purpose. By early 1915, as Frank McCoy rejoined the Third Cavalry at Fort Sam Houston, Texas, a somewhat chastened American president no longer saw himself as the ultimate arbiter of Mexico's destiny. Yet, having once become involved in the revolution, Wilson found that he could not easily disengage from it.[3]

While still in Washington, McCoy had not shared the prevalent enthusiasm for interfering with events in Mexico. He chided friends such as Gutzon Borglum for their belligerence. Mocking the noted sculptor for "reek[ing] with fighting blood," McCoy observed that "if it were not for us altruistic soldier missionaries, you jingoes would have forced us into an unjust war against the poor, downtrodden peons of Mexico." Writing to Hugh Scott, now a brigadier general, McCoy commended Wilson's "watchful waiting policy" and foresaw little likelihood of its changing. McCoy admitted that Mexico might have difficulty in restoring political stability but added that "I don't see myself any need of there ever being war over that." Moreover, he asserted, "the President certainly does not anticipate any warlike intervention." Here McCoy underestimated Wilson's determination to unseat Huerta: A month later, American forces occupied the Mexican port of Veracruz.[4]

Only after experiencing firsthand the spillover of the revolution along the border did McCoy become more militant. His return to the Third Cavalry coincided with a pronounced increase in tension throughout southern Texas. January 1915 saw publication of the so-called Plan of San Diego, a scheme of reputed Mexican origin that called for an uprising of Mexican-Americans to secure the independence of Texas, New Mexico, Arizona, Colorado, and California. Whites living in the lower Rio Grande Valley reacted to the threat posed by this fantastic scheme with utter seriousness and demanded federal troops for their protection.[5]

McCoy's regiment was among those tasked to respond to this call. On March 1, he led two cavalry troops out of Fort Sam Houston and headed for the border. Two weeks later, after a demanding march of over 300 miles, his column established a base at Mission, Texas, a small town near the Rio Grande, 60 miles northwest of Brownsville. McCoy's detachment arrived to find that, although no rebellion had occurred, the Plan of San Diego had left the valley awash with racial animosity. McCoy's assignment to uphold order in the Mission Patrol District translated into one of keeping Anglos from launching a race war against Mexican-Americans. This, he soon realized, was best accomplished by establishing a military presence sufficiently visible to convince the white population that it had nothing to fear. McCoy made the best of this hard and thankless task, assuring Stimson that he felt "the enthusiasm of a youngster" about being back with troops and urging the former secretary—whom he now addressed as

Harry—to visit the border. Yet the daily grind of operations aimed at keeping Americans from each other's throats strained even McCoy's usual equanimity. By August, his appraisal of the situation betrayed a certain testiness:

> The women all up and down the valley are hysterically afraid of shadows, the men all pack arms, patrol with the troops, and shriek through their representatives for more soldiers. I am still . . . chasing rumors, and . . . so far there hasn't been an untoward happening in my district. And I don't think there will be [because] the greasers are worse scared if possible than the whites. . . . never again let me hear about the brave Texans, whipping their weight in wildcats. . . . I feel so ashamed of this white livered lot. Not a bit do I show it though. . . . We go barging out most every night, chase down the rumor, let them see the soldiers and give them a sleep.[6]

McCoy's sense of missing out on large events and his growing disenchantment with Wilson did nothing to improve his mood. In the spring of 1915, while McCoy pursued phantoms and calmed overwrought civilians, the German U-boat campaign was threatening to involve the United States in the European war. Meanwhile, from its headquarters in New York harbor, Leonard Wood's crusade to rearm the United States was gaining momentum. Despite the appeal of serving with troops, McCoy chafed at his exclusion from such developments: "All sorts of wondrous things are going on in the great world and for the moment I seem very out of them," he lamented.[7]

The German sinking of the *Lusitania* on May 7, 1915, with 124 Americans among the nearly 1,200 fatalities, outraged McCoy. So, too, did Wilson's subsequent refusal to combine his diplomatic efforts to solve the U-boat problem with preparations for military contingencies. "The President's note was a fine one of course, why shouldn't it be," he told his family on May 24. "But you and the whole country have been jumping with relief over words. . . . Here we are on the verge of war, on which brink we'll be balancing for years to come and this idealistic wordmaking administration is not doing one solitary thing towards preparing for its great and dangerous part." Wilson's greatest predecessors all recognized the role of military power in resolving international disputes, McCoy believed, yet "the President at a time like that of the Lusitania [says] 'We are too proud to fight.' Bosh."[8]

The *Lusitania* crisis turned McCoy against Wilson and planted him firmly in the camp of Theodore Roosevelt, whose calls for a holy war against the Hun put him far out in front of public opinion. "Don't feel badly over T.R.," McCoy told his mother. "I love him for the mistakes he makes, for he speaks the truth and is not afraid." During the summer of 1915, Roosevelt began laying plans for raising a volunteer division of mounted riflemen that he hoped to lead either into Mexico or to France, wherever the United States got in a fight first. The former Rough Rider enlisted as key subordinates the bright lights of the officer corps: James G.

Harbord, Henry T. Allen, Fox Connor, and Peyton March, among others. As division chief of staff, "the most important position under me," Roosevelt wanted McCoy. His former aide, disgruntled with the inactivity of his border mission and angered by Wilson's caution, accepted with alacrity. Over the next year, McCoy corresponded frequently with the former president and with Henry Stimson, another Roosevelt Division recruit, in formulating plans for the unit.[9]

The *Lusitania* affair also increased McCoy's enthusiasm for Wood's preparedness drive. Through the summer of 1915, McCoy carefully followed the experiment in voluntary military training at Plattsburg, New York, which he saw as "the beginning of a great movement . . . throughout the nation." Wood and his aide, Gordon Johnston, kept McCoy up to date, as did those Family members who endorsed Wood's campaign. A number of 1718's "civilians"—Willard Straight, Basil Miles, and George Marvin, a Family journalist—trained alongside other bluebloods under Wood's tutelage at Plattsburg. The Family's citizen-soldiers provided McCoy with detailed training reports—"As a fellow soldier I salute you," wrote Straight—and exchanged optimistic forecasts on the prospects of the preparedness movement.[10]

Straight tried to cheer McCoy with predictions of armed intervention in Mexico in the near future. To McCoy, although poised to participate in such an operation, intervention seemed unlikely. To Straight, anxious to share in such an adventure, only a suitable pretext was wanting. With such a need in mind, Straight became a driving spirit behind the Red Cross's National Committee for Mexican Relief, hoping that "somehow or other we are to be the parties responsible for intervention in Mexico." Revealing a cynical understanding of American antimilitarism, he explained to McCoy: "You will of course appreciate that it is a very different thing to send the brutal and licentious soldiery across the border to protect people handing out loaves of bread and dried fish to the starving populace than it would be if said soldiery were to go over first and be followed by a pack train of Angels of Mercy."[11]

By September, the rumors that McCoy's troops had been pursuing for months began to take on substance. No longer did Straight's prophecy of intervention seem quite so improbable. No longer did his unit's presence on the border seem quite so pointless. Parties of armed Mexicans launched a series of attacks throughout the lower Rio Grande Valley, looting villages, holding up trains, and ambushing isolated American patrols. Although the raiders depicted themselves as advance agents of a revived Plan of San Diego, they probably pursued more limited aims prescribed by Venustiano Carranza, first chief of the Constitutionalists, foremost among the factions vying for control of Mexico.[12]

With his two cavalry troops deployed along a 32-mile stretch of river, McCoy lacked the strength to prevent Mexican attacks, most of which took place at night. Whenever local civilians reported an incident, McCoy could only mount a reaction force and give chase—typically tracking down his quarry only after it slipped back across the river. In at least one instance, he watched as Carrancista soldiers on the far side "welcomed back the looting band . . . with open arms." Although under orders not to initiate hostilities, McCoy's soldiers used the slightest provocation as an excuse to fire across the river, venting their frustration and inflicting occasional casualties on the defiant raiders.[13]

Such skirmishing inspired journalistic predictions of war with Mexico. The increased unrest stirred up further racial animosity. It also meant long days and sleepless nights in the saddle for McCoy's soldiers—in his view the only ones who "kept their heads, and tried to keep the peace without excitedly . . . shooting greasers or giving encouragement to that pastime." September's raids also persuaded senior commanders to bolster their forces. By November, 20,000 American troops were patrolling the border. Two more cavalry troops and a signal company joined the contingent that McCoy commanded at Mission. With so many detachments chasing bandits and generally patrolling disturbed neighborhoods, McCoy traded his horse for an automobile to keep track of his command. When the level of activity thereafter subsided, McCoy reported hopefully that "the border war of the Press is squashed for a few moments and the excitement and fright of the neighbors of Hidalgo county allayed. Enough at any rate to give us a few peaceful nights in bed, and to suspend the habit of shooting stray greasers on sight."[14]

Actually, McCoy had little confidence that beefed-up military forces alone would guarantee harmony along the border. In September, Herbert Croly, editor of the *New Republic,* the journal founded by Straight in 1914, asked for McCoy's views of the situation for use without attribution. The probable result, entitled "On the Mexican Border," appeared in the journal's issue of October 9. Like McCoy, the anonymous author of this piece believed that the crux of the border conflict was race: "The Mexican is as suspicious of the Gringo as the latter is contemptuous of the Greaser," he wrote. Given the contrast between prosperity north of the border and near starvation to the south, the temptation to raid the American side would continue to be irresistible. Carranza's followers lacked the authority to prevent such incursions and at times even sympathized with them. Hence, looking to the future, "raiding is more likely to increase than to diminish."[15] Within days, events proved this prediction correct as raiders again struck in McCoy's district. A party of thirty attacked a small outpost at Ojo de Agua, killing or wounding all but four of the American soldiers stationed there. For once, McCoy and his relief column reached the scene when the fight was still in progress. Surprised by the reinforcements, the enemy "scattered like quail in the brush," leaving behind five dead.[16]

Although Mexican crossings again declined after the Ojo de Agua fight, McCoy's outfit continued its patrols. To Wood, he boasted that his troops had killed twenty-seven raiders since September 1. By the time his troopers were pulled off the line in November 1915, they had assumed responsibility for fully 90 miles of river front with "every out-post linked up with wire-less, telephone, and rockets and quick relief." In January 1916, McCoy—still a captain—assumed command of the entire Third Squadron, Third Cavalry. For the next several months, he found no little satisfaction in leading the squadron as it rotated between tours of border patrol and visits to the more hospitable environs of Brownsville to refit and break in recruits.[17]

Wilson's dispatch of the Punitive Expedition after Pancho Villa's raid of March 9, 1916, on Columbus, New Mexico, increased tension along the lower Rio Grande yet again. To reinforce the forces on the border, Wilson on May 9 activated the national guard of Texas, New Mexico, and Arizona. That same month, Brig. Gen. James Parker arrived at Brownsville to assume command of all units deployed in the lower valley. These included not only the Third Cavalry but also four regiments of regular infantry, two regiments of Texas militia, and two battalions of field artillery. "Galloping Jim" Parker, Medal of Honor winner and the army's premier exponent of the horse, looked the part of a cavalry officer with his luxuriant head of silver hair and well-groomed mustache. Noted more for panache than for clear thinking, Parker was perfect for leading any would-be charges into Mexico. But when it came to molding his conglomeration of diverse units into a coherent force, Parker badly needed help. Whatever polish Parker lacked, McCoy had. So when the general decided to form a provisional headquarters to assist in controlling his growing command, he shrewdly turned the job over to McCoy, appointing him to serve as his chief of staff.[18]

The troop build-up and the advance of General John J. Pershing's expedition into Mexico created a heightened sense of expectation along the border. American tactics became more aggressive. The War Department authorized Parker to cross the Rio Grande in hot pursuit, instructions that Parker interpreted loosely. When Mexican irregulars on June 15 inflicted several casualties on an American patrol at San Ignacio, he alerted a squadron of 400 cavalrymen, who splashed across the river—a full two days later—on June 17. General Alfredo Ricaut, in charge of local Carrancista forces, demanded that the Americans withdraw immediately. According to McCoy, when Parker responded by threatening to "attack him with his whole force," the Mexican commander backed down. The American squadron returned of its own volition a day later, but the event seemed to set a precedent for similar operations on an even larger scale. Wilson gave added credence to that view by mobilizing the rest of the national guard on June 18. "We are all on [our] toes to cross over at the word," wrote McCoy. "Here's the gala . . . long needed to clear and clean the atmosphere. All Mexico . . . is seemingly wild with anti-gringoism. . . . If only we go in with a big and strong sweep." Yet McCoy's lack of confidence in Wilson gave rise to second thoughts. "The air will be full of notes and compromises and arbitration," he predicted. "I wish we were inspired and backed up by a civil administration made for war, and not for highfalutin sentiments about humanity in [the] abstract."[19]

McCoy's premonition of compromise proved well-founded. Both nations drew back from the brink of a war neither wanted. As a result, rather than launching boldly into Mexico, Parker's command found itself struggling to survive inundation by the additional militiamen mobilized to meet the crisis and for whose care the regulars now assumed responsibility. By July 31, 110,000 national guardsmen had arrived on the border, over 30,000 of them in Parker's sector. By summer's end, his command had swollen to include nineteen regiments of infantry plus cavalry, artillery, and support units.[20] McCoy initially viewed the arrival of these reinforcements as a mixed blessing. "We are practically disorganizing our regulars to receive and train state troops," he wrote in early July, "but if it were not done, they would be helpless." At the same time, for an officer disappointed by his exclusion from Wood's preparedness campaign, here was an ideal laboratory in which to test Wood's hypothesis—that a mass of virtually untrained citizens could be quickly and efficiently transformed into a competent military force.[21]

Much work needed to be done. To McCoy's eye, "the state troops came pouring in ready for a picnic, not for war." Yet the regulars, believing that the guard was joining them for a Mexican invasion of which the Punitive Expedition represented only the first increment, embraced their new responsibilities wholeheartedly. As McCoy reported in August: "Regular officers are with each regiment—as guides, philosophers & friends, non-coms with the companies, our cooks teaching their cooks, our horseshoers shoeing their horses, etc, etc, etc." Training citizen-soldiers proved to be "a fine game," McCoy told Wood in November. "If we are able to hold them a few months longer," he added, "[we] will have accomplished much of the same sort of training and propoganda [sic] as you have so successfully done at Plattsburg."[22]

Remarkably, McCoy also found time during this period to compile his own contribution to preparedness propaganda, *Principles of Military Training*, published the following year as part of a series called the National Service Library. McCoy's 381-page work covered such wide-ranging subjects as discipline, field hygiene, tactics, and training methods picked up over the course of nearly twenty years of service. A book of no great originality, it was instead a compendium of proven techniques and inherited wisdom ("an infantryman is only as good as his feet"). McCoy asserted that a soldier's "mind is at least as useful as his body and its training must not be forgotten." Toward that end, he offered a list of suggested readings extending to over 200 titles, interesting as a reflection of the thoroughness with which he himself had studied his profession over the years. Starting with *On War* ("the most profound analysis and description of war that has ever appeared in any language"), it included works by Homer, Shakespeare, Francis Parkman, Helmuth von Moltke, Emory Upton, and Leo Tolstoy, among others. In his introduction, McCoy observed that the war in Europe demonstrated the importance of "training whole nations on the right lines of progressive systems." Yet Americans had never developed the framework of an adequate military policy. As a result, throughout the nation's history, "the only consistent school of war in the United States [had] been war itself," a school in which the lessons were usually painful. *Principles of Military Training* provided practical advice for citizens who aspired to create at last a progressive military system suited to the United States.[23]

For the guardsmen assigned to Parker's tutelage, rigorous training throughout the summer and fall of 1916 climaxed in November with a nine-day tactical maneuver. This exercise culminated with an impressive ceremony on November 25 when McCoy paraded two full national guard divisions in a massive review before Parker. By now, McCoy was far more upbeat about the capabilities of his citizen-soldiers. Although the enlisted soldiers as yet remained "far ahead of their officers," he reported that five months of training had made the guardsmen into "a wonderful body of men."[24] Whatever the success of this experiment at developing citizen-soldiers, McCoy could view his own role with satisfaction. Completion of the guard's training program concluded that role and marked the end of McCoy's border tour. In December, he left for a new assignment, a posting directly attributable to Family connections.

In October 1915, President Wilson appointed Family member Henry P. Fletcher ambassador to Mexico—a position vacant since July 1913—thereby providing 1718 H Street with a considerable opportunity. The events of 1916, especially the presence of the Punitive Expedition on Mexican soil, delayed Fletcher's departure for Mexico City. When he finally did take up his post in February 1917, the staff accompanying him illustrated both the usefulness of Family connections and the opportunities for military men to cross over into diplomacy. Two diplomatic secretaries assisted Fletcher in Mexico: George T. Summerlin, a West Point graduate of the class of 1896 and a resident of 1718, and Matthew Elting Hanna, also a West Pointer and a classmate of McCoy's. A member of Leonard Wood's clique, Hanna designed the Cuban public school system created during the first occupation and had only recently left the army for a diplomatic career; he also maintained close connections with 1718, although his marital status precluded full membership. To fill the post of military attaché, Assistant Secretary of State William Phillips turned to the Family's military contingent and recruited Frank McCoy. It was thus with some justification that McCoy reported after arriving in Mexico City that the four-member mission bestowed upon the reopened American embassy "a distinctive 1718 character."[25]

The traditional function of a military attaché is to report to his government on military activities within the host nation. In Mexico, where the regime still devoted most of its energies to eradicating insurgents like Villa and Emiliano Zapata, the line separating civil and military affairs was ill-defined if not invisible. With Mexican military leaders playing a large political role, McCoy's responsibilities assumed particular importance. For the Mexican revolution as a political or social movement, McCoy—finally promoted to major—possessed neither understanding nor sympathy. Analyzing the radical Mexican constitution of 1917 soon after his arrival, he reported that it contained "much social reform stuff" and "individual rights and States Rights carried to the extreme." McCoy did not take such rhetoric seriously, contending that "as usual there won't be much attention paid to it in practice." McCoy viewed the revolution as a façade behind which self-anointed generals who had spent their lives in utter obscurity competed for power merely to exploit it for personal gain. "For the successful revolutionist," he wrote, "this is a great country for graft and topside opportunity."[26]

The head of the War Ministry and hence the key official to whom McCoy required access was General Álvaro Obregón, Carranza's best field commander. On March 14, after the first of several meetings with Obregón, McCoy described him as "a man of strong personality and a good deal of reserve force." Obregón amused the American attaché with his attempt "to play the Cincinnatus act." Despite his protests "as to his pure patriotism and desire for the simple life of yore," McCoy believed—correctly—that the general considered himself "a good rival or successor to the Primer Jefe [Carranza]." McCoy boldly suggested to Obregón that, as the only military attaché accredited to the Mexican government, he be given special consideration so as to get "the correct dope on what happened in military affairs." But Obregón was no more impressed with this pose than McCoy had been with the general's.[27]

The reopening of the embassy in Mexico coincided with the final crisis over German U-boat policy leading up to the American declaration of war. Once the publication of the Zimmermann Telegram on March 1 thrust Mexico into the middle of the German-American conflict, McCoy concentrated on determining the extent to which local German activity threatened American security. No matter how fanciful Zimmermann's proposal that Mexico regain control of Texas, New Mexico, and Arizona, German-Mexican collaboration was not altogether implausible. In November 1916, Carranza had informed Germany of his nation's sympathy for the Reich and expressed interest in some form of German-Mexican cooperation. He even offered to permit the German navy to construct permanent bases for U-boats in Mexico.[28]

Through the spring of 1917, American consuls, customs officials, intelligence agents, and private citizens deluged Washington with reports of sinister German activity in Mexico. The cumulative impact of such information—usually overstated and unconfirmed—was to fuel heightened concern among responsible American officials. The State Department counselor, Frank L. Polk, passed a report to Fletcher claiming that Mexican leaders were "under the domination and under the pay of Germans," who were "the real brains and initiative in Mexico." From Arizona, Pershing passed along rumors that Carranza had contracted with German officers to organize and train the Mexican army. Secretary of State Robert Lansing informed Wilson that "the military party" controlling Mexico was "intensely pro-German." He predicted that Mexico would deny the United States access to American-owned oil fields in Mexico, an attempt that "may result in an open declaration of war or in an ultimatum which will result in war."[29]

Reports of German operations in Mexico fell generally into three categories: sabotage directed against American-owned oil fields; construction of submarine bases on the Gulf coast; and establishment of wireless stations to coordinate U-boat operations. It now became an important part of McCoy's job to determine the veracity of such reports. While still maintaining his contacts in the Mexican War Ministry and accompanying Fletcher to the inevitable round of diplomatic social events, McCoy began devoting the bulk of his attention to "keeping track of German and Mexican intrigues and following the trail of 1001 rumors."[30]

Through extensive contacts with American businessmen and consultations with friendly diplomats, McCoy reached conclusions about the German threat at variance with those emanating from Washington. He refused to equate anti-Americanism in Mexico with support for Germany. "Of course the Mexicans are rather flattered by the international notice given them in the Zimmerman [sic] note," he observed in April, and Carranza, "whose long suit is saying nothing while sitting and taking notice," could be counted on "to try to keep everybody guessing." Yet keeping in mind the precarious stability of the Constitutionalist regime and its reliance upon American-supplied military equipment, McCoy believed that the First Chief was "too canny to invite any break with us." McCoy also discounted reports that Obregón, whom he saw as the real power in Mexico, entertained a special fondness for the Germans. "I don't think he likes any foreigners," McCoy observed of Obregón, "but is using them for his own purposes."[31]

Further investigation confirmed these conclusions. McCoy fully expected Germany to use Mexico as a base for espionage, and he agreed that it was of "the utmost importance to keep discriminating watch" over such activities. Yet he cautioned his superiors not to overreact. As he told Fletcher in May, American newspapers were exaggerating the threat that such activity posed to American interests. As time passed, Carranza's "absolute economic dependence" on the United States and "the great and vigorous war policy outlined for America" would weaken Mexican sympathy for Germany. In McCoy's view, Germans in Mexico were too few and too weak to threaten the oil fields near Tampico. American oil companies were "well able to look after themselves and their interests." Concerning the rumored U-boat facilities along the Mexican coast, McCoy was "unable to find any basis whatsoever." Although the German legation had indeed established a wireless station in Mexico City, it was "never . . . in communication with Berlin, contrary reports notwithstanding." All in all, McCoy did not see "German activities at present or future as a weighty menace, provided the neutrality of Mexico be strict or friendly, which may safely be assumed."[32]

Whatever the fascination of running a large-scale intelligence operation, the fact remained that American entry into the war in April transformed Mexico from a diplomatic hotspot into a military backwater. Anxious to join the American forces bound for France, McCoy sought to curtail his tour as attaché. Turning first to his military contacts, he asked his old friend Hugh Scott, now the army chief of staff, to secure his return. When Scott's request foundered on Secretary of State Lansing's objection that the attaché could not be spared, McCoy shifted to Family channels. He persuaded Fletcher to write the State Department, volunteering to release him, and also asked Assistant Secretary of State Phillips to use his influence. This tactic proved much more successful, and on June 1, 1917—after only three months in Mexico—McCoy departed for home. Two weeks later, after a hasty farewell at 1718 and a personal send-off by Straight in New York harbor, McCoy was enroute to France for duty with the American Expeditionary Forces (AEF).[33]

McCoy's contact with the Mexican revolution—an event whose significance quite exceeded his comprehension—had ended. Yet his dealings with Latin America did not. Ten years after his departure from Mexico City, he returned to the region at the head of yet another American mission created to sort out a political tangle, this time in Nicaragua. McCoy's contempt for Latin American politics and his belief that corruption and self-interest alone motivated Latin American politicians—conclusions he reached during his service in Cuba and Mexico—both colored his actions in this later episode and limited his effectiveness.

# 6

# World War
# and Its Aftermath

In traditional military biography, campaigns and battles play a crucial part, framing the narrative and often furnishing its climax. The protagonist's actions over the course of a few days or weeks of combat define his historical significance. But Frank Ross McCoy was no typical soldier. Not battlefield exploits but his career's overall dimensions provide the measure of his importance. His signal achievement in the decades before World War II lay in straddling the then supposedly unrelated worlds of soldier and statesman, obliging us to revise our notion of the military's role in that era. Although noted for his contributions as a diplomat and colonial administrator, McCoy remained in his own eyes first and foremost a military officer, "one of those lucky individuals who love to call themselves 'poor soldiers.'" Nor was he an unblooded diplomat in uniform in the mold of Generals Tasker Bliss and Enoch Crowder. To a greater extent than other officers favored with opportunities for unconventional service, McCoy succeeded in establishing impressive credentials in the strictly military realm as well.[1]

The pattern of McCoy's career prior to 1917, punctuated with assignments of visibility and substance, established his reputation as one of the most promising officers of his generation. He served in the right places for the right people and performed well throughout. Yet the professional capital accrued over twenty years would have amounted to little had McCoy not proved himself yet again in World War I. In a profession in which shared experiences are key determinants of individual status, active service in France became a critical rite of passage. To remain in 1917-1918 on the wrong side of the Atlantic was not only embarrassing personally but also seemed a fatal blow to a military career. Able soldiers such as Dwight D. Eisenhower and Matthew B. Ridgway would overcome their lack of combat experience in World War I. Yet even decades later, in memoirs written after they achieved high office, their disappointment and chagrin at being kept from France still lingered. Unlike Eisenhower and Ridgway, McCoy had the personal connections to preclude relegation to a stateside assignment. Indeed, barely two weeks after the first contingent of the AEF reached France on June 13, he arrived in Paris.[2]

During their first year at war, Americans engaged in little actual fighting. Instead, under the tutelage of General Pershing, the AEF progressively grew in strength and prepared for combat. The instrument devised to assist Pershing in transforming an untested American army into a battleworthy force was his General Headquarters (GHQ), located originally in Paris, but after September 1917 at Chaumont. Assignment to GHQ became a mark of distinction. Not surprisingly, many of the service's brightest officers gravitated to Pershing's staff: James G. Harbord, Hugh Drum, William D. Conner, Fox Connor, George Van Horn Mosely, Billy Mitchell, and John McCaulay Palmer, among others. Collectively, they would become the "Chaumont circle"—envied and resented by those less favored. For many among them, this identification with Pershing early in the war became the first step toward continuing prominence in the army of the interwar period.[3]

Assigned to GHQ as soon as he arrived in France, McCoy felt no qualms about joining such distinguished company. Members, like himself, of the elite of the officer corps, their paths had often crossed his in the past. "Every one of them I know well," he remarked, "and have served with before." Such common background made for a personal compatibility that eased the process of melding the staff into a team. It also added to the congeniality of life at GHQ. By the time McCoy arrived, his friend James Logan had already established himself as Pershing's personnel officer. Sharing a villa at Chaumont, the two Family members dubbed their quarters "abri [dug-out] 1718" and made it a stopover for old friends now in uniform, such as Henry L. Stimson and Willard Straight. (In Straight's biased view, "Thanks to Logan and McCoy largely," the GHQ staff was "running everything over here.") McCoy renewed his acquaintance with Robert Bacon, the former secretary of state and ambassador to France who was now a major on Pershing's staff. Beginning each day with a prebreakfast gallop through the countryside around Chaumont, the two became close friends. Bacon described McCoy as "a perfect corker," and told his wife, "I am crazy about him." Of the old friendships McCoy now reclaimed, the most important was that of James G. Harbord, Pershing's chief of staff and McCoy's immediate superior. Bluff, influential, and highly respected, Harbord was GHQ's self-made man. Failing to get into West Point, he enlisted and earned a commission from the ranks in 1891. He made his name in the army during extended service with the Philippine constabulary. The two officers had kept in touch since their days in the Moro Province where Harbord had been another of Leonard Wood's admirers. In his new job as secretary of the general staff, McCoy coordinated the administrative functioning of GHQ while serving as Harbord's key assistant. The chief of staff especially appreciated McCoy's buoyant sociability and his refusal to let the pressures of Chaumont interfere with an occasional meal at a fine restaurant or an outing away from the office. To his family, McCoy confided in September, "My personal and official relations with Harbord . . . are closer than ever."[4]

Certainly, in the nearly two decades that had elapsed since he embarked for Santiago de Cuba, McCoy had lost little of his enthusiasm for war. "The times are great and glorious," he wrote in July. "We feel sorry for everybody before and hereafter for missing [the war]." In October he commented in a similar vein: "It is not done to confess it now-a-days I know, but I do love war and this war beats the Dutch both figuratively and literally, and is the grandest performance [there] ever was, and every day I'm thanking my lucky stars I'm all in it, and hope to be to the bitter end."[5]

Duty at GHQ was important, comfortable, and rewarding—promoted twice in short succession, McCoy was soon a colonel—but it kept him far from the front. As the AEF inched closer to actual combat, he became restive. Encountering his friend in Paris in January 1918, Stimson found McCoy "hungry to get into the line." The desperate German offensive begun in March 1918 that forced the hasty commitment of American troops only added to his anxiety. To be a staff officer at such a time, he reflected, was "not . . . comforting to the soul." Hearing of an opening in the First Infantry Division, he volunteered to give up his colonel's eagles in return for command of a battalion. Although Harbord, himself jockeying for a frontline billet, endorsed the proposal, Pershing rejected it. Discouraged, McCoy could only comment: "Everything but the fighting seems banal."[6]

Finally, in late April, the American commander in chief relented. Interrupting McCoy's plea for a friend seeking command of the 165th Infantry, Pershing surprised his subordinate by abruptly announcing, "I have selected you myself for that particular regiment." It was the opportunity for which McCoy had waited. Better known as the Fighting Sixty-ninth, the 165th was one of four regiments composing the Forty-second (Rainbow) Division. After a farewell given by Stimson and Straight, McCoy hurriedly left Chaumont "full up with pride and happiness" and reported to the division at Baccarat.[7]

The 165th was a national guard outfit composed of equal parts tradition, sentiment, and boisterousness. The regiment's two previous commanders "had their heads cut off" for failing to restrain the Irish New Yorkers filling its ranks. As a "rank outsider," McCoy judged it a "sporting proposition" to see whether or not he could succeed where his predecessors failed. Emphasizing his identification with his troops, McCoy declared half seriously that overnight he "changed from a canny Scot to a very hot hearted Irishman." More relevant to his prospects for success was his relationship with Father Francis P. Duffy, the regimental chaplain. Father Duffy—in McCoy's description, "a spicy and charming personality"—wielded great influence among the rank and file. His backing was essential if McCoy were to establish more than nominal authority over his command. Fortunately, the two hit it off immediately. Father Duffy was taken by his colonel's "dignity of bearing, charm of manner and . . . alert and wide-ranging intelligence." For his part, the new regimental commander soon learned to appreciate the value of a chaplain who "not only . . . preach[ed] the gospel, but expounded with much force the rules of military discipline."[8]

Because the Baccarat sector was a quiet one, McCoy had the opportunity to become acquainted with other key subordinates while putting the finishing touches on the regiment's training. To judge from Father Duffy's account—one admittedly generous in praising anyone associated with the 165th—the men of the regiment soon held their new commander in high regard. "It is a delight to go to our mess with McCoy's stimulating wit," the chaplain recorded in his diary, and to discuss "the various aspects of war and life opened up by all sorts of interesting people—Bishops, diplomats, soldiers, and correspondents who drift in from afar, drawn by the magnetism of our colonel." McCoy's injunction to his officers—"to enjoy this war—the only war most of them can hope to have"—went well with the bellicose temper already existing in the regiment.[9]

The last spasms of the German spring offensive interrupted the 165th's stay at Baccarat and brought it into the fight for the first time. As part of an effort to reconstitute a reserve depleted by successive German attacks, the Forty-second Division in early July was reassigned to the French XXI Corps. The division assumed positions east of Rheims, on the shoulder of a salient that a German drive six weeks earlier had pushed south to the Marne River. While the bulk of the division remained in reserve, one of McCoy's three battalions occupied the forward defensive line alongside two French divisions. By July 7, the French determined that an attack toward Rheims, designed to widen the Marne salient, was imminent. All indicators pointed to the night of July 14 as the probable time of the assault.[10] Alerted to the prospects of a major action, McCoy confessed that July 14 was "a very tense day." To ease that tension, he invited several Allied officers to lunch in the regimental mess and broke out some vintage French wine. By evening, the troops retired to their battle positions and McCoy to his command post to wait.[11]

General Henri Gourad, to whose Fourth Army the Forty-second Division was assigned, had no intention of waiting passively for the Boche to strike. To disrupt the offensive, Gourad unleashed an artillery barrage shortly before midnight against German attack positions. The enemy responded in kind but with little effect because his shells, in McCoy's words, were roaring over the regiment's positions "like freight trains." An hour before dawn, the Germans emerged from their trenches, and over the next six hours, the French 170th Division, with McCoy's Second Battalion, beat off seven separate German assaults. Further efforts to breach the Allied lines over the next two days were also repulsed. Failing to achieve a breakthrough, the German high command on July 18 suspended the attack. Although most of McCoy's unit remained out of the fight, his Second Battalion had been severely battered while fighting alongside the

French. Sustaining most of the regiment's 269 casualties over the four-day battle, the battalion won high praise from Gouraud.[12]

This baptism of fire was a mere prelude. Once the German offensive exhausted itself, the Allies took the initiative. To reduce the Marne salient, the Allies launched on July 18 a counteroffensive—the first in which the AEF figured prominently. Two American divisions—one of them commanded by Harbord—pierced the salient's western face toward Soissons. Their line of communications threatened by the Allied thrust, the Germans withdrew their exposed units. By July 25, they had pulled back to strong positions on the high ground north of the Ourcq River near Sergy. Units deployed along the southern tip of the salient, including the U.S. I Corps, now received orders to pursue the retreating Germans.[13]

Having rested briefly after the fight at Champagne, the Rainbow Division joined U.S. I Corps, assigned to the French Sixth Army. On July 25, the division relieved the Twenty-sixth (Yankee) Division and the French 167th Division and assumed the corps mission of pursuing the Boche. As the Fighting Sixty-ninth began occupying the sector previously held by the 167th, departing French officers informed McCoy that the enemy was still retreating. McCoy passed this information to Col. Douglas MacArthur, the division chief of staff. MacArthur replied that the Forty-second's general officers were temporarily absent, which made McCoy the senior officer present in the division. With that, McCoy announced that "the pursuit would be pressed with everything I could find at the front." Throughout July 27, McCoy's regiment advanced northward, delayed only by scattered German machine guns in otherwise abandoned positions. By nightfall, the regiment reached the Ourcq, where heavy shelling from the far bank and strafing German aircraft indicated that the enemy intended to make a stand.[14]

Anxious to keep pressure on an enemy it mistakenly believed was still withdrawing, French Sixth Army headquarters ordered a hasty crossing of the Ourcq to seize the heights overlooking the river. The pell-mell advance of the previous two days left the Rainbow Division in no condition to mount a coordinated attack, but the army commander was insistent. Still without support on either flank and short of artillery, McCoy received orders to cross the river before daybreak on July 28. Although the Ourcq itself did not present a major obstacle, the well-prepared German positions stretching along the commanding terrain on the far side made it a formidable challenge. McCoy questioned the wisdom of such a hastily prepared operation, but was told that the attack would be executed as planned and indeed that "if necessary, I must sacrifice my command to the effort."[15]

Thus, the Fighting Sixty-ninth "was made the spearhead of the entire army and pushed forward by a most explicit order as a forlorn hope against a whole German division." At 3:45 A.M. on July 28, supported only by a handful of mortars, McCoy attacked with two battalions. His remaining unit, Maj. William J. "Wild Bill" Donovan's First Battalion, stayed in reserve. The audacity of assaulting across the river with a single regiment won some initial gains. As

McCoy observed, "The attack was executed with such quickness and spirit that the Germans were entirely surprised, the crossings forced, and their machine gun company and defensive detachments captured with only a few casualties on our side." Although pleased to have gained a precarious hold on the far bank, McCoy knew that such an easy success merely signified the lull before the storm. In short order, the Germans counterattacked, aiming to throw the Americans back across the Ourcq. This began a bitter four-day sequence of attack and counterattack that, in McCoy's words, "tried the Regiment from colonel to private." Though alone initially, McCoy's regiment was soon reinforced. By midday on July 28, the remainder of the Forty-second Division had joined the battle. Eventually, elements of three other American divisions were thrown into the fight.[16]

Like any good commander, McCoy positioned himself far forward on the battlefield. With his command post exposed to enemy fire, several members of his staff were killed or wounded, but McCoy himself remained unscathed. By the end of the first day, he had established telephonic communications with brigade headquarters and each of his battalions, giving him some control over the fight for the first time. For the rest of the battle, he maneuvered his units, provided for their logistical needs, inspired the downhearted (according to Father Duffy), and above all coordinated fire support as more and more field artillery was committed to the fight. Although surrounded at one point by most of the Fourth Prussian Guards Division, the regiment held on and even expanded its foothold on the north bank. Finally, American tenacity paid off. On the night of August 1-2, the Germans abandoned their positions and broke contact. The battle of the Ourcq was won.[17]

At once, the high command pressed forward units in pursuit. Its ranks decimated, its survivors exhausted, the 165th limped forward several miles toward the Vesle River. Here, on August 3, the U.S. Fourth Division relieved the Rainbow in the line. As his weary regiment moved toward the rear, McCoy halted it to allow Father Duffy to deliver a "fiery and stirring sermon." Despite their success, McCoy's soldiers might well have needed some cheering up. In this one engagement, the 165th suffered nearly 2,000 casualties—about the same, McCoy observed, as the entire army had sustained throughout the Santiago campaign of 1898.[18]

The 165th settled near Bourmont for a much-needed refit. McCoy emerged from the Aisne-Marne offensive, as it came to be known, with only a touch of mustard gas, but the stress of combat showed in the twenty pounds that he had lost. Envious friends who visited from GHQ reported that he was well but thin. Despite the stress and recollection of the casualties that the regiment had suffered, McCoy found combat command exhilarating. To his family he wrote: "I'm having the time of my life."[19] Yet his days as a regimental commander were numbered. As the combat of 1918 revealed the strengths and frailties of American military leaders at every echelon, shifts in personnel became frequent. Commanders found wanting were shunted off to less-demanding responsibilities.

Those proving themselves in battle advanced rapidly. Thus, by the time that the Rainbow Division prepared to return to the front in late August, McCoy was no longer in its ranks. Instead, he was assuming command of the Sixty-third Brigade, one of two brigades composing the Thirty-second (Red Arrow) Division. It took McCoy fourteen years of service as a captain to win promotion to major in early 1917. Now, barely a year and a half later, he pinned on the star of a brigadier general.[20]

The Sixty-third Brigade comprised the 125th and 126th Infantry Regiments, each formed from elements of the Michigan National Guard. McCoy took command on August 29 with the Thirty-second Division in the midst of the Oise-Aisne offensive. Having been battered in recent fighting near Juvigny, his unit spent several days in support of its sister brigade, the Sixty-fourth, which was leading the attack. Even in reserve, McCoy's unit lay within range of enemy artillery. According to one witness, however, McCoy "strolled about the area with every evidence of unconcern." He pointedly engaged in long conversations with his subordinates, drawing them out of their dugouts "to stand in the open with their brigade commander and set an example of steadiness." On September 2, the division pulled out of the line and moved to Joinville to recuperate. Later that month, the Red Arrow became part of the newly formed First U.S. Army and moved to the vicinity of Verdun to prepare for the Allied counteroffensive scheduled to begin on September 26.[21]

At the beginning of the Meuse-Argonne offensive—the name given the American portion of the overall Allied attack—the Thirty-second Division formed the reserve of V Corps. On September 30, the Red Arrow relieved the Thirty-seventh Division near Nantillois and made contact with the enemy. On the following day, the division attacked with the Sixty-third Brigade in the van—a position it retained through the next nineteen days. McCoy's brigade advanced methodically against a stubborn, entrenched foe and enjoyed considerable success. One of his regiments, the 126th, captured nearly 500 Germans in a single day in the Tranchée de la Mamelle. Similarly, the 125th mopped up 200 prisoners while penetrating the Kriemhilde Stellung, part of the Hindenburg Line. McCoy's own performance was superb. From the vantage point of GHQ, one of Pershing's aides reported that "McCoy has done awfully well[;] . . . he is winning fresh laurels continually." Yet the brigade also sustained heavy casualties. In just under three weeks of fighting, 585 of McCoy's men were killed and 1,780 wounded.[22]

The armistice found the Sixty-third Brigade across the Meuse River pursuing a crumbling German army. At the designated hour on November 11, McCoy reported, "we gathered under a tree nearby, flung out the colors and gave our heartiest cheer." The officer who earlier described the war as "great and glorious" now admitted that he was "overwhelmed by Peace."[23] Although the Sixty-third Brigade marched on to the Rhine as part of the Allied occupation force, it did so without McCoy. James G. Harbord, now commanding general of the Services of Supply (SOS), faced the complicated task of returning the AEF to

*McCoy as brigade commander during World War I: The strain of combat has taken its toll. (Courtesy U.S. Army Military History Institute)*

the United States for demobilization. He needed help. Pulled out of division command by Pershing in July to straighten out a deteriorating logistical situation, Harbord discovered that his chief problem was a dearth of leadership. The logistics command, he complained, was staffed by a "constant stream of misfits . . . from the front. Every man tried out and discarded up there comes back discredited and with a grouch." In his attempts to upgrade the SOS, Harbord told McCoy in September, "I have been sorely tempted to howl for you on several occasions. . . . You can take it as an extraordinary tribute to my interest in your upward flight that I have not insisted to General Pershing that you be sent back here to me." Once the fighting ended, such considerations no longer carried much weight, so Harbord wasted no time in summoning McCoy to his headquarters at Tours and appointing him director of the Army Transport Service (ATS). Disappointed at losing his command literally at the moment of victory, McCoy "gulped the bitter medicine" and did as he was told.[24]

A problem of monumental proportions awaited him. As he wrote in late November, with "124 ships in ports now, unloading 30,000 tons of cargo daily; and 2000000 men etc. to go home, I foresee I shall be busy." Getting those troops home quickly was an issue to which the American command attached considerable importance. Writing to Maj. Gen. James W. McAndrew, Pershing's chief of staff, Harbord noted that any ill feeling that the AEF carried back to civilian life would "have an influence on the future of the Regular Army and on any policy for proper preparedness." He continued: "We of the Regular Army are tied up together in this matter and it is our duty . . . to send these two million men homeward bound in a friendly mood toward a proper military policy."[25]

McCoy measured up to the task. The ATS easily surpassed initial projections that at most 250,000 troops could be sent home per month. In June 1919 alone, 400,000 doughboys completed the return passage to the United States. In all, 600,000 troops reached home well ahead of schedule. McCoy's work especially impressed his immediate superior, Brig. Gen. William W. Atterbury, the vice-president for operations of the Pennsylvania Railroad who had served as the AEF's director general of transportation. Contemplating his imminent return to mufti, Atterbury nominated McCoy to be his successor.[26]

Along with new responsibilities, the end of the war brought new honors. In January 1919, Marshal Henri-Philippe Pétain decorated McCoy with the Légion d'honneur and the Croix de guerre with palm. That same month, Pershing personally awarded McCoy and nine other general officers the Distinguished Service Medal. Perhaps the most meaningful tribute came from Father Duffy, who reported from the Rhineland that, although the Fighting Sixty-ninth was now serving under its seventh commander since entering federal service in 1917, "you were our only colonel."[27] In January, McCoy became deputy director general of transportation under Atterbury. "If constant travel makes a transportation man, I am it," he reported. The pace of his activities after the armistice on top of the campaigns of 1918 may well have increased his susceptibility to the influenza that laid him out later that month. The influenza epidemic that was sweeping much of Europe and the United States took the lives of thousands, including the effervescent Willard Straight. Although ill enough to be hospitalized, McCoy recovered. Released in mid-February, he left France on convalescent leave, which he spent in Rome and Sicily as a guest of Thomas Nelson Page, American ambassador to Italy. Refreshed and reinvigorated by "the most leisurely gentlemanly loaf I've ever had," he was back on the job in early March.[28]

From France, McCoy corresponded with Wood, cheering up his old mentor and commenting on international developments, especially those pertaining to the ongoing Paris Peace Conference. (Wilson and Pershing deprived Wood of the wartime role that the latter believed ought to have been rightfully his. The most distinguished American soldier of the previous decade and a half had spent the war supervising trainees in Kansas.[29]) One such letter, written in March 1919, revealed McCoy's support for the League of Nations—somewhat surprising given his prewar impatience with Wilsonian idealism. His only reservation stemmed from a concern that the United States enter the world organization on "a proper and American basis." He applauded the debate over the League at home because it guaranteed that "the American people are going to know what they are about and are not going to accept . . . the probable surrender of certain sovereign rights without a thorough thrashing out of the whole affair." As to the outcome of that debate he had no doubt: "Whatever the result . . . , the League of Nations is here and America cannot stay out of it." In passing, McCoy also predicted that the peace conference would grant the United States a mandate to provisionally govern Armenia and possibly other parts of Turkey, telling Wood that with his background in colonial affairs, the Wilson administration might see in such a new responsibility "a good place to bury you and hide your light under a bushel for some time to come."[30]

McCoy's expectation in early 1919 that the United States might accept a mandate for Armenia was not as fantastic as it appears in retrospect. The currents of Wilsonian idealism, American public opinion, Allied disagreement, and rising nationalist aspirations in Asia Minor coincided briefly to make just such an outcome appear possible. As used by the victors in Paris after World War I, "Armenia" referred to the rugged, undeveloped area of the Ottoman Empire bounded by present-day Iran on the south, the modern Soviet republics of Georgia and Azerbaijan on the east, and the Black Sea on the north, with a western edge along a line drawn from the southeastern tip of the Black Sea to the Mediterranean near the city of Adana. The 3 million or so people inhabiting this region divided into several ethnic groups. Most numerous were the Turks and Kurds, both Moslem, and the Armenians themselves, who were Christian. In tracing the establishment of their church to A.D. 301, the Armenians claimed that theirs was the oldest of all national Christian churches.[31]

For reasons only partially rooted in religious differences, these people found it impossible to live with one another in peace. Beginning in the late 1870s, their long-standing antipathy erupted into genocidal atrocities directed against Armenians. Attacks by Turks and Kurds escalated in scale and brutality, culminating in 1915 when the Turkish government ordered the extinction of the Armenian population remaining in the Ottoman Empire. This directive resulted in the massacre or starvation of from 600,000 to 1 million victims, with a further half million pouring into neighboring countries as unwelcome refugees. Word of these events received in the predominantly Christian United States provoked a wave of revulsion against Turkey, already tainted by its wartime alliance with Germany. Church groups and humanitarians mounted campaigns to provide relief for the targets of Turkish persecution. Not surprisingly, the Armenians' plight enlisted the sympathy of the humanitarian in the White House. Point 11 of Wilson's Fourteen Points promised both "undoubted security of life" and "an absolutely unmolested opportunity of autonomous development" for nationalities currently under Turkish rule. Thus, for many Americans, Armenia by 1919 came to symbolize not merely a place name but a cause.[32]

To Allied statesmen convened in Paris to negotiate the peace, Armenia was never more than a peripheral issue, although one involving complicated political as well as humanitarian considerations. During the war, Britain, France, Italy, and czarist Russia agreed secretly to partition the Ottoman Empire into spheres of influence—an arrangement whose implementation Wilson resolutely opposed. The American president proposed instead that areas detached from Turkey become mandates to be administered by disinterested powers with the welfare of the local population uppermost in mind. Under such an arrangement, the Armenians would establish a homeland carved out of remnants of the Ottoman Empire, live for a time under the tutelage of a great power, and eventually gain full independence. Wary of each other's ambitions in the Near East and therefore unable to agree upon a division of spheres, the Allies reluctantly accepted Wilson's alternative. On January 30, 1919, the Council of Ten adopted a draft resolution that called for the creation of several mandates out of Turkish territory, one of them to be set aside for the Armenians.[33]

With Britain and France checking one another's designs in the region, the European powers looked to the United States as the logical candidate to undertake the mandate for Armenia. In the European view, because the United States lacked a tradition of imperial involvement in the Middle East, it could be counted on to administer an Armenian mandate impartially. Having acquiesced in the president's scheme, the Allies now pressed him to accept his country's share of the responsibility. Notwithstanding the domestic clamor to do something for Armenia, Wilson balked, citing the uncertainty of both popular and congressional reaction to the reality of a mandate. In all likelihood, the president decided to defer a decision on Armenia until the more important issue of American membership in the League had been resolved.[34]

Yet the issue could not be disposed of quite so neatly. Throughout the spring of 1919, reports from Armenia spoke of widespread famine among the survivors of Turkish persecution. In addition, the Allied-supported Greek landings in Smyrna in May—a development ostensibly unrelated to Armenia—incited Turkish nationalists and raised fears that the Turks's desire for retribution against Christian enemies could lead to a recurrence of the bloody events of 1915. The perception that the long-suffering Armenians were about to be engulfed by yet another wave of terror evoked concern in the United States and increased the pressure on Wilson to take some action in Armenia before returning home from Paris. A cable sent to the president on June 22, 1919, illustrates the political sensitivity of the Armenian question. "When the unspeakable Turks were perpetrating their diabolical crimes [in 1915]," the message said, "American hearts were stirred with impotent horror." American entry into the war ended that impotence. With the war over, the United States needed to act. "Without regard to party or creed the American people are deeply interested in the welfare of the Armenian people and expect to see the restoration of the independence of Armenia." The cable was signed by a bipartisan group of American leaders. Heading the list were Elihu Root, elder statesman of the Republican party, Charles Evans Hughes, Wilson's opponent in the campaign of 1916, and Henry Cabot Lodge of Massachusetts, chairman of the Senate Foreign Relations Committee.[35]

The president could not ignore the views of Republican leaders whose support he sorely needed if the United States were to enter the League. Even before the signing of the Treaty of Versailles, the opposition party signaled its dissatisfaction with the League Covenant, most tellingly with the famous Senate "Round Robin" of March 1919. Wilson could ill-afford to give further offense over Armenia. On the other hand, for the president to embrace the role of Armenia's protector too enthusiastically could jeopardize ratification by giving credence to fears that Wilsonian internationalism knew no bounds. The president needed to satisfy the pleas of those calling for Armenia's rescue while avoiding any irrevocable commitment that could provide ammunition to those skeptical of the growing American role in world affairs.[36] The president's solution, urged upon him by Henry Morgenthau and Herbert Hoover, was to dispatch a military mission to assess conditions in Armenia. Such a mission would serve three purposes: It would demonstrate Wilson's support of the pro-Armenia lobby; as an expression of official American interest in Armenia, the mission might deter renewed attacks against the Christian minority; and the mission's findings would provide information on which to base future policy, including a possible American mandate.[37]

While President Wilson was seeking a way to dispose of the Armenian issue, Frank McCoy, his work as director general of transportation nearly complete, prepared to assume command of the Second Brigade, First Infantry Division, the last AEF unit to return home from France. But when Harbord received word on August 2 of his appointment to head the Armenian mission, he told McCoy to scrub his plans. Harbord needed someone to serve as his chief of staff, and he drafted McCoy for the job.[38] McCoy's specific assignment makes it difficult to analyze his contribution to the mission. A chief of staff serves as his commander's alter ego. He must be loyal and self-effacing. Disagreements between a commander and his chief remain behind closed doors. Barring Harbord himself, McCoy enjoyed more influence and authority than any member of the mission.

Yet, because he consistently used that influence to support Harbord, differentiating between the views and roles of each is next to impossible. Given their common background and long association, differences were probably rare. An attempt, therefore, to isolate McCoy's personal contribution to the mission holds little promise. A better approach is to accept the episode as Harbord's mission, remembering that if McCoy's impact was seldom decisive, nowhere was it absent.

Harbord and McCoy spent most of August in Paris preparing for their expedition. Gathering background information on Armenia—most of which was biased or badly dated—took up much of McCoy's attention. He also assembled a staff to accompany the mission and report on the various military, political, and economic facets of the region. The team he recruited included regular officers, citizen-soldiers awaiting discharge, and civilian academics. In the first category was Brig. Gen. George Van Horn Mosely, like Harbord and McCoy, a veteran of the Philippines and Chaumont. The second group included Capt. Stanley K. Hornbeck, a political scientist from the University of Wisconsin and later a prominent State Department official; Lt. Col. Jasper Brinton, a noted Philadelphia lawyer; and Lt. Col. John Price Jackson, former dean of the School of Engineering at Pennsylvania State University. McCoy recruited Benjamin Strong, governor of the Federal Reserve Bank of New York and a member of the Family, to assess economic conditions in Armenia. When ill health forced Strong's withdrawal, William Wilson Cumberland, an economist at the Univer-

*The American Military Mission to Armenia, 1919. In front, from left, are an intense George Van Horn Mosely, a jovial James G. Harbord, and McCoy. (Courtesy Library of Congress)*

sity of Minnesota and adviser to the American mission at the peace conference, agreed to fill in. Other members of the mission included former Harvard football All-American Edward Bowditch, who spent several years as aide to the Philippine governor general. No member of the mission, either military or civilian, had previously visited Armenia.[39]

Meetings with American officials in Paris gave Harbord and McCoy a more detailed understanding of their assignment. General Tasker Bliss told Harbord that the administration hoped to persuade Americans "that pending action by Congress the President was doing all he could by sending someone for moral effect." Harbord agreed that an expression of American interest in the region might exercise some restraining influence, but he worried about the effect if such interest was not followed up by action.[40] The American Mission in Paris also provided Harbord with recent reports from Asia Minor, giving, in the words of one staff member, "a terribly black, but I fear truthful picture of the region." Such a characterization was appropriate. The situation was "fast approaching crisis," wrote American relief officials from Constantinople, and without prompt action, Armenia would "succumb to starvation and aggressions of neighboring peoples." An American diplomat who advocated a mandate predicted, "Unless prevented, the Turks apparently intend the total extinction of [the] Armenian race."[41]

Forewarned by such bleak predictions, the American Military Mission to Armenia departed Brest on August 24. Their ship, the *Martha Washington*, was a seedy, cockroach-infested ex-Austrian transport. The party consisted of fourteen principals, a number of aides and enlisted men, and a French chef, Louis Lutard, who purportedly cooked for Marshal Pétain during the war. The ship stopped briefly at Gibraltar where, recalled Cumberland, Harbord and McCoy "regaled us by explaining how they felt sure they could capture the place." Proceeding to Constantinople, the mission arrived on September 3. Harbord and McCoy immediately set to work, spending the next few days calling on Allied representatives and local leaders. Harbord then divided the mission into two groups: Personnel assigned to examine questions of trade, finance, and government remained in Constantinople, the region's political and commercial center, while the main body, including the three generals, mounted in motorcars and armed with sawed-off shotguns, set off on a firsthand inspection of conditions in Turkish Armenia and the Caucasus.[42]

For the next five weeks, Harbord's party covered the length and breadth of Asia Minor from Constantinople to Baku on the Caspian Sea. In all, according to Mosely's log of the trip, the mission travelled 8,734 kilometers (5,415 miles) by rail, automobile, and horseback, stopping at most of the region's major cities and numerous villages. Conditions were miserable. Vehicles broke down or were hung up on primitive roads; on one occasion, Kurds ambushed the caravan, wounding two Americans. Worst of all, Monsieur Lutard's talents soon proved "unequal to turning out bacon and fried onions" in quantity over an open campfire.[43] Despite such inconveniences, the mission took its responsibilities seriously.

*The Harbord mission in deepest Turkey, 1919. McCoy, second from left, is following
directly behind Harbord. (Courtesy Library of Congress)*

According to Harbord, "We literally dreamed Armenia and massacres." Yet,
whatever their dreams, Harbord's party drew from their own observations and
from numerous interviews with missionaries, relief workers, and local officials a
picture that, although harsh, differed greatly from what they expected. "We
heard the sad tale of deportation and sad return," wrote McCoy from Adana on
September 11. "But I must say that now there is no sign of hunger or misery nor
present complaint." Ten days later, Harbord expressed a similar view: "Nothing
I have seen thus far indicates to me that any state of danger exists." Armenians
returning home were meeting with no violence.[44]

In addition to concluding that the immediate plight of the Armenians had been
exaggerated, the mission's members developed two other general impressions that
informed their overall conclusions. The first concerned the Turks. Journalistic
opinion and diplomatic reports relentlessly portrayed them as the villains of the
Near East; that there was more to the story came as a revelation. As McCoy told a
British official in Constantinople near the end of the mission, "He had been
prepared to find that the Christians had suffered greatly, but not to discover that
the Turks had suffered quite as much or more." Indeed, he attributed the region's
surprising tranquility to the exhaustion of the Turkish people as a result of war.
Harbord estimated that not more than 20 percent of the men who went to war
returned. Typhus alone killed 600,000 Turkish soldiers. In the eyes of these
Americans, some manner of Turkish salvation was at hand in the nationalist
movement of Mustapha Kemal Ataturk. Harbord and McCoy had a lengthy
interview with Kemal on September 20 at Sivas in Turkish Armenia. Telling the

Americans what they wanted to hear, Kemal made a favorable impression. He pledged that there would be no new attacks against Armenians. Vowing to resist any attempt to dismember Turkey, he persuaded Harbord that his aim was to preserve "the integrity of the Ottoman Empire under the mandate of a disinterested great power, preferably America." McCoy had the wit to recognize that the sincerity of Kemal's "eulogy" of the United States was on a par with that of "a Mexican . . . talking face to face with an American." Yet he too was impressed by the nationalists and believed that "the people are all solid for Mustapha Kemal."[45]

The second matter requiring attention concerned the long-term prospects of an independent Armenian state. Completing its tour of Turkish Armenia in late September, the Harbord mission proceeded to Transcaucasia to visit Georgia, Azerbaijan, and the Republic of Armenia. These small, struggling nations had achieved a tenuous existence following the overthrow of the czar. Though created from territory traditionally Russian, the new Armenian state declared its intent to encompass Turkish Armenia as well, providing a single homeland for people of Armenian origin. If the United States were to accept a mandate for Armenia, this embryonic republic would constitute its basis. Thus, the outlook for its survival demanded careful scrutiny.[46] In fact, conditions in these three states were dismal. Russian Armenia still contained some 300,00 hungry refugees from Turkey, the countryside lay in ruin, and, with no crops planted, starvation seemed imminent. The vulnerability of the three republics ought to have inspired cooperation, but their governments instead bickered about conflicting territorial claims. Each was "corrupt, inefficient, [and] bankrupt," and all were surviving only on the "salvage from [the] Russian collapse" and showed signs of Bolshevik influence. As for the Armenian republic's expansionist aspirations, Harbord advised the American Mission in Paris that the Armenians "cannot govern themselves much less Turks . . . who are in [the] actual majority."[47]

By October 15, the mission reassembled on the *Martha Washington* for the return to France. During this voyage, the members of the mission refined their conclusions and prepared the report that Harbord had been ordered to present to the president. The result was imposing: Harbord's portion ran to forty-three pages of typescript, supplemented by eleven voluminous appendices. Yet, however thorough, it was a perverse, even outlandish document. Apart from the domestic political purposes it served, Woodrow Wilson had sent the mission to Armenia to gain a realistic, dispassionate appraisal of conditions in the Near East. Perhaps to avoid the hyperemotion that Armenia regularly evoked, the mission had been explicitly organized as a military one—its leaders were hardheaded soldiers, well-versed in the problems of ruling subject peoples. Yet the florid rhetoric of the final product recalled nothing so much as a missionary tract. And its conclusions overreached any that the progenitor of "missionary diplomacy" himself might have drawn.

To the modern reader, the Harbord Report's most striking characteristic is its sententious and melodramatic tone. Embroidering a brief historical narrative of Armenia—a nation "evangelized by apostles fresh from the memory of our Lord"—Harbord wrote, "mutilation, violation, torture and death have left their haunting memories in a hundred beautiful Armenian valleys; and the traveller in that region is seldom free from the evidence of this most colossal crime of all the ages." Surely, he continued, "no faith has ever been put to . . . harder test or has been cherished at greater cost." Turning to the current situation in the Near East, Harbord decried "political conditions which shriek of misery, starvation, ruin and all the melancholy aftermath . . . of beastial [sic] brutality unrestrained by God or man." Conspicuous by their absence are references to the surprisingly tranquil countryside or to Turkish suffering, views that Harbord and McCoy earlier expressed through official channels.[48]

The report envisioned only one possible remedy to this appalling situation: to designate a disinterested power to control the area. Yet Harbord boldly proposed not merely protection for Armenians but "a single mandatory for the Turkish Empire and the Transcaucasus" stretching from Constantinople to the Caspian Sea. Economic realities and political tensions dictated that the region be treated as a unit. Harbord did not intend to understate the difficulty of such an undertaking—to accept such a responsibility would mean "facing a long period of tutelage for possibly unappreciative and ungrateful pupils, much expense, probably diplomatic embarrassment . . . , and little reward except the consciousness of having contributed to the peace of the world and the rehabilitation of oppressed humanity."[49]

What nation would accept such a mandate? Of necessity, it would be one motivated by "a strong sense of altruism and international duty to the peace of the world, [willing] to steadfastly carry out a continuity of policy for at least a generation and to send only its most gifted sons to leadership in the work." What nation in 1919 could claim such ideals? Describing Europe as "without pretensions to altruism or too much devotion to ideals," Harbord discounted the likelihood that one of the traditional Western powers would assume the mandate. If, on the other hand, the United States were to accept the responsibility, Harbord observed that other nations would "expect of America . . . the same lofty standards shown in Cuba and the Philippines—the development of peoples rather than material resources and commerce." The mission concluded that Americans alone possessed the capacity for such an undertaking and that others wished the United States to take on the job. Harbord believed that the United States possessed advantages "enjoyed by no other great power." Similarly, Hornbeck wrote that other nations viewed the United States "as the one great power which can approach the local problems with unbiased mind and without ulterior motives."[50]

Indeed, Hornbeck believed that the job could be accomplished with comparative ease, a view with which others on the mission concurred. Harbord estimated that an American mandate for the entire region would initially require 59,000 American troops and would cost $275 million in its first year. In his appendix on military considerations, Mosely wrote that establishing the mandate would require 69,450 troops supported by an air service and a dozen naval vessels. Both the expense of administering the mandate and the size of the garrison would decrease over time. According to Harbord's projections, the total costs over the first five years would be $756,014,000.[51]

But should the United States actually commit itself to accept such an obligation? Here, Harbord became coy. "This mission has not felt that it is expected to submit a recommendation," he wrote. The reason for this reticence is not entirely clear. One possibility is that opposition to a mandate existed within the mission itself. Cumberland later recalled that an attempt to poll the members on the question produced seven votes in favor of a mandate and seven opposed. Or perhaps Harbord received oral instructions not to state an opinion. Whatever the reason, Harbord concluded his report with an ostensibly objective cataloging of those factors favoring an American mandate and those against. Although not including an outright recommendation, this exercise effectively signalled Harbord's clear support of a mandate.[52]

Harbord listed thirteen reasons militating against an American mandate. Generally, these cited the need to husband American resources for problems closer to home and the undesirability of involvement in an area of marginal strategic importance. Couched in understated terms, they suggested an attitude of prudent realism. With little subtlety, the report also provided President Wilson with fourteen points in favor of a mandate. The significance of that number can hardly have been lost on either Harbord or his intended reader. In discussing the reasons favoring a mandate, Harbord reverted to his previous grandiloquence and emphasized moral responsibility, divine mission, and the capacity of American idealism. The Near East was the "greatest humanitarian opportunity of the age"; the United States was Armenia's "only hope"; a mandate would provide Americans with an "outlet to a vast amount of spirit and energy." Reason 13 quoted Cain's question to God: "Am I my brother's keeper?" And reason 14—the only one not balanced against a corresponding drawback—stated: "Here is a man's job. . . . America can afford the money; she has the men; no duty to her own people would suffer. . . . Shall it be said that our country lacks the courage to take up new and different duties?"[53]

Mosely, for one, supported Harbord's conclusions. "From a disinterested, humanitarian point of view," he argued, the mission had "convinced [him] it is our duty to step in and take over the task entirely." "If the American people could witness what we have witnessed," he added, "I do not believe they would hesitate for a moment to accept the task, gigantic though it is. No nation has ever been offered such an opportunity." As for McCoy's views, the evidence is sparse. He never committed himself on paper to a particular position. But Cumberland recalled years later that McCoy viewed the prospect of a mandate skeptically

because he "saw America wedged in between Russia[n] . . . and British interests
. . . without its own communications, thousands of miles from the United States
and utterly indefensible." Although such considerations argued against a
mandate restricted to the Transcaucasia, they were less relevant to the mandate
for the Turkish empire outlined in the Harbord Report. Moreover, Harbord's
correspondence with McCoy after the mission suggests that he considered
McCoy an ally regarding Armenia.[54]

Delivering its report to the American Mission in Paris in late October, the
American Military Mission to Armenia ceased to exist. In large measure, it
accomplished its short-term objectives. By sending Harbord to the Near East,
Wilson placated those calling for American action in behalf of Armenia. And
certainly, so long as the mission remained in Armenia, the renewed violence that
many observers feared did not occur. Indeed, the mission discovered that such
fears had been largely misplaced. Yet events occurring during the life of the
mission ended any possibility that the mission's report would be useful as a brief
in favor of an American mandate. Whatever the prospects for a mandate during
the summer of 1919, by autumn they had evaporated. Even before the mission's
departure, the *New York Times,* itself favoring a mandate, noted the nation's
shifting mood. "The American people are eager to save Armenia," the paper
commented, but only "if it can be done without any trouble or inconvenience to
us." Wilson's own recognition of the country's changing attitude regarding the
role of the United States in world affairs inspired his decision in September to
take his case for the League directly to the people. The subsequent train of
events—Wilson's stroke and incapacity, the Senate's partisan debate of the
League, and ultimately the rejection of the Versailles Treaty on November 19,
1919—buried the idea of an American mandate for Armenia once and for all.[55]

A month before, Secretary of State Robert Lansing ordered the American
Mission in Paris to forward Harbord's findings as soon as possible, saying that
they were urgently desired for a Senate subcommittee. By the time the report
became available, such urgency no longer existed. It is doubtful that the
president ever read the report. Had he done so, he would have found little use for
it. The report's crusading spirit and the breadth of its conclusions ran directly
counter to the emerging postwar temper of the country. If rejection of the
Versailles Treaty obviated efforts to secure a mandate for Armenia, publication of
the Harbord Report would only have hindered efforts to resuscitate the League.[56]

Only after the Senate's second and final rejection of the League in March 1920
did the Harbord Report briefly resurface—and then for partisan rather than
substantive reasons. In a gesture designed to signify its interest in Armenia,
Congress petitioned Wilson to release Harbord's findings. On April 3, Wilson
honored the request, sending the report to the Senate, in the words of the *New York
Times,* "several months after it had ceased to have any practical value." The report
did retain value as political ammunition for use against Wilson himself. The
following month in a quixotic gesture probably intended to embarrass Congress by

exposing the shallowness of its concern for Armenia, Wilson formally proposed that the United States accept a mandate. Rejection of the proposal was a foregone conclusion. In the brief debate that preceded final congressional action, opponents of a mandate repeatedly cited data from the Harbord Report to support their views. The religiosity and idealistic rhetoric that characterized the report retained no more cogency in the late spring of 1920 than did Wilson's own Fourteen Points. Yet Harbord's projections of troops to be deployed and dollars to be spent possessed concrete meaning. According to the *New Republic,* "General Harbord's report . . . has been quoted by half the editorial writers in the United States to combat our acceptance of a mandate." During congressional debate, speaker after speaker cited facts and figures from the Harbord Report to substantiate his opposition to an Armenian mandate. As expected, on May 31, by a margin of fifty-two to twenty-three, the Senate denied President Wilson the authority to accept a mandate. Similar action by the House soon followed.[57]

The congressional action sealed the demise of a cause whose decline began the previous summer. For Harbord, however, the lack of support for his position was difficult to accept. In a futile effort to drum up interest in Armenia, he published a series of articles that called attention to Armenia's plight and to the work of his mission. Even after formal congressional rejection of the mandate, Harbord insisted that the issue was not dead. "The American conscience will not stand for more than a certain amount more of Armenian atrocities," he told McCoy. He disputed the conventional wisdom on the public's fading interest, arguing that it "underestimated the number of church people of all denominations who wish America to do something for Armenia besides lend or give her money." He predicted that there would be a revival of the question in Congress.[58] With greater realism—and evident regret—McCoy accepted Congress's action as final. He placed the real blame for the abandonment of Armenia on Britain and France. Although many "fine Britons are in sympathy with their government," he told James L. Barton of Near East Relief, "these men talk one thing and their government does another." Until European policies changed, "no individual American would be safe in touching" any scheme to assist Armenia.[59]

The American Military Mission to Armenia illustrated again the involvement of soldiers in foreign policy. Although the principal product of the mission, the Harbord Report, was overtaken by events before its completion, it is not entirely without interest. The report vividly illustrates the military's support for expanding American global presence—even into an area of marginal strategic and economic importance to the United States. Officers who twenty years before enthusiastically civilized Cuba and the Philippines welcomed a similar opportunity in the Near East. Only the rationale had changed: The ideals of Wilson superseded those of Kipling. The report also shows how completely the mission misread public opinion. As a brief in favor of American assistance to Armenia, the Harbord Report was irrelevant. Only as a source document for those opposing a mandate did it achieve a brief, ironic usefulness.

# 7

# Return to the Philippines

*Earthquakes in Japan, revolution in China, and
bunk from Manila, are mere incidents
in the cycles and centuries of these old countries.*
FRANK ROSS McCOY TO ELIOT WADSWORTH[1]

The army that awaited McCoy once the Harbord mission disbanded bore scant resemblance to the self-assured establishment that existed just a year earlier. Headlong demobilization coupled with an emergent antimilitary mood across much of the United States all but wrecked the army as a usable instrument of policy. Many soldiers who endured this period became profoundly disillusioned about what their wartime sacrifices had achieved. Those who saw the AEF as culminating the rise of the United States to great-power status now witnessed their country walk petulantly off the world stage. Officers for whom victory in France had vindicated years in the wilderness felt betrayed and humiliated as the nation rewarded its returning regulars with neglect. Although unavoidable, reductions in the army were exacted brutally and without any sense of a phased, orderly process. Congress slashed the army's strength to less than 10 percent of what it had been in 1918. Surviving units were undermanned. The purchase of new equipment came to an end. Morale plummeted. Drawn to glittering civilian alternatives, officers in large numbers resigned their commissions. Even Harbord left, trading his uniform for the presidency of RCA.[2]

Returning from Europe in January 1920, McCoy assumed command of an amorphous entity known as the Arizona District. Given the circumstances, he could hardly have contemplated with much optimism his immediate future as a soldier. If he retained any illusions in this regard, the War Department's action

91

in abruptly reducing him to his prewar rank of major destroyed them. From the narrow perspective of his own advancement, the war might never have occurred. McCoy could easily have followed Harbord in joining the exodus of those leaving the service. Given his civilian connections, challenging and lucrative opportunities were his for the asking. Yet he never seriously considered resignation; indeed, he seems hardly to have given the matter much thought. A forty-five-year-old bachelor without fortune or fame, McCoy willingly—even happily—soldiered on. He loved army life, especially the invigorating physical routine that marked the soldier's existence in that day. The peremptory transfer from one duty station to the next— so upsetting to some officers—always excited him as a harbinger of some new experience. And however outsiders might view a military career, McCoy judged his service to have been worthwhile and rewarding. Above all, as a source of day-to-day gratification, he rejoiced in the varied and colorful people encountered along the way. McCoy's gift for making friends was prodigious. Acquaintances made in the course of accomplishing his duties routinely remained friends for life.


McCoy's stay in Arizona proved to be a brief one. As a mere major, he was now too junior to head a district. Yet, if McCoy regretted giving up his command, the prospect of his next assignment brightened his outlook considerably. In late March, he joined the staff of an old friend who not only commanded the Central Department at Fort Sheridan, Illinois, but was also the front-runner for the Republican presidential nomination.[3] Campaigning vigorously for the presidency while still on active duty, Leonard Wood had long since abandoned any notions about the desirability of an apolitical soldiery. In the weeks preceding that summer's Republican national convention, McCoy himself edged closer to partisan politics. With whiffs of yet more trouble with Mexico in the air, McCoy took the incumbent commander in chief to task in a lengthy analysis that he provided to Wood. "Mr. Wilson [had] practically repudiated the time honored duty of protecting American lives and property," McCoy wrote. He recommended that Wood stand for a get-tough policy. The United States should demand assurances of Mexican protection for American interests. In the event of further attacks on American lives and property, Washington should reply with punitive measures leading to a Cuban-style military occupation. Among Wood's supporters, Stimson for one did not hesitate to call on McCoy to take a direct hand in the campaign. The former secretary of war worried that Wood's candidacy would suffer if the general appeared to neglect his military responsibilities. Stimson wanted someone close to Wood to advise him on the political implications inherent in his official military actions. "You must be the real information center," he told McCoy.[4]

Wood's attempt to assume Theodore Roosevelt's mantle as leader of the Republican party's progressive wing eventually foundered on the ineptness of his campaign and even more on the country's changing temper. His advocacy of military preparedness no longer generated enthusiasm. Hoping to capitalize on the nativist, antiradical fervor of 1919, Wood proclaimed himself the candidate of 100-percent Americanism. That cause also fizzled before the year was out. Wood arrived at the Chicago convention in June bearing only his reputation as an intimate friend of TR, as a successful colonial administrator, and as a soldier who received shabby treatment at Wilson's hands during the war. None of these was potent enough to win the nomination. Although in the early balloting Wood enjoyed a substantial lead over Gov. Frank L. Lowden of Illinois and Sen. Hiram W. Johnson of California, he lacked the strength to gain a majority. To avert a deadlock, the party's professionals—who disliked Wood's amateurism and feared his maverick tendencies—settled on a compromise candidate of agreeable temperament: Sen. Warren G. Harding of Ohio. To McCoy fell the unenviable task of informing Wood of Harding's triumph on the tenth ballot. Listening to McCoy report that "so far as he was concerned, the thing was over," Wood burst into a rage. "Like a lion at bay," Gordon Johnston recalled, he angrily vowed "to tell the delegates the theft that had been committed." Only by physically restraining his chief could McCoy dissuade him from marching into the convention hall.[5] Although the convention squelched Wood's presidential prospects, it did not end his political aspirations. As a leading Republican, he would be a contender for a cabinet post—logically that of secretary of war—if Harding won in November. So Wood swallowed his bitterness and supported the party ticket. Still on active duty, he publicly endorsed Harding, declaring that in the upcoming election, "the one great issue is the success of the Republican Party."[6]

Motivated more by loyalty than ambition, McCoy remained with his chief. On July 1, 1920, he was restored to the grade of colonel and thus no longer confronted the limited horizons of the junior field grade officer. New opportunities presented themselves. From the American legation in Warsaw, Hugh Gibson, a career diplomat and Family friend, tried to cajole McCoy into becoming military attaché in Poland. With "the military questions . . . so mixed up with the political," Gibson promised an interesting assignment. The offer was an attractive one, but when Wood asked that he stay on, McCoy turned it down.[7] McCoy's future was again tied to his general's. But Harding's landslide victory in November yielded disappointing results for Wood. Their candidate elected, GOP kingmakers no longer needed to court Wood's favor. Indeed, the general's unreliability as a team player persuaded the incoming administration to keep Wood at arm's length. Appointment to the War Department was out of the question. Nor was any other cabinet post available. Still, a man of his prominence could scarcely be ignored altogether. As Theodore Roosevelt discovered in 1902, finding a niche suitable for Wood posed a delicate problem. Like Roosevelt, Harding found his solution in the western Pacific.[8]

In his last annual message to Congress on December 7, 1920, Woodrow Wilson recommended an immediate grant of independence to the Philippines. Although the proposal evoked little support among the Republican majority, it represented a logical culmination of Democratic actions over the previous eight years. The cornerstone of Wilson's Philippine policy was the Jones Act of 1916. This measure committed the United States to freeing its largest possession as soon as Filipinos demonstrated their ability to maintain a stable government. The provisions of the Jones Act meshed nicely with the antiimperialist predisposition of Wilson's appointee as governor general, Francis Burton Harrison. From 1913 to 1921, Harrison pursued a policy of "filipinization," designed to provide the islands with de facto autonomy even before a formal grant of independence. Chief among the beneficiaries of this policy were Manuel Quezon and Sergio Osmena, leaders of the Philippine legislature who built their careers on the cause of Philippine nationalism. With Harrison's acquiescence, these two politicians effectively eclipsed the governor general as the ultimate authorities in the islands. Privately, Quezon and Osmena retained serious doubts about the ability of the Philippines to survive a grant of outright independence. They recognized all too well their country's military vulnerability and the fragile nature of its economy. The dynamics of Philippine politics, however, demanded the commitment of all politicians to immediate independence, whatever their personal feelings.[9]

Republicans followed these developments with a mixture of skepticism and outright disapproval. Harding, former chairman of the Senate Committee on the Philippines, doubted that the islands were ready to go it alone. Yet Democratic policies imparted a momentum to the independence movement that the new administration had to reckon with. As a prelude to constructing a new Republican policy, Harding decided to send a mission to investigate conditions in the islands. He saw in Leonard Wood the man he needed to lead such a mission.[10] Even before the inauguration, Wood turned down an offer to become Philippine governor general, viewing it as a transparent attempt to send him into political exile. Deprived of any chance to exercise real power in Washington, he considered leaving the army to accept an appointment as provost of the University of Pennsylvania. Yet, when Harding asked Wood to head a mission to provide recommendations on Philippine policy, he accepted—overriding objections by McCoy, who thought the appointment beneath his dignity. In Wood's eyes, the job promised to be an interesting one. The position at Penn could await his return.[11]

Complicating the picture was the fact that Harding had already invited W. Cameron Forbes, governor general during the Taft administration, to lead the proposed mission. Fortunately, the gregarious and agreeable Forbes consented that he and Wood act as coequals. (In fact, Forbes ended up playing a secondary role.) In choosing personnel to assist them, Wood and Forbes turned to the army's old Philippine hands. McCoy's intimacy with Wood and long acquaintance with Forbes made him the obvious choice to be chief of staff. Other recruits were McCoy's old friends Col. Gordon Johnston and Maj. Edward Bowditch.

Johnston left Princeton in 1898 to enlist with the Rough Riders, won the Medal of Honor at Bud Dajo, and served as Wood's aide during the preparedness campaign. Bowditch, known as Peter, had been Forbes's personal secretary in the Philippines and later served in the Moro Province. More recently, he accompanied McCoy on the mission to Armenia. To provide a semblance of balance, several outsiders were added: Ray Atherton, first secretary of the American legation in Peking; H. Otley Beyer, an ethnologist at the University of the Philippines; and Lt. Comdr. Stewart F. Bryant. No Filipino served on the mission in any capacity.[12] In late March, McCoy traveled to Washington to coordinate administrative details and draft the mission's letter of instructions. That document, signed by Secretary of War John W. Weeks, instructed Wood to render judgment on the conflicting testimony concerning the readiness of the Philippines for independence. Weeks specifically asked the mission to examine Philippine economic conditions and prospects for political stability, as well as such matters as health, education, and public works.[13]

The Wood-Forbes mission sailed from Seattle on April 9. After a brief layover in Japan, it arrived at Manila on May 4 and set to work immediately. As with any project undertaken by Wood, the mission pursued its goal with thoroughness and frenetic energy. Over the course of the next four months, its members traveled some 15,000 miles by sea, rail, automobile, and horseback, visiting all but one of the forty-nine provinces and conferring with leaders in 449 municipalities. Frequently, the mission divided in two groups, each led by one of the principal investigators. As a rule, McCoy accompanied Wood. On occasion, however, he operated separately as the nucleus of a third element. The mission's method upon sweeping into some provincial village was to see as much as possible as rapidly as possible. As McCoy described it, Wood held court and was entertained with luncheons, speeches, and testimonials while his subordinates dug beneath the surface, "Gordon taking schools and Constabulary, while I sized up General Administration, and set in with Treasurers, collectors of Customs, Judges, Fiscals, Engineers, padres, missionaries, merchants, and heard complaints from downtrodden citizens."[14] In the end, the complaints of the downtrodden informed the conclusions of the mission less than did the views of the well-to-do that the mission made a point of soliciting. McCoy devised a confidential questionnaire sent to prominent Filipinos not involved in politics, asking for their views on political conditions in the islands and on the issue of independence. Members of the American business and commercial community did not wait for a questionnaire. They told the mission that conditions in the Philippines under Harrison had steadily deteriorated, that politicos such as Quezon and Osmena were untrustworthy, and that independence would be a disaster.[15]

Military officials in the Philippines agreed with the business community. American officers gave short shrift to the narrow question of an independent Philippine state's ability to defend itself. Instead, the military advocated retention of the Philippines by fashioning a wide-ranging argument that touched

*The Wood-Forbes mission, 1921: Wood and McCoy return to Zamboanga. (Courtesy U.S. Army Military History Institute)*

on economics, strategy, and race. Col. Charles D. Rhodes, chief of staff of the Philippine Department, started from the premise that the United States stood "on the threshold of an era of marked commercial development." To adapt itself to this new era, he believed, "our country must insist on equal opportunity for our merchants, the 'open door,' in markets of the Far East." Exploiting that open door required a series of stepping stones for American shipping. Rhodes believed that the Philippines were the most vital element in that series. Maj. Gen. Francis J. Kernan, the department's commander, described the Philippines as a way station but also saw them in their own right as a field for the investment of surplus capital and a source of raw materials. Both officers echoed the views of Adm. Joseph Straus, commander in chief of the Asiatic Fleet, who worried that Japan, with "her lust for national wealth and power," would fall on the Philippines if the United States withdrew. Straus predicted that "if the Philippines are granted their absolute independence now or in the near future . . . [they would] fall into the hands of the Japanese in a short time." The Japanese maintained "a burning desire for the Philippines," alleged Kernan.

Filipino incapacity for resisting such foreign incursions was self-evident. American officers viewed the Philippine people as inferior. In a memorandum on psychological characteristics, Maj. John P. Smith, Kernan's intelligence officer, described Filipinos as "generally helpless, indolent in the extreme, [and possessing] no moral sense." The people's enthusiasm for independence was not authentic, reflecting instead the rabble rousing of demogogic politicos whom the military mistrusted. "It would manifestly be a crime against humanity," wrote Kernan, "to withdraw our protecting supervision and leave these people prey to the small oligarchy now in power." Furnishing that note of missionary zeal favored by military imperialists, he added: "Our moral duty to persevere in the work of leading this backward people to a higher plane of civilization cannot be shirked [without] shame to ourselves."[16]

In addition to consulting the resident military, the mission interviewed numerous officials and private citizens and was swamped by petitions both for and against independence. "We are absorbing much," McCoy reported, "and interpreting things to ourselves and to each other in a way that will easily crystallize ideas into opinions." By July, that process was well under way. Wood and his assistants identified a series of deficiencies that rendered the Philippines, in their view, unfit for independence. Moreover, the mission believed that it had isolated the specific causes of Filipino ills and had settled on a remedy that would form the basis of a new American policy.[17]

Assessing the conditions that had evolved by the end of the Harrison regime required some basis of comparison. Inevitably, the mission's members turned to the years prior to 1913 for their standard. During that period, many of them had figured prominently in governing the islands. Naturally, the mission claimed high marks for the administration of that earlier period. Up to 1913, wrote McCoy in a memorandum summarizing his views, the islands made "remarkably rapid progress . . . due to the tutelage of American officials who, despite Kipling, did hustle the East." Until Harrison became governor general, "effective supervision by Americans with a high sense of duty and the burning spirit of crusaders"—men who acted "without a thought of political partisanship"—secured advances in all aspects of Philippine life. The filipinization policy—a "leap into the dark" by inexperienced men ignorant of conditions in the islands—ended all that. Permitting Filipino control without careful American supervision allowed the quality of government to deteriorate. Indeed, "the deterioration seems to have kept pace with the Filipinization of the services."

*The controversy over Philippine independence: McCoy solicits the views of Filipino villagers, 1921. (Courtesy National Archives)*

The "infection of politics" replaced the high-mindedness of American administrators, bringing with it bloated job rolls, graft, spoilsmanship, and general
inefficiency.[18]
       McCoy's views, including his concern for the "infection of politics," pervaded
the final report prepared by Wood and Forbes.[19] The report described in detail
the decline suffered under Harrison. In 1913, "honest, highly efficient"
Philippine government "set a high standard of energy and morality." Eight
years later, the Wood-Forbes mission found an administration "top-heavy in
personnel and enmeshed in red tape"; a politicized and demoralized civil service
and constabulary; a system of justice in which politics and family carried undue
weight; prisons that were unsanitary and overcrowded; and schools staffed by
incompetent teachers. The incidence of preventable diseases such as typhoid,
malaria, and beriberi had risen steadily.[20]
       Worse yet were existing economic conditions and the government's economic
policies. Relying heavily on the export of sugar, hemp, coconut oil, and tobacco,
the Philippine economy suffered tremendously from the postwar collapse of
commodity prices. The islands' usually favorable trade balance reversed itself
dramatically. As the mission noted, "the country is suffering from the general
world-wide depression at the present time." Yet the Wood-Forbes Report did not
dwell on the islands' dependence on commodity exports as a possible root of
their difficulties. Nor did it see the need for structural remedies to salvage the
economy. (On the contrary, the report argued that without free trade with the
United States, the islands' principal commercial partner, economic conditions
would have been still worse.) Instead, as a scapegoat for economic failures, the
report took aim again at the Harrison administration. The mission especially
criticized government enterprises that competed with the private sector. Ventures
such as the state-owned Manila Railroad and the National Coal Company were
regularly losing money, straining the government's already precarious finances.
Above all, the mission singled out the virtual insolvency of the Philippine
National Bank as proof of Philippine incompetence and of the unwisdom of
thrusting government into areas better left to private enterprise.[21]
       What caused conditions to reach such a state? McCoy's answer was twofold:
race and politics. The Philippine people had not yet developed the capacity for
self-government. Given adequate direction, the Filipino was a good worker, but
"as yet, in most cases, he is unable to direct." As public servants, McCoy
believed, Filipinos were lacking in initiative, constructive spirit, and energy. They
compared unfavorably to Cubans—in McCoy's eyes, hardly a lofty standard.
With the people naive and malleable—in the words of the final report, "free from
worries . . . , light-hearted and inclined to be improvident"—they were easy
marks for manipulative politicians like Quezon and Osmena. This was Harrison's
greatest crime: By providing only shadowy and fitful supervision of his charges,
he encouraged the "interference and tacit usurpation by the [Philippine] political
leaders of the general supervision and control of . . . the government granted

by law to the Governor-General.'' Introducing politics into such a society inevitably brought in its train corruption, inefficiency, and an end to progress.[22]

Such findings provided all the support needed for a recommendation that the United States retain the Philippines. Yet, despite this emphasis on unsatisfactory internal conditions as a rationale for retention, the mission also asserted positive reasons for opposing independence. The mission entertained its own vision of a Japanese-American rivalry as well as hopes for commercial advantage. Although it would have been impolitic to include such factors in the final report, in remarks made on July 2 to the American Chamber of Commerce in Manila, McCoy succinctly described the breadth of the mission's viewpoint:

> We must remain here for the benefit of ourselves, for the benefit of the Filipino and for the benefit of every people whose countries are washed by the waters of the Pacific. If we leave the Philippine Islands the Far East becomes a Japanese province. We are not imperialists. . . . But America must remain the sovereign nation. Either that or we must get out absolutely, not only out of the Philippines, but out of the Orient, and we may as well burn up our shipping.[23]

If independence was out of the question, what was to be done to clear away the debris of the Harrison years? To McCoy, the answer was clear: Re-establish the sovereignty of the United States by a determined exercise of the governor general's powers; get the government out of big business as soon as possible; restore nonpartisan, in other words, American, supervision to the various departments, thereby upgrading their efficiency; increase the role of the army and navy in governing the Philippines by making senior commanders ex-officio members of the advisory council of state; and provide ''consistent and proper encouragement'' for ''American capital to play its important part in the development of the Islands.''[24]

Once again, McCoy's recommendation to liquidate the government's ''ill advised experiments in state socialism'' appeared in the Wood-Forbes Report. His belief that stronger apolitical supervision would increase government efficiency recurred throughout that document. But the final report softened McCoy's recommendation that the governor general assert his powers to the fullest, remarking ambiguously that the executive should ''have authority commensurate with the responsibilities of his position.'' An open proposal to increase American power at the expense of local leaders would needlessly inflame Philippine opinion. Yet, while muted in the final report, this appeal for a reinvigorated governor generalship, along with interest in expanding the American presence in the islands, became the hallmarks of U.S. policy for the next several years.[25]

With the mission's final report on its way to Washington, Wood and McCoy embarked upon a tour of the Far East, stopping at Hong Kong, Shanghai, Peking,

Manchuria, Korea, and Japan. McCoy's first visit to China since 1906 gave him a fresh appreciation of the continuing turmoil of the revolution. An audience with the empress of Japan provided the trip's other highlight. McCoy compared the formalities involved in meeting that august personage to "one of Walter Camp's bending and stretching exercises."[26] In Washington, meanwhile, Harding had already decided to reverse the Wilsonian drift toward Philippine independence. Instead of serving as the basis for a reexamination of existing policy, the Wood-Forbes Report served to justify changes that were already under way. Yet questions remained as to how the United States would persuade Filipinos to accept indefinite American retention of the islands. Closely related was the question of who would act as Harding's agent in this delicate undertaking. The administration once again concluded that only Wood possessed the stature and experience needed for the job. Once again, Harding asked him to accept appointment as governor general. At first, Wood resisted, but repeated urging from Washington wore him down. By the time he and McCoy returned to Manila in October, Wood had acceded to the president's request, although with certain conditions attached. Still intending to accept the position at Pennsylvania, he insisted that his term as governor general be for one year only. And to assist him in governing the Philippines, he persuaded the War Department to permit McCoy, Johnston, and Bowditch to stay on as personal assistants.[27]

Wood did not really expect to eliminate the problems identified by the Wood-Forbes mission in a single year. He hoped to persuade Harding to appoint McCoy as vice-governor and "to have him take over the Governorship as soon as the machine is once more moving forward," thereby freeing himself to return home. Because McCoy shared "the basic principles which I have always employed in all work of this kind," Wood could count on him to carry on the right policies. Throughout the late summer and fall of 1921, Wood campaigned for McCoy's appointment. Back in the United States, Forbes also worked in McCoy's behalf. Their efforts failed, due in part to a reluctance to have military men fill both of the leading offices in the Philippine administration. Some in Washington may also have realized that depriving Wood of control over his successor could keep him in the Philippines.[28]

Although denied the vice-governorship, McCoy remained in Manila until 1925 as the leading figure in Wood's "cavalry" or "khaki" cabinet. Though without official status or statutory authority, the soldiers on the governor general's staff emerged as influential and eventually controversial figures in the Wood administration. McCoy and his fellow officers at the Malacanan Palace drafted legislation to sort out the islands' tangled finances. They headed investigatory missions into remote areas. They represented Wood at meetings with Filipino officials or at civic functions, in the opinion of one Manila resident, "too consciously bearing 'the white man's burden.'" In effect, they protected an aging chief executive whose health eroded the longer he stayed in Manila. They served as a buffer in his uneasy relations with Filipino leaders. If need be, they

*Khaki cabinet: McCoy and Gordon Johnston in Manila, 1921. (Courtesy U.S. Army Military History Institute)*

talked him out of impetuous decisions, especially McCoy, "from General Wood's point of view the only man essential to him." Perhaps most important to one whose ambitions had been thwarted (he believed) by unworthy opponents, they gave unstinting loyalty and affection. They were Wood's protégés come of age: Unlike others, they would not betray him.[29]

For an influential member of the governor general's household, duty was not without its rewards. Even for an old Far East hand, the varied attractions of the

*The Malacanan Palace: Wood and McCoy entertain a guest on the veranda. (Courtesy U.S. Army Military History Institute)*

Philippine capital retained fascination. Although tame by comparison, the Army-Navy Club overlooking Manila Bay provided well-appointed surroundings for socializing with other Americans. To stay fit, McCoy played polo regularly, becoming president of the exclusive Manila Polo Club. In the countryside, game was plentiful, and the *Apo*, the governor general's dispatch boat, could be commandeered for fishing nearby waters. Moreover, whenever the coastal heat became oppressive, McCoy joined Wood's family at their mountain retreat in Baguio.

Still, these comfortable remnants of privilege could not disguise the aura of imperial twilight engulfing Wood's administration. In retrospect, the premises from which Wood operated seem unreal. Certainly, his hopes for the Philippines appear hardly relevant to the reality taking shape beyond the gates of Malacanan. McCoy described the administration's goal as "bringing order out of chaos." Yet, however ruinous, the social and economic disarray of the Philippines in the aftermath of World War I did not compare in significance to the irrevocable political transformation then under way. The conditions existing in the decade after 1902 when American power in the Philippines reached its zenith no longer pertained, having been undermined by Harrison's passivity and growing Filipino assertiveness. Neither Wood nor McCoy, however, could accept that fact.[30]

The near absence of serious American interest in the Philippines further complicated the Wood administration's problem. A decade before, guiding the islands toward maturity had been recognized as an important American responsibility. By the 1920s, true believers in the American mission to uplift the

Philippines had become few in number, either within government or outside it. The miniscule size of the American community in the islands—fewer than 7,000 U.S. citizens resided there—suggests the extent to which Americans had lost interest in their great Pacific possession. Even Harding paid scant attention to the Philippines. Having made the political point of reversing Woodrow Wilson's Philippine policy, the Republicans by and large were willing to let Wood work out the specifics of the policy replacing it. Thus, in embarking on his crusade, Wood could expect little help from Washington. In the event, he received little help from anyone other than his intimates in the khaki cabinet, all of whom shared his views.

Historians have yet to give the Wood administration the detailed scrutiny that it deserves. Beginning in 1921, Wood and his advisers sought to repeat his Cuban successes on a grander scale. With 11 million Filipinos scattered among 3,000 islands, divided further among themselves by religious and ethnic rivalries, their task was not easy. While Americans at home busied themselves with the fruits of normalcy, these army officers labored to create in the Philippines an efficient, humane capitalist order reminscent of the now-faded ideals of American progressivism. Opposed by local nationalists far more interested in power for Filipinos than in imported ideals, they failed.[31]

Wood outlined his goals in his inaugural address of October 15, 1921. Economy, efficiency, and true progress were the broad objectives that his administration would pursue. Its hallmarks would be honesty, morality, and an appreciation that public office is a public trust. Yet he would not slight human needs. Citing as a "frightening indictment of our sanitary and health conditions" the fact that nearly one out of three Filipino children died in infancy, he called for improvements in medical care, public works, and treatment of the chronically ill. Education, too, needed to be improved and extended; Wood proposed that English be taught as a common language to unify the diverse population. In education as well as in other aspects of Philippine life, he told his listeners, "your women must be given equal opportunity with your men." Regarding economic policy, he vowed to encourage, not discourage, private enterprise. Toward this end, he would disengage the government from such ventures as railroad ownership and cement production while working to attract foreign capital.[32] Wood and his inner circle were uncompromising in their support of private enterprise as the vehicle for economic development. Yet they were no mere conservative defenders of business interests. Their advocacy of a positive state committed to human welfare, of women's rights, and of education to achieve cultural homogenization put them squarely in the tradition of American progressivism. What marked them above all else as progressives was their constant refrain of efficiency as the highest attribute of government performance.[33]

In their own eyes, these military progressives were qualified to serve as the agents of humane, efficient rule because of their expertise and nonpartisanship, both of which further emphasize their links to domestic progressivism. They had already demonstrated their administrative skills as colonial administrators, and they expressed confidence in their ability to transfer their previous experience to a new situation. "It seems like the old Cuban game," McCoy remarked within a month of Wood's taking office. Only those already well versed in the game could lay claim to play it. Indeed, intrusion by novices drew their contempt. As McCoy commented later concerning an attack on American policy in the Philippines, "Like . . . other theoretical friends of the Filipinos," the authors of the critique had "never sweat[ed] nor suffered with them nor taken the trouble to go see them with their own eyes." Having done their share of sweating, these soldiers believed that they possessed the expertise needed to rule.[34]

Beyond technical competence, progressive leadership required breadth of vision. As Robert H. Wiebe comments, although the ideal progressive leader could "comprehend the details of a modern specialized government, he was much more than an expert among experts. His vision encompassed the entire nation, his impartiality freed him from all prejudices, and his detached wisdom enabled him to devise an equitable and progressive policy for the whole society." Partisan politics, which inevitably involved conflicts between interest groups, compromise, and the promotion of parochial interests, obscured the common good. According to Samuel P. Hayes, progressives sought as leaders "experts [who] could transcend the 'petty' bickerings of political strife, rise above a welter of grassroots interests, and produce the greatest good for society as a whole." Ignoring their own recent involvement in a presidential campaign, Wood and his circle believed that the military's traditional nonpartisanship uniquely fitted them to provide rational, disinterested administration best suited to the interests of all Filipinos.[35]

On the surface, the military's authoritarian style appears at odds with progressivism's democratic leanings. This contradiction was more apparent than real. Although progressives at home professed support for democratizing reforms, in practice they enfranchised only those deemed capable of responsible political behavior. This standard excluded blacks, Asian-Americans, or immigrants from southern and eastern Europe. When applied to the Philippines, where Americans viewed the entire population as inferior, this rule of thumb logically absolved progressivism of its democratic component entirely. With the people incapable of self-rule, enlightened American military administrators would rule for them.[36]

Thus, reasserting the governor general's authority became a prerequisite to the application of progressive principles in the Philippines. Yet, given the rein that Harrison permitted Philippine leaders, any threat to their prerogatives would invite resistance. Wood and his disciples recognized that circumstances in the Philippines were not precisely those of Cuba twenty years before. As a result of American rule, Filipinos had become less malleable. "We have made them energetic and have made them work and have [made] them ambitious," McCoy told Katherine Mayo, a sympathetic journalist. "In the accomplishment of this,

we have made them bumptious and half-baked and unpleasant in many cases."
"Bumptious" political leaders like Quezon and Osmena would not automatically
do the governor general's bidding, yet Wood fully expected that in a test of
strength, he would prevail.[37]

Initially , the new governor general enjoyed surprising support from Filipino
leaders. The legislature saw utility in certain aspects of Wood's program,
especially those aimed at salvaging the country's finances. Less-agreeable
proposals could simply be deferred until the governor general's one-year term
expired. Thus, at the end of the legislative session of 1922, McCoy reported to
George Van Horn Mosely that the financial program that he and Bowditch
prepared for Wood passed "without being altered or punctured in a vital spot."
The legislature approved measures floating new bond issues, reorganizing the
Philippine National Bank, and providing financial assistance for the ailing
government-owned Manila Railroad. "The spirit of the legislature," reported
Wood in his annual report for 1922, "has been one of cooperation."[38]

The administration devoted the preponderance of its energies not to drafting
legislation but to devising ways to replace sloppiness with order and efficiency.
Wood reduced government expenditures, arguing that the heavy losses sustained
by the national bank "necessitated the most rigid economy in the administration
of government"; public works absorbed the brunt of these cuts. Wood examined
ways to consolidate provinces and municipalities to trim the number of
government employees, and he launched vigorous campaigns against gambling
and prostitution. He financed improvements to the leper colony at Culion (a
project to which he devoted great personal attention) and also expanded public
health programs—for example, increasing smallpox vaccinations from 25,000 in
1921 to 1,744,000 in 1922.[39]

In Wood's view, 1922 was a year of significant progress. Yet, even with
spending cuts, the budget remained in deficit. The government failed to divest
itself of its commercial enterprises, whose poor condition rendered them
unsalable. The national bank was operating at an annual loss of 600,000 pesos.
Wood's efforts to infuse Americans into the Philippine constabulary and the
ranks of teachers languished for want of qualified volunteers. Attempts to attract
American capital enjoyed little success. Much, therefore, remained to be done.
Failing to get McCoy designated as heir apparent, Wood concluded that he alone
could carry on the work. Abandoning the idea of a quiet retirement to academia,
he told Washington that he would stay in Manila indefinitely.[40]

Unfortunately, the harmony of Wood's relations with the legislature in 1922
was deceptive. Bowditch, for one, observed the governor general's uneasiness
with Philippine leaders. "One thing you can be sure of," he wrote Forbes,
"General Wood and his family will never get into . . . close touch with the
filipinos. . . . Their race prejudice is too strong and too apparent." Wood's
imperious manner too often ruffled the feathers of those with whom he dealt: "To

him a good Filipino is one who agrees with him, [whereas] one who has his own mind . . . is disloyal and dangerous." Given the delicacy of the political situation, remarked Bowditch, McCoy provided the administration's "anchor of safety and hope."[41]

Wood's decision to continue as governor general triggered the eruption that Bowditch feared. Viewing Wood's presence as an obstacle to their aspirations and knowing that he would not permit even the level of autonomy permitted by Harrison, Filipino leaders orchestrated a political clash to discredit the governor general.[42] Criticism of Wood, growing through the first half of 1923, followed two lines. Filipino leaders accused the governor general of exceeding his authority by insisting that the cabinet, all but one of whose members were Filipino, was responsible directly to him. This reversed the Harrison administration's practice of permitting the cabinet to report to the legislature—in effect, to Quezon and Osmena. In addition, they said, Wood abused his veto power by refusing to sign bills concerned purely with local issues rather than restricting its use to matters relating to American sovereignty or international obligations. Harrison rarely used the veto. The frequency with which Wood did so reflected his own broader conception of the governor general's role.[43]

Discord between Wood and the Philippine leaders reached a climax in July 1923. The incident bringing events to a head was a trivial one, involving Wood's intervention in behalf of an American named Ray Conley, a member of the Manila police vice squad, whom Filipino authorities accused of misconduct. Yet Wood's action in restoring Conley to duty symbolized the growing reach of his authority that nationalists so resented. On July 17, the council of state (less its single American member), comprising the cabinet, the president of the senate (Quezon), and the speaker of the house (Manuel Roxas), marched into Wood's office and quit in protest over his handling of the Conley affair. Denouncing the action as "an organized and preconcerted attack" on his authority and "as a challenge and a threat," Wood nonetheless accepted their resignations. As the Philippine leadership filed out of the governor general's office, they left Wood's plans for reconstructing the islands in a shambles.[44]

Wood's lack of political dexterity, his petulant treatment of Filipinos, and his own physical decline produced a reaction that played into the hands of his opponents. They now had a cause—cast in nationalist hues—that they would exploit as long as he remained in office. No one had been able to save the old general from himself. Recounting these events in a letter to Mosely, Harbord commented,

> My theory has always been that General Wood got into trouble when McCoy was away from him, and that he never got into trouble when McCoy was around. . . . I have heard several times that General Wood was getting rather forgetful, and that McCoy is really the key man in the whole situation

out there. Admire [Wood] as we will, . . . the bald facts are that the lameness of his is in his head and not in his leg.

Unfortunately for Wood, during the troubled summer of 1923, McCoy was not around. Instead, he was home on leave, celebrating his recent promotion to brigadier general. McCoy left Manila in April, intending to return by late summer.[45] Had he done so, McCoy might have been able to save Wood from himself. But other events intervened to prolong his absence.

The end of August found McCoy in Japan enroute back to the Philippines. As his ship, the *President Pierce,* was leaving Kobe on September 1, he felt a slight tremor. Only when he reached Shanghai did he learn that the tremor had been a disastrous earthquake that leveled much of Yokohama and Tokyo. Judging himself "the nearest and freest American official" who could offer assistance, he immediately reboarded the *Pierce* and sailed for Yokohama.[46] He arrived on September 7 to find a scene of "awe-inspiring destruction and desolation." Yokohama had been "obliterated, leaving behind nothing but smoking ashes and heaps of ruins." Nothing he had seen in France compared to the devastation. Fires burned out of control for two days, wreaking even greater damage than the quake itself. Eighty percent of the buildings in Yokohama were destroyed. In Tokyo, fires gutted 300,000 residences. Thirty-three thousand people died in Yokohama; authorities in Tokyo estimated their losses at 120,000 dead or missing, another 35,000 injured, and 2.5 million left homeless.[47]

Having cabled both the secretary of war and Wood of his return to Japan, McCoy received orders putting him in charge of American relief efforts. His responsibility was to coordinate the transfer of supplies being rushed from Manila and the United States and to do it without treading on local sensibilities. Although the Japanese welcomed short-term assistance, they would resent any meddling that implied an inability to manage their own affairs. To maximize the humanitarian and diplomatic value of American contributions, it was essential to conduct the operation in the proper spirit.[48]

*The Japanese earthquake of 1923: the smoldering ruins of Yokohama. (Courtesy Osaka Mainichi)*

The earthquake had destroyed the American embassy, so McCoy set up headquarters in the Imperial Hotel, designed by Frank Lloyd Wright and one of the few structures to survive intact. He spent the next six weeks assisting Americans and Filipinos stranded by the earthquake, supervising the unloading of supplies in Yokohama bay, arranging the construction of the field hospitals that were the centerpieces of the American contribution, and coordinating with Japanese officials the transfer of relief matériel. Typhoons, aftershocks, and red tape in Washington and Tokyo slowed operations, but, in all, $16 million of aid was turned over to the Japanese. Included in this sum were three hospitals erected by American troops and staffed temporarily by seventy American doctors and nurses.[49]

Within weeks, McCoy saw signs of recovery. "Like all Orientals," he remarked, the Japanese were "most adaptable to what to us would be impossible . . . conditions." Wary of overstaying his welcome, McCoy decided to terminate relief operations by mid-October. Before departing, he escorted the prince regent, the future emperor Hirohito, on a tour of the American-donated hospitals and called on the Japanese war minister to receive the thanks of the Japanese government. The two generals expressed their mutual hopes that the American reaction to Japan's distress would mark the beginning of improved relations between the two countries. McCoy believed that such an outcome was genuinely possible. In his final report, he pointed to a new cordiality observable toward Americans in Japan. He detected "a distinctly new attitude toward all Americans on the part of all classes of the Japanese." Perhaps, for the moment, such a new attitude did exist. A newspaperman long resident in Japan reported that because of the American response, "there never has been a time when the feeling throughout the country . . . has been so sincerely friendly toward the United States." With calculations of national interest inevitably erasing the memory of past good will, however, such affection proved short-lived.[50]

However transitory McCoy's contribution to Japanese-American friendship, his success there far exceeded any he would achieve in mending the fortunes of the Wood administration. Returning to the political wars of Manila in November, McCoy warned his family that "most of that appearing in your newspapers [about the Philippine situation] is bunk." Protective of his chief, McCoy was determined to be optimistic. In truth, by the time McCoy rejoined Wood, relations between the governor general and the Philippine leaders had been shattered beyond repair. The crisis that began in July sputtered along for the rest of Wood's tenure, sapping the energies of his administration.[51]

On one level, the dispute was a constitutional one, a disagreement between the governor general and the legislature over how much authority each was permitted under the Jones Act of 1916. Philippine leaders, citing Harrison as their model, argued that the governor general's role was to symbolize American

*Earthquake relief: The future emperor Hirohito inspects American-donated field hospitals in Tokyo, 1923. (Courtesy National Archives)*

sovereignty while exercising little real authority. They depicted Wood's efforts to assert broad powers as the actions of an autocrat. They accused Wood of creating his khaki cabinet to supplant local political leaders, reducing their own role to that of ineffectual observers. Wood and his defenders—of whom McCoy remained always the foremost—claimed that Harrison perverted the Jones Act by failing to fulfill the obligations of his office. Wood was merely attempting to restore the balance between the executive and legislative branches that the framers of the Jones Act had intended. Seen in this light, the legislature was the usurper. As McCoy told a *New York Times* correspondent, Filipino politicians sought "to diminish our control without diminishing our responsibility, and to gain control of the government by intrigue and misleading interpretations of the [Jones] Act. . . . The attitude of the Governor-General has been to keep the flag at the top of the pole where Congress has placed it, until Congress decides to the contrary."[52]

Yet such legalistic arguments concealed the true substance of the disagreement. The underlying reasons for the clash were more visceral and thus less

subject to compromise. For at least a decade, the pursuit of immediate independence had dominated Philippine politics. Independence became a cause no
less fraught with emotion than slavery had been to Americans on the eve of the
Civil War. Out of principle and a prudent concern for his own career, no
Philippine politician could regard the expansion of American authority as
anything other than illegitimate and unacceptable. The purpose for which that
authority might be used was irrelevant. As Quezon notoriously remarked, he
would prefer a "government run like hell by Filipinos to one run like heaven by
Americans." What Philippine leaders demanded of Wood was not a compromise
interpretation of the Jones Act that could smooth over their differences with him,
but abandonment of the concept of Philippine-American relations that he and the
Republican party represented.[53]

Likewise, for the soldiers at Malacanan, the legal issue was only secondary.
Their commitment to the governor general's authority and their opposition to
nationalist aspirations flowed not from devotion to the Jones Act but from
conviction. Upbringing and experience convinced them that nonwhites were
incapable of self-government. Only generations of comprehensive supervision
could possibly prepare the Philippines for independence. Publicly, McCoy stated
that the administration's opposition to freeing the Philippines rested on their
unpreparedness "either economically or from the standpoint of defense." Yet his
real reservation—and Wood's as well—concerned the people themselves. Of
necessity, he had to argue that the Filipinos had made progress over the course of
a quarter-century of American tutelage. But, as he told Katherine Mayo,

> the only point that is doubtful in my mind is whether it has gone far enough.
> Those things are part of the important imponderables . . . that are habits of
> mind and customs that have grown up after years, and in many cases
> generations, of thinking . . . on certain lines, and I doubt whether we have
> been here long enough to create that habit as against the primitive habit of
> going out and killing a landlord.

American withdrawal would jeopardize whatever advances had been achieved. "If
American control were entirely removed at present," he told Mayo, "there would
be an easy slipping-back" into primitive habits.[54]

The Americans acknowledged the racist assumptions underlying their position. According to McCoy, "the root and branch" of Philippine-American
differences was "a racial thing." The well-to-do, educated Filipino, he said,
"feels the racial superiority bearing down on him. There is not a day in the week
that it is not impressed on these fellows in some way, and they resent the
Americans here." The clamor for independence stemmed in part from a desire of
the upper class to be freed of reminders of their inferiority. McCoy thought it
perfectly natural that race should play such a role in determining both politics
and interpersonal relations. As he explained to Katherine Mayo: "I don't have

any physical repugnance for the Malay. I do for the Negro. But I have watched the thing and I can detect no physical repugnance in myself for a Malay or an American Indian. If I were surrounded by them and had to associate with them closely, it would probably come. You just can't get away from it under certain conditions." Racial differences created racial tension and that, in turn, spawned nationalism. The sequence was "a normal thing, sure to happen under like conditions with any people," said McCoy. "It was marked in Cuba, where the Cubans were white people. And the conditions here . . . have been consistently normal right from the start—the desire to get rid of the white man." Bowditch shared this view. "Did we consider the Filipino our equal socially," he remarked to McCoy, "our problem would be fairly simple. But taint [sic] so and won't be so while we live anyway."[55]

Somewhat inconsistently, the Wood administration also argued that the entire independence movement was contrived and insincere. The Americans contended that cynical politicians had manufactured the movement by using their naive countrymen for selfish ends. Wood termed the issue a "purely local and artificial agitation produced by a small group fanning the very natural desire of the people for independence, but absolutely failing to enlighten them as to . . . the costs or responsibilities which independence involves." The discrepancy between the politicians' public and private views only confirmed the disdain that the Americans in Manila felt for the likes of Quezon and Osmena. "In private and practically without exception," McCoy said, "they say very frankly that they are not ready for independence and will not be for years to come, but that for local and political reasons they are obliged to continue to talk and advocate on their line of ultimate aspirations." Such hypocrisy shocked military progressives, who expected public officials to subordinate partisan or selfish concerns to the common good. To indorse such conniving would be unconscionable.[56]

The net effect of this political dispute was to create an insurmountable impediment to the fulfillment of Wood's plans for the Philippines. Attacking the governor general and his khaki cabinet preoccupied the legislature. Replying to such charges became the chief concern of the governor general and his household. McCoy even felt obliged to provide the War Department with a brief refuting Filipino attempts to depict Wood's assistants as a "brutal and licentious soldiery [of] Boche-like appearance." McCoy portrayed Wood as a man of great forbearance, patiently withstanding the slings of his opponents. The governor general put up with abuse "that would have driven most other white men crazy," said McCoy. "He has never as yet allowed his temper to show with these people. I know that he has a terrific temper. He wouldn't stand this from white people. He would knock them down probably." To Forbes, McCoy reported that Wood "stood the gaff without a sign of weakness. It was a fine Anglo-Saxon performance as against . . . the meanness of Orientals, egged on by American politicians."[57]

Yet no defense of Wood could conceal the fact that the goals of the military progressives remained unfulfilled. The cabinet crisis of 1923 ended Wood's chances of gaining passage of significant legislation. The government never succeeded in shedding its business interests. The bank kept "barging along," wrote McCoy, "hopeless in the long run" but propped up for the moment by rebounding sugar prices. Higher commodity prices also enabled Wood to balance the budget from 1923 onward, taking the edge off the financial crisis that existed in 1921. Yet the teaching corps and the constabulary remained without their American leaven, and efforts to attract new capital to the islands collided with Filipino fears of foreign exploitation. Even McCoy's attempts to call on business friends such as Harbord produced negligible results. So long as Philippine agitation made independence a possibility, few American businessmen would risk long-term investment in the islands.[58]

Granted, under Wood the legislature no longer dominated the Philippine government as it had during the Harrison years. Yet it retained enough power to deny Wood the latitude that he had exercised in Cuba or the Moro Province. As a result, his imprint was less far-reaching. "I should suggest," he told Katherine Mayo in 1924, "that during the next twenty-five years there . . . be no discussion of [freeing] the Philippines. . . . There would be a sigh of relief. In twenty-five years, . . . the question [could] be opened again." To his chagrin, Philippine nationalism could not be wished away so easily.[59] By 1925, McCoy was claiming victory—Wood had "beaten the politicos at every turn," he asserted. But this was pure bluster. Even Gordon Johnston admitted that the Filipino leaders had defeated Wood. "They played with him as a sportsman plays with a trout," he said. Wood had "put up with all manner of indignities, believing always that he could persuade these men to work harmoniously with him."[60] Not least among the blows that Wood suffered was the loss of McCoy himself. As part of their attack on Wood's khaki cabinet, Filipino representatives in Washington challenged the legality of assigning military officers as civil advisers to the governor general. In ruling on the matter, the comptroller general of the United States affirmed the Philippine position. Despite outraged cries from Wood and attempts by the secretary of war to circumvent the ruling, McCoy was ordered home. On April 17, 1925, he left the Philippines—and Wood—for the last time.[61]

Wood stayed on for two more years. The strain of governing the Philippines in the face of concerted opposition by the local political establishment took its toll. The gimpy leg and periodic seizures—symptoms that had twice been relieved by surgery to remove brain tumors—recurred with greater severity. Even before his own departure, McCoy urged his chief to return home for another operation. Wood refused to give his opponents the satisfaction of driving him from the islands, telling McCoy, "I am going to fight this thing through and die in harness."[62] In the end, the American attempt to revive the governor general's authority foundered on the opposition of a handful of Filipino leaders whose political agenda consisted of a single issue: independence. These men would not acquiesce in a return to an era of near-total American control. During the Harrison years, they acquired the clout and the savvy to prove more than a match for Wood. Once ruptured in 1923, relations between the governor general and the legislature would not recover so long as Wood remained in the Malacanan Palace. Wood's stubborn determination only sealed the failure of Republican policy in the islands.

# 8

# Mission to Nicaragua

McCoy did not return alone from the Philippines in 1925. Developments toward the end of his tour in Manila effected a fundamental change in his life. Even in his correspondence with his family, McCoy was reticent in discussing his personal affairs. Certainly he enjoyed the company of women. But in his gentlemanly way, he refrained from recording the details of his relationships with them. Although there had been romances, the sparse surviving evidence makes it difficult to evaluate their seriousness. To be sure, McCoy's papers contain numerous letters from a Texas schoolteacher, E. Bliss Baldridge, whom he met during his tour on the Mexican border. She was smitten, but how McCoy responded is unclear. Similarly, there are hints of a romantic attachment between McCoy and Daisy Harriman, the worldly, attractive, and politically active widow who was a Family friend and had followed the AEF to France.[1] In the overall context of McCoy's life, however, the importance of such episodes was negligible. Since leaving West Point, he had subordinated the needs of his private life to the demands of his profession. Among other things, this priority led McCoy to value highly his independence. To preserve that independence, it made sense to avoid long-term relationships with the opposite sex. Always on the move, surrounded by male associates, McCoy appears to have been quite content with the arrangement.

By the time McCoy returned to the Philippines in 1921, however, he had grown weary of bachelorhood. For a time, he shared quarters with Peter Bowditch in Manila and thus had someone's company while off duty. But in 1922, Bowditch went home, and McCoy thereafter lived alone. To his family, he remarked glumly,

An earlier version of this chapter appeared as "The American Electoral Mission in Nicaragua, 1927-1928," *Diplomatic History* 4 (Summer 1980): 241-261.

"If it were my habit, I think I should cast about to find someone to marry," adding quickly, "but it isn't so don't be alarmed."[2] A year and a half later, without having given the slightest inkling of what was afoot, he addressed the subject of matrimony a second time. "Dearest Mother," he wrote,

> I was married yesterday to Frances Judson after some weeks of stress and strain, for though I had been proposing daily and determinedly, Frances did not want to be married and did want to go home to Mother, sailing . . . on the 28th. That was more than I could bear, so yesterday morning while driving her about . . . and in a moment of weakness, of sympathy for my evident distress, she allowed herself to become engaged, and before she knew it I had . . . the Bishop ready, telephoned for the General and Mrs. Wood . . . and [we] were married at 12:30. . . . We drove back to Malacanan for lunch, and drove off right after to Baugio where the General has given us the house for our honeymoon. We are very happy and always will be.[3]

By all accounts they were. The twenty-eight-year-old bride from New York City was spirited, outspoken, and accustomed to living her own life. Having made her decision, however, she became an ideal companion for McCoy, willingly adopting his itinerant life, sharing his interests, and making his friends her own. In appearance, according to her husband, she was a "tall, slim, red head, lovely in face and figure."[4] Beyond her attractive personal qualities and charm, Frances was an intriguing choice as a bride for McCoy. Although he told Cameron Forbes that "falling in love was the last thing I anticipated," McCoy's decision to marry was not as impulsive as it appeared. Twenty-one years her senior, he had known Frances since she was a young girl; she was in fact a favorite niece of Wood and his wife—almost another daughter. Indeed, one of her periodic visits with the governor general's family provided the occasion for McCoy to fall in love and to court her. Thus, marrying Frances in effect formalized what had been heretofore an unofficial claim to membership in Wood's immediate family. Long McCoy's mentor, role model, and chief, Leonard Wood became something like McCoy's father as well. If binding himself more closely to Wood's family gratified McCoy, Wood no doubt returned the feeling. His own sons, Osborne and Leonard, Jr., repeatedly disappointed him. Now the man whom above all others the governor general would have chosen for his son symbolically became just that.[5]

The McCoys used their return to the United States as an excuse for a European honeymoon. In Rome, they visited Fletcher and Summerlin, family friends who were both assigned to the American embassy. The couple continued on to Venice, Florence, and Paris where they stayed with William Phillips and James Logan. In July, the McCoys finally reached New York. They spent the rest of the summer calling on relatives, first in Lewistown and then in Newport, Rhode Island, where Frances's family was living. When McCoy completed his vacation, he was slated to assume command of an infantry brigade at Fort Sam

*Frances Judson before her marriage: independent, outspoken, and, for McCoy,*
*irresistible. (Courtesy U.S. Army Military History Institute)*

Houston, Texas. Yet, even before leaving for his new assignment, orders from the
War Department diverted him to Washington.[6]

McCoy had been tapped to serve on the court-martial panel that would try Col.
William Mitchell, an old friend from Pershing's staff in France. Mitchell, of
course, was the great publicist for the concept of air power. Frustrated by the lack
of support for his ideas in the War Department, Mitchell devised a bold plan to
generate interest in his cause. Determined to bring his dispute with official

Washington before the public, Mitchell called a press conference on September 5, 1925, and read a lengthy statement denouncing the War and Navy departments for "incompetency, criminal negligence, and almost treasonable administration" in running their air services. As Mitchell had anticipated, such insubordination left the War Department with no choice but to bring charges against him.[7] The court-martial itself, beginning on October 28, greatly inconvenienced McCoy and his wife. They took up temporary quarters at 1718 H Street and then lived for awhile with friends assigned to Washington. When "the Mitchell court-martial began to look like the length of a deep sea cable rather than a piece of string," they rented a house on I Street.[8]

McCoy approached the trial with ambivalence. On the one hand, he understood and to a degree sympathized with Mitchell's motives. While waiting for the trial to begin, McCoy predicted to Wood that the Philippines would become a topic of much discussion in the near future. He went on to remark that he considered such discussion "good as a matter of education—pretty much like the air investigation and Billy Mitchell—good for everybody but Billy."[9] With this in mind, McCoy kept his sense of humor throughout the presentation of the airman's long, combative defense. Mitchell's attorneys, McCoy admitted, handled the case so adroitly that "to the public, the War Dept. is on trial instead of the festive Bill." McCoy found himself cast as one of the villains of the piece while the accused had contrived to become "the town and national hero." Only the trial's duration evoked any expressions of discontent. "The court-martial keeps me sitting as I never sat before," he told Cameron Forbes in November. McCoy complained of feeling "like Mrs. Page's darky 'sometimes setting and thinking, and sometimes just setting.' And the end is not in sight."[10]

When the end did come on December 17, the court found the defendent guilty. McCoy's correspondence contains nothing to suggest that he dissented from the majority. Indeed, for a man who placed discretion and obedience high on his own scale of professional traits, it would have been out of character for him to have done so, whatever his sympathy for Mitchell's views. Yet McCoy valued personal loyalty as well. Thus, his friendship with Mitchell survived the court-martial intact. The following spring found Mitchell, since resigned from the service, enjoying a long visit as McCoy's guest at Fort Sam Houston. (McCoy confided to Wood that Mitchell had "allowed [that] he never would have had to break the china had you been in the W[ar] D[epartment].") McCoy later became godfather for one of Mitchell's children, and at Mitchell's funeral in 1936 he served as a pallbearer—the only former court member to do so.[11]

In early 1926, McCoy assumed command of the Third Infantry Brigade, Second Division, at Fort Sam Houston. He remained there for more than a year, until May 1927 when he was reassigned to command the First Artillery Brigade at Fort Hoyle, Maryland. This return to troop duty provided a quiet interlude in an otherwise hectic career. Besides troop training and garrison duties, McCoy supported Reserve Officer Training Corps (ROTC) and Citizens' Military

Training Camp (CMTC) activities and participated in infrequent maneuvers with the rest of the division. The schedule provided adequate time for leisure, a situation of which McCoy strongly approved. He told his officers that each of them "should have some avocation or sideline of interest that will . . . distract his mind occasionally from, and refresh him for, the labors of his chosen profession." McCoy insured that those labors would not be excessive. In a memo that captures the flavor of the army of the 1920s, he directed that "the policy of this brigade will be so far as possible to leave the afternoons and evenings to the discretion of the individual officer." The brigade commander set the example in his own activities. Polishing up his tennis game, McCoy entered the Corps Area Tennis Tournament and "was too successful for my age and condition," reaching the semifinals in the singles competition and the finals in the men's doubles. Evenings were spent with Frances, frequently at the movies. As a result of his years overseas, McCoy told his family, he was "very much behind on all the famous pictures" and so was "enjoying even those which seem old to the rest of you."[12]

The summer of 1927 reunited McCoy briefly with Leonard Wood when the governor general returned to the United States. Yet even unmistakable signs that Wood was ailing did not prepare McCoy for the news of his mentor's death on August 7. Vacationing in the Adirondacks with Henry Stimson, McCoy received word that Wood had died on the operating table during a third attempt to relieve the painful and debilitating effects of a brain tumor. McCoy rushed back to Washington, took charge of the funeral arrangements, and served as a pallbearer during the ceremony. Wood's death left McCoy with a sense of irreplaceable loss. "I shall always miss him," he told Mrs. Wood a year later. "My whole life and work were wrapped up in him, much of the savor of life has gone with him."[13]

Wood's death set off a flurry of speculation that McCoy might become governor general. Even before Wood's funeral, the *New York Times* touted McCoy as a leading candidate for the job. A bit later, the *New York American* reported "a steady stream of letters . . . pouring into the White House from all over the United States and the Philippines" in McCoy's behalf. In the Philippines, too, McCoy picked up the endorsement of papers such as the *Mindanao Herald,* which lauded "his suaveness, his facility for making friends, his gracious demeanor . . . , and the courteous manner with which . . . he can administer a rebuke and make the patient feel like a dog, but like it." McCoy remained silent as to his own preferences in the matter, promising only that should an offer from the president materialize, "I shall be ready with a decision."[14] In all likelihood, McCoy would have accepted an appointment to serve as governor general. But whatever his final decision might have been, he never had reason to reveal it. A presidential call for his services did come in the fall of 1927, but instead of returning McCoy to the Far East, it set him off on a new tack—to Nicaragua.

*Back in the United States for surgery in 1927, an ailing Wood visits McCoy for the last time. (Courtesy U.S. Army Military History Institute)*

U.S. military involvement in Nicaragua began in 1912 when U.S. Marines landed in the midst of civil war to restore order and protect American lives and property. Although the occupation was not intended to be a long one, an American garrison remained for over a decade, propping up the increasingly unpopular regime that had invited the United States to intervene. Once the ill effects of this extended military presence became evident—particularly its corrosive impact on relations with the rest of Latin America—Washington committed itself to terminating the occupation at the first suitable opportunity. When Calvin Coolidge finally ordered the last troops home in August 1925, Americans believed that their Central American military ventures had ended once and for all. Such hopes, however, proved illusory.[15]

The stability that permitted the withdrawal collapsed immediately, with civil war erupting within a month. By March 1926, the Nicaraguan president had resigned, the vice-president had fled the country, and Emiliano Chamorro, the unscrupulous but charismatic leader of the Conservative party, had installed himself as chief executive. The State Department, citing the unconstitutionality of Chamorro's actions, denied him diplomatic recognition, thereby effectively declaring open season on the new regime. Internal order—briefly reestablished by the Conservative strong man—again disintegrated. Although Chamorro struggled to consolidate his position, in October 1926—bankrupt, harried by a Liberal party insurgency, and frustrated by American nonrecognition—he resigned the presidency. Turning to the problem of designating a successor, the State Department threw its support behind Adolfo Díaz, a pliant Conservative and former president who had welcomed the intervention of 1912. When vigorous lobbying in the Nicaraguan Congress secured his election on Armistice Day of 1926, American recognition followed.

Unfortunately, the ouster of Chamorro did not end the episode. No happier with the new American-sponsored president than they had been with his predecessor, the Liberals continued their "revolution" without pause. As Díaz's position deteriorated in the face of Liberal pressure, the American commitment to his survival increased. To prevent the outright collapse of the Díaz government, on Christmas Eve of 1926 U.S. Marines began returning to Nicaragua on an unprecedented scale; by February 1927, the number of American military personnel stationed in Nicaragua or enroute had swollen to nearly 5,500.[16] On the surface, this second intervention, following hard on the heels of the previous year's long-awaited withdrawal, seemed inexplicable. More than mere loyalty to Díaz had triggered the sudden reversal. Other hemispheric developments (specifically, the erratic course of the Mexican revolution) altered the State Department's perception of the real issues being contested in the Nicaraguan civil war—and of the real contestants.

By 1926, relations with Mexico had fallen to another low, the ostensible bone of contention being President Plutarco Calles's determination to reclaim Mexican oil properties controlled by American investors. Yet American concern extended far beyond simply protecting the holdings of a few Yankee oil barons. Mexican nationalism potentially threatened American political hegemony, the acceptance of American economic ground rules, and the universality of the American model of national development.[17] To a suspicious State Department, Mexican radicalism lurked behind the uprising in Nicaragua. In December 1926, Mexico audaciously recognized the "government" of former Vice-President Juan B. Sacasa, the leading Liberal claimant to the Nicaraguan presidency. Accusations soon followed that Calles was covertly providing the insurgents with arms and ammunition as well. To officials in Calvin Coolidge's administration, this alleged support of the revolution in Nicaragua posed a direct challenge to the United States. Mexico's actions, they argued, transformed Nicaragua into a critical "test case" of American prestige and influence throughout the Caribbean and hence required a forceful and determined response.[18]

Yet the mere presence of American troops would not suffice to contain this supposed spread of radicalism. Liberal resistance showed no signs of wilting just because the marines had landed. Coolidge attempted to forestall a further widening of American involvement by sending Henry L. Stimson to Managua to mediate a solution. But the resulting Tipitapa Agreement of May 1927 that Stimson engineered was only a partial success at best. Although the Liberal military commander, General José M. Moncada, agreed to disarm in exchange for an American pledge to supervise the 1928 Nicaraguan election, many insurgents rejected out of hand any settlement underwritten by the Yankees.[19] They vowed to continue the struggle and rallied to the leadership of a hitherto obscure Liberal general, César Augusto Sandino. Within weeks, the Nicaraguan countryside was again in turmoil. As the American minister in Managua reported to the State Department, Sandino "preached communism, Mexican brotherly love and cooperation, and death to the Americans until the rabble . . . joined him in his plan to massacre Americans . . . and to set up his own government."[20]

Abandoning any pretense of neutrality, the Marine Corps confidently launched a full-scale pursuit of the remaining rebels. Although ill-equipped and outnumbered, the Sandinistas proved aggravatingly elusive. In classic guerrilla fashion, they capitalized on their familiarity with the rugged local terrain and on the sympathy of the Nicaraguan people. Inaccurate intelligence, a sparse road network, and dependence on the cumbersome logistic train all conspired to hamper marine effectiveness. Sandino shrewdly encouraged the Americans to expend themselves on grueling, futile expeditions into the mountainous interior and then pestered his exhausted adversaries with hit-and-run ambushes and raids. In July 1927, a spectacular siege of an isolated marine garrison in the village of Ocotal convinced many that the struggle in Nicaragua had settled into a frustrating stalemate.[21]

Support for American policy at home, never great, evaporated as the military failed to make good on its optimistic predictions. By mid-1927, criticism of the administration—much of it from the president's own party—had become intense.[22] Privately, the administration was as unhappy as its detractors. By the end of 1927, even the most enthusiastic proponent of reintervention recognized the policy for what it was: a blunder of the first order. Panicked by the phantom of Mexican radicalism, the United States plunged headlong into a sticky guerrilla war that threatened to drag on for months or even years. Diplomatic attempts to untangle the situation not only failed to resolve the military problem but actually deepened the American commitment by pledging supervision of the Nicaraguan election of 1928. The ensuing marine campaign to destroy the Sandinistas failed. At home, efforts to rally public support misfired completely. Abroad, the reintervention damaged U.S. diplomatic relations throughout Latin America and in much of Europe. Noting the gap between his preaching and the marines' practice, some Europeans even began questioning the seriousness of Secretary of State Frank B. Kellogg's advocacy of a worldwide treaty to outlaw war.[23] Thus, an early end to the American presence became a matter of vital importance. The administration disagreed with its critics only on the manner in which the withdrawal should be accomplished. The wreckage of the previous year notwithstanding, any disengagement needed to take place amidst the trappings of political and diplomatic success. Neither the Republican party nor the United States could tolerate even the suggestion of humiliation. Acting on Stimson's advice, President Coolidge turned to McCoy to salvage his Nicaraguan policy.

The mission to Nicaragua inaugurated a new phase in McCoy's career as a military diplomatist. Coming into his own as heir to Leonard Wood, he no longer would stand off-stage as someone else's aide, assistant, or chief of staff. Henceforth McCoy would gain diplomatic employment as a principal in his own right. For McCoy personally, however, growing prominence provided less gratification than did the opportunity to carry on his mentor's work. As he confessed to a friend, "General Wood's death has distressed and shocked me even more than I would imagine." As a device to help McCoy overcome his sense of loss, the timing of the Nicaraguan mission was fortuitous. That the enterprise itself would surely have won Wood's endorsement was a source of added consolation.[24]

On June 26, 1927, Kellogg handed McCoy his commission as personal representative of the president. Formally, his mission was simply to carry out the promise made by Stimson a month earlier to supervise the Nicaraguan presidential election of 1928, thereby expediting the withdrawal of American forces. Such a withdrawal required that McCoy first restore domestic harmony, reduce the level of political corruption, and administer an election of such procedural correctness as to gain the support of Nicaraguans of all political persuasions. In addition, McCoy was to advise the American government on matters pertaining to Nicaragua and to "do everything possible to assist the Nicaraguan Government in electoral and military matters."[25]

The administration's commitment to the mission's overt purpose was not insincere. Credible evidence of evenhandedness would restore some luster to the tarnished American image as sponsor of democracy in Latin America and, by mollifying domestic critics, might prevent Nicaragua from being a source of further Republican distress. Yet, beyond staging a graceful exit for U.S. occupation forces, the Coolidge administration also viewed the mission as a vehicle for achieving a more substantial goal, namely, upholding American regional hegemony. Here, success hinged on different requirements: the liquidation of Sandino, a symbol and potential model for other anti-American movements in the region; installation of a pro-American regime; and the creation of instruments of power capable of sustaining that regime after the marines departed.

After a month spent preparing for his assignment, McCoy departed New York on August 10 to assess the situation in Nicaragua at first hand. Arriving in Managua on August 27, McCoy spent the following month investigating local conditions. To his eyes, Nicaragua recalled "Santiago de Cuba in '98 and '99." Although a backward country, it had "stirring possibilities if we can help out for some time." Deprived of American support, he predicted that Nicaragua would "go forward like a crab." With the countryside in disarray due to continuing attacks by Sandino and other bands of chronic outlaws and violent political partisanship rife among the people, restoring order and preventing renewed flare-ups of political violence would demand a firm hand. In an interim report, McCoy cautioned Kellogg to defer plans to reduce the marine garrison and urged the administration to augment Nicaragua's embryonic national police force—the Guardia Nacional—with more American officers and increased financial aid.[26]

Returning to Washington in October to report on his findings, McCoy began assembling a staff, for the most part choosing old army acquaintances, with "a few civilians to take the blight of militarism off the affair."[27] At the same time, he mapped out his overall strategy. Guaranteeing an orderly campaign with an agreeable outcome required that McCoy exercise absolute control over Nicaragua's electoral machinery. Armed with such authority, he could block the candidacy of any Nicaraguan unacceptable to the United States and discredit political elements inclined to question the election's legitimacy. In addition, convincing American guarantees of the election's honesty would conceivably persuade the losing side to accept the outcome of what had been presumably a fair fight. Mindful of these requirements, McCoy and Harold W. Dodds, a political scientist who served as his chief technical adviser, soon drafted an election law defining the prerogatives of the electoral mission. This law, according to Kellogg, was the sine qua non of the American effort. It created, as the *New York Times* reported, "an American dictatorship over the coming elections," giving McCoy, as president of the National Electoral Board, virtually unlimited authority.[28]

Developments in Managua during McCoy's absence, however, threatened the mission's success virtually before it began. As soon as the United States committed itself to supervising the elections, Emiliano Chamorro petitioned the State Department to permit him to run for president. His plea met with little sympathy. Because of Chamorro's systematic oppression of political enemies in the past, the Liberal party would never accept him as president. Given that his election in 1928 would be a disaster, in all likelihood rekindling the civil war, the State Department staunchly opposed his candidacy.[29] Although informed of this verdict in late October, Chamorro refused to accept it. Hoping to extort a change in the American attitude toward him, he mobilized his influence within the Conservative party to bottle up the American-designed election law *(la ley McCoy)* in the Nicaraguan Congress. Simultaneously, he began undermining Díaz's position by criticizing the president's submissiveness to American demands. Deprived of *la ley McCoy* and the incumbent president's cooperation, McCoy's mission would be seriously jeopardized.

By mid-January 1928, as McCoy again sailed from New York, Chamorro's intrigues culminated in a full-fledged crisis. *La ley McCoy* passed the Nicaraguan Senate but appeared irretrievably stalled in the Chamber of Deputies. Caught between Chamorro's insistent attacks and pressure from the American legation, Díaz announced his intention to resign. Apprised of this news during a layover in Panama, McCoy cabled Dana G. Munro, the chargé in Managua, to do whatever was necessary to "prevent or retard" the resignation of the president.[30] He then scrapped his own itinerary and seized upon the fastest available transportation, a navy ammunition ship, to hasten his arrival in Nicaragua.

McCoy reached Managua on January 22 and plunged into a series of conferences with Díaz, Moncada, and Chamorro. For the moment at least, Munro had allayed the president's anxieties. Expressing his absolute confidence in Díaz, McCoy bolstered the wavering president's commitment to remain in office. Efforts to persuade Chamorro to allow passage of *la ley McCoy* proved less successful. Chamorro remained adamant in his opposition, arguing that it was unconstitutional to surrender control of Nicaragua's internal affairs to a foreigner. The Nicaraguan's pose as an "apostle of the constitution" struck McCoy as ludicrous. The real motive behind the former dictator's ploy was unvarnished personal ambition. Whatever his purpose, such obstructionism irked McCoy: "My carefully laid plans are all awry," he grumbled privately.[31]

The stumbling block of greatest immediate concern was the Nicaraguan Congress's adjournment, scheduled for March 13. Failure to gain favorable congressional action by that date would require drastic measures to enact *la ley McCoy.* Unfortunately, the prospects for weakening Chamorro's grip on the legislature were poor unless pressure could be brought to bear on obstructive deputies. McCoy's hopes that Díaz would apply that pressure on his Conservative colleagues were disappointed. Although Díaz was outwardly cooperative, McCoy cabled Kellogg, the president's real attitude remained open to question. Certainly, he was doing less than his utmost to break the congressional log jam.[32] As adjournment neared, McCoy himself began twisting the arms of recalcitrant Conservative deputies. The manner in which he did so, however, suggests that he had already reconciled himself to proceeding without congressional consent. Meeting with groups of Chamorrista deputies on March 12, McCoy demanded a yes or no vote on the measure. Yet whether or not the law was enacted, he warned, the United States had no intention of reneging on its commitment to supervise the election.[33]

*Adolfo Díaz, president of Nicaragua, 1928 (left). His timid look parallels his approach to matters of policy. Emiliano Chamorro, 1928 (right): a shrewd and conniving adversary. (Courtesy National Archives)*

Chamorro, in fact, overestimated the importance that the Americans attributed to having Nicaraguan legislators enact *la ley McCoy*. Although congressional endorsement would lend legitimacy to the electoral mission, such legal niceties were not essential to its success. Above all, the State Department and McCoy as its chief agent were determined to adhere to the original American plan—without Chamorro for certain, and without the Nicaraguan Congress if necessary. Already in mid-February, Munro was insisting that the United States inform the Nicaraguan Congress "very strongly and very specifically that we are going to go ahead with or without a law." The State Department concurred, stating that the United States would not be thwarted "by any man or group of men in Nicaragua playing the game of party politics with purely selfish motives." If the Nicaraguan Congress refused to act, McCoy could persuade Díaz "to arrogate to himself practically dictatorial powers," implementing *la ley McCoy* by executive decree. Failing that, "the only remaining course would be for the United States to take matters into its own hands and give General McCoy full powers."[34]

On March 13, McCoy got his vote. The lower house decisively rejected the American election law and adjourned shortly thereafter. As elated Chamorristas converged on Managua's cathedral and rang the bells, tolling in honor of the death of McCoy's law, the man after whom the measure was named began prodding Díaz to enact the election law on his own authority. Although admitting that the legality of such a decree might be questioned, McCoy maintained that its "strictly legal status" was of "distinctly secondary importance." After all, the Nicaraguan constitution, representing "abstract statements of political theory rather than practical and effective guides for governmental action," was hardly sacrosanct. And although executive decrees were "not in accord with Anglo-American custom," they had long been common features of Latin

American politics. More to the point, *la ley McCoy* was critical to the electoral mission's success, and implementation by presidential order was preferable to the only other practical course, namely, for McCoy to issue the law on his own authority.[35] Whatever the merits of McCoy's arguments, Díaz quickly assented, if only to avoid having the Americans arbitrarily seize complete control of the country—as they were clearly prepared to do.[36] A member of McCoy's staff drafted the proclamation, and, after some minor haggling, Díaz enacted it on March 21, 1928.[37]

The decree vested authority for supervising the 1928 election in a National Electoral Board. It recognized McCoy as president of the board and Ramon Castillo and Enoc Aguado, representing the two major parties, as members. In practice, the Nicaraguans played a largely decorative role: The board could not meet without the president in attendance; no action by the board was valid without his concurrence; and in an emergency—as defined by the board's president—he could act alone to take whatever actions he deemed "indispensable to the conduct of a free and fair election." The decree also gave McCoy authority over the Guardia Nacional.[38]

Having, in the words of the *Washington Herald*, "been made the Mussolini of Nicaragua," McCoy at last possessed the authority to get on with the business at hand.[39] The one problem demanding attention above all others was Sandino. By the spring of 1928, the rebel leader had attained international stature, with an especially warm following among critics of American policy in the United States. Support for Sandino reached even the floor of the U.S. Senate, where Burton K. Wheeler of Montana applauded the Nicaraguan's struggle for "the same principles of liberty and free government for which our forefathers fought in 1776."[40] Admiration for Sandino grew the longer he mocked the military's claims that his demise was imminent.

Members of the electoral mission in Nicaragua did not share that admiration. According to Capt. Matthew B. Ridgway, one of McCoy's trusted subordinates, exposure to Mexican radicalism had infected Sandino with "the bolshevism that aims at [the] brotherhood of all men and control by the present laborers." Having absorbed a "fanaticism that wants to make the world over in a day by destroying all that opposes it," the guerrilla leader was "eager to grasp the opportunity to establish bolshevism in Nicaragua." Yet, as McCoy emphasized, it was not ideology alone that made Sandino the object of concern, but his emergence as "the symbol of opposition to United States policy throughout Latin America and at home, a useful figure to those who desire to attack us." For those inveighing against American domination of the Caribbean, Sandino was the subversive archetype of the patriot fighting for his native land against the United States as oppressor.[41]

On March 3, Kellogg requested McCoy's personal assessment of the military situation in Nicaragua. The secretary of state voiced the fear that the insurgency would go on indefinitely with a continuing sacrifice of American lives and without concrete results. The optimistic reports regularly issuing from the Navy Department satisfied him no more than they did the administration's critics. "People cannot understand why the job cannot be done," he complained, "and frankly I do not understand myself."[42] McCoy shared Kellogg's concern about the lack of progress being made against Sandino. Yet he was sensitive to the "extreme delicacy" of his position in regard to strictly military measures—a polite way of saying that the marines would resent outsiders prying into their affairs.[43] Although mindful of the need to reinvigorate the sagging American military effort, McCoy had waited for a suitable opportunity—one such as Kellogg's query provided. Not surprisingly, within forty-eight hours, he cabled a detailed reply.

In general, McCoy reported, the military outlook was dismal. Recent successes had so enhanced Sandino's prestige that he threatened to "greatly embarrass our electoral program." Yet the Sandinista problem, he admitted, posed more than ordinary difficulties. The advantages that Sandino enjoyed were not to be underestimated: superior mobility, knowledge of the local terrain and language, genuine popular support, and the ability to fight largely at times and places of his own selection. Nevertheless, McCoy found severe deficiencies in the marines' performance, particularly their inability to collect accurate intelligence and their "failure to maintain continuous contact with Sandino forces once they have been located." The root of the problem, in McCoy's view, was leadership, especially the lackluster performance of the marine commander, Brig. Gen. Logan Feland.[44]

In the weeks following this report, McCoy began concerning himself more directly with marine operations. The weekly conferences of senior officials over which he presided at the American legation became increasingly acrimonious whenever military issues arose. According to Rear Adm. David F. Sellers, Feland's immediate superior as commander of the Special Service Squadron offshore, McCoy galled the marine commander with his searching inquiries about what the marines were doing or intended to do about Sandino. Sellers himself, already resentful that a one-star general should be his temporary superior, complained loudly when McCoy assigned his principal deputy, Col. Frank Le Jau Parker, to investigate marine operations for the State Department. That an army colonel should be reporting on the command of a rear admiral was almost unbearable.[45]

Yet polite efforts to spur Feland and Sellers had no noticeable effect. In a letter to Stimson in April, McCoy complained that "Sandino still flies around like a mosquito. . . . There seems to be no chance of getting him except by a stroke of good luck." Exasperated, McCoy provoked a showdown at a legation conference on April 18. "Where is Sandino?" the captor of Datto Ali demanded of Feland. "You don't know. Your intelligence service is a failure and we stand just where we did six months ago." He accused Feland of having lost touch with the situation by remaining in Managua instead of taking to the field. Finally, he delivered his ultimatum. "I am the Special Representative of the President," he

*Rear Adm. David F. Sellers, USN (on left), and Brig. Gen. Logan Feland, USMC, in Nicaragua, 1928. Duty there was rarely amusing. (Courtesy National Archives)*

reminded the marine commander. "If you haven't gotten Sandino in a month from now . . . you will have failed and I shall so report to the State Department."[46] The shock waves of this encounter, passing through Sellers back to the chief of naval operations, did little to endear McCoy to the Navy Department. Whether or not the attempt to intimidate Feland was itself beneficial beyond establishing the primacy of McCoy's own authority, the overall American military effort did improve thereafter. For one thing, McCoy asked for and received reinforcements, 1,000 more marines in mid-March and an equal number in June. Employing these forces with greater aggressiveness, the American command stepped up the pressure on Sandino, soon forcing him to seek refuge outside Nicaragua.[47]

When aerial reconnaissance into neighboring Honduras located a concentration of Sandinistas, apparently secure in the belief that they were beyond American reach, McCoy asked the American minister in Tegucigalpa, George T. Summerlin, to secure permission for the marines to strike across the border. Summerlin was unresponsive—he had not "really grasped [sic] that this was our war in Nicaragua and that getting Sandino was a matter of vital importance"—so McCoy dispatched Munro to confer with the Honduran leaders. Munro quickly cajoled President Miguel Paz Barona into permitting American forces to pursue Sandino into Honduras and even to attack him from the air—"with the understanding however that the matter be kept absolutely quiet." Not even the Honduran foreign minister was informed.[48] The marines' ability to disregard this international boundary undoubtedly made it more difficult for Sandino to maintain a secure base from which to launch attacks back into Nicaragua.

As part of this revitalized campaign against Sandino, McCoy accelerated the development of the Guardia Nacional. The State Department had emphasized that the Guardia was "the most vital feature of the entire [American] program" because it would constitute "the cornerstone of stability for the whole country long after the election."[49] During the period of the electoral mission, the Guardia tripled in size and made considerable strides toward improved training and effectiveness. Although McCoy gave Feland operational control of elements pursuing Sandino in the field, he did not surrender his overall responsibility for the Guardia. Through its *jefe director*, Brig. Gen. Elias R. Beadle, he took daily interest in its activities and progress. Whereas Feland viewed the Guardia as a conventional military force that should help the marines by taking a more active and larger part of the campaign against Sandino, McCoy envisioned it primarily as a constabulary devoted to preserving order and enforcing the law. Realistically, the Guardia lacked the competence to render more than marginal assistance against Sandino. With an eye on the election, moreover, McCoy was anxious to replace the local police, who "have been used as an instrument of oppression, a source of graft, and often a cause of disorder," with a national police force free of corruption. To make the American presence less intrusive, meanwhile, the marines would refrain from the "exercise [of] civil police functions if it can be avoided." In short, McCoy believed that "it was much more important for the success of the elections, to have the guardia police the cities, small villages, and districts in which the elections were actually taking place, leaving to the marines the job of keeping Sandino covered."[50] Beadle agreed with McCoy. Consequently, the Guardia adhered to the orientation that they, rather than Feland, thought appropriate. The improvement in police and military capabilities orchestrated by McCoy paid dividends. During the summer of 1928, over 1,600 guerrillas surrendered. By autumn, the level of Sandinista activity had fallen dramatically. Marine and Guardia casualties declined. By late October, McCoy could claim that Sandino had been effectively eliminated as a factor in the election.[51] And yet—much to McCoy's annoyance—Sandino himself eluded capture.

Hopeful that the threat posed by Sandino was being reduced, McCoy returned to Washington in May for consultations. The purpose of his visit was twofold. On the one hand, it provided an opportunity to neutralize domestic opponents of the intervention who remained wary of the McCoy mission. Back in the capital, McCoy participated in a series of briefings for journalists, congressmen, and prominent businessmen.[52] Such proselytizing formed only a part of a larger public relations offensive. To the administration, mustering support for the electoral mission was no small matter. McCoy later recalled that, in first sending him to Managua, Coolidge had been "very definite in directing me to change the public opinion" regarding Nicaragua. Stimson believed that the best way to convert the administration's critics was to "invite the sunlight of publicity as an antiseptic [to] all this backdoor gossip" about the intervention. He even proposed that representatives from the Pan-American Conference, then meeting in Havana, be invited to observe the election. But McCoy demurred. Outsiders would be receptive to anti-American propaganda, he argued. Their mere presence "would probably result in complicating very seriously our supervision."[53]

McCoy was less interested in inviting outside scrutiny than in reshaping the image of the American role in Nicaragua that was being projected back to the United States. His intention was to manage carefully the type of information provided for public consumption. As a first step toward properly informing the public back home, he added to his staff a full-time public relations adviser, Walter Wilgus, an old friend and former editor of the *Manila Times*. Next, McCoy, in an effort to gain the support of key opinion makers, bombarded a long list of prominent Americans with carefully constructed explanations of what his mission was doing and why. The targets of the campaign included such diverse figures as Walter Lippmann, Frank Knox, Felix Frankfurter, William Howard Taft, and the president of Standard Oil of New York. The flattering attention that McCoy paid these men, many of them acquaintances, proved surprisingly effective. "There was gladness when I read that you were put in charge of America's honor and good sense in Nicaragua," wrote Frankfurter in reply, adding that "it seemed like an old family party that you should succeed Stimson in the task." And the old progressive Newton D. Baker responded: "I do not know where the white man's burden begins and ends and I have no clear conviction as to whether we have a manifest destiny in the election you are supervising . . . but I dismiss all these questions because you are there."[54] Had the marines continued to sustain a high level of casualties, of course, public relations techniques alone would have been ineffective. Combined with improved conditions in the field, however, they helped defuse much of the unfavorable attention Nicaragua aroused throughout the previous year. By the fall of 1928, success was virtually complete: Americans had lost interest in Nicaraguan politics—a situation most gratifying to a Republican party preparing for a presidential election.

The second purpose of McCoy's Washington visit was to discuss the steps to be taken after the election to insure a stable pro-American Nicaragua. McCoy himself urged that the United States "guard against the unduly optimistic belief that a fair election is a panacea for Nicaragua's troubles." Rather, he said, "the election itself is but one detail of the country's general problem." Having seen firsthand in Nicaragua the same awful backwardness that he had encountered in Cuba and elsewhere, McCoy recognized that arranging an orderly political succession of itself would accomplish little. He went on to outline an ambitious program of internal development reminiscent of the reforms sponsored by American proconsuls in the Philippines and Cuba in years past. To build a stable and progressive Nicaragua, he called for "the preservation of order, the development of communications, . . . the elimination of widespread corruption of the government, the improvement of health conditions and the extension and modernization of schools."[55]

Implementing such a reform package would require money—inevitably, American money. To McCoy and most other American officials in Managua, a made-to-order vehicle for generating that money already existed in the Cumberland Plan, a State Department-sponsored survey of Nicaragua whose outlines were familiar through much of the Caribbean. In return for a sizable loan, an American-controlled commission would direct key areas of the Nicaraguan economy—customs, currency, governmental expenditures—creating a new climate of expansion, with political order as a by-product. McCoy argued for the plan to both Kellogg and "the terrible Wall Street bankers who are strangling poor Nicaragua." The secretary of state, however, feared that the proposal would provide a powerful weapon to critics who were charging that Americans were "taking advantage of a so-called military occupation of Nicaragua to impose upon it a permanent economic domination." When he refused to associate the American government with the loan, Wall Street backed away from the proposal. The demise of the Cumberland Plan, despite McCoy's assertions of its importance, emphasizes Kellogg's reluctance to extend American involvement in Nicaragua beyond the life of the electoral mission. Kellogg's timidity, contrasting sharply with his earlier rashness, frustrated McCoy, who saw himself charged with establishing a new order in Nicaragua while denied the wherewithal to do so.[56]

Although disappointed by the lack of enthusiasm for Nicaraguan development, McCoy could spare little time worrying about the setback. In Managua, further political problems awaited his return. An election providing a satisfactory outcome to the United States required from the outset two "acceptable" candidates. The identity of the Liberal nominee was a foregone conclusion: The accommodating General Moncada received his party's endorsement even before the decree of *la ley McCoy.* Finding an equally agreeable leader for the Conservative ticket proved more difficult. Chamorro still refused to count himself out.

As Munro noted, Chamorro remained still the real leader of the Conservatives, exercising full control of the official party machinery.[57] The Nicaraguan made no secret of his intention to parlay this influence into the nomination of a Conservative candidate personally loyal to him. Díaz, for once willing to stand up to Chamorro, was equally determined that as president he should designate the party's nominee. When attempts to nominate a candidate in May 1928 resulted in a deadlocked convention, the party divided into two factions and rump sessions nominated separate tickets. Each then petitioned the National Electoral Board for recognition as sole legitimate representative of the Conservative party.

At about the same time, two other factions, identified with neither traditional party, began to coalesce, insisting that a free and fair election would grant them a place on the ballot in November. These new splinter parties, called Liberal-Republican and Conservative-Republican, along with the split in the Conservative party, raised the possibility that no candidate would receive an absolute majority of the vote, thereby throwing the contest into the Nicaraguan Congress beyond McCoy's control. It was incumbent upon the National Electoral Board, therefore, to thin out the suddenly crowded ranks of Nicaraguan party politics. Later McCoy would recall that he had sidestepped the recognition of any third party. In fact, his action was much more direct. Ignoring existing Nicaraguan statutes that would have recognized the two new splinter parties, McCoy denied their viability, flatly declaring in each instance that no bona fide party existed.[58] There would be no new parties in the 1928 election.

The problem posed by the split in the Conservative party was less easily solved. Recognition of a Conservative representative was necessary to avoid the farce of a noncompetitive election. Nonetheless, the prospect of choosing between the Conservative claimants based strictly upon the credentials that each could muster was an unattractive one. A decision made in strict accordance with a "technical legal determination of the issues," Parker told McCoy, would oblige the board to side with that faction whose actual head had openly stated his purpose of obstructing the electoral plan—Chamorro. Such a rebuff to President Díaz "might result in the withdrawal of his financial and other cooperation and even in his resignation." On the other hand, to ignore the Chamorristas would expose American claims of impartiality as hypocritical.[59]

Although McCoy disavowed any intention of acting privately as an arbiter to resolve the Conservative squabble, he had no intention of remaining passive. On July 23, McCoy opened a session of the board by reading a draft resolution "giving [the] Conservative Party til 25 July at noon to get together." Beyond that deadline, the board would refuse to consider the application of any additional candidates. Failure to agree on a unified ticket, in other words, would exclude the

Conservative party from the election altogether. Castillo, the board's Conservative member, stated his opposition to the proposal in the strongest terms. The effect of its passage "would be liquidation of [the] Conservative Party and his own resignation." Chamorro, he insisted, was the sole obstacle to party unity: "Had it not been for him, an agreement already would have been made." To permit a final attempt to resolve the situation, McCoy temporarily tabled his resolution, providing Castillo with a copy for Chamorro "in order to make him realize what will happen unless action is taken soon to get [the] party together."[60]

Armed with this ultimatum, Castillo brought his party to heel. McCoy, he warned, was prepared to declare that "the historic Conservative party had ceased to exist." Facing the prospect of political extinction and lacking the nerve to call McCoy's bluff, the party leadership capitulated. Both factions abandoned their candidates and, on July 27, nominated a compromise figure, Adolfo Benard, acceptable not only to Chamorro and Díaz but to the United States as well. McCoy had forced the Conservative party to heal its split, reported the *New York Times*.[61] The assessment was a fair one. His stratagem secured the party's participation in the election while avoiding the pitfalls of either recognizing Chamorro or disaffecting Díaz.

By August 1928, McCoy could finally turn his attention to the details of voter registration and the actual balloting. To insure order at the polls and minimize procedural irregularities, McCoy intended to saturate Nicaragua's electoral machinery with Americans. Each of Nicaragua's thirteen departments received its own electoral board, headed with one exception by U.S. Army officers. Grouped under each department were district boards for each of the 352 precincts—enough, remarked McCoy, that "no blooming native will have far to go to vote."[62] American military personnel headed these boards as well. Voter registration, scheduled for five days in late September and early October, provided the first test of the American scheme. The outcome was encouraging. Only two incidents of violence marred the otherwise uneventful period. In all, some 150,000 Nicaraguans registered, 25 percent above the 1924 totals; the increase persuaded some observers that many would-be voters had been recorded on the rolls more than once. McCoy defended the totals as accurate and credited the increase to the success of marine and Guardia efforts to protect citizens from intimidation by their political opponents.[63]

The election on November 4 went even more smoothly. As during the registration period, marine ground and air units deterred any intrusion by Sandino. To counter expected allegations of an inflated final tally, McCoy devised a method of discouraging "repeaters." Before casting his ballot, each voter dipped his thumb into Mercurochrome—a gimmick sufficiently novel to attract favorable editorial notice. Predictions of widespread violence on election day proved completely unfounded. An obviously pleased McCoy informed Kellogg that "the only case of disorder reported [was] . . . the death of a steer which ran amuck . . . and was shot by a marine"—an incident culminating in nothing more

*American marines load out to supervise the election of a Nicaraguan president, 1928.*
*(Courtesy National Archives)*

ominous than an impromptu barbecue.[64] The large turnout—88 percent of those
registered—resulted in an unequivocal Liberal victory. More important, the
defeated Conservatives professed their willingness to abide by this outcome. A
Conservative spokesman, calling the election both fair and honorable, laconically
explained the results with the simple admission that "our party lost." Indeed,
both parties were so pleased with the supervision of the campaign that, even
before election day, Moncada and Benard publicly called upon the Americans to
supervise succeeding presidential contests.[65]

   To most observers, the mission achieved an impressive success. With few
exceptions, the press enthusiastically commended the U.S. supervision and
especially the role played by McCoy. But, even in the midst of continuing
accolades—the Managua city council entertained a resolution to erect a statue of
McCoy in the city plaza—unresolved questions began to intrude.[66] The overt
premise of American strategy had been that supervision of an "honest" election
would allow the United States to pull out. Although McCoy delivered that
election, he recognized that little of substance had changed. "This election is a
good step in the right direction," he told Henry Cabot Lodge, Jr., "but . . . it is
neither the first nor the last"; "until we . . . take some permanent steps to

establish peace and order," he added, "we have not finished the job."[67] Yet any serious attempt to address the fundamental problems that perennially convulsed Nicaragua (and tangentially raised doubts about the effectiveness of American power) would require a prolonged presence of the very type that McCoy had been commissioned to avert. Not surprisingly, McCoy's superiors showed little interest in his proposals for a sustained commitment to Nicaraguan development. They refused to see Nicaragua as a latter-day Cuba, with McCoy in the role of Leonard Wood.

Nonetheless, his awareness of the mission's cosmetic accomplishments and of the limited headway made toward achieving its larger goals nagged at McCoy. What nagged above all was the knowledge that however reduced the scope of the Sandinista movement, McCoy's efforts to destroy the insurgency and Sandino himself had failed. "Strictly speaking," McCoy acknowledged after the elections, "the obligations of the United States have been carried out." But a second implicit requirement—the elimination of Sandino and other bandit leaders—was essential to any stable peace in Nicaragua.[68] That obligation remained all too clearly unfulfilled. In an angry encounter with Feland and Sellers, McCoy betrayed his obsession with Sandino. Shortly after the election, the naval and marine commanders drafted a dispatch to the Navy Department recommending an immediate reduction of American forces in Nicaragua. Given the election's ostensible success, the step seemed logical enough. But the proposal infuriated McCoy. After reading the dispatch, he "threw it on the table and stated emphatically that he did not agree at all." Then, according to Sellers, McCoy "started on a tirade." The proposed reduction showed once again that the navy and marines had never fully grasped the situation in Nicaragua. McCoy personally had never had the slightest concern over his ability to hold a successful election. The principal problem, he said, had been to catch Sandino, who had successfully defied the authority of the United States. Indeed, "until Sandino . . . had been killed, captured, or run out of the country the Marines had signally failed in their mission." Sandino's forced inactivity of recent months was not enough. "All of the armed forces of the U.S. in Nic[aragua] have been organized into an expeditionary force with the announced purpose of getting Sandino." Mere survival against such an onslaught evoked plaudits throughout Latin America.[69]

McCoy was convinced that a premature troop withdrawal would jeopardize the meager progress toward stability that his mission had achieved. On November 14, he cabled Kellogg to urge that the marines remain "at full strength . . . until Sandino and the major armed groups of bandits have been eliminated or the Guardia [is] sufficiently developed to handle the situation." The next months would be "critical with regard to our friendly efforts here," he emphasized. "Any changes . . . should be made with great caution."[70] By calling for the retention of American troops in Nicaragua, McCoy tacitly conceded his mission's failure. He had been unable to demonstrate the futility of challenging the United

*Our man in Managua, 1928: Sandino eluded his grasp, and Washington rejected his strategy. (Courtesy National Archives)*

States in Central America. Nonetheless, as McCoy embarked for home in mid-December 1928, few recognized the limited nature of the mission's accomplishments. Observers in the United States for whom the election of a Nicaraguan president without bloodshed seemed success enough gave the returning emissary an impressive reception. Touting McCoy to succeed Stimson as Philippine governor general, the *New York Times* bestowed on the general its supreme absolution, declaring him "free from the characteristics which are usually held to the disadvantage of army officers in civilian posts."[71] More substantively, due largely to his services in Nicaragua, McCoy was promoted to major general and became the first American officer to receive a second award of the Distinguished Service Medal.

Such laurels notwithstanding, Sandino had bested McCoy. He had set out to wreck the American plan for the election of 1928. In the end, because the insurgent remained at large, McCoy felt compelled to ask the administration to scrap its hopes for disengaging from Nicaragua as soon as the balloting was complete. However wary of the sweeping commitment implicit in McCoy's admonition about Sandino, the new administration of Herbert Hoover could not ignore his warning altogether. Although the strength of the marine brigade gradually declined during 1929, substantial forces remained. By January 1931, the American garrison had stabilized at approximately 1,400 marines. For the United States, this middle course produced the worst of both worlds: an occupation force too feeble to deal with a resurgent Sandino but large enough to insure that Nicaragua remained an embarrassment.[72] Thus, despite its trappings of success, the McCoy mission was doubly disappointing. It failed either to demonstrate beyond question the strength of American dominion or to terminate decisively an intervention that virtually everyone conceded had been a mistake in the first place. For the United States, the legacy of the mission was merely to prolong an error. For Nicaragua, the consequences would be tragic: The American-created Guardia ultimately became an instrument of oppression and the base of power for the Somoza tyranny.

# 9

# Troubleshooting
# for Stimson

Within days of McCoy's return from Nicaragua, the State Department drafted him for yet another mission. This time the problem concerned fears that a dispute between Bolivia and Paraguay over the Chaco Boreal region would soon lead to war. The episode is worth examining, not only because it further illustrates the military's role in foreign policy, but also because it outlines the geographic limits of American hegemony in Latin America. Washington's reaction to the Chaco question differed markedly from its response to Nicaraguan unrest the previous year. That difference defines in a rough way the State Department's views on what was and was not important in the western hemisphere.

Equivalent in size to the state of North Dakota, the Chaco Boreal was a parched and largely unsettled region wedged between four republics of lower South America. Its inhospitable character may account for the lack of interest that Argentina and Brazil showed in the area. The other two contiguous nations, Bolivia and Paraguay, were too poor to disdain even such a dubious treasure. Each of them had asserted claims to the Chaco since the collapse of Spain's empire a century before. Developments in the early twentieth century—including reports of oil deposits in the Chaco, Bolivia's need for an outlet to the sea, and rising national chauvinism—bred a mutual determination to resolve the issue once and for all. By the 1920s, this determination had resulted in an arms build-up, the planting of rival occupation forces, and, ultimately, open hostilities. On December 5, 1928, Paraguayan forces overran the small Bolivian installation of Vanguardia, killing or capturing numerous members of the garrison and putting the rest to flight. Bolivia retaliated by attacking two of Paraguay's outposts. Amid a clamor for revenge and the redemption of national honor, the two governments severed diplomatic relations. By the end of December, they stood on the brink of war.[1]

That same month, coincidentally, the International Conference of American States on Conciliation and Arbitration convened in Washington under the auspices of the United States. All of the hemisphere's republics except Argentina sent representatives. With the objective of adding substance to the idea of Pan-Americanism, this gathering, with Secretary Kellogg as chairman, sought to devise mechanisms for the peaceful resolution of hemispheric conflicts. This effort produced two agreements. The first called for the submission of inter-American disputes to commissons of inquiry and conciliation. The second treaty required signatories to submit disagreements of a juridical nature to binding arbitration. Of course, subsequent application alone would determine the practical value of such accords, if any. Recognizing the skirmishing between two of its conferees as an opportunity to validate the conference's work, Kellogg called for an investigation into the Chaco affair.[2] His initiative gave birth on Janaury 3, 1929, to a protocol creating the Commission of Inquiry and Conciliation, Bolivia and Paraguay. Mexico, Cuba, Uruguay, Colombia, and the United States—collectively known as the "neutrals"—each provided a delegate to this body. Both contending parties, meanwhile, were entitled to two represen-tatives. The commission's charter assigned it ambitious goals while severely restricting its prerogatives. On the one hand, the commission was to investigate the incident of December 1928, settle the incident amicably, and thus restore the conditions that existed prior to the outbreak of fighting. On the other hand, the commission would expire six months after it first convened, regardless of the situation existing at the time. The charter also forbade the commission to address the underlying territorial dispute regarding ownership of the Chaco. Worst of all, in McCoy's view, the commission could act only by unanimous vote, a stipulation that, combined with the presence of both protagonists as voting members, "almost wrecked the Commission's work."[3]

Fresh from Nicaragua and awaiting reassignment, McCoy seemed well suited to serve as the American delegate. Personally, he preferred to return to military duties, but when Kellogg asked him on January 5 to accept the assignment, McCoy dutifully agreed. Though the State Department nominated McCoy to serve on the commission, the panel's status as an international body meant that the American delegate operated "entirely at liberty and unhampered by instructions." In practice, however, McCoy enjoyed less freedom of action than his nominal status implied. As in Nicaragua, his real role was to serve as an agent rather than a maker of foreign policy. Toward this end, he kept the State Department regularly informed about the commission's progress, a habit that became all the more natural once his friend Stimson became secretary of state in the incoming Hoover administration. More importantly, McCoy sought to coordinate the commission's work with the broader outlines of American policy.[4]

Shaping the character of policy toward the hemisphere's southern cone was the scantiness of perceived American interests there. In contrast to the Caribbean, where vital interests produced a policy of uncompromising domination, the importance of southern Latin America was slight. American interests in the Chaco Boreal itself were virtually nil. Although Bolivia had granted concessions to Standard Oil of New Jersey, the overall economic stakes were so meager as to play no discernible part in determining the U.S. position in the dispute. Nonetheless, American efforts to avert war between Bolivia and Paraguay cannot be ascribed merely to humanitarianism. Conflict between any American republics jeopardized the edifice of Pan-Americanism that the United States had erected to keep order in its half of the world—especially in those remote corners where the direct projection of power was undesirable. Success by the Commission of Inquiry and Conciliation would show that Pan-Americanism worked.[5]

Kellogg personally convened the commission's opening session at the Pan-American Union in Washington on March 13, 1929, and remained long enough to see McCoy elected as the panel's chairman. With the American delegate thus situated to guide its activities, the commission plunged into the investigative phase of its work. Throughout April and May, the delegates heard testimony from the contending parties, usually bombastic memorials blaming the other side for the skirmishing in December and proclaiming the justice of its own claim to the Chaco. Despite such protests of innocence, the neutral delegates soon agreed that Bolivia and Paraguay shared in the culpability for December's fighting. To spare national sensibilities and preserve an environment conducive to meaningful negotiations, however, the commission withheld its findings. On a more practical tack, the delegates sought to arrange a prisoner exchange as a preliminary to an overall settlement. The successful conclusion of this effort in mid-May yielded the first positive fruits of the commission's work.[6]

McCoy hoped that the agreement on prisoners would lead to the evacuation of captured fortifications and the renewal of diplomatic ties. Instead, resolution of the prisoner issue left the talks stalled. By late June, McCoy admitted that the commission's work "had been going badly for several weeks." The problem, he concluded, lay with the group's charter. To expect the commission to resolve the conflict while ignoring the question of who owned the Chaco was hopelessly unrealistic. Given the privately expressed willingness of both Bolivia and Paraguay to permit the commission to address this so-called basic question, the restriction was also unnecessary. McCoy knew full well that "under the protocol we were forbidden to take up the fundamental question of settling the boundary between the countries concerned." Nonetheless, at his urging, from July onward the commission attempted to do just that.[7]

With the territorial question at the top of its agenda, the commission at least was taking aim at the real issue. In itself, this did not guarantee success. Although closed-door negotiations continued throughout July and August, progress was slow. In Washington's sweltering heat, tempers grew short. Half-humorously comparing himself to Grant at the Wilderness, McCoy promised to have "determination enough to last if 'it takes all summer.'" He rejected suggestions of impatient neutrals that he simply call upon overwhelming

American power to force a settlement, replying that in such a "Pan-American undertaking" the proper role for his country was simply a "position of international equality." Indeed, McCoy intentionally stayed in the background during the negotiation's early stages, asking Cuba and Mexico to take the lead in determining the disputants' minimal demands. Such cooperative tactics contrast strikingly with the highhanded unilateralism that McCoy practiced in Nicaragua. Yet he was not being disingenuous in appraising the intended American role as one of equality. McCoy's less coercive approach reflected not a change of heart since the previous year but the comparatively trivial American stakes in the Chaco.[8]

From the outset, several factors militated against the commission's efforts to resolve the basic question. Most fundamental was the complexity of the dispute itself—the layers of claims and counterclaims and of past proposals accepted by one side but not by the other that had built up over the previous century. Adding to the difficulty of the negotiations was the rigidity of the Bolivian and Paraguayan governments, which hesitated to make any concessions that might offend nationalists at home and undermine their own legitimacy. Third, and most frustrating to McCoy personally, was the conduct of his fellow delegates. For some, a lack of authority necessitated consultation with their governments even on the most trivial matters. In the case of Uruguay's delegate, delay amounted to outright obstructionism. Such behavior resulted in negotiations that were awkward, time-consuming, and inefficient.[9]

In the end, McCoy's attempt to divide the Chaco Boreal on some historical basis foundered when the nonnegotiable demands on each side collided. On August 26, the commission abandoned any hope for a directly negotiated settlement and began considering schemes for submitting the dispute to formal arbitration. This effort produced a draft treaty that McCoy presented to Bolivia and Paraguay on August 31, two weeks before the commission's scheduled adjournment sine die. McCoy's proposal provided for a five-member court to rule on the claims of the two countries, with the court's decision to be binding. But the plan also attempted to protect interests vital to each country. It awarded outright to Bolivia the port of Bahia Negra on the Paraguay River, thus giving Bolivians their long-sought access to the sea. Conversely, it removed from the court's purview that portion of the Chaco awarded to Paraguay in 1878 by President Rutherford B. Hayes in defining Paraguay's border with Argentina. McCoy's proposal also extended the commission's life until such time as the court assumed its responsibilities.[10]

Throughout the next week, McCoy lobbied to persuade the Bolivian and Paraguayan delegates to commend the proposal to their governments. Eventually, he extracted promises of unqualified support from each. At the same time, working through the American ministers in La Paz and Asunción, Stimson undertook a similar effort aimed directly at the contending governments. Despite encouraging signs in Washington, the responses received from the two Latin American capitals were disappointing. Although both countries professed support for arbitration in principle, each rejected McCoy's specific proposal. Neither side would accept the territorial guarantees that the plan provided to its rival. Each objected to that aspect of the plan permitting the court to define the overall limits of the territory to be arbitrated. Such authority, announced the Bolivian delegate, was "destructive of the right of sovereignty since it does not place any limitation whatever on any claims which Paraguay may wish to make to the territory of Bolivia."[11] With the expiration of the commission's charter fast approaching, McCoy made a final effort to salvage arbitration. He deleted from the draft treaty those provisions guaranteeing Bahia Negra to Bolivia and the Hayes award to Paraguay. To provide further reassurance that arbitration would not jeopardize vital interests, McCoy proposed that the court's decision be nonbinding. These changes met the chief objections to the original proposal. Although Paraguay showed interest in the revised draft, Bolivia still insisted upon prior definition of the arbitral zone as an absolute requirement. Bolivia, it was now evident, opposed arbitration in any form.[12]

Anticipating the rejection of arbitration but determined to have something to show for his efforts, McCoy turned his attention during the commission's final days to the more limited objective of conciliation. With the exchange of prisoners now completed, he presented a protocol calling for "mutual forgiveness of the offenses and injuries caused by each of the Republics to each other," evacuation of captured fortifications, and the restoration of diplomatic relations. Anxious to hurry the commission out of existence and realizing that such an agreement would not compromise its freedom of action, Bolivia quickly agreed. Paraguay, still hoping for arbitration, attempted to force a prolongation of the commission's life by delaying its answer to the proposal for conciliation. Recognizing, however, that refusal to sign such an innocuous document would place Paraguay in a bad light, its delegation eventually agreed to the protocol in the waning hours of the commission's existence.[13] Thus, the commission did succeed in bringing about the diplomatic reconciliation of Bolivia and Paraguay, providing a token testimonial to the efficacy of Pan-Americanism.

Yet McCoy knew that his accomplishment was superficial. Without a solution to the territorial issue, war would follow, exposing Pan-Americanism as a sham. Bolivia promised to continue negotiations through direct bilateral talks. McCoy believed that without the participation of the commission's neutrals "to watch over and guide the negotiations," such talks could not succeed. With this in mind, McCoy proposed at the commission's closing session on September 13 that the five neutrals extend their collective good offices to Bolivia and Paraguay to keep alive their efforts to resolve the Chaco dispute. At McCoy's urging, moreover, Stimson pressured both Bolivia and Paraguay to reconstitute the commission.[14] Stimson's efforts ran up against Bolivian determination to prevent the commission's revival. The Bolivian minister in Washington indicated politely that, because "spectacular conferences have the inconvenience of exciting [the] national spirit," his country preferred to rely on private bilateral talks. When the

United States insisted on a direct role in the negotiations, Bolivian representatives began justifying their opposition to the commission by accusing McCoy of bias against their claims. The State Department refuted such accusations—which had never been made during the commission's life—and recognized them for what they were: an attempt to exclude the United States from an affair that Bolivia concluded it could best handle itself.[15]

American attempts to revive the commission continued sporadically through the end of the year. In October, McCoy was assigned as commanding general of the IV Corps Area with headquarters at Fort McPherson, Georgia. During the fall of 1929, he returned to Washington several times to assist in drafting notes that attempted without success to pry Bolivia away from its uncompromising stand. McCoy attributed the failure of these efforts and of his commission's work to two sources. The first was domestic politics. He told former Secretary Kellogg that Bolivia's "backing and filling" illustrated the impact of "local politics influencing a very weak government." To another correspondent he wrote: "It was perfectly evident that both Governments wanted to reach a reasonable arrangement which our Commission proposed to them, but [tentative agreements were] later on cancelled due to popular clamor against both Governments which were weak and could not withstand the nationalistic opposition." Such views both reflected and reaffirmed McCoy's low opinion of politicians as a class.[16]

The second reason that McCoy cited related to the limited power wielded by the United States. In his confidential final report, McCoy lamented that "no means by which our Government could exert direct pressure on the parties to the dispute was obvious or even discernible." More accurately, although means were at hand, the game was not worth their application. Far and away the hemisphere's most powerful nation, the United States possessed a range of diplomatic, economic, and military levers that it could employ, either directly or through third parties. McCoy knew that, but he was also sufficiently realistic to realize that the modest character of American interests in the southern cone limited him to accepted diplomatic practices. Bombing Sandinistas could be justified by virtue of American vital interests in Nicaragua, but similar action against Bolivia was inconceivable—a point that goes far in explaining the relative equanimity with which the United States accepted Bolivian defiance of its peacekeeping efforts.[17]

The Commission of Inquiry and Conciliation was only the first of several instances in which McCoy assisted his friend the secretary of state. Stimson's confidence that McCoy shared his viewpoint, combined with the army general's tact as a negotiator and his experience in Latin American and East Asian affairs, led the secretary repeatedly to call on his friend's services. Yet care must be taken not to exaggerate McCoy's influence—he remained an army officer, not a State Department official. Despite frequent trips from Fort McPherson to

Washington, he did not participate regularly in policymaking. Rather, he functioned as a consultant, called in periodically to consider problems falling within his particular area of competence. The secretary himself acknowledged the limits of McCoy's role in an entry in his diary in February 1931. Temporarily short-handed due to the illness of Joseph Cotton, the undersecretary of state, Stimson called up McCoy at Atlanta,

> to see whether he would be available for an emergency, in other words whether he would give up military work to come into the Department and help me temporarily in Cotton's absence, which would seem to be long.
>
> Like the good friend and soldier that he is, he said that he was ready to obey orders and do whatever would help me. We both see the dangers and difficulties of bringing a military man into the Department, but he has such a level head and has been so helpful in everything that I have ever consulted him in, that I am very strongly tempted to do it.[18]

McCoy's work for Stimson ranged from the sensitive to the comic. As indicated above, his involvement in the Chaco dispute continued beyond his service on the commission. McCoy also advised Stimson in Nicaragua, and he figured frequently in issues relating to Philippine-American relations—for example, in the abortive appointment of Nicholas Roosevelt to be vice–governor general in 1930.[19]

A member of the *New York Times* editorial board, Roosevelt was notorious among Filipinos as the author of an influential book critical of their aspirations for independence. President Hoover's announcement of his appointment in July 1930 evoked anger in the islands. Filipino leaders denounced Roosevelt and sponsored rallies in which copies of his book were ceremoniously burned or dumped into Manila Bay. Reacting to this criticism, the Senate Insular Affairs Committee refused to recommend Roosevelt for confirmation, leaving both the president and his appointee dangling in considerable embarrassment.[20]

Strictly speaking, neither the president nor the Senate was obliged to consider Filipino preferences in appointing top officers in Manila. Yet it was soon evident that forcing Roosevelt onto the islands would rekindle the sort of animosity in Philippine-American relations that had lain dormant since the end of Leonard Wood's rule. Prudence, therefore, demanded that the administration disengage itself from such a potentially dangerous situation. To McCoy, Stimson assigned the delicate task of persuading Roosevelt to withdraw voluntarily. Along with Brig. Gen. Frank Parker, chief of the Bureau of Insular Affairs, McCoy held a series of conversations with Roosevelt, out of which emerged a solution. In return for eating humble pie for the administration's sake, McCoy told Stimson, Roosevelt wanted a position in the State Department. Acceptable to all parties, this proposal culminated on September 24 in Roosevelt's request to have his name withdrawn from consideration to be vice–governor general and in his simultaneous appointment by Stimson as minister to Hungary.[21]

Hoover's inability to appoint his own man to be vice–governor general indicated the drift of Philippine-American relations by 1930. Advocates of continued colonial status for the islands found themselves increasingly on the defensive. Filipino opposition to the Roosevelt appointment should have surprised no one. Certainly the momentum of the Philippine independence movement had not slackened in the years since McCoy left Manila in 1925. What had changed, however, was domestic opinion in the United States. To ailing American economic interests, the islands had come to represent a liability. The sugar, dairy, and cottonseed oil industries, all struggling as a result of the Great Depression and resenting supposed Filipino competition, joined organized labor in a noisy coalition that campaigned to get rid of the Philippines. This independence lobby generated enough support in Congress to make some change in the islands' status all but inevitable.[22]

Hoover, Stimson, and Secretary of War Patrick J. Hurley, whose department administered insular possessions, were dead set against freeing the Philippines. The islands were simply not ready for independence, they believed. Moreover, to set them adrift would affect adversely the strategic balance in the western Pacific by reducing the American presence there just as concern over Japanese intentions was increasing. Although the administration's leaders in public remained uncompromising in their insistence upon maintaining the status quo, privately they recognized the need to strike a bargain with independence forces. The only question was whether long-frustrated Philippine nationalists would be content with anything less than full independence.[23]

Next to Stimson, who followed Wood as governor general, and W. Cameron Forbes, Hoover's ambassador to Japan, McCoy was the best known of the old Philippine hands still in public life. His participation in the final disposition of the Philippines came as a matter of course. In fact, Stimson invited McCoy's participation both in an executive and an advisory capacity. Before and after the Nicholas Roosevelt affair, he sought McCoy's return to the Philippines as governor general. In June 1930, he asked McCoy to accept an appointment as vice-governor general with the prospect of elevation to chief executive within a year. Hoover, Stimson said, would be guided by his own and Hurley's recommendations. But McCoy was uninterested. In October, Hoover himself suggested McCoy as a replacement for Roosevelt, again with the idea of being subsequently promoted. Stimson replied that McCoy preferred to go as governor general, but "would of course do what the President wanted." It remained only to determine whether McCoy would be acceptable to the Filipino leadership. In his diary, Stimson noted that "it would be an error of the first importance to rush the McCoy appointment rudely or roughly on the Filipino people." He cautioned Hoover to clear the nomination with Quezon before making it public.[24]

Unfortunately, word of the consideration being given McCoy reached Manila before the necessary groundwork had been laid. John M. Switzer, a friend of Hoover's and president of the American Chamber of Commerce in Manila, leaked word of McCoy's pending appointment among leading Filipinos. Stimson believed that Switzer and his associates were attempting "to pose as kingmakers in regard to the appointment of [the next] governor general and to trade on the influence they were supposed to have." Yet, as the secretary observed, nothing would incite Philippine opposition with greater certainty than to have the appointment attributed in any way to the members of the American Chamber of Commerce, an organization long in the vanguard of opposition to Philippine independence. Thus, as a result of "Switzer's butting into this affair," Stimson felt obliged to shelve McCoy's appointment for the time being.[25]

Within months, however, Stimson revived the idea of sending his friend to Manila. In a conversation with McCoy on May 19, 1931, the secretary of state remarked that he and the president were "afraid Congress had made up its mind to do some irresponsible thing" concerning the Philippines. In that event, they both "wanted McCoy out there . . . in the thankless task of holding the bag while we were getting out." Despite such pessimism, Stimson's subsequent instructions indicated that he had not given up hope of making a deal with Filipino leaders that would satisfy their aspirations without severing the islands' links to the United States. In 1929, Quezon told then Governor General Stimson of his willingness to accept some form of dominion status in return for promises of continued free trade with the United States. The secretary of state asked McCoy to sit down with Quezon, currently in the United States, to explore ways of working out such an arrangement.[26]

As a result, the summer of 1931 once again found McCoy temporarily quartered at 1718 H Street. Throughout the first two weeks of June, he conferred with Quezon, bringing Stimson up to date when they met for golf at Burning Tree Country Club. McCoy's assignment was a thorny one. He knew that Quezon's public enthusiasm for independence was matched by serious reservations about the viability of the Philippines if deprived of American protection and access to American markets. McCoy also understood the rules of Philippine politics. Quezon had risen on the political ladder by putting himself at the head of the independence movement. Any sign of infidelity to that cause could destroy his career.[27] The concept that McCoy presented to Quezon was a simple one: In return for greater autonomy, Filipinos would accept the indefinite extension of American sovereignty as well as the preservation of certain American prerogatives reserved for emergencies. It was a proposal that Quezon approached with utmost wariness. To protect his rear, he insisted that McCoy make it clear to Stimson and Hurley that the conversations did not mean that he had changed his well-known stand on independence. Yet he went on to stipulate his hope of gaining from the negotiations "a more liberal government *under the present Organic Act* [the Jones Act]" while "settling the Philippine question in a manner that will satisfy the aspirations of the Filipinos [and] protect their economic interests." The last reference reflected his determination to preserve Philippine exclusion from American tariff barriers, a privilege that would be jeopardized if Congress granted the islands independence.[28]

Notwithstanding Quezon's gingerly approach to the subject, McCoy succeeded in striking an apparent bargain with the Filipino leader. By June 18, they had agreed to a proposal that McCoy presented to Hurley in a lengthy memorandum. While acknowledging a moral commitment before the world to grant the islands eventual independence, McCoy argued that to do so now or in the near future would be disastrous for both Philippine and American interests. Moreover, he argued that the Jones Act was inadequate to prepare the Philippines for freedom because it lacked "sufficient flexibility to permit gradual evolution by trial and error." Yet, whatever the islands' prospects for survival and the liabilities of the Jones Act, popular demand for self-rule—a "product of racial self-consciousness"—was so strong that, unless satisfied, insurrection could occur. To avert such a calamity, McCoy proposed a British imperial solution of converting the Philippines into a dominion. The office of governor general, an offending symbol of American authority, would be abolished, and the islands would enjoy broad political autonomy. The American presence would remain only in the form of a high commissioner who would refrain from involvement in day-to-day matters of state but would be "clothed with explicit reserve powers to protect the interests of the United States." Thus, Filipinos would govern their own affairs while still enjoying a measure of American protection, both military and commercial. The United States would maintain the status quo in the western Pacific while defusing Philippine political agitation. It was a compromise that would meet the needs of both sides.[29]

Although Stimson judged the plan very good indeed, Hoover was un-enthusiastic. Ultimately, however, its fate was contingent less on American support than on its acceptability to Filipino leaders. Could Quezon persuade his colleagues to take a realistic view of the future and accept something less than absolute independence? Quezon told Hurley that he would attempt to do so. Even after returning to Manila in the autumn of 1931, he continued privately to profess his support for the dominion plan. Quezon may even have convinced Osmena and Manuel Roxas of its benefits. Yet in the end, political expediency won out. The partisan advantage to be accrued from letting Quezon alone sponsor the dominion plan—and then attacking him as a lackey of the Americans—was too great for his rivals to pass up. Quezon recognized this danger, and when Osmena and Roxas refused to support the proposal publicly, he, too, abandoned it in favor of the old cry for complete independence. In the end, McCoy's plan for a Philippine dominion came to nothing. Yet the plan possessed real merit and its rejection resulted less from its own shortcomings than from the shortsightedness of Filipino politicians.[30]

Not all of McCoy's assistance to the Hoover administration was quite so weighty as seeking the orderly liquidation of the American empire. In one instance, his role did not involve external affairs at all—unless the U.S. Marine Corps and the Navy Department can be considered rival sovereignties. Credit for McCoy's assignment in early 1931 to umpire a dispute between these two institutions belongs first of all to Maj. Gen. Smedley D. Butler, USMC. "Old Gimlet Eye," the most colorful marine officer of his day, won fame and two Medals of Honor during a career that took him from China to the Caribbean. He was best known, however, for his undisciplined tongue, a weakness that repeatedly attracted the wrath of his civilian superiors.[31] Butler supplemented his marine pay by travelling the lecture circuit, charging a $250 fee for each appearance. Showman enough to understand what it took to fill a hall with cash customers and vain enough to enjoy their attention, Butler delighted audiences by skewering senior administration officials, especially over U.S. policy in the Caribbean. Characterizing his own service in the region as dishonest and pernicious, he lent credibility to the most extreme criticism of American foreign policy.[32]

Butler's insubordinate grandstanding did not endear him to the strait-laced Hoover and Stimson. When newspapers quoted Butler describing American policy in the Caribbean as "hypocritical and oppressive . . . a policy imposed by force and fraud," the administration decided it had had enough. Secretary of the Navy Charles Francis Adams officially reprimanded Butler and directed him to refrain from public comment on controversial subjects. For a brief period, Butler complied. The Marine Corps was about to get a new commandant, and Butler naively hoped that with a demonstration of good behavior he might win the job. When another officer was chosen instead, the bonds restraining Smedley Butler fell away.[33] In January 1931, Butler returned to the headlines in typical fashion as a result of a speech in Philadelphia. Expressing his opinion that "mad dogs" among Europe's leaders made the prospects for peace appear bleak, Butler proceeded to illustrate his point by recounting an anecdote that portrayed Benito Mussolini, Italy's premier, as a callous hit-and-run murderer of little children. Word of the remarks leaked out and a diplomatic flap ensued. When the Italian ambassador protested the insult to Il Duce's good name, the State Department apologized for Butler's "discourteous and unwarranted utterances." But the incident did not end there. Hoover and Stimson wanted Butler court-martialed. Stimson was particularly adamant, complaining in his diary of the "shilly-shallying" of Secretary of the Navy Adams, who doubted the wisdom of bringing charges against Butler. In the face of Stimson's insistence, however, Adams had no choice but to give in.[34]

When Adams ordered Butler relieved as commander of the marine base at Quantico, Virginia, and placed under house arrest, the ensuing outcry suggested that the navy secretary's reservations had been well founded. Marine leaders were outraged at what they believed was unjustified persecution of a brother officer. Veterans' groups and congressmen rose to Butler's defense. Franklin D. Roosevelt, the governor of New York, and former navy secretary Josephus

Daniels both volunteered to testify in Butler's behalf. The affair was ideally designed to distract, however briefly, an economically depressed nation, many of whose citizens found in hating the Hoover administration one of life's remaining pleasures. The *New York Times* reported that newsreel footage of Butler was drawing cheers in movie houses, while pictures of Stimson "met with signs of disapprobation." A *Times* correspondent in Washington noted, "The case occupies first rank in public interest here." The Butler affair "sizzles . . . satirically, on editorial pages," reported the *Literary Digest* in its survey of press opinion, "at times sputtering into a chortle of ridicule."[35] Highly sensitive to criticism, Hoover soon regretted the court-martial decision. By February 4, concerned that Butler's defense counsel would further embarrass the State Department by airing the remarks about Mussolini in court, Stimson reached the same conclusion. He now told Secretary Adams that administrative rather than judicial proceedings against Butler would suffice. But Adams, having ordered a court-martial only at Hoover and Stimson's prodding, now saw no way of withdrawing from that position without looking like a fool. The initiative had now become Butler's: What price would he demand in return for letting the affair drop?[36]

After a cabinet meeting on February 6, Hoover suggested that Stimson recruit McCoy to act as an emissary to the Butler camp. While noting the anomaly of appointing an army officer to arbitrate a matter that was essentially internal to the Navy Department, Stimson agreed with the president that McCoy's "wisdom and tact" were well suited for the task. McCoy was already in Washington consulting with the State Department on Nicaraguan matters, so Stimson was able to brief him on his mission that same day.[37] With instructions giving him "practically carte blanche" so long as he squelched the court-martial, McCoy went quickly to work. First, he called on Adams to get the navy's viewpoint. He then met with Butler's chief counsel, Maj. Henry Leonard, to solicit Butler's terms. Over the next two days, McCoy continued these negotiations, first with one side and then with the other, eventually hammering out a formula acceptable to both. On Sunday morning, February 8, Leonard delivered to McCoy at 1718 H Street a letter in which Butler apologized to Adams for having "caused embarrassment to the Government." That same afternoon, McCoy met with Adams and secured the secretary's signature to a reprimand that spent as much time commending Butler for his record of distinguished service as it did chastising him for his recent misbehavior. The mildness of the reprimand is not really surprising: Leonard drafted it himself. Yet Butler had admitted culpability, however slight, thus providing the administration with a shield to deflect further criticism of its handling of the matter. In return for his admission, charges against Butler were dropped and he was restored to command without prejudice. The "court-martial" of Smedley Butler sank mercifully into oblivion.[38]

Unquestionably, the affair had been a silly one. Yet, as Hoover recognized, there existed the real chance that Butler's court-martial "would make a great mess" such as his administration could ill-afford. By arranging what Stimson thought was "a very good and satisfactory ending of a very disagreeable matter," McCoy averted that mess. In so doing, McCoy again proved his usefulness to the administration. Certainly, Stimson was in his debt; the secretary of state repaid his friend in short order by assigning him to represent the United States in one of the century's pivotal diplomatic crises.[39]

# 10

# The Lytton Commission

For those who seek to understand (or assign blame for) the origins of World War II, the Asian city of Mukden holds special significance. On the night of September 18, 1931, an explosion near Mukden tore a gap in the tracks of the South Manchurian Railway. No one was injured and damage was so slight that a southbound express passed by unhindered a short while later. Yet, for the Kwantung Army, protector of Japanese strategic and economic interests in Manchuria, the incident triggered a systematic offensive against the remnants of Chinese sovereignty over the region. Within weeks, the Japanese established themselves as the new masters of Manchuria. These occurrences, writes one historian in a recent study, "initiated a chain of events leading directly to world war."[1] Although others have cautioned against attempts to draw a straight and unbroken line from Mukden to Pearl Harbor, such views have long enjoyed wide credence. Certainly, contemporary observers considered the Japanese conquest of Manchuria to be a watershed in post-World War I international relations. Scholarly interest in the incident has scarcely diminished since. The result has been a copious body of literature that has variously traced the course of the Japanese "conspiracy," examined the role of the League of Nations, and assessed the parts played by individual nations or leaders.[2] This study will not duplicate efforts of other scholars who have produced detailed analyses of this complex episode. To do so would result in a book altogether different from this one in structure and focus. Instead, this chapter will limit itself to three issues: first, the relationship of the League of Nations Commission of Inquiry on Manchuria to the overall Asian policy formulated by Secretary of State Stimson; second, McCoy's success in coordinating the commission's findings with Stimson's requirements; and third, the results of this collaboration between McCoy and the secretary of state.

151

Neither American resistance to Japanese expansion after Pearl Harbor nor the Sino-American partnership necessitated by the Pacific war should obscure the ambivalence and circumspection of the initial American response to the Manchurian crisis. In the face of raw Japanese aggression, several factors interposed to temper the American reaction. For example, despite sympathy among missionaries and admirers of China's ostensibly republican revolution, few Americans (among the minority who thought about such things) held the Middle Kingdom in high regard. Perennial domestic turmoil, an alien culture, and, above all, a seeming inability to master the essentials of Western methods created in the United States an image of Chinese backwardness and inferiority. Few Americans believed that the Chinese could exploit Manchuria's economic potential to best advantage. Many doubted that China deserved the region at all.[3] In contrast, although many Americans shared McCoy's wariness of the Japanese as the most aggressive of the "yellow races," they also admired Japan's spectacular modernization over the previous half-century, a feat attributed to that nation's facility for imitating the West. Moreover, Japan by 1931 had become easily the most important U.S. trading partner in the Far East as well as an attractive field for investment, which only added to American reluctance to criticize Japan too hastily over Manchuria.[4]

Prevailing domestic conditions compounded American wariness of becoming involved in Asia. In 1931, the United States had yet to reach the bottom of the Great Depression. The overriding importance of checking the economic slide seemed to dictate a foreign policy that would husband American energies and resources for urgent problems at home. Surging congressional interest in cutting loose the Philippines typified the isolationism that gripped the country. Even had the nation been willing to support a forceful response against Japan in 1931, American military forces—most notably the navy—were under strength and ill prepared to face any respectable opponent.[5]

Not surprisingly then, the secretary of state reacted cautiously to the events unfolding in Manchuria. Convinced that Japanese actions constituted "the first major blow at the new system of war limitation and prevention" created since the World War, Stimson could hardly pretend that American interests were uninvolved. Yet he recognized the constraints that limited the American role and hoped initially that the Japanese themselves would resolve the crisis. Stimson based this hope on the belief that responsibility for the events subsequent to Mukden rested with renegade military officers who were acting in defiance of "liberal" civilian leaders. According to this view, the interests of the United States and other Western countries would be best served by permitting political leaders such as Foreign Minister Kijuro Shidehara the opportunity to reassert control over the military and return Japanese policy to a more pacific course. Interested observers, Stimson believed, should tread lightly to avoid aggravating Japanese nationalism. Any attempt to coerce Japan would undercut the position of those Japanese who opposed expansionism. Above all, Stimson intended to avoid any action that threatened to arouse Japanese ill will against the United States.[6]

At the headquarters of the League of Nations in Geneva, Stimson's counsel to leave Japan alone reinforced the prevailing mood among the European powers. Preoccupied like the United States with problems that were much closer to home, these nations had no inclination either to rescue China or to antagonize Japan. The unfavorable American opinion of China and respect (not liking) for the Japanese was, if anything, even more pronounced in Europe. Although China would not permit the League to overlook completely the fact that two of its members were engaged in open hostilities, no action beyond solemn discussions and high-sounding pronouncements was likely to be forthcoming from the world organization. Indeed, when some of the League's lesser members boldly suggested in late September that a commission of inquiry be dispatched to Manchuria, Stimson ordered American diplomats to scotch the idea. The ease with which they did so showed the importance that the League's members attached to American support. It also exposed the timidity of the organization's leading members. The withholding of American support became a facile justification for inaction.[7] Unfortunately, the premise underlying this wait-and-see policy proved invalid. Events in October and November demonstrated that there existed no significant disagreement within Japan about the importance of controlling Manchuria. Despite Japanese pledges of an early troop withdrawal, the fighting steadily expanded in range and intensity.

Japan's bombing on October 8 of Chinchow, far from Mukden, jolted Stimson from his policy of conciliation. Though not abandoning altogether the hope that enlightened civilian leaders would salvage the situation nor forgetting the danger of arousing Japanese nationalism, the secretary of state embarked on a course intended to align the United States with an international effort to reproach Japanese misbehavior. Surely, he believed, a great demonstration of solidarity by the West in condemning the events in Manchuria would awaken Japan to the error of its ways. In the absence of any spontaneous international gesture, Stimson was willing to orchestrate the rebuke himself.[8] This shift in tactics brought in its trail a series of initiatives: the unprecedented decision in October to permit an American diplomat to participate in League discussions on Manchuria; the Stimson doctrine of nonrecognition in January 1932; and the letter to Sen. William E. Borah the following month affirming the U.S. commitment to the Washington treaties as inseparable adjuncts of the traditional Open Door policy. Stimson designed each of these measures to rally "the united moral disapprobation of the world" against Japan's wanton disregard of its treaty obligations.[9]

American support for what came to be know as the Lytton Commission can best be understood in the context of this policy of moral coercion. Indeed, in Stimson's mind, the commission represented his best hope for success. Unlike the nonrecognition doctrine and the Borah letter, whose unilateral character left the United States exposed and unsupported, the Lytton Commission was a joint effort that originated in the League Council and even had Japanese endorsement. The risks involved in supporting such an undertaking thus appeared to be minimal, whereas the potential benefits in terms of rallying international opinion promised to be correspondingly great. As Stimson told Sen. David Reed of Pennsylvania, a unanimous report holding the Japanese responsible for the events since September 1931 would provide the basis for condemnation of Japan by the League Assembly. The weight of such an adverse judgement would make it almost certain that the Japanese "would listen to reason . . . and it would prevent Japan from raising any outside financial support." Despite all the discussion of Manchuria, the League had thus far reached no real conclusions. Stimson believed that

> We cannot discuss punishment until there has been a judgment. . . . If they make that judgment we can then discuss punishment and tell them we will go along with them [the League's members] as far as a universal declaration of non-recognition of any treaties, etc. . . . The President thinks that this would have enormous and controlling effect upon an Oriental nation like Japan.[10]

In Stimson's view, Frank McCoy was "the best man in America" to represent the United States on the Lytton Commission. The secretary of state had no trouble persuading his friend to accept the position—although doing so required McCoy to forego an assignment to become superintendent of West Point. When Stimson telephoned with the offer on December 22, McCoy "said that all he wanted to know was that the President and I would like him to go, and in that case he would." McCoy told Stimson that he had no illusions about the undertaking and fully expected that "it would be a hell of a job."[11] The League showed less enthusiasm at McCoy's appointment than did Stimson. Aristide Briand, France's foreign minister, objected to McCoy's nomination on two counts. First, McCoy was an army general and the commission already had one of those in the French representative. Second, Briand feared that McCoy's recent service in Nicaragua would reduce the willingness of the League's Latin American members to support the commission's efforts.[12] Stimson bluntly rejected Briand's objections. The Lytton Commission "would be a success only if we do not try to fill it with trades or professions, but with men," he told the French ambassador in Washington. Because McCoy was the best man for the job, "it didn't make any difference whether he was a general or not." As for Nicaragua, Stimson contended that inasmuch as McCoy had "transform[ed] an imperialistic policy into a truly great reform," Latin America would not take exception to his appointment. Whether or not Briand was much persuaded by such arguments is problematic. Given Stimson's insistence and the League's determination that the commission include an American, the French leader was obliged to concede to the secretary's preference.[13]

Later, Stimson asserted that McCoy served on the Lytton Commission "solely because he had been appointed as such by the League. We had no right to participate as a government in the inquiry. [As a result,] in what he did, General McCoy was responsible to the League, not to us." Such an explanation overlooks not only Stimson's role in imposing McCoy on the League but also McCoy's consultations with Stimson prior to the mission. In January and February 1932, McCoy and Stimson met on at least four occasions to discuss Manchuria: twice at Woodley, Stimson's home in Washington; once at the State Department; and once at the White House with President Hoover. The atmosphere of the conversations was intimate and low key. After dinner at Woodley, the secretary and his friend would enjoy "a good old-fashioned talk together over the fire," permitting Stimson to explain his views in detail. Stimson's contention that McCoy represented only himself on the Lytton Commission may have been strictly correct. Yet unofficially McCoy was performing his familiar role as a responsible agent of his government, charged in this instance with insuring that the commission's findings complemented the American policy of mobilizing world opinion to restrain Japan. As he had in Nicaragua, McCoy enjoyed broad freedom of action; yet in practice, he adhered to the overall goals prescribed by the secretary of state.[14]

The League of Nations Commission of Inquiry that McCoy joined in New York on February 9, 1932, after its voyage from Le Havre was an august body to which each of Europe's principal powers contributed. Great Britain provided the commission's chairman, Victor Allen George Robert Bulwer-Lytton. A product of Eton and Cambridge, the Earl of Lytton had served as first lord of the admirality, undersecretary of state for India, governor of Bengal, and briefly as viceroy of India. The French representative was General Henri Claudel, like McCoy a professional soldier with broad experience in colonial matters. During World War I, Claudel served as a corps commander and an army group chief of staff. Albert Schnee, the German representative, was a career diplomat whose primary expertise lay in colonial affairs. He was a former director of the colonial ministry in Berlin and from 1912 to 1919 served as governor of German East Africa. Italy, too, was represented by a career diplomat: Count Luigi Aldrovandi-Marescotti. Aldrovandi's background included assignments as secretary general of the Italian delegation at the Paris Peace Conference and, more recently, as Rome's ambassador to Buenos Aires and Berlin.[15] A small staff was provided to assist the commissioners in their work. Of its members, the most important to McCoy was another American, George H. Blakeslee. A well-known professor of international relations at Clark University, Blakeslee in effect acted as McCoy's political adviser.[16]

After adding McCoy to their number, the commissioners traveled by rail to San Francisco where they embarked on February 13 aboard the *S.S. President*

*Coolidge.* Upon arrival in Yokohama on February 29, the group proceeded to Tokyo and set to work, interviewing diplomats, businessmen, and senior government officials, both civilian and military. As he would throughout the mission, McCoy immediately began maintaining close contact with U.S. government agents, among them his old friend W. Cameron Forbes, the American ambassador. The Japanese made a rather obvious play for McCoy's support through elaborate expressions of appreciation for his assistance at the time of the earthquake of 1923. Of greater importance in shaping McCoy's attitude, however, was the assassination on March 5 of Baron Takuma Dan, a leading Japanese industrialist. McCoy had become well acquainted with Dan in 1923 and called on him the day before he was murdered by right-wing militants.[17]

In a series of meetings with the commission, officials in Tokyo presented their version of events in Manchuria. The Japanese claimed that it was "their national mission to maintain peace and order in the Orient" against the threat of Chinese irresponsibility and Bolshevik expansionism. If given a free hand, Japan promised to maintain order in Asia without violating the concept of the Open Door, which promised developed nations equal opportunity in China. Lt. Gen. Araki Sadao, the minister of war, assured the commission of Japan's desire for "a world without restrictions and frontiers."[18] Although Japanese promises to honor the Open Door did not persuade McCoy, the American representative did share Japanese concern about the Soviet Union. Interviewing Yoshizawa Kenkichi, Shidehara's successor, McCoy remarked that "we have to consider the existence of Russia as a shadow in the background of this problem." The Japanese foreign minister responded to this opening by citing his government's concern about Soviet penetration into Manchuria. "If Manchuria were Bolshevized," he said, "Korea would be exposed to great danger." Japanese interest in limiting the spread of Soviet influence struck a responsive chord with both McCoy and Lytton.[19] Despite such appeals, McCoy left Tokyo with a distinctly negative opinion of Japan's leaders and of the course on which they had set their country. A party of "youth, irresponsibility, and fanaticism" had come to power, intent on redeeming Japan from the influences that contact with the outside world and rapid Westernization had brought about. Although army officers occupied the forefront of the movement, "the term 'Military Party' . . . was a misnomer" because its support extended far beyond the military establishment. The triumph of this reactionary nationalism accounted for "the course of events in Manchuria, the anti-American agitation, and other examples of unfriendliness and lack of rational control."[20]

One day after McCoy and his colleagues left Tokyo on March 8, the birth of Manchukuo was announced to the world. The creation of this transparent Japanese puppet state was surprising only in its timing, which seemed a calculated expression of contempt for the Lytton Commission. Despite this further evidence of Japan's unwillingness to compromise over Manchuria, the commission proceeded undaunted to China. At Shanghai, the next stop on its itinerary, further complications awaited. In late January, Japanese naval units and marines landed there in retaliation for a Chinese boycott of Japanese goods. Fighting erupted and continued until early March. Japanese air attacks and artillery devastated Chapei, the Chinese quarter of the city. Such disregard for civilian life outraged the West—Stimson likening its impact on public opinion to that of Germany's invasion of Belgium in 1914. The fighting also frightened Shanghai's International Settlement, the quarter controlled by Western nations including the United States. Although a fragile ceasefire existed by the time the commission arrived on March 14, the city remained an armed camp.[21]

Sir Eric Drummond, the League's secretary general, warned against the commission becoming bogged down in a peripheral matter such as Shanghai. Similarly, the State Department informed McCoy that it wanted the commission to steer clear of the affair. Nonetheless, some attention to the events of the previous months was unavoidable. With the exception of the Japanese, Shanghai's multinational community welcomed the commission with hopeful anticipation. Japanese aggressiveness so flustered and intimidated Western officials, remarked McCoy, that "all their complications were passed to us, and we had to struggle against being lost in an Oriental jungle."[22] Although the commission did not attempt to arrange for a disengagement of the forces at Shanghai, it remained in the city for thirteen days, hoping through its show of concern "to create a propitious atmosphere" for negotiations. Other than the refugees camped in public buildings and the large number of soldiers in the streets, McCoy and his colleagues found little evidence of recent fighting in central Shanghai. Chapei, however, was another matter. After inspecting that ravaged part of the city, McCoy remarked that it was as if "the Bronx [had] been destroyed without Manhattan, Brooklyn and Jersey City showing signs of war."[23]

While in Shanghai, the commission established the routine to which it adhered throughout its subsequent travels in China and Manchuria. In their quest for information, the commissioners availed themselves to the views of virtually any group with an opinion on Sino-Japanese relations. Given that few of these groups made even a pretense of disinterest, sorting out fact from propaganda was no easy task. For McCoy and his colleagues, each day became a continuous round of interviews and conferences with local officials, diplomats, businessmen, bankers, journalists, civic groups, educators, and missionaries. The commission interrupted its routine only for luncheons and dinners, "which were also loaded [with] propaganda." Those moments when the commissioners were freed from their collective responsibilities found McCoy consulting with local American representatives such as Nelson T. Johnson, the minister to China, and Adm. Montgomery M. Taylor, commander of the U.S. Asiatic Fleet.[24] From Shanghai, the commission proceeded to Nanking, seat of Chiang Kai-shek's Nationalist government. Over the course of several meetings with the commission, Chiang and his ministers made a favorable impression. "They are a brilliant lot of revolutionaries," McCoy told his family, "and Chiang, much the best of the lot, a

*The Manchurian crisis, 1932: McCoy and Lord Lytton search purposefully for a solution. (Courtesy U.S. Army Military History Institute)*

Cromwellian character." A new generation of Chinese leaders was emerging, McCoy believed, "a change from the older mandarin type to the young revolutionist," schooled by missionaries and frequently graduates of American universities.[25]

From Nanking, the commission proceeded to Peking, arriving on April 9. Here the commissioners met with officials of Manchuria's deposed Chinese administration, including the warlord Chang Hsueh-liang. Although McCoy and his colleagues intended to stop only briefly in Peking, their departure was delayed by Japanese obstructionism that henceforth hindered their attempts to gain a comprehensive picture of conditions in Manchuria. The League Council had authorized Japan and China each to designate an "assessor" to assist the Lytton Commission in its work. A Japanese assessor escorted the commission throughout Japan, and his Chinese counterpart, Wellington Koo, joined the party in Shanghai. Now in Peking, Japanese officials informed Lytton that they would not permit Koo, a close associate of Chiang Kai-shek, to enter Manchukuo. When the commissioners insisted that Koo accompany them, a brief impasse ensued. Eventually, on April 19, the Japanese relented, and the commission resumed its travels. Seven months after the incident at Mukden, the League of Nations Commission of Inquiry arrived at its destination.[26]

"When the commission went into Manchuria," recalled Professor Blakeslee, "the outstanding fact was the protection which was given to the party." He went on to explain:

On nearly every railroad an armored train went ahead of us about ten minutes. . . . On the commission's special train sometimes as many as two cars were filled with soldiers and every car had both platforms guarded with from one to four soldiers or police armed with rifles. . . . Nearly everywhere we went the track was guarded. For hundreds of miles Manchokuo [sic] troops, coolies in uniforms they looked like, were guarding the track; they were stationed every few hundred yards . . . fac[ing] away from the track pointing their rifles toward the horizon.

Actually, as the commissioners soon recognized, the Japanese made such elaborate provisions less to protect the commission than to isolate it. The new lords of Manchuria were determined to prevent the commission from unearthing any evidence of opposition to the Japanese occupation.[27]

Foremost among the commission's many stops in Manchuria was Mukden itself. McCoy described the city as "a drab place [of] howling winds and impalpable dust." Security in Mukden, as throughout Manchuria, was tight. "This place is worse than Russia," McCoy told his family, "in the air of suspicion, and the number of police and S[ecret] S[ervice]." Japanese security officers sealed off the Oriental Hotel to prevent Koo from having any contact with the populace. Chinese brave enough to attempt to see the commissioners were harassed and often arrested. Guards outside of local post offices intercepted letters intended for McCoy and his colleagues. Japanese agents rifled any mail that did reach the commission and, according to Blakeslee, "they opened our trunks in the hotel at night when they thought we were not around." Japanese surveillance was so all-encompassing that, when one commissioner complained privately in a letter to his wife of a broken radiator in his room, repairmen appeared unbidden the following morning to fix it.[28]

Like their nominal superiors in Tokyo, Japanese army officers in Manchuria emphasized the threat of Soviet expansionism. "We feel that we are on the frontier line for the protection of Western culture and civilization," said Lt. Gen. Honjo Shigeru, commander of the Kwantung Army. The Red propaganda of the Third Internationale failed in Europe, so the Soviets now directed their attention to the East. If Japan left Manchuria, China would be bolshevized. Other officers warned the commission that, without Japan's presence as "a barrier against the penetration of red influence," foreign investments and interests throughout the region would be endangered. Soviet influence would mean that the door would be closed to foreign investments. These Japanese soldiers predicted that Communist infiltration would not stop in China but could well "reach down to Indo-China, India, and the Philippine Islands."[29]

These elaborately staged efforts were unavailing. In the commissioner's eyes, Japan remained unalterably oriental, and hence the image of Japan as a bulwark of Western civilization was literally incredible. Likewise, dire warnings about the Soviet threat to the Open Door rang hollow in the face of a deliberate Japanese campaign to eject Western economic interests from Manchuria. Even the rigid security measures designed to deny the commissioners access to contrary opinion succeeded only in antagonizing them. Despite Japanese efforts, McCoy and his colleagues obtained convincing testimony from consular officials, businessmen, and missionaries that Manchukuo was a sham. McCoy's secret meeting in Harbin with a leader of Chinese guerrilla forces still resisting the Japanese occupation reinforced this view. As McCoy noted, even the Chinese who spoke in support of Manchukuo "informed us indirectly, later, that what they had said in public did not represent their true feelings—quite the contrary!"; "of course, the coolies do not care," McCoy added, "but the representative Chinese are almost unanimously against the new government which they regard as the puppet of Japan."[30]

The commission spent six weeks in Manchuria, visiting such cities as Harbin, Dairen, Port Arthur, and Chinchow and conscientiously interviewing interested parties and officials up to Henry Pu Yi, the last emperor of China, now installed by Japan as nominal ruler of Manchukuo. In early June, the commission returned to Peking, and McCoy and his colleagues began to compose their final report, a task that commanded their attention for the rest of the summer. Only once did they interrupt their labors. In early July, the commission again visited Tokyo, ostensibly seeking the views of the newly formed cabinet of Viscount Saito Makoto. In fact, the investigators by this time had passed beyond the point of seeking information: The visit actually combined a final appeal for Japanese concessions with a forewarning of what the commission's findings would be. Although the visit elicited no positive response from Japan, it did provide McCoy the opportunity to communicate his own conclusions to Japanese officials and to Joseph C. Grew, the new American ambassador in Tokyo.[31]

McCoy never challenged Japanese assertions of Japan's pre-eminent interests in Manchuria. Nor did he dispute Japanese grievances against the Chinese. McCoy sympathized with the Japanese, he told Grew. "The Chinese are devils to work with. They have not played the game with the Japanese [and] have had a most irritating policy in Manchuria." China had undermined the privileges to which Japan was entitled by treaty. Contemplating the disorder that existed in Manchuria and the corruption and lethargy of the Chinese bureaucracy, McCoy conceded that "it was enough to drive anyone crazy." Yet McCoy also believed that Chinese "pin-pricking . . . posed no immediate danger to Japan's vital interests." He rejected the idea that Japan seized Manchuria out of self-defense. "If Japan were to tell the League that it merely acted in self-defense," he told Foreign Minister Uchida Yasuya on July 14, "it would be the duty of the Commission to say that there had been no immediate threat to her vital interests but there had merely been the culmination of a long series of irritations."[32]

*The Lytton Commission confers with Henry Pu Yi, titular ruler of Manchukuo, 1932. To Pu Yi's right are Lytton and McCoy; to his left are Count Luigi Aldrovandi-Marescotti, Dr. Albert Schnee, and General Henri Claudel. (Courtesy National Archives)*

To justify their actions in Manchuria, the Japanese cited the analogy of U.S. intervention in Latin America. This infuriated McCoy. "They are always bringing up the Nicaraguan case," he told Grew. "But the cases are not parallel." Why not? "First, our interference took place some years ago," he explained, ignoring the continued presence of American marines in Nicaragua. Second, "we were not committed not to do it" through treaties promising nonintervention; "we were rather committed to do it" under the terms of the Roosevelt Corollary to the Monroe Doctrine. "Also we were always asked by both sides to the dispute to intervene *and we always got out when the job was finished.* Japan was not asked to do what she did." At root, McCoy objected less to Japan's purpose than to its methods. "Times have changed," he told Grew, implying that the heavy-handed interventionism that had once been acceptable no longer was. "The Japanese [had] had a good case [in Manchuria] but they went about it the wrong way."[33]

McCoy not only objected to the propriety of Japanese methods in Manchuria but also doubted their efficacy. The dispute over who should control Manchuria, he told the Japanese foreign minister, could not be solved unilaterally. Although weak, China would never relinquish its claim to the contested region. Viewing Manchuria as "unalterably Chinese," the government of China remained serenely confident "that eventually, in a hundred or five hundred years, the matter would be straightened out, to China's advantage. Time . . . was no object in the dispute." In McCoy's eyes, this determination, combined with Japan's "fanatic patriotic fetish" to control Manchuria, would pose an ongoing threat to Asian stability. Japan would insist that China recognize its claims. Although China's army was ineffectual and corrupt, McCoy reminded Grew that "the Chinese have tremendous powers of passive resistance." He went on to predict: "If the Japanese tried to invade China, they would run up against the same thing that invaders of Russia have always found. They could take the ports but could not get into the interior." In short, Manchuria would become "like Alsace-Lorraine, a festering sore," the basis not of a new Japanese order but of ever-widening conflict.[34] Such arguments left Japanese leaders unmoved. As Foreign Minister Uchida told the commissioners, for his countrymen, Manchuria was "a question of life and death." Just as other nations acted without consulting Japan on issues they considered vital, so the Japanese considered themselves justified in proceeding unilaterally in this instance. The League's hopes for stability in Asia would be fulfilled only "if Japan were given [a] free hand to deal with China alone."[35]

Uchida's revelation of Japan's projected diplomatic recognition of Manchukuo evoked the full measure of the commission's disapproval. McCoy made no attempt to sugarcoat his objections. "In the eyes of other countries," he told Uchida, "the recognition of Manchukuo would be regarded as a violation of the Covenant of the League, the Nine Power Treaty, and the Kellogg Pact." In taking such a step, the Japanese would "ignore the well-considered opinion of the rest of the world." McCoy hoped that Japan would realize the implications of that fact. What were those implications? McCoy did not even pretend that the West would do more than simply state its disapproval. As he told Uchida, "There was of course no question of other countries taking up threatening attitudes. They knew it was a complicated action and that Japan's vital interests were involved." It was merely "from the moral sense that Japan would find the opinion of the world against her."[36] Coming from an authoritative source, such remarks must have eased Japanese fears about the likelihood of the League or the United States resorting to military or economic sanctions. McCoy had assured the Japanese that they had to contend only with world opinion—anything else was bluff.

The Japanese did not fear moral condemnation. If anything, the reverse was true. Uchida took pains to explain that Japan would proceed on its course in Manchuria despite an adverse report by the commission and unfavorable reaction in the West. Yet McCoy departed Tokyo hoping that the commission's warning to Uchida would have a salutary effect on the Japanese leaders. Discussing the popular support for the Japanese army's hard-line position regarding Manchuria, McCoy predicted to Grew that a change in sentiment was likely. Cabinet members supposedly hinted that there was some chance of a compromise. Once back in China, McCoy went so far as to tell Nelson T. Johnson that Uchida had been "quite shaken by the arguments which Lytton and the other members of the Commission had put up. . . . There were even intimations . . . that the Commission should delay any action in order to give Japan an opportunity to think things over." As a last resort, McCoy, too, was betting on the reassertion of enlightened, that is, Westernized opinion: "Staunch liberals," he told Johnson, "had more than intimated that a delay on the part of the League in taking action . . . would strengthen the hands of liberals in Japan who hoped to influence actions by the Government." However illusory these hopes appear in retrospect, they constituted in 1932 the framework of Stimson's Asian policy: the importance attributed to moral positions, the avoidance of coercion, the belief that Japanese leaders were susceptible to world opinion, and the confidence that liberalism would ultimately eclipse militarism in Japan.[37]

The Lytton Commission's return to Peking on July 20 found McCoy confident that its members had reached conclusions indistinguishable from those guiding American policy in the Far East. On July 22, McCoy passed the good news to Stimson: "There will be no blinking the facts, and no minority report," he assured the secretary of state. Furthermore, McCoy wrote, the commission's "report will be in harmony with American policy, and . . . it may strengthen it."[38] For the rest of July and all of August, the commission worked hard at finishing its report. With the investigative phase of the commission's work complete, Frances arrived from the United States to join her husband. The couple settled into a comfortable villa in Peking, for McCoy a welcome respite after weeks spent in Pullman sleepers and hotels and countless meals in restaurants and banquet halls. Before he could get too comfortable, however, unexpected difficulties arose. The harmony to which McCoy had confidently alluded came precariously close to unraveling. Earlier, McCoy reported that he and his colleagues "live[d] and work[ed] together like warm friends." Now, as their mission drew to a close, the friends quarreled.[39]

In Peking, Lytton fell seriously ill and was hospitalized for six weeks. Despite severe pain and a fever, he continued to work intensely and continuously on the report. Lytton's illness also affected him emotionally, leaving him, in Blakeslee's words, pathologically irritable and stubborn. Because the report would carry his name into history, Lytton was adamant that it bear his personal imprint. He intended to write the document himself in his hospital room; the others were welcome to call there, inspect Lytton's work, and give their assent. Such procedures were totally unacceptable to the remaining commissioners, who began to feel "as if Lord Lytton regarded them as assistants rather than his colleagues." They insisted upon having a direct hand in drafting the report. But when the remaining commissioners convened outside of the confines of Lytton's hospital room, they succeeded only in provoking their chairman's ire. As McCoy remarked with characteristic understatement, the commission's "work and range [had] been very much cramped by the illness of Lord Lytton."[40]

The disagreement between Lytton and his colleagues involved substance as well as ego. McCoy, Schnee, and Aldrovandi objected to the sarcasm and vituperation that Lytton directed at Japan in his draft. They did not disagree with Lytton's thesis, which found no justification for Japan's actions in Manchuria; however, the three commissioners wished to avoid indicting Japan outright and,

*McCoy and Frances share a quiet moment in China, 1932. (Courtesy U.S. Army Military History Institute)*

*The long summer of 1932 in Peking: McCoy passes time with a friend. (Courtesy U.S. Army Military History Institute)*

hence, preferred a subdued, unemotional style. General Claudel, on the other hand, wished to purge the report of the least hint of anti-Japanese bias. The French representative was wholly unsympathetic to the idea of restoring Manchuria to Chinese control and wanted to avoid a report that favored China even by implication. Although he did not accept Japan's description of Manchukuo as a spontaneous creation of the Manchurian people, he believed it foolhardy to pretend that the new state did not exist. Any report that took such a view, according to Claudel, would be idealistic and largely impractical. Claudel called for a pragmatic approach: What the commission "had to deal with was an illegitimate child," and, in the final analysis, "their problem was the legitimizing of this child." He believed, in short, that any resolution of the Sino-Japanese dispute would necessarily use the existing government of Manchukuo as the basis of settlement.[41] The other commissioners rejected this view categorically. To recognize Manchukuo would be to indorse Japanese violations of the League Covenant, the Nine-Power Treaty, and the Kellogg Pact. In his intolerant mood, Lytton had little patience for Claudel's opinions. He and the French general were soon at odds. When Claudel threatened in late August to attach "reservations" to the report as a precondition for signing it,

Lytton told him to "write your own report." At that moment, prospects for unanimity appeared bleak.[42]

McCoy believed, as did Stimson, that only a report indorsed by all the Western powers could possibly have the impact that the secretary of state sought. With that support in jeopardy, McCoy intervened to prevent the two extremes on the commission from getting too far apart. His task compared to what it had been in Manila during Wood's term as governor general: working behind the scenes to prevent the self-destruction of a prominent figure whose judgment was clouded by illness. Closer personally to Lytton than any of the other commissioners, McCoy capitalized on his relationship with the chairman to chide him for being too abrupt with his colleagues and to remind him of the importance of unanimity if the report were to carry the weight that Lytton hoped. McCoy also arranged for a three-member committee to draft the report. While Lytton participated as one member, Blakeslee and Robert Haas, the commission's secretary-general, insured that other opinions (not least of all McCoy's) received consideration as well. The other members no longer complained that Lytton monopolized the drafting process. In addition, McCoy mustered his reserves of tact and patience to nudge General Claudel into taking a position less at odds with that of the other commissioners. It was McCoy who devised the formula whereby Aldrovandi—the nearest thing to a bridge between Claudel and the rest of the group—redrafted key segments of the report to merge aspects of the Frenchman's position with that of the majority. Recounting these events, Blakeslee wrote: "To General McCoy . . . probably more than to any other man, the Commission owes its unanimous report."[43]

"As in all commissions," McCoy reported to his family, "there was a terrible jam in the last two weeks, but we finally reach[ed] unanimity, and finished our report after midnight sittings" on September 4. The result was a remarkable document: comprehensive in scope, evenhanded in tone, calibrated to expose Japanese transgressions while refraining from naming a transgressor. It carefully noted that "the issues involved in this conflict are not as simple as they are often represented to be." Acknowledging the exceptional character of Japan's interests in Manchuria, the report cited the validity of certain Japanese grievances. Japan, it said, suffered more than any other power from the lawless conditions existing in China. At the same time, the Lytton Report refused to accept Japan's claim that its actions following the explosion at Mukden were measures of legitimate self-defense. The subsequent creation of Manchukuo, the report said, resulted not from a genuine and spontaneous independence movement but from intrigues conceived, organized, and carried through by Japanese officials. The report stopped short of accusing Japan of violating its various treaty obligations, but by declaring Manchuria an integral part of China, it said as much by implication.[44]

The report agreed that Japan's security was irrevocably linked to its Manchurian "life-line." But it suggested that Japan could protect its interests in ways "more in keeping with the principles on which rests the present peace organization of the world." Specifically, the report proposed a ten-point formula to guarantee Japan's Manchurian interests without granting it the right to control the country either economically or politically. Key points were the demilitarization of Manchuria in conjunction with the creation of an internationally supervised constabulary to maintain order in the region; Chinese acceptance of the free participation of Japan in the economic development of Manchuria; and the negotiation of Sino-Japanese commercial and nonaggression treaties. The proposed commercial agreement would forbid Chinese boycotts of Japanese goods. In return, Japan would dismantle Manchukuo and recognize the autonomy of Manchuria under Chinese sovereignty. In return for acknowledging that Manchuria was inalienably Chinese, Japan was promised first claim in the economic exploitation of the region. If implemented, the Lytton Report's authors believed, such an arrangement would not only resolve the dispute immediately at hand but could become the starting point of a new era of close understanding and political cooperation between Japan and China.[45]

McCoy was delighted with the finished report. The commission stated its findings so dispassionately, he believed, that even the Japanese would be pleased with the tone of the report. He predicted to Nelson T. Johnson that the way the facts had been set forth might influence the Japanese to ameliorate their attitude. Yet, he warned, "if the present fanatical leaders of the [Japanese] Army continued [in] control of the situation anything was possible," even an eventual Japanese-American war.[46] Whatever the report's ultimate effect, McCoy delivered what Stimson wanted: a unanimous report that found against Japan but refrained from direct criticism. As McCoy accompanied the commission back to Geneva to deliver the report to the League, Blakeslee assured Stanley Hornbeck at the State Department that the commission's findings and recommendations would "be gratifying to the Secretary of State and your own good self." Hornbeck passed on Blakeslee's digest of the report to Stimson, who found it a fascinating paper, so much so that "it kept me so wide awake that I didn't sleep much during the night afterwards." Emphasizing the unanimity of the commissioners and the fact that the report found against the Japanese on all important issues, Stimson predicted that it would be "an epoch making document." He was especially pleased to note that "the paper cannot help but justify the position I have taken right along." It was, of course, in hopes of such justification that he agreed to American representation on the commission in the first place.[47]

Having received the report on October 1, the League released it the following day. Reaction to the document in the United States was favorable. Like Stimson, most American commentators interpreted the report's conclusions as a vindication of American policy. An article in the *Boston Herald* typified editorial opinion: "While the Lytton Commission did not represent this government, its findings strongly support our government's position on the Manchurian question." Of far greater importance, however, was the reaction of Japan. On September 15, as Uchida had warned the commission, Tokyo recognized

Manchukuo, thereby offering further proof of its truculence over Manchuria. By taking this action before the League even received the Lytton Report, the Japanese not only signaled in unmistakable terms their unhappiness with its contents but also showed their disdain for the League's peacekeeping efforts as a whole.[48] Despite Japan's action, the League persisted, treating the report as if it held the key to resolving the crisis. For six weeks, the League's members studied the contents of the document—and delayed its consideration by the council in hopes that Japan's anticipated reaction would soften. But the Japanese remained obdurate and so intimidated the council that, when its members addressed themselves to the report on November 21, they only referred the matter to the League Assembly. The assembly convened in early December. Despite strong sentiment among many of the League's members to adopt the report along with a resolution of nonrecognition, the uncertainty of the great powers led to more delay and the creation of a Committee of Nineteen to study the report further.[49]

The United States deliberately kept its distance from these developments. In Stimson's view, the Lytton Commission pointed the League in the proper direction, one aligned with American policy. Now it was up to the League to find the courage to move decisively, thereby confronting Japan with a united opposition. It was imperative that the initiative for such a move come from the League collectively rather than from any single state. Stimson wished especially to avoid the appearance that the United States was pushing the League in an anti-Japanese direction. Thus, when Hugh Wilson and Norman Davis, American diplomatic observers at Geneva, suggested that McCoy sit on the Committee of Nineteen, the idea was rejected. Indeed, although McCoy remained in Switzerland until December, he played no role in the debate over the report, remaining outside of Geneva, aloof from the League's deliberations.[50]

In reality, no amount of resolution on the League's part would deflect Japan from its policy in Manchuria. Japanese representatives in Geneva made that point as clearly as had Japanese officials in Tokyo in their conversations with the Lytton Commission. As did many others, McCoy refused to accept Japan's stated position at face value. Instead, he remained hopeful that a united expression of Western opinion would bring Japan to its senses, as Stimson had predicted. In a conversation with Hugh Wilson and Norman Davis before leaving Geneva, McCoy summed up his views. As Wilson reported to Stimson,

> McCoy believes that the Japanese have discounted a nonrecognition declaration and that thus we need not fear that the issue of such a declaration [by the League] will cause further irritation with the resulting stiffening of their attitude. [Furthermore,] if the Japanese expect such a declaration and it does not come they will feel that there is a disunion . . . on the part of the . . . members of the League and will not feel the necessity for compromise as they would if they faced concerted action.

McCoy's views thus remained consistent with those of the secretary of state. Like Stimson, he was dead wrong.[51]

On December 31, nearly eleven months after his departure, McCoy returned to Washington. He received Stimson's congratulations for a job well done and briefed the secretary on the impressions garnered during his travels. McCoy bolstered Stimson's confidence in the correctness of his policy. In his diary that night, Stimson recorded with satisfaction McCoy's assurances "that Japan could not get away with it in Manchuria." And, during a golf outing with Stimson two weeks later, McCoy reiterated that "the policy of careful non-irritating resistance in lining up the Powers against Japan is the one that is going to win out. . . . The moral pressure upon Japan is really more effective than the economic pressure which she is up against in having bitten off more than she can chew." In sum, McCoy assured Stimson that his efforts to mobilize world opinion against Japan still promised to yield favorable results.[52]

With his return to Washington, McCoy's connection with the crisis in the Far East ended. Yet the crisis itself ground on, exposing in short order the false premises of American policy. In February 1933, the Committee of Nineteen concluded its deliberations, indorsing the Lytton Commission's conclusions. The League Assembly proceeded to approve the Lytton Report and refused to recognize any change in the Asian status quo occurring at the expense of China's territorial integrity. However oblique the language, Japan stood condemned as an aggressor by the community of nations. Stimson's policy, based upon the sanctity of international agreements and the presumed efficacy of world opinion, was now the League's as well. Yet Japan knew, as did the nations who stood in judgment, that beyond the words of censure stood a void. As McCoy had admitted to Uchida, neither the League nor the United States would employ military force or economic sanctions. The West lacked the will and perhaps the means to enforce its wishes in such a distant quarter. Thus assured, the Japanese defiantly abandoned the League, more than ever determined to pursue their vital interests in Manchuria. Japan stood alone against the West, resentful at being branded an international outlaw.[53]

Months before, an assistant U.S. military attaché in Tokyo speculated on the consequences of the Lytton Report. Lt. Thomas G. Cranford already anticipated in July 1932 the report's essentially anti-Japanese character. "This will make Japan withdraw from the League and defy the whole world," he predicted. But, he added, "the worst of it is that they will blame the United States more than anyone else." Cranford, of course, proved correct. Stimson's belief in Japanese sensitivity to world opinion was utterly misplaced. Moreover, his attempt to use the Lytton Commission to camouflage the role of the United States in leading the opposition to Japan failed completely. The Japanese now identified the United States as their principal foe. Despite the patent American unwillingness to do anything substantive to check Japan, this perception of hostility cast an ineradicable pall over Japanese-American relations.[54]

McCoy performed his role as the American representative on the Lytton Commission with considerable skill. But it had been a creditable performance in support of a flawed policy. Some months later, McCoy expressed to Lytton his hope that their work would yet "point the way for the nations involved as it has already done for the League." Lytton dourly replied that, with no settlement in sight, "it looks very much . . . as if our work has been wasted." Certainly, Lytton's was the more realistic appreciation. Whatever its intent, the Lytton Report brought the Far East no nearer peace and pushed Japan farther along the road to war.[55]

# 11

# New Directions

Blaming Herbert Hoover for the Great Depression, the electorate in November 1932 repudiated both the president and his party, thereby ending the Republican era that began in 1920. When McCoy returned to the United States several weeks after the election, he discovered a nation waiting expectantly for President-elect Franklin D. Roosevelt to fulfill his pledge to restore economic prosperity. Meanwhile, the GOP's discredited leaders were bracing themselves for what promised to be a long political exile. For an army officer who had enjoyed ties with every Republican administration since Theodore Roosevelt's, the change in power did not lack personal significance. Notwithstanding the American military's supposedly apolitical character, McCoy's intimacy with such men as Wood and Stimson and his services to Coolidge and Hoover marked him indelibly as a Republican general. Although acquainted with the incoming president, McCoy could hardly expect to play in a Democratic administration the role that he performed for Franklin Roosevelt's predecessors. For McCoy, too, an exile of sorts seemed in the offing.

The general returned home to take command of the First Cavalry Division, the largest formation in the depleted army of the Great Depression. General Douglas MacArthur, the army chief of staff, had promised McCoy the division, describing it with typical flourish as "a magnificant [sic] unit now at the apex of its splendid efficiency." Although others might have characterized horse cavalry as then approaching the apex of obsolescence, the officer corps viewed the command as a plum assignment. Geographically, it left something to be desired. The First Cavalry was garrisoned at Fort Bliss, located alongside El Paso in the farthest reaches of western Texas. Commanding even a prestigious unit in such a remote locale promised to limit McCoy's access to the centers of national influence to a greater extent than had any assignment since the last time a Democrat occupied the White House.[1]

Gracefully accepting his fate, McCoy looked forward to serving again with troops. He told Stimson that he was eager to get out of Washington before the Democrats took power. He did not intend to provide the sensitive MacArthur with any pretext to claim that McCoy was ingratiating himself at the chief of staff's expense by "pulling wires with Franklin Roosevelt." On March 2, two days before the inauguration, McCoy made a final call on Stimson at the State Department. Perhaps fearing that Roosevelt's inauguration marked the close of his own career of government service, Stimson recorded his friend's leave-taking in valedictory tones. "It was rather sad," wrote the outgoing secretary of state in his diary, "to think that this was our last official intercourse." Yet, he added, "it was encouraging and cheerful to think that there was a man in the world like McCoy, and that he is on such terms with me. We have been comrades in so many, many things together." Recalling the high points of their association, Stimson praised McCoy as "a man with a broad vision" who had come to be "recognized as the most unique soldier in the United States."[2]


For McCoy, commanding a division turned out to be "a real picnic." His responsibilities for training the unit and administering an installation as large as Fort Bliss did not tax him unduly. The commanding general found time to ride and hunt, and at age fifty-nine he still played polo occasionally. He and Frances entertained guests such as the Stimsons, who spent two weeks at Fort Bliss in the spring of 1933 in order to recuperate from the strains of public life. The New Deal enlivened McCoy's official routine by assigning to his supervision some sixty Civilian Conservation Corps (CCC) camps scattered throughout Texas, Arizona, and New Mexico. Inspection tours of CCC camps provided a handy excuse for visiting the Southwest's scenic attractions along the way and touring old historical sites. All in all, the division commander's lot was a pleasant one.[3] To McCoy's regret, the picnic proved to be short-lived. In October 1933, the War Department reassigned him to command the Seventh Corps Area with headquarters at Omaha, Nebraska. According to the organizational charts, the move was a step up, but McCoy accepted the job with more resignation than enthusiasm. The Seventh Corps commander's responsibilities encompassed army activities within a seven-state region, including not only a number of regular, reserve, and national guard units but also ROTC detachments and over 150 CCC camps. In practice, however, his duties tended to be of a broad supervisory nature. McCoy noted that his new routine did "not have the keen pleasure for me that the actual command of troops has had."[4]

Occasionally his duties did depart from the ordinary. In the spring of 1934, for example, MacArthur worked himself into a lather over a proposal by the Farmer-Labor party of Minnesota to convert ROTC at the state university from a mandatory to an optional student activity. Ever wary of conspiracy, MacArthur suspected that, far from being an isolated matter of little consequence, the attempt to deemphasize military training at Minnesota "synchronizes with the drive throughout the country against the R.O.T.C. movement." The chief of staff ordered McCoy to look into the matter.[5] As a result, in April 1934, McCoy spent a week in Minneapolis and St. Paul. There he met Farmer-Labor chief Floyd B. Olson, then Minnesota's "very radical Governor," and Lotus D. Coffman, the university's "very conservative President," as well as others "in that mixed up state." McCoy soon concluded that MacArthur's fears were greatly exaggerated. Coffman and a majority of the Board of Regents steadfastly supported the retention of compulsory military training at the university. Although Governor Olson opposed mandatory ROTC, he assured McCoy that he had no intention of making a public issue of the matter. The real opposition to ROTC centered in the Committee on Militarism in Education, led by a small number of "so-called Liberals and intelligentsia" whom McCoy dismissed as ineffectual. All in all, he reported to MacArthur, "there is no immediate cause for concern." ROTC would weather the crisis.[6]

A less-interesting but regular part of McCoy's job was to keep the army and its needs before the public. As the army's senior spokesman in the Great Plains, McCoy was called to address numerous civilian groups. To the students of Kansas State College, for example, he extolled the soldier's opportunities for public service in peacetime, using the career of a Kansas State alumnus, James G. Harbord, as an illustration. In an April 1934 Army Day address to the Kansas City Chamber of Commerce, he reviewed recent army contributions to the civilian community such as CCC camps, engineering projects, and air mail delivery. Speaking engagements formed part of the routine of senior officers throughout the army; however mundane the occasion or banal the sentiments expressed, such efforts were part of the army's efforts to keep in touch with the people.[7]

Nineteen-thirty-five brought McCoy yet another new assignment, this time as commanding general of the Second Army in Chicago. Here McCoy's duties remained largely unchanged: the supervision of maneuvers, unit inspections, visits to CCC camps, and speaking engagements, all now on a grander scale. Chicago lay closer to mainstream American society than did El Paso or Omaha. Describing visits by Eleanor Roosevelt and Secretary of War George Dern, McCoy remarked, "This busy place has me in its grip, and keeps me going too fast." McCoy's neighbor in Chicago was a friend from World War I—Col. George Catlett Marshall. Currently the senior instructor with the Illinois National Guard, Marshall's career seemed to have reached a dead end. According to Marshall's biographer, McCoy was instrumental in salvaging Marshall's fortunes. McCoy arranged the interview for his friend with Secretary Dern during which Marshall made the impression that secured his first star.[8]

In the fall of 1935, Douglas MacArthur's term as army chief of staff expired. Although an oft-mentioned contender for the post, McCoy was not selected, an outcome in which partisan considerations may have figured. A friend at the War Department told McCoy that, although "it appears that you are the President's real choice. . . , the question seems to have become largely a political one." He warned that "some politicians are pointing out your long connections with Republicans and the Republican Party." Whatever the reason, Maj. Gen. Malin Craig ultimately succeeded MacArthur.[9]

Although McCoy did not become chief of staff, realignment at the top rippled through the general officer ranks and soon had him on the move again. In the spring of 1936, the War Department shifted McCoy to command of the Second Corps. With headquarters on Governor's Island in New York harbor, this assignment was the most prestigious of the army's area commands. In a short time, while remaining at Governor's Island, he took on the added responsibility of commanding the First Army, encompassing the entire eastern seaboard as well as Puerto Rico.[10] This move to the east coast brought few changes in McCoy's military duties. By placing him in the intellectual and financial center of the nation, however, it provided the opportunity to renew his involvement in public affairs. The changes in the world situation by the mid-1930s—German rearmament under Adolf Hitler, continuing tension in the Far East, and the beginnings of an intense foreign policy debate at home—provided further incentive for McCoy to participate in public discussions of international affairs. During earlier visits to New York, he accompanied Stimson to occasional meetings of the Council on Foreign Relations (CFR), the hub of the east coast foreign policy establishment. Now residing in New York, he accepted an invitation to join that influential institution. Nor was his membership purely honorific. McCoy participated actively in the council's affairs. In the autumn of 1936, he chaired a council study group that examined Japanese competition in international trade. The following spring he presided at a CFR gathering to discuss American policy in the Far East. In December 1937, with such luminaries as James T. Shotwell and Allen W. Dulles sharing the dais, he presided at a council dinner held to consider ways of staying out of war. Six months later, following the German annexation of Austria, he joined the CFR research project on the mobilization of American resources in time of war.[11]

Thus, command of the First Army offered its own unique compensations. But here, too, McCoy's stay was brief. Reaching the mandatory retirement age of sixty-four, he ended his forty-one years of commissioned service on October 31, 1938. An impressive array of honors marked his departure from active duty. The *New York Times*, chief organ of the establishment, reviewed McCoy's career as "the army's pacificator and clean-up man" and cited achievements that made him "the complete embodiment of the American soldier-diplomat . . . as ready and resourceful in peace as in war." That same month, Washington and Jefferson College awarded McCoy the first of several honorary degrees that he would receive. Over the next four years, Princeton, Brown, Clark, Columbia, and Yale followed with similar honors. And, in 1939, the Theodore Roosevelt Memorial

Association awarded its annual medal for distinguished national service to McCoy, along with George Washington Carver and Carl Sandburg.[12]

Often, of course, such tributes are merely tokens contrived to console once important figures confronting the end of their prominence. Fulsome editorials, honorary degrees, and medals are the gold watches of the elite. McCoy was lucky. Continued deterioration of the international situation saved him from obscurity. By the winter of 1935/36, Italy had overrun Ethiopia. The following spring, Germany remilitarized the Rhineland. In July 1937, Japan invaded China proper. German and Italian forces fought alongside Franco's Fascists in the Spanish Civil War. In March 1938, Germany annexed Austria, and just prior to McCoy's retirement, Great Britain and France surrendered to Hitler's demands that Czechoslovakia yield the Sudetenland to the Third Reich. To McCoy as to many others, these events heralded the coming of another world war that would inevitably involve the United States.

After leaving the army, the McCoys settled in Lewistown. As he told Cameron Forbes, "The old veteran has returned home after 45 years of being most everywhere else." Yet the move was not as final as the remark implied. In the face of what he saw as a growing crisis, he had no intention of slipping into silent idleness. So McCoy continued to contribute to discussions of world affairs, attempting like Leonard Wood a generation before to build support for increased military preparedness. In an article in the *St. Louis Post-Dispatch* shortly after his retirement, for example, he warned that respect for international law and the treaty system that formed the basis for postwar stability had now "gone by the board." In Asia, "the 'open door' has been shut in our faces," leaving vital American interests at risk. Because the nation's "standard of living and habits of life have become directly dependent on the sale of surplus products overseas, as well as on the secure flow of imports," it must be American policy not only "to defend our territories and people [but] to protect our world wide commerce, and to insure respect for our peaceful policies of open and equal opportunity." Given this definition of the national interest, McCoy assessed existing American defenses as entirely inadequate. As he told his audience at the *New York Herald-Tribune*'s annual public affairs forum, the army since 1920 had "lived on its war-time fat." Making do with obsolete weapons would no longer suffice. "What, then, is the best insurance against war?" he asked. "There can be only one answer to this—adequate preparedness." For McCoy, preparedness meant not only improving the size and quality of the military services but also streamlining the nation's ability to employ force. Chief among his recommendations in this regard was the "elimination of the unnecessary hampering restrictions which bind the hands of the [chief] executive." As he explained to the Council on Foreign Relations in January 1939, "I don't want to suggest that we turn our Commander-in-Chief into a dictator, but I do want to find some way that he can exercise his war powers without his being hampered and hindered by either the people or Congress." McCoy reiterated this theme in a paper read to the

Academy of Political Science in May 1939. To provide greater freedom of action on the part of the president, he called upon Congress to study its war powers and how it could best support the commander in chief, the State Department, and the army and navy.[13]

In public forums and in private institutions such as the Council on Foreign Relations, McCoy participated in the controversy over national policy that became increasingly heated in the late 1930s. His was not a decisive voice nor an especially original one. Rather, it was but one of many contributing to a complex and emotional debate that encompassed foreign policy, military preparedness, and domestic priorities. Yet McCoy's involvement in that debate and the acceptance of the propriety of his doing so are themselves important. Consider the standard view of the officer corps in the 1930s as expressed by Russell F. Weigley. The historic tradition of the officer corps, writes Professor Weigley, "was one of isolated military professionalism that carefully abstained from involvement in the turmoils of civilian life and the vicissitudes of national policy making." The Great Depression only exacerbated these tendencies, so that "by the 1930s [the military's] passivity had come to seem an unbreakable tradition." According to Professor Weigley, the army played virtually no role in shaping American foreign policy in the 1930s—"nor did it seek to do so." As a result, Weigley assigns partial responsibility for the coming of World War II to the officer corps for "failing to perform consistently its duty to acquaint the civil government with the military dimensions of national policy."[14]

Although not entirely without merit, Weigley's view is incomplete. It fails to recognize the existence of a second, activist tradition within the officer corps— the tradition of Emory Upton, Leonard Wood, Billy Mitchell, and others, including a generation later, Matthew B. Ridgway and James M. Gavin. Although these men differed from one another in many ways, they shared this belief: Each refused to accept a parochial definition of his responsibilities as an officer. Rather than shunning the vicissitudes of national policymaking, they attempted to influence its formulation. McCoy's public statements on the eve of World War II, which together constituted a modest attempt to "acquaint the civil government with the military dimensions of national policy," confirmed his place in this activist tradition.

In the summer of 1939, McCoy acquired an institutional base that permitted him to expand his efforts to influence, at least indirectly, the formulation of foreign policy. In the process, he gained an opportunity to remedy a problem that he had discussed years before with Stimson. Summarizing his views on the quality of American public opinion, McCoy had complained that "there is generally too much of a sectional feeling, too little broad concern about the nation, and outside of a handpicked few, practically complete oblivion to international issues and their particular effect on economic life." This lack of interest suggested a need to educate Americans as to their stake in world affairs and to provide them with the information needed to consider foreign policy issues intelligently.[15]

Since the end of World War I, there existed in the United States one organization devoted exclusively to the twin objectives of improving public understanding of foreign policy and circulating information on world affairs—the Foreign Policy Association (FPA). The FPA was second only to the Council on Foreign Relations among institutions devoted to international relations, yet to equate the organizations would be misleading. As one journalist remarked in comparing the two, "The difference is like that between the New York phone book and *Who's Who in America.*" The council, distinctly the more prestigious and influential, is an exclusive guild in which prominent business, academic, and political leaders gather privately to discuss international issues. The FPA, on the other hand, exists to encourage the average citizen to take an interest in world affairs. With membership open to anyone, the association devotes itself to the widest possible dissemination of information about foreign policy issues of interest to the United States. This difference in focus has obviated the need for any competition between the association and the council. Indeed, between them, a symbiotic relationship has flourished. The wealthy New Yorkers who have financed the FPA have been closely linked to the council. In addition, council members have frequently served as directors of the Foreign Policy Association. For its part, the association has often provided a forum wherein leading figures of the council could air their views to the public at large.[16]

The Foreign Policy Association forms part of the legacy of the progressive era. Near the end of World War I, a group of New York intellectuals and journalists of progressive bent formed the League of Free Nations Association. The organization's founders—men such as Herbert Croly, Charles A. Beard, John Dewey, and Walter Weyl—intended it as a vehicle to advocate a more active and constructive role for the United States in the postwar world, specifically through membership in some form of international peacekeeping organization. By 1919, the association was devoting its energies to supporting American entry into the League of Nations. The Senate's rejection of the Versailles Treaty and the subsequent elevation of Warren G. Harding to the presidency represented sharp defeats for the American internationalist movement. As a result, by 1921 the association found that both its audience and its access to the checkbooks of wealthy liberals were dwindling. The association's leaders remained committed to internationalism but recognized that their struggle would be a protracted one. To enable their creation to survive for the duration, they gave it a new identity. The association renounced its earlier support for American membership in the League and declared that henceforth it would avoid taking any particular position on specific issues. Rather, it would concentrate on disseminating objective, nonpartisan information on a broad range of foreign policy questions. To symbolize this shift from advocacy to education, the organization chose a bland, uncontroversial name: the Foreign Policy Association.[17]

The organizational metamorphosis succeeded. Throughout the 1920s and 1930s, public support for the FPA's programs grew steadily, as did the organization's reputation. The association sponsored important research into such topics as disarmament, war debts and reparations, and the World Court. It administered the Bok Prize, which offered $100,000 for the best plan to secure world peace, and it gave monetary awards for the year's best article on foreign policy. Well-known speakers at FPA luncheons and meetings discussed world affairs, with their addresses often broadcast to a larger audience. Most important, the organization produced a wide variety of publications—the *Foreign Policy Bulletin, Foreign Policy Reports,* and the *Headlines* series of pamphlets.[18] By and large, the Foreign Policy Association honored its pledge of nonpartisanship. At the same time, the organization remained faithful to its internationalist origins, for the premise underlying virtually all of the association's activities— that Americans could no longer afford to ignore world affairs—itself had partisan implications. The FPA sought to wean Americans from the belief that the nation could remain apart from the world. As one historian wrote, the association was thus attempting throughout the interwar era "to keep alive the Wilsonian vision of an international world." Or, as the *New York Times* succinctly put it in the headline of a recent anniversary assessment, the history of the Foreign Policy Association has amounted to "60 Years of Wrestling with Isolationism."[19]

Responding to a recommendation by Henry Stimson, the FPA's board of directors chose McCoy in the summer of 1939 to succeed Raymond Leslie Buell as the association's president. In September, with German panzers rolling across Poland and most Americans hoping to stay out of this new European war, McCoy took office. At that time the FPA's rolls listed 14,600 total members distributed among seventeen branches, most of which were located in the Northeast. Unquestionably, McCoy's appointment enhanced his stature within the foreign affairs community. Whereas previously his views represented the opinion of a single, retired officer, they now reflected the views of a large and respected institution. Yet, paradoxically, his new position obliged McCoy to become less outspoken. Although he continued to speak through 1939 and 1940 on such topics as national defense and "the British Empire under fire," he avoided controversy. In October 1939, for example, when McCoy inaugurated a series of FPA broadcasts on network radio with a speech entitled "Democracy and Foreign Policy," he confined his remarks to considering the importance of accurate information as a precondition for understanding foreign affairs. It was, in other words, simply a plug for the FPA.[20]

The reason for McCoy's reticence at a time when he was enjoying greater prominence is clear. The need to preserve the FPA's reputation for nonpartisanship imposed real limits on the president's prerogatives to engage in public debate. To entangle the association in such issues as rearmament, intervention, and the virtues of neutrality would undermine the credibility of the organization's educational activities, activities that remained the heart of the FPA program. McCoy's own sensitivity to this problem is evident in his directive to FPA members that use of the organization's name in connection with any circular, protest, or petition was entirely unauthorized. Such actions, he warned, endangered the association's status as an entirely nonpartisan educational group.[21]

McCoy's role was to manage the affairs of a going concern, not to strike out in any radically new direction. Given the requirement that the FPA's president set the example of nonpartisanship, his interests revolved largely around fund raising, administration, internal governance, and liaison with other institutions such as the Council on Foreign Relations and the State Department. The FPA suffered from chronic budgetary problems and depended heavily on support from the affluent to maintain its operations. A major responsibility of the president was to solicit contributions from potential patrons who might make sizable donations. Moreover, in meetings of the FPA's board of directors, McCoy played a leading role in determining how the association would expend its resources. The outbreak of another world war and especially U.S. entry into it in December 1941 confronted the American people with a host of new foreign policy issues. An understanding of world affairs was becoming more important than ever before. The war, therefore, demanded a redoubling of FPA programs. With considerable success, McCoy sought to broaden the reach of the association's activities. FPA membership steadily increased; by 1945, his last full year as president, it had more than doubled to 31,000. To capitalize on the influence of radio, McCoy persuaded the National Broadcasting Company to present a series of FPA-sponsored Sunday afternoon foreign affairs programs. He also expanded the association's publications program, introducing a major new periodical, the *Pan American News*. By the FPA's own standards, the flood of pamphlets and newsletters produced during McCoy's tenure remained nonpartisan. That they also retained a unifying theme is suggested by these titles of *Headlines* series pamphlets: "The Struggle for World Order" (1941), "Unity Today for Tomorrow" (1942), and "On the Threshold of World Order" (1944).[22]

To the FPA's directors, World War II signaled the imminent demise of American isolationism. Convinced that the nation and all mankind would benefit from a postwar era of cooperative internationalism, the FPA leadership believed that advocating such an idea could hardly be deemed partisan. The association staked out its wartime role in unmistakable terms in December 1941 with a pledge to "endeavor in every way to assist in the task of rebuilding world order." The *Foreign Policy Bulletin* added that Americans would contribute to this new world order only "by abandoning once and for all the illusion that we can ever again isolate ourselves from the rest of humanity." Mrs. Bayard James, an FPA director, elaborated on the association's position at a board meeting in January 1943: Given the FPA's "commit[ment] to an anti-isolationist policy," she said, "we have an interest in world cooperation. . . . Our program should, therefore, try to educate the public to that state of mind." The association's resolute pose of disinterest reflected the lessons of experience rather than any uncertainty as to its position. The singlemindedness of the League of Nations Association in pursuit of American entry into the League had proved counterproductive; the FPA learned from its parent's failure that the effective lobby was the one that avoided the lobbyist's identity. As another board member commented in indorsing Mrs. James's view, the association learned to recognize that "it [is] easier to educate people if they are not antagonized from the start by too strong a position." To this, McCoy added that, after all, "our aim . . . was to help promote sound opinion on foreign affairs." To the FPA in the early 1940s, the promotion of sound opinion meant propagating the gospel of internationalism.[23]

What impact did the FPA's efforts on behalf of internationlism have during the war? The triumph of internationalism by the end of World War II proves nothing. Various groups recognized the war as Wilsonianism's "second chance" and threw themselves into making the most of the opportunity.[24] The conversion of the American people to internationlism by 1945 derived from a number of other factors as well, among them the decline of the traditional European powers, the prominence of the American contribution to victory, and the support given the idea by President Roosevelt. The relative influence of each factor is problematic. Yet, given the FPA's reputation as an authoritative source of information about foreign affairs as well as the vitality of its wartime programs, the association's contribution to changing the climate of public opinion was probably considerable.

Thus, the war became the pivotal episode in the FPA's institutional life, the moment for which it had been created. That fact adds interest to the association's selection of McCoy to lead it through the war years. When McCoy accepted the FPA presidency in 1939, the demise of isolationism was by no means certain. Indeed, at that moment, a vigorous amalgam of isolationist and antiwar sentiment animated a large part of public opinion. Given that the FPA was anxious to preserve its reputation of remaining above the partisan battle, one might have expected the organization to shun any identification with soldiers whose background supposedly stamped them collectively as warmongers and interventionists. The association would not have engaged McCoy if such an appointment risked saddling the FPA with the image of being led by an American Colonel Blimp. The FPA clearly expected that McCoy's reputation would enhance its own stature. McCoy's partnership with the FPA further illustrates American willingness to permit soldiers a broad field of participation in foreign affairs.

On several occasions, the war interrupted McCoy's routine as FPA president. Although of little consequence individually, brief mention of these instances will provide an appreciation of the scope of his wartime activities. Beginning in December 1939, McCoy participated in the CFR's War and Peace Studies Project. Funded by the Rockefeller Foundation and including leaders such as

John Foster Dulles, A. Whitney Griswold, William Langer, James Shotwell, and Hanson Baldwin, the project undertook studies intended to provide the State Department with long-term projections on issues stemming from the war.[25]

Early 1941 found McCoy on a 28,000-mile junket around Latin America, entirely by air. This expedition had two sponsors: the State Department's coordinator of commercial and cultural relations between the American republics, Nelson A. Rockefeller; and the Inter-American Escadrille, a private group promoting the expansion of aviation in Latin America. The escadrille's directors included Allen W. Dulles, Laurence S. Rockefeller, James P. Warburg, and James R. Angell, president emeritus of Yale. Nelson Rockefeller's office defrayed the expedition's operating expenses; his brother Laurence provided the twin-engine amphibious aircraft that McCoy used.

The rationale for the trip, which carried McCoy to the principal capitals of Central and South America, combined economics and security. One objective was to improve the access of U.S. airlines and aircraft manufacturers to Latin America. As McCoy noted upon his return, "At the end of the war the United States will have a vast airplane productive capacity . . . [and] an almost unlimited supply of trained operating, maintenance, and manufacturing personnel." Full use of that capacity would require new peacetime markets. McCoy's survey convinced him that the postwar development of private and commercial flying in South America would be enormous. It only remained to insure that the main direction and impetus for that development were from the United States rather than from Europe. By publicizing American technology in talks with aviation ministry officials and businessmen, McCoy's mission was a step in that direction. Yet his careful coordination with American military attachés in embassies and legations along with the interest he expressed throughout the trip in airfield construction suggests a second objective as well. By 1941, the United States had become increasingly concerned about the Axis threat to South America. A prerequisite for American assistance in the event of an attack on Latin America would be air facilities available for rapid conversion to military use. McCoy's mission assessed conditions relating to that problem as well.[26]

In 1940, in a gesture of bipartisanship, President Roosevelt recalled Henry L. Stimson to governmental service as secretary of war. George C. Marshall, now the army chief of staff, immediately telephoned McCoy for advice on how to get along with the new secretary. Once back in office, Stimson revived his practice of calling on McCoy for counsel. During the war years, the secretary consulted McCoy on matters such as the promotion of general officers, the suitability of Joseph W. Stilwell to command American forces in China, and the type of military government that the United States should establish in occupied territories. He also tried to bring McCoy into the War Department on a full-time basis as director of the draft. This attempt failed when FDR appointed Lewis B. Hershey instead. Despite this setback, McCoy's connections in the War Department did provide other opportunities for service.[27]

The first such opportunity followed the Japanese bombing of Pearl Harbor on December 7, 1941. Hoping to pre-empt any prolonged controversy over responsibility for the disaster, President Roosevelt in mid-December established a commission to investigate the attack. Known as the Roberts Commission after its chairman, Supreme Court Justice Owen J. Roberts, the group was predominantly a military body composed of four senior officers: Adm. William H. Standley and Adm. Joseph M. Reeves, both retired; Brig. Gen. Joseph M. McNarney of the Army Air Corps; and McCoy. Although the commission's members were well known as men of integrity and professional competence, they were hardly the sort to dig too deeply into the conduct of their superiors, especially when there was a war to be won. It was natural for McCoy, for example, to be more concerned with supporting his friends Stimson and Marshall than with second-guessing their conduct at such a crucial time. There is no evidence to suggest that the Roberts Commission was told in advance what verdict to deliver, but its members undoubtedly realized that a large part of their role was to demonstrate appropriately decisive corrective action as a way of limiting any political damage that Pearl Harbor may have caused. Certainly, the administration was expecting such a report. It was also counting on the personal credentials of the commission's members to win acceptance of their findings and thereby prevent questions about Pearl Harbor from undermining either the nation's commitment to the war effort or its confidence in the administration.[28] However much they might try to approach their task with an open mind, Roberts and his military colleagues did not undertake the investigation without some opinions already formed. Certainly this was true in McCoy's case. The day after the Pearl Harbor attack he told a friend that responsibility for the tragedy was "not even a debatable question, that the Navy [had] failed to make good and must shoulder the blame." McCoy's professional training inclined him to look to the commander in the field as the one obliged to bear the brunt of responsibility for defeat.[29]

Beginning its work in Washington on December 18, the commission initially took nonverbatim, unsworn testimony from senior Navy and War Department officers, McCoy's friends Stimson and Marshall among them. Having completed these interviews, the commission immediately departed for the west coast and Hawaii. By December 22, Roberts and his associates had established themselves at Honolulu's Royal Hawaiian Hotel. They remained there for two-and-a-half weeks, diligently conducting their inquiry. With instructions to confine its investigation to negligence on the part of military personnel directly involved, the commission focused its attention on errors made in Hawaii rather than any that may have been made in the nation's capital. In the process, the commissioners examined some 3,000 pages of documents and interviewed 127 witnesses who generated 1,887 typewritten pages of testimony. On January 9, the last witness stepped down. A day later, the commission took off for San Francisco, eventually arriving back in Washington on January 15. After recalling several officials for additional testimony, the five commissioners signed the finished report on January 23. Justice Roberts presented it to President Roosevelt the next day.[30] The report that FDR received and soon released to the public reached precisely the conclusions for which the administration had hoped. It explicitly exonerated senior officials in Washington; the commission assigned the onus of responsibility for the tragedy to the commanders on the scene. In particular, the Roberts Report cited Adm. Husband E. Kimmel and Lt. Gen. Walter C. Short—both already relieved—for dereliction of duty.

Initial public reaction to the commission's findings was quite favorable. As Stimson remarked with satisfaction, although "Congress and the press are showing signs of going through a ghost hunt . . . and the isolationists are beginning to take up that cry in Congress, . . . the report met virtually all such trails." Administration leaders took particular encouragement from the favorable editorial treatment that the report received. The *New York Sun* applauded it as "masterly in form and lucid in its findings." The *New York Times* complimented the investigators on a "remarkably candid, thorough and able document." Yet the *Times* also registered a significant reservation, wondering whether Roberts and his coauthors may not have been "too sweeping in exculpating their superiors in Washington from blame."[31] Despite the general approval that initially greeted the commission's efforts, doubt soon spread. Acceptance of the Roberts Report as the authoritative explanation of the Pearl Harbor disaster was short-lived. Of more immediate interest to the administration, the political value of the report in deflecting attention from its own responsibility for Pearl Harbor soon declined. Unresolved questions of cause and culpability dogged the administration throughout the war.[32]

McCoy's next foray into government service was more successful. It began on June 27, 1942, when J. Edgar Hoover, director of the Federal Bureau of Investigation (FBI), announced the capture of eight Nazi saboteurs along the Florida and Long Island coasts. Acting on a Justice Department recommendation, President Roosevelt directed the army to determine the fate of the captives. On July 2, the president signed an order creating a military commission of eight general officers to try the prisoners. Roosevelt recalled McCoy to active duty to preside as the commission's president.[33] No one doubted the outcome of the proceedings. The elaborate preparations for the trial reflected the administration's desire to maintain even in wartime the appearance of due process. As the government candidly noted, given that "enemies caught behind the lines without uniform need not be tried at all," the proceedings of the military commission were "merely a matter of grace . . . , in recognition of our own respect for democratic procedures." Similarly, Stimson noted in his diary that the trial was designed to demonstrate that "there is no railroading of the defendants to their death and no star chamber."[34]

Less agreement existed with regard to how McCoy would carry out his charge. Attorney General Francis Biddle, who headed the government's team of

*The military commission presiding at the trial of the Nazi saboteurs, 1942. To McCoy's left is Maj. Gen. Blanton Winship; to his right are Maj. Gen. Walter G. Grant, Maj. Gen. L. Gasser, and Brig. Gen. John T. Lewis. (Courtesy U.S. Army Military History Institute)*

prosecutors, wanted maximum publicity given to the proceedings. Likewise, J. Edgar Hoover, who planned to attend the trial to "assist" Biddle, hoped to exploit the saboteurs to garner publicity for the FBI. Allied with Biddle and Hoover was the chief of the Office of War Information (OWI), Elmer Davis. As head of the federal government's domestic propaganda agency, Davis intended to use the trial to give Americans a minor but welcome success against Germany. In contrast, the War Department's concern was to insure that the proceedings revealed no information that could adversely affect national security. Stimson, therefore, asked McCoy to minimize the publicity given the trial. To the distress of the press and the OWI, McCoy responded to Stimson's guidance by barring from the courtroom all but the actual participants in the trial.[35]

McCoy's decision touched off a brief bureaucratic skirmish. Davis complained to the president, who called Stimson over to the White House to confer on the matter. At FDR's urging, Stimson promised that McCoy would at least issue periodic communiqués describing the progress made in the courtroom. But Davis's victory was a hollow one. Although McCoy began releasing statements to the press, they were so enigmatic that, according to one newspaper, they "barely went beyond the admission that the trial was being held." For all practical purposes, the commission carried on in virtual secrecy, much to the irritation of Biddle, Hoover, and Davis.[36]

The results of the trial were foreordained. Permitting a standard of evidence that McCoy acknowledged was "far more flexible . . . than prevails in ordinary criminal trials or in courts-martial," the commission found the eight defendants guilty. Stimson was pleased with the outcome and praised McCoy for setting an important precedent for the "protection of the national interests against dangerous and subversive attacks." Although in a letter to Col. Robert McCormick, publisher of the *Chicago Tribune*, McCoy commented on "the more or less star chamber" character of the trial, he was speaking in terms of peacetime standards. In war, of necessity, results outweighed methods in such matters, and McCoy delivered the desired results. Two of the convicted saboteurs received long prison terms; the remaining six, whom McCoy sentenced to death, were electrocuted on August 8, 1942. A rough sort of justice had been done.[37]

# 12

# The Far Eastern Commission

To contemporary observers, the Axis collapse of 1945 marked the beginning of a new historical epoch. World War II destroyed the prewar balance of power. The struggle that laid waste to Germany and Japan also exhausted Great Britain, France, and China among the nominal victors. Although the Soviet Union's vast resources left it in somewhat better shape, that nation, too, faced the long and arduous task of repairing the devastation suffered at the hands of the Third Reich. Only the United States emerged from the war intact. Indeed, the war enhanced American power many times over. American economic and military supremacy—the latter resting largely on a monopoly of atomic weapons— appeared unassailable. This realization of American potential at the expense of the declining traditional powers had important diplomatic consequences. The end of the war offered the United States that second chance for which groups such as the Foreign Policy Association had labored. As George F. Kennan remarked, it now seemed inevitable that the American people would shoulder "the responsibilities of moral and political leadership that history plainly intended them to bear." To many Americans, the opportunity to reclaim the legacy of Woodrow Wilson and create a new world order seemed theirs for the asking. In short, Henry Luce's promised American Century was at hand.[1]

With the destiny of mankind thus apparently in the balance, the United States in 1945 set out to incorporate American notions of how the world should operate into a new structure of international relations. The results of this effort—the United Nations, the Bretton Woods Agreement, and the various allied diplomatic councils and occupation authorities—were intended to blend distinctly American political and economic values with the Wilsonian ideal of international coopera- tion. A brand of leadership that prescribed specific norms while simultaneously inviting cooperative multilateral control promised to be difficult at best. As events would show, few Americans were inclined to concede that the interests of other nations might legitimately differ from those of the United States. When differences arose, Americans typically attributed them to obstinacy, wrongheadedness, or the willful desire to undermine world peace. Reluctant to see its vision of a better world frustrated, the United States replied to such opposition by resorting to unilateral action—all without dropping a syllable of its professed devotion to international cooperation. In this way, in the late 1940s, the United States usually achieved its ends, but at a cost of damaging any hope for genuine international harmony.

We most often associate the demise of postwar harmony with the rise of Soviet-American hostility and the onset of the Cold War. For the past forty years, no other phenomenon has approached the Cold War in its overriding significance for world affairs. But the Soviet Union was not the only nation that bridled at the U.S. assertion of global leadership. Nor does the Cold War provide the sole example of how the American response to such opposition contributed to international disharmony. In the Far East, for example, World War II left in its wake widespread economic dislocation, surging nationalism, and renewed civil war in China. Of greater importance than any of these to the United States, however, was Japan and the policies to be pursued in occupying, reforming, and rehabilitating this former enemy. Given its predominant contribution to victory in the Pacific, the United States expected to assume primary direction of occupation policies in Japan. Yet the other nations that had fought Japan—China, Great Britain, the Philippines, Australia, and New Zealand, in particular—also insisted upon a voice in the occupation. The professed American commitment to international cooperation made it difficult for the United States to ignore these claims altogether. But combining American control with allied participation in occupied Japan would prove workable only so long as allied interests coincided with those of the United States. In practice, such an identity of interests never existed. The subsequent American response to allied independence regarding Japan illustrates an important contradiction of postwar U.S. policy. From his vantage point at the nexus of that contradiction, Frank McCoy labored for four years to find some common ground between the United States and allied positions regarding Japan. His failure provided a frustrating and in some ways ignominious denouement to his career.

Preliminary jockeying for control of postwar Japan began during the war; however, not until August 1945 did the allies seriously attempt to reach an agreement on the issue. At that time, the United States proposed to the other members of the Big Four that the nations actively engaged in hostilities against Japan should form a Far Eastern Advisory Commission (FEAC) to oversee the occupation. With this device, the United States hoped to satisfy its allies by offering them an honorific role in the occupation while retaining real control for itself. The operative word in the commission's title was *Advisory*. Charged with making recommendations regarding the policies and principles that would guide the occupation, the FEAC would exercise no real authority. Given the commission's purely advisory character, the American proposal received a cool reception. Among the great powers, only China offered unequivocal support. Britain applauded the concept of an allied commission for Japan but objected to the limited powers envisioned for it by the United States. The Soviets, too, anticipated that the FEAC would be impotent and refused to join. The lesser allies—Australia, Canada, France, India, the Netherlands, New Zealand, and the Philippines—accepted invitations to sit on the commission. Yet they, too, objected not only to the weakness of its charter but also to the Big Four's failure to consult them in formulating the commission.[2]

Frank McCoy's connection with these events began with a telephone call from Secretary of State James F. Byrnes on October 9, 1945. Byrnes said that President Harry S Truman wanted to know if McCoy was available to represent the United States on the FEAC. Accepting the position would require McCoy to give up his post as president of the Foreign Policy Association and leave the comfortable life that he and Frances enjoyed in New York. Still, the offer was an attractive one: Neither hungry for power nor craving a return to the limelight, McCoy yearned at seventy-one to contribute to this new age of international relations. Disqualified by age from active service in the war just ended, he remained in spirit young enough—in his way, idealistic enough—to be excited by even a modest role in shaping the postwar world. The scope of the task at hand—the expectation that the United States would lead its allies toward a global order based on the values for which they had fought—gave the prospect added appeal. Nor was McCoy inclined to renounce his long-standing principle of acceding to presidential requests for his services. Without hesitation, he accepted.[3]

McCoy took up his new duties in time to attend the FEAC's opening session in Washington on October 30, where he listened to Byrnes reiterate the American promise of cooperation and joint action in dealings with other nations. With the lesser powers feeling slighted, the British rejecting the commission's terms of reference, and the Soviets absent altogether, the FEAC seemed ill-suited to redeem the secretary's pledge.[4] At the commission's second meeting, the delegates unanimously chose McCoy to serve as permanent chairman, an acknowledgment of American primacy in the Far East. From the beginning of his tenure, however, McCoy found himself caught between the conflicting views of the commission's role held by his own government and by the other member nations. The commission's effectiveness would depend largely on McCoy's ability to align the two views.[5]

From the outset, McCoy recognized the deficiencies of the FEAC. The United States would be naive to expect its allies long to support arrangements that bestowed the appearance of collective indorsement upon actions stemming in fact from unilateral American decisions. Soviet refusal to join the FEAC constituted a second, equally serious flaw. The commission's deliberations, remarked McCoy to a friend, were like "a play without Hamlet when Russia is absent from the table." So, to his own government, McCoy advocated a policy of broadening allied participation in the occupation, thereby giving substance to American promises of international cooperation. In a memorandum written prior to the FEAC's first meeting, McCoy cautioned Secretary Byrnes that "unless further steps are taken to meet the desires of our Allies there is serious doubt as to whether the commission will be able to function satisfactorily." To remedy the FEAC's inadequacies, he proposed that the commission be given power to formulate policies, principles, and standards to govern the occupation of Japan instead of merely making recommendations. In conjunction with this change of responsibilities, McCoy suggested that the word *Advisory* in the title of the commission be omitted. And, not least of all, he called for elimination of the veto that the FEAC charter granted to the Big Four powers.[6]

In commission proceedings, however, McCoy found himself obliged to defend the existing FEAC to delegates who soon felt restless and irrelevant. On November 7, Assistant Secretary of War John J. McCloy, just back from Japan, bluntly informed the commission that "Gen[eral Douglas] MacArthur had expressed the view that the FEAC was no concern of his." Given such an attitude on the part of the supreme commander for the allied powers (SCAP), the delegates had difficulty imagining just what any advisory body could accomplish. To make matters worse, the commission found itself unable to get to work due to continuing disagreement over its terms of reference. The allies recognized, of course, that while the FEAC dawdled, the actual occupation was proceeding apace under SCAP's control. The Australian ambassador to the FEAC and to the United States, Herbert V. Evatt, complained that while the commission talked, policy was being put into effect every day. He warned that "the time would come . . . when no Government could remain on such a Commission." In reply, McCoy could only observe that Japan's hasty surrender had required the United States to exercise a certain amount of initiative. He promised that once the FEAC got on its feet, American policies would revert to a more cooperative plane.[7]

Dissatisfaction was thus so great that, virtually as soon as the FEAC came into existence, the allies launched a concerted effort to change it. Two distinct approaches to strengthening the allied character of the occupation soon emerged. The Soviets challenged the practicality of relying on a body located in Washington to supervise events in Tokyo. They advocated the formation of an Allied Control Council in Japan to complement the FEAC by monitoring the day-to-day business of the occupation. Great Britain supported the concept of a Washington-based commission but wanted to provide it with real authority—the British wanted a commission empowered to determine rather than merely recommend occupation policy. Soviet and British unhappiness with existing arrangements undoubtedly carried greater weight in American government circles than did McCoy's own critique. Although loath to see its authority diminished, the United States recognized the need to compromise if it hoped to preserve a semblance of allied unity in Japan.[8]

Negotiations among the three powers produced a solution in time for the December meeting of the Council of Foreign Ministers in Moscow. At first glance, the agreement seemed to contain generous American concessions. In exchange for Soviet membership on the commission in Washington, the United States agreed to the creation in Tokyo of an Allied Council, consisting of representatives from the United States, the USSR, China, and the British Commonwealth. Responding to British criticism, the United States also accepted several changes in the FEAC's terms of reference. Indicative of the commission's new role was a new name—the Far Eastern Commission (FEC). As McCoy suggested, the word *Advisory* was dropped. Furthermore, the foremost prerogative of this new FEC was the authority to formulate the policies, principles, and standards for the conduct of the occupation.[9] Yet upon closer examination, the American concessions lose much of their apparent significance. The Soviet victory in gaining acceptance of an Allied Council in Tokyo was a hollow one. Deletion of the word *control* from the original Soviet proposal signified more than a semantic detail. The Moscow agreement strictly limited the Allied Council to consulting with and advising the supreme commander. The council possessed no authority to overrule or restrain MacArthur, who in any event served as the body's chairman. The council's terms of reference stated explicitly that the supreme commander remained "the sole executive authority for the Allied Powers in Japan." Although it was hoped that MacArthur would consult with the council when "the exigencies of the situation permitt[ed]," he alone would determine whether or not such consultation was appropriate. According to the council's charter, SCAP's decisions upon these matters would be controlling.[10]

Similarly, even though the Council of Foreign Ministers had apparently vested in the FEC ultimate responsibility for making occupation policy, the United States was counting on certain provisions of the Moscow agreement to minimize any real loss of American authority in Japan. First, by requiring the FEC to use the existing chain of command from Washington to Tokyo, the revised terms of reference inserted several layers of American bureaucracy between the commission and MacArthur. Second, the new FEC charter prohibited the commission from issuing instructions directly to SCAP. Rather, the commission was expected to forward its policy decisions to the U.S. government, which would draft and transmit specific implementing directives to MacArthur. Third, the commission could take no action without the approval of the United States because FEC decisions required unanimous American, British, Chinese, and Soviet concurrence. And last, should urgent matters arise not covered by policies already formulated by the commission, the United States unilaterally could issue interim directives with the force of policy. Thus, the United States could circumvent the commission by finding that "urgent matters" existed requiring immediate action.[11] These safeguards preserved the substance of American power in Japan.

Yet in allied eyes, the Moscow agreement created expectations that the FEC would function as a policymaking body. The revised terms of reference seemed to reaffirm the American promise to include the allies in the occupation in a meaningful way. Any subsequent attempt to hamstring the commission by exploiting the loopholes in the FEC charter would appear to be a breach of good faith. As one member of the commission remarked, in such an event, the allies would feel as though they had "been invited to dinner [by the United States] and then given nothing to eat."[12]

Revision of the FEC's charter formed just one part of the effort to salvage allied cooperation in Japan. A cooperative occupation under U.S. control required the support not only of the other Pacific allies but also of the American potentate currently installed in Tokyo. Douglas MacArthur, however, hotly opposed allied involvement in Japan, so, while Byrnes met in Moscow with his British and Soviet counterparts, the FEAC dispatched emissaries to Tokyo to mend fences with SCAP. Accompanied by representatives from each FEAC member nation, McCoy with Frances flew from Washington to Hawaii on December 26, 1945.[13] At Pearl Harbor, the party boarded the U.S.S. *Mount McKinley* for the voyage to Japan, arriving on January 10. McCoy and his colleagues remained in Japan for three weeks, where they met with Japanese officials and "were lectured by General MacArthur and all the members of the occupation staff." According to George H. Blakeslee, serving as he had in Manchuria as McCoy's political adviser, the FEAC's members generally liked what they saw in Japan, though with important reservations. Conceding that "the Occupation authorities are the real government of Japan," the allies still believed that SCAP should make an effort to "consult the Japanese before the issuance of directives." Several commission members also objected to the high priority that MacArthur assigned to political issues at the expense of economic ones. As Blakeslee summarized the commission's views: "The immediate problem is economic. A sane democracy cannot rest on an empty stomach." Failure to meet the essential needs of a jobless and hungry people invited political extremism. Yet, even as it called for attention to Japan's economic problems, the commission insisted that the issue of war reparations be resolved first. Stated simply, a final determination of the resources and facilities that Japan would forfeit seemed necessary before full use could begin of those that the Japanese would retain. Given that several FEAC nations were counting on spoils from Japan to facilitate their own recovery, the allied emphasis on economic issues generally, and reparations specifically, was hardly disinterested.[14]

Allied reservations regarding SCAP were eased by the surprisingly warm reception that MacArthur gave to the commission. In an audience granted on Janaury 30, the general employed his considerable charm to convince McCoy's party that he now "looked upon the relationship between himself . . . and the

*The Far Eastern Advisory Commission arrives in Japan to consult with SCAP, January 1946. Facing McCoy is Sir Carl Berendsen of New Zealand. (Courtesy National Archives)*

Commission as a relationship of a team." MacArthur "spoke feelingly about the international character of his mission" and indicated that he "was deeply conscious of his responsibility to each and every nation participating in the occupation." The supreme commander even expressed enthusiasm for adding allied officers to his staff. Indeed, he promised that "any personnel that might be offered would be more than welcome to him and to his organization." Quite unexpectedly, a sound relationship between SCAP and the commission seemed possible.[15]

In mid-February, the commission returned to Washington, prepared at last to begin catching up with an occupation that began months before. The adoption of revised terms of reference, the addition of a Soviet member, and the opening of new headquarters at the former Japanese embassy on Massachusetts Avenue appeared to herald a real chance for success. Secretary Byrnes reinforced the prevailing sense of optimism at the opening session of the officially redesignated FEC on February 26 by affirming that the United States had "always desired that the control of Japan should become an Allied responsibility." The secretary of state described the commission's conversion to a policymaking group as one of the major accomplishments of the Moscow conference. He told the assembled delegates that "the Terms of Reference agreed to . . . in Moscow placed the final and ultimate responsibility for formulating the policies and principles upon which the peace and security of the Pacific may well be based, in your hands."[16] Yet, by the end of 1946, American policies had destroyed the FEC as an effective body. MacArthur's pledge of cooperation proved meaningless, and the State and War departments chose to take advantage of flaws in the Moscow agreement to paralyze the commission. Although examples abound of how the United States undercut the FEC's position, the issue that was most important in the commission's eyes—the drafting and ratification of a Japanese constitution—provides the best illustration.

The FEC considered its claim of responsibility for constitutional reform to be unassailable. Commission members, including McCoy, believed that in giving the FEC authority to establish basic occupation policies, the Moscow agreement had placed constitutional matters well within the commission's purview. Statements by American officials lent support to that view. In Tokyo, MacArthur told the commission that "the question of constitutional reform . . . had been taken out of his hands by the Moscow Agreement." And in a press conference on March 12, Byrnes promised that "before the Constitution becomes constitutionally effective, it will in some way or other come before the Far Eastern Commission."[17] Despite such assurances, American officials consistently excluded the FEC from constitutional matters. Concerned lest a mature FEC someday impair his own authority, MacArthur concluded that pre-empting the FEC's claim to constitutional reform would enable him to bludgeon the still-frail commission into submission before it acquired real strength. Within five days of his meeting with McCoy and the FEC in Tokyo, MacArthur without fanfare directed his staff to begin writing a new constitution. By early March, senior Japanese officials had approved SCAP's draft. MacArthur immediately and brashly announced that adoption of the draft constitution—which had his full approval—would proceed forthwith. Toward that end, SCAP scheduled the election of a new Japanese Diet on April 10. A top priority of this Diet would be to ratify SCAP's handiwork.[18]

MacArthur's announcement caught the FEC by surprise. Recognizing that SCAP's action threatened to present it with a fait accompli, the commission reacted vigorously. Objections to SCAP's initiative dominated FEC meetings throughout March. Allied members attacked the draft as fundamentally defective. Sir Frederic Eggleston of Australia characterized it as "one of the most sketchy documents that has ever been put forward." The British representative described it as "rather idiotic." The allied members voiced particular criticism of MacArthur's public indorsement of the draft. They feared that SCAP's approval foreclosed the possibility of giving equal consideration to any alternative—such as one the FEC itself might devise. Last, McCoy's colleagues objected to the date set for electing a new Diet. They argued for postponement on two counts: first, to allow the participation of Japanese soldiers still returning from overseas; and second, to permit more time for the Japanese people to assimilate democratic principles. To those who argued—as McCoy was obliged to do—that details such as scheduling elections lay beyond the FEC's competence, Sir Carl Berendsen of New Zealand replied: "I defy anybody confidently to construe the order of reference of this Commission—that remarkable document, that remarkably ambiguous document, that remarkably ill-drafted document. [But] if there is one thing that is clear it is that any matter of policy is within the purview of this commission." He concluded that there could be no matter of policy more important than one relating to providing liberal government for Japan. More was at stake than simply Japan's future political structure. If the FEC permitted SCAP to wrest responsibility for constitutional reform away from the commission, the prospects for any *real* allied participation in the occupation would fade.[19]

McCoy loyally tried to support SCAP. He defended MacArthur's indorsement of the constitution as personal rather than official. He told Berendsen that the FEC was too far removed from events in Japan to concern itself with election dates. Moreover, he suggested, whatever its imperfections, a new Diet would surely be preferable to the one currently sitting—its members had been in office since 1942. Above all, McCoy tried to convince his colleagues that the FEC's prerogatives were secure. "In any case," he promised them, "no Diet can adopt the constitution without [it] being passed on by this commission."[20] McCoy's assurances failed to placate the allies. They insisted upon some collective expression of their displeasure with MacArthur. In addition, they wanted the commission to affirm that "the Far Eastern Commission must be given an opportunity to pass upon the final draft of the Constitution . . . before it is finally approved by the Diet and becomes legally valid." Convinced that such an assertion was within the commission's prerogatives, McCoy supported a motion containing that language. On March 20, the motion passed unanimously. McCoy also concurred with a suggestion to SCAP that he delay the election of the new

Diet. McCoy asked only that he be permitted to draft the message himself to avoid getting MacArthur's "back hair up."[21]

Although respectful to a fault, McCoy's message infuriated the supreme commander. The FEC's impudence in presuming to tell him how to run the occupation was intolerable. MacArthur's reply was abrupt and arrogant. Backhandedly dismissing the FEC, MacArthur began by defining the basis of occupational policy as "the utilization of the Japanese Government to the fullest extent under SCAP supervision and control." Notwithstanding the fact that the election of a new Diet had already been twice delayed, he warned that any postponement would have a profoundly adverse reaction. As for the constitution, MacArthur disclaimed responsibility for that document. He chided the FEC for "laboring under a confusion of thought" in believing that the draft represented the views of any single individual. The supreme commander defended the draft as the work of men from many different groups and many different affiliations. Therefore, he concluded, "my own approval of it will have no slightest effect in any way." In sum, MacArthur rejected the commission's concerns out of hand and would proceed as he had planned.[22]

MacArthur's reply did little to mollify the FEC. The Soviet delegate, Mikolay V. Novikov, termed the response evasive and with Berendsen called for FEC action to suspend the elections. McCoy answered that for the FEC to begin "intervening at every point . . . captiously" would be wrong, especially if doing so might endanger the progress already achieved in Japan. If the FEC had intended to make an issue of the election, it should have done so during its visit to Japan. With the balloting now less than two weeks away, any action was likely to be ill-considered. Reluctantly, the allies went along with McCoy. In fact, they had no alternative. After all, the commission lacked the authority to override MacArthur. The FEC's charter prohibited it from issuing orders, and SCAP proved serenely immune to polite suggestions. The commission's members recognized that their chances of winning a direct confrontation with MacArthur were poor. Certainly the general's nominal superiors in Washington evidenced no inclination to rally behind the FEC. So the commission acquiesced in the election as scheduled.[23]

Despite having lost the skirmish, the FEC did not give up on the issue of constitutional reform. The commission's hopes for effectiveness hinged on its ability to establish a relationship with SCAP based on mutual respect. On one level, general accord existed. None of McCoy's colleagues disagreed with his assertion on March 27 that "ours . . . is a problem of [formulating] broad policy." Nor did they dispute his comment that "General MacArthur is charged with the daily dozen"—that is, with day-to-day implementation. But, in practice, no clear-cut line existed between policy formulation and policy implementation—especially because SCAP had habitually exercised both functions in the months before the FEC's creation. McCoy believed that the commission needed to jump ahead in the policy formulation process by addressing issues as yet untouched by

SCAP. "The only way we can function and do what our terms of reference had given us the power to do," he said, "is to get together on some problems for the future." Concerning relations with MacArthur, McCoy concluded, "We can't expect him to follow our ideas . . . until we lay down some broad policy." Yet McCoy's colleagues believed that MacArthur's action in drafting a constitution— after claiming that the matter was no concern of his—had denied them the chance that was rightfully theirs to make policy in an area of fundamental importance.[24] So the commission resolved to seek a new accord with MacArthur. In early April, the allied members requested McCoy to communicate their concerns to SCAP. The result was two FEC messages sent to MacArthur on April 12, each suggesting ways to improve communications between SCAP and the commission. In a separate personal message to MacArthur, McCoy discussed allied unhappiness more candidly. He outlined the role that the allies expected to play in constitutional reform and concluded that "unless [the] Commission has full opportunity to express itself before final adoption of [the constitution], there is grave danger that it will not be approved by the Commission."[25]

MacArthur's reply to McCoy on April 15 removed any doubts as to his opposition to the FEC. The supreme commander rejected the assumption that the allies were acting in good faith. Rather, FEC intrusion into constitutional questions represented "a planned and concerted attack" on American authority in Japan "under the veneer of diplomacy and comradeship." By insisting that it approve the draft constitution prior to its ratification, "The Far Eastern commission is reversing American policy," MacArthur wrote.

> The purpose underlying such requirement is not clear, but its effect is capable of doing immeasurable harm to the occupation as it will undoubtedly prejudice many Jap[anese] people against the instrument itself who will therefore look upon it as a thing forced upon Japan at the point of Allied bayonets. . . . There can be no free will when the threat of disapproval by the Allied powers overhangs all deliberation, discussion and debate of the constitutional issue.

MacArthur rebuked McCoy for failing to prevent FEC interference in occupation affairs. He concluded with typical bombast: "Appeasements, small as they may seem, rapidly become cumulative to the point of danger. If we lose control of this sphere of influence under this policy of aggressive action [by the FEC], we will not only jeopardize the occupation but hazard the future safety of the United States."[26]

If anyone was "reversing American policy," of course, it was MacArthur, through his implacable hostility to allied participation in the occupation as had been agreed upon at Moscow. American officials were too timid to take issue with the general. In commenting on MacArthur's message, the director of the Office of Far Eastern Affairs, John Carter Vincent, proposed that the State Department straddle the FEC-SCAP dispute, disagreeing with neither side. "Concurrence should be expressed with General MacArthur's general approach," Vincent told Secretary Byrnes, while also "indicating simply, without legalistic argument," that the department supported the FEC's claim to have a say on the constitution. Yet, by making such a distinction, McCoy's reply to MacArthur, revised by Vincent and approved by Byrnes, read like an apology. While telling MacArthur that the constitution would in some way come before the FEC, the message also said that "our view is in full accord with yours that the Commission should take no formal action on a new Constitution" *unless* it failed to meet the criteria of the Potsdam declaration. McCoy concluded with assurances to MacArthur that "I will always protect your flank and rear."[27]

MacArthur had addressed his reply to McCoy personally. Therefore, McCoy was not obliged to reveal its contents to the commission. Indeed, given the cable's insulting tone, he would have been foolish to do so. For several weeks, however, MacArthur did not respond to the FEC's queries of April 12. SCAP's silence provoked further resentment among the allied members, who now felt that MacArthur was simply ignoring them.[28] The allies vented their resentment with new demands for recognition of the commission's right to set the terms for constitutional ratification. McCoy opposed such expressions of assertiveness, fearing that they would reinforce SCAP's view of the FEC as a threat. He deflected a proposal by the Soviet and Indian delegates to use a constituent assembly or plebiscite rather than the Diet as the instrument of ratification. McCoy described the issue as a procedural one and therefore of concern to the Allied Council rather than the FEC. Likewise, McCoy opposed a motion by New Zealand on May 13 declaring that "no Constitution for Japan shall be finally adopted until it has been approved by the Far Eastern Commission." According to McCoy, such a declaration would "prevent us from getting that complete cooperation that I am trying to get" because it called into question promises already made by American officials. Byrnes and MacArthur had publicly stated that the constitution must be approved by the Far Eastern Commission, McCoy told his colleagues; "I can assure you that there is no doubt on the part of the United States or General MacArthur . . . that we have that authority and that the Far Eastern Commission will have to approve the Constitution." McCoy spoke in good faith, but he was promising more than he could deliver.[29]

In part, the FEC's irritation at receiving no reply to the April 12 messages was misdirected. After some prodding, MacArthur had sent the FEC a lengthy cable, routing it according to standard practice through the Joint Chiefs of Staff. In it the supreme commander rejected the FEC proposals and reiterated his views regarding the proper role of the commission. Although milder in tone, the substance of the message followed closely MacArthur's April 15 cable to McCoy. Certainly, SCAP showed no signs of relenting in his determination to deny the FEC a role in constitutional reform: "The Commission could render no better service to the cause of democracy," he wrote, "than to permit the Japanese

Government and people . . . to proceed unshackled, unhindered, and in complete freedom to work out their constitutional reforms, examining the situation only after action thereon has been completed.''[30] Anticipating an adverse FEC reaction, the State-War-Navy Coordinating Committee (SWNCC), the principal coordinator of American foreign and defense policy, suppressed the message. Meanwhile, the allied members continued to press McCoy for a reply from SCAP. Finally, on June 5, the State Department released the text of MacArthur's reply— postdated to June 4 to conceal its delay by SWNCC. As anticipated, its content only angered the allies further. Sir Carl Berendsen spoke for all in predicting the consequences of letting SCAP define the FEC's role: "What we are facing now is nothing less than the continued usefulness and authority of this Commission." He continued: "Here is a Commission set up with the consent of our governments, including the United States Government, given certain powers. It has got to find a means of exercising those powers . . . or it has got to resign itself to the fact that it cannot perform its functions. . . . We cannot go on like this."[31]

The commission was facing, as Berendsen said, a trial of strength between itself and SCAP. It was not a contest to which the FEC looked forward with relish. Nor was it one the commission could hope to win without strong support from the U.S. government. Such support was not forthcoming. Instead, when SWNCC threw its weight into the dispute, it did so by attacking the prerogatives of the FEC's chairman. Before the commission began prying into serious issues, McCoy enjoyed a measure of autonomy. A State Department memorandum of March 2, for example, noted approvingly that, as chairman of an international body, McCoy was not subordinate to any single government. Now that the FEC had become troublesome, however, SWNCC imposed strict controls on McCoy. As a result of a May 7 decision, the FEC's American representative was directly subordinated to SWNCC. Henceforth, the committee would dictate in detail the positions of the American delegation. If the commission balked at an American proposal, McCoy was to shut off discussion and turn to SWNCC for guidance. Furthermore, SWNCC had no sympathy for the FEC's challenge of MacArthur. Therefore, its intervention in FEC affairs only reinforced SCAP's efforts to undermine the commission.[32]

With both SCAP and the American foreign policy apparatus in Washington arrayed against it, the FEC by the summer of 1946 was fighting for survival. The commission's frustration regarding constitutional reform was repeated in numerous other areas: reparations, economic recovery, food supplies, education, agrarian reform, and the return of looted cultural objects. American responsibility for the commission's problems was plain. Citing the arrogance and inflexibilty of American behavior toward the FEC, one dissenter within the State Department complained of the lack of discretion permitted U.S. representatives "who must interrupt negotiation of all issues before the Far Eastern Commission in order to obtain, step by step, approval of the most minute verbal changes from several departments." Such restrictions reduced the negotiator's role to that of "a humiliated clerical stooge." This unwillingness to permit the American delega-tion any latitude reflected Washington's fear of MacArthur and "the habit of measuring all policy controversies in terms of [his] imagined desires, prejudices, and objectives." Adopting SCAP's perspective injected into negotiations "an element of narrow self-interest . . . which corrupts honest discussion of every important policy issue." The American attitude succeeded only in creating "strains, distrust, suspicion and complications" in American relations with the other FEC members.[33]

John Kenneth Galbraith, the noted economist who was then a member of the FEC's American delegation, offered a similarly scathing indictment. The commission's activities, Galbraith wrote, "consist[ed] mostly of laborious debate and either ultimate rubber stamping of pre-existing United States positions or indefinite delay." Attempts to confine FEC jurisdiction to absurdly narrow limits required American representatives "to assert arguments that are casuistical if not phony." Preoccupied with doing nothing to offend SCAP, the United States had "stalled, delayed, or otherwise interfered with [the] efficient functioning of the Commission." Such behavior convinced the allies that the United States had no real interest in their opinions while suggesting an American determination "to assert the same monopolistic influence in Japan that the Soviet Union asserts in Eastern Europe."[34]

Galbraith wanted his government to revitalize the FEC, thereby living up to its commitments at Moscow. The United States found it more convenient to ignore its allies, however, and permit the commission to shamble along, hamstringing it further whenever it threatened to interfere with the occupation. For example, on constitutional reform, the FEC doggedly kept trying to catch up with SCAP, despite the futility that marked its efforts. The newly elected Diet began considering SCAP's constitution on June 20. Two weeks later, the FEC solemnly passed a policy decision mandating the "Basic Principles for a New Japanese Constitution"—as if that document were yet to be written. MacArthur received this FEC decision, blandly announced that the draft constitution conformed in every respect to FEC requirements—a view with which the commission emphati-cally disagreed—and urged Washington to prevent publication of the FEC decision. MacArthur claimed that such a "restrictive and mandatory directive would . . . provoke a revulsion of the Japanese people" against the constitution because it "would instantly become clothed with the taint of Allied force." SWNCC agreed and ordered McCoy to block publication. SCAP could ignore an unpublished decision virtually without penalty, again permitting the United States to frustrate the commission's intent.[35]

By way of a minor victory, the FEC did secure several amendments to the draft constitution, aligning it more closely with the commission's "Basic Principles." But, in conceding to demands for more explicit guarantees of universal suffrage and popular sovereignty—and in rejecting several other commission objec-tions—MacArthur did not overlook the opportunity to attack the FEC yet again.

The commission's attempt "to force perfection in detail," he told the secretary of state on July 26, threatened to "vitiate our very aim and purpose to secure adoption of a constitution which expresses the free will of the Japanese people." As a member of the FEC's American delegation dourly noted, "MacArthur's position of objecting to amendments to the constitution made by the Commission as 'interfering with the will of the Japanese people' was slightly inconsistent with the fact that he himself was responsible for having written the constitution and having handed it to the Japanese Government to enact."[36]

The United States had thwarted the FEC's hopes of either drafting the constitution or determining the method of its ratification. Yet the allied members clung to the provision in the policy decision of March 20 that required the commission to "pass upon" the constitution before it became valid. In July, the United States sought to sap the meaning from even that modest assertion of authority. To the allies, the March 20 policy decision meant that no constitution would go into effect without some positive act of indorsement by the FEC. In avowing American recognition of the commission's right to approve the constitution, McCoy reinforced that view. Now the United States began an effort to narrow even further the commission's role. In what even Blakeslee characterized as an exercise in "Mediaeval casuistry," the U.S. government argued that the new Japanese constitution did not need the formal approval of the FEC in order to become effective. Rather than a positive indorsement, the March 20 policy decision merely required the commission's acquiescence. So long as the commission did not disapprove the constitution, it would go into effect. This distinction was a crucial one. If actual approval were required, a majority of the commission's members or a veto by one of the Big Four could stall ratification. But to have the FEC "pass upon" the constitution through its silence would permit the United States to use the veto to muzzle any attempt to disapprove it.[37]

By early September, after weeks of examining SCAP's draft, the FEC turned to this question: Would it acquiesce in the Diet's ratification of the constitution? Or would it attempt to block ratification and invite yet another confrontation with SCAP and the U.S. government? The most vocal allied members retained serious substantive reservations about the draft. Australia believed that SCAP's constitution still contained several important flaws and labeled the provision renouncing war "somewhat of a joke." The Soviets considered the draft to be inconsistent with both the Potsdam Declaration and the FEC's own "Basic Principles." Great Britain said that there was "no question of [giving the document] positive approval." New Zealand restated its view of the Diet's inadequacy as an instrument of ratification. Despite such reservations, the allied members shied away from forcing the issue through any collective assertion of disapproval. Instead, they indicated a willingness to accept even a defective constitution *on the condition* that the commission be permitted to review it after its promulgation.[38]

By conceding this authority to review the constitution, the United States could purchase the unopposed acceptance of its ratification. The United States promised to pay the allies' price—not now, but later. SWNCC's position, as related by McCoy to the FEC on September 19, was that the commission should postpone any action on the question of review until after the constitution had been promulgated: "Deferment of action, [however, was] entirely without prejudice to the right of the commission to review the constitution at an appropriate time." To demonstrate American sincerity, McCoy on September 21 offered a motion—for discussion rather than immediate action—that affirmed the continuing jurisdiction of the FEC and called for the commission to review the constitution after it had been in effect a full year. The allies accepted this bid as the best they could expect.[39]

The Japanese Diet ratified the constitution on October 7. Consistent with McCoy's promises, the FEC immediately sought to establish its review authority. On October 17, the commission unanimously approved a policy decision identical to McCoy's proposal of September 21. The United States then exasperated its allies by announcing that it would not publish the decision until MacArthur approved it. Only through publication would the Japanese government and people be notified of the commission's review authority—hence the issue's importance to the FEC. MacArthur took advantage of this opportunity to declare his opposition to announcing the decision for at least a year. He then denounced the specter of any review by the FEC as threatening to reduce the constitution from a "genuine expression of the popular will" to a "frail skeleton of temporary expedience overshadowed by the threat of forced abrogation or revision at the point of Allied bayonets."[40]

American refusal to publish the decision of October 17 produced yet another volley of allied protests. As the Australian representative remarked, those nations that "made a condition of our acquiescence in the constitution that this decision should be passed" resented the manner in which the United States had abused their trust. Moreover, MacArthur's "contemptuous language"—in British representative Sir George Sansom's phrase—infuriated the allies. Australia, New Zealand, and India joined Britain in denouncing SCAP's message. Virtually without exception, the allied members agreed that MacArthur's reply was "weak in its argument and insulting in its tone." Privately, McCoy confessed that he was inclined to agree with this interpretation. By way of apology for the message's bluntness, McCoy explained lamely that MacArthur's response "had actually been addressed to the Joint Chiefs of Staff and this accounted for its somewhat peremptory tone."[41]

Frank McCoy possessed to a high degree the soldier's virtue—and limitation—of obedience. Over the course of fifty years of service, he fulfilled his responsibilities as an agent of American foreign policy with diligence and dependability. During the summer and fall of 1946, he loyally supported SCAP and his government in their attempts to protect American interests in Japan—even though the effort required the emasculation of the commission he headed. His loyalty was not, however, without personal cost. McCoy's duties required him to assist in perverting the Moscow agreement, to renege on commitments made to his colleagues, and to subject himself to their scorn. By the end of 1946, he had had enough.

McCoy broke ranks over the issue of implementing legislation. Putting the constitution into effect would require the Diet to enact a series of measures dealing with everything from judicial organization and a criminal code to human rights and financial regulations. As early as September, the FEC had indicated its interest in examining such legislation to insure its consistency with the Potsdam Declaration and the commission's policies. McCoy agreed that the commission possessed the authority to exercise such oversight and notified the State Department of his position. Nothing more was said of the matter until November when, with the constitution ratified, the Diet began to consider the means of implementation. The War Department instructed MacArthur to provide the FEC with copies of the draft legislation before the Diet. MacArthur ignored the order. When allied members began badgering their chairman to produce the drafts, McCoy was left once more to make excuses. When McCoy subsequently asked that the War Department prod MacArthur into compliance, the department's Civil Affairs Division suggested instead "that the United States try to dodge its prior commitment and try to keep the commission from sticking its nose into implementing legislation." McCoy protested that such a policy would keep the commission out of what took place in Japan until it had been passed. He continued: "This was what General MacArthur had tried to do with respect to the Constitution, and it had put the U.S. members of the Commission in a very embarrassing position. . . . The Commission was charged with making policy and General MacArthur ought to remember that fact." The following month, McCoy presented his case in a letter to Assistant Secretary of State John H. Hilldring, the State Department member of SWNCC. McCoy argued that to deny the FEC the authority to review implementing legislation "would challenge its rights . . . and needlessly irritate the members of the Commission." McCoy's responsibility was to make the FEC function as a successful organization. He could do so only by fostering a spirit of cooperation between the FEC and the United States: "It would embarrass General McCoy to be forced to take a position contrary to the strongly held views of most of the other members of the Far Eastern Commission on an issue which the commission is convinced involves its rights . . . and it would hamper him in his efforts to maintain cordial relations within the Commission."[42]

McCoy's appeal produced no results. MacArthur continued to ignore the commission's requests for drafts of the legislation. By the end of December, reports reached the commission that the Diet was enacting implementing measures. The inevitable blowup in the FEC occurred on January 2, 1947, with Sir Carl Berendsen leading the way. "Mr. Chairman," he began, this is the last, and so far as I am concerned the word is accurate, the last of a lengthy series of instances in which successive attempts by the Far Eastern Commission to exercise . . . its functions have been stultified. . . . I am making no criticism of General MacArthur. . . . Indeed, I cannot believe . . . that what have . . . appeared to be deliverate [*sic*] discourtesies have indeed been intended to be such. . . . [Yet] it was unquestionably known to the Supreme Command that the Commission . . . considered itself, rightly or wrongly, to be concerned with the text of the implementing legislation. And this was not the view of one or two members of the Commission, perhaps ignorant or ill-advised—it was the unanimous view of the whole Commission, including the representative of the United States.

Now the Diet had begun passing the measures without the FEC ever having seen them, "leaving to the Commission no option but to accept the situation as it is or . . . to embark upon the much more difficult task" of persuading the Diet to alter legislation already enacted.[43] After the New Zealander concluded, the Australian delegate observed that Berendsen's "disquiet is shared by every member around this table today. The Commission has made known from the very beginning of its existence its interest in the constitution and in the implementing legislation." He assured McCoy that MacArthur had little "to worry about in referring things to the Commission. We are not here to snipe at him." But, he concluded, "we do want the right to participate in the formulation of policy in Japan." Sympathizing with his colleagues, McCoy made no reply.[44]

By the end of 1946, MacArthur had won his trial of strength with the FEC. It had been no contest. Although several of the commission's members refused to accept the verdict, further resistance was ineffective. Henceforth, the United States dropped all pretense of treating the commission with seriousness. For example, when the commission demanded publication of its policy decision on reviewing the constitution, the United States agreed in March 1947 to publish it everywhere but in Japan, the only place where it mattered. When the FEC in 1948 indicated its determination to reexamine the constitution anyway, the United States announced that it would permit such a review only if conducted "as inconspicuously as possible and with a minimum of debate." The United States refused to entertain the notion that such a review might actually change the constitution. The commission's impotence with regard to the constitution continued to be matched in other areas in which it took an interest. When the FEC, contrary to American wishes, attempted to raise a new issue, SWNCC simply refused to provide McCoy with an American position on the matter. As a result, items languished on the commission's agenda for months without action. When the United States did want the commission to act, it was merely to indorse American proposals without amendment. But American officials soon lost patience with the FEC's cumbersome method of reaching decisions. Vowing, in the words of the secretary of war, that the United States would no "longer be balked by the FEC," SWNCC began attaching an ultimatum to each position paper sent to the commission. The United States gave the FEC a period of time, usually twenty-one days, to adopt an American proposal as a policy decision. Otherwise, the United States would issue it unilaterally as an interim directive.[45]

For its part, the commission continued to hold weekly meetings, circulate memoranda, and even make "decisions." But by 1947 an air of unreality permeated its undertakings. The FEC's most notable achievement of that year was to adopt the "Basic Post-Surrender Policy for Japan" on June 19. In Blakeslee's retrospective view, this decision ranked among the commission's "most important." In fact, it signified only a belated and meaningless acceptance of principles that the United States had been unilaterally applying to Japan for nearly two years. As Berendsen remarked, the commission invited the derision of public opinion in passing a measure that events had long overtaken. Even McCoy admitted that its passage would serve historical purposes and little else. The Americans would have been happy to dissolve the FEC and be done with it. But scrapping the commission required unanimous concurrence of the veto powers and such consent was not forthcoming. As a next best solution, one State Department official in 1948 suggested that the commission be packed off to Tokyo. Chief among the benefits expected from such a move was that "an end would be put to the existence of several hundred government officials whose role and primary responsibility in Washington has been to keep some activity going in the Far Eastern Commission." But SCAP opposed the idea, so the commission remained where it was.[46]

As he had over the issue of constitutional review, McCoy continued to serve as an advocate for the FEC to his own government—though with negligible effect. He protested, for example, American misuse of so-called interim directives. Continued use of this method to circumvent the FEC, he told Hilldring, "would antagonize the other states on the Far Eastern Commission . . . and above all . . . would be inconsistent with a basic policy of the United States and my own instructions: to support the principle of International Cooperation." McCoy admitted that a multilateral body "normally reaches its conclusions more slowly than does a single state." Such delay, he believed, was the price that any state must pay for the recognized advantages of a policy of international cooperation. Moreover, American criticism of delay in the FEC was especially inappropriate given the American tactic of intentionally withholding policy papers from the commission for months at a time. This practice caused repeated postponements of matters before the commission. At the other extreme, McCoy cited instances in which the FEC had responded promptly to American requests that it adopt a measure "as a matter of urgent importance," only to have SCAP neglect to implement the policy.[47] McCoy's appeal had no effect. By the autumn of 1947, the attachment of deadlines to American proposals in the FEC had become standard practice. By the end of the year, SWNCC had gone a step further, deciding that, in the absence of an FEC policy decision, MacArthur possessed the "authority to make the necessary policy decision himself and take appropriate implementing action thereon."[48]

This increasing boldness of American efforts to bypass the FEC in 1947 and 1948 matched the hardening of U.S. attitudes toward the Soviet Union. Still pursuing the goal of international cooperation, McCoy failed to appreciate the Cold War's impact on American diplomacy. Although he sensed that his government's lack of support for the commission by 1947 stemmed in part from "the belief that the Russians took an intransigent and uncooperative attitude in the FEC," he insisted that such a belief was unwarranted. In fact, he said, "the Australians and New Zealanders had been more difficult on the Commission than had the Russians." According to Blakeslee, throughout 1946 and 1947, the Soviets behaved in a "surprisingly cooperative and conciliatory fashion." In March 1948, one American on the FEC staff could still defend the commission as a valuable forum for showing the Soviets that "they have more to gain by sitting down and negotiating their differences with us . . . than by proceeding entirely on their own." The unifying theme of McCoy's chairmanship, he wrote, had always been "the assumption that international cooperation is essential, and that agreement with the Russians is not only desirable but possible." A full year after the promulgation of the Truman Doctrine had committed the United States to combating the spread of communism, such sentiments betrayed the extent to which Americans on the FEC had lost touch with the current premises of American foreign policy.[49]

American absorption with the Cold War insured the failure of McCoy's attempts throughout 1948 and 1949 to revive international cooperation by reminding his government of its obligations under the Moscow agreement. In May 1948, McCoy took his case directly to George C. Marshall, now secretary of state. McCoy assured his old friend that "until recently the active Soviet member [had] appeared anxious to cooperate with other delegations." It was only after the United States initiated a more unilateral policy in regard to Japan that the Soviets became increasingly critical of SCAP and the United States. "The problem of the United States in the Far Eastern Commission," he continued, "is not the Soviet Union, but the other nine states whose general friendship it is to our interest to maintain." American inflexibility, intentional obstruction of the commission's work, unilateral shifts in basic policy, and, above all, SCAP's penchant for exceeding his legal authority all eroded that friendship. McCoy suggested a number of proposals to salvage the situation: to submit new basic policy problems regarding Japan to the FEC in accordance with the terms of reference; to annul the apparent decision to encourage SCAP whenever possible to take independent action; to refrain from using interim directives; and, generally, to adopt a more cooperative attitude toward the FEC, showing "a willingness to give reasonable consideration to the views of the other states."[50]

However much Marshall may have sympathized with McCoy's plight, the State Department that he headed had little interest in fuzzy notions of international harmony in the Pacific. To be sure, the department sought solidarity, but it was the ideologically charged solidarity of American-led resistance to expanding Soviet influence. The accelerated revival of the Japanese economy formed an essential component of that effort, aimed at converting Japan into a Western-aligned bulwark of anticommunism. This goal required that real authority over occupation policy reside in Washington, not in Tokyo where MacArthur's whimsical reformist agenda reflected his own political ambitions as much as it did any rigorous strategic vision. So Marshall's more assertive State Department set about wresting control of occupation policy from SCAP. Yet, if this initiative represented an important shift in American policy, it did not imply State Department support for a more muscular FEC. On the contrary: To the extent that MacArthur's nominal subordination to the allies created opportunities for him to play off his own government against the commission, policymakers in Washington were determined to keep the FEC weak.[51]

Not surprisingly, therefore, Marshall was willing to respond to only part of McCoy's critique, promising to eliminate delays in stating U.S. positions on matters pending before the FEC. Yet even Marshall's intervention had no effect. Six months later the commission was still waiting for numerous papers that the United States had promised from fourteen to twenty-three months earlier. The American attitude regarding the "Concentration of Economic Power in Japan" illustrates the problem. The commission waited from August 1946 to May 1947 for an initial statement of American views on this subject. Shortly after the FEC received that statement, the American position changed and the American delegation withdrew the paper and suspended negotiations, pending submission of a revised version. The United States promised the new version by October 1947. A year later, the FEC was still waiting for it. Eventually, in November 1948, the United States rewarded the commission's patience by announcing that it had no intention of giving its views on economic concentration until the FEC demonstrated why any paper on the subject was actually necessary.[52]

In January 1949, McCoy brought the FEC's problems to the attention of yet another secretary of state, Dean Acheson. McCoy prefaced his memorandum for Acheson by quoting at length the president's State of the Union message of January 5. "Our guiding star," Truman said, "is the principle of international cooperation. To this concept we have made a national commitment as profound as anything in history. To it we have pledged our resources and our honor." With that as background, McCoy recounted the FEC's demise, which he attributed to American "delays in submitting policy papers . . . , delays in reaching [U.S.] positions on papers pending in the Commission . . . [and] delays due to a change in [U.S.] policy." American obstructionism had convinced the allies that the United States was not acting in good faith, preferring instead to "carry out important measures in Japan under SCAP's . . . authority without regard for the

Far Eastern Commission which has the right to formulate policy." McCoy objected to such cavalier treatment, arguing that the United States was legally and morally bound to support the FEC. Criticizing U.S. attempts to coerce the commission, McCoy pointed out that the FEC's charter did not "warrant the United States Government assuming or demanding that the Commission should adopt a policy introduced by the United States. The other states have not only rights under the Terms of Reference but often . . . have national interests involved." In the FEC, as in other international organizations, therefore, "discussion, compromise, [and] agreement" should guide American conduct. McCoy called for increased American flexibility and cooperation, a "policy of making concessions to our friends on minor matters in order to advance a major objective: gaining their cordial support in the critical situation in the Far East."[53]

Although conceding the accuracy of McCoy's diagnosis of the FEC's failure, the State Department dismissed it as irrelevant. No one would, of course, wish to quarrel with the principle of international cooperation, wrote Assistant Secretary of State Charles E. Saltzman in summarizing McCoy's memorandum for Acheson. Saltzman admitted that the United States had disrupted the efficient functioning of the commission (though he placed most of the blame on MacArthur and the army). Yet he insisted that these were peripheral issues. More important was the fact that "General McCoy takes inadequate account of the extent to which circumstances have changed since 1946 and early 1947." Since then, he continued, "the Soviet Union has adopted an open policy of world aggression, [using even] the FEC as a propaganda sounding board to attack the United States' policies in Japan and elsewhere." In response to this threat, the Truman administration "adopted a policy of firm resistance to Soviet aggression, a policy which must be applied in the FEC as at all other points where U.S. and Soviet interests meet." As part of that resistance, the United States decided to rebuild Japan, converting its former enemy into the linchpin of its anticommunist strategy in the Pacific. As Saltzman noted, this decision had been made without consulting the allies of the United States, many of whom opposed it vehemently. For this reason, he wrote, "the time would seem to have come for [the FEC] to restrict its policy-making activities so as to permit the Japanese to proceed in their own way with the implementation and assimilation of the measures already directed." With the onset of the Cold War, in other words, the FEC lost its usefulness as a vehicle for sharing responsibility and fostering international harmony. Henceforth, the commission could be of use only as a minor propaganda outlet. American diplomats would not negotiate but merely debate with their adversaries. According to Saltzman, the United States should stand up to the Soviet Union in the commission "even at the cost of contributing to U.S.-U.S.S.R. friction."[54]

By January 1949, while Harry Truman proclaimed his nation's dedication to international cooperation, State Department officials were blaming the Soviet

Union for the absence of American cooperation in international councils. Yet the attempt to explain American unilateralism as a product of the Cold War is unconvincing. Since the establishment of the FEC, the United States had systematically undermined the commission. Before the Cold War began, American policy toward the FEC helped destroy any chance for harmony in the Pacific, however slight that chance may have been. Forced to choose between honoring its promises to its allies and implementing its own design for Japan, the United States without hesitation chose the latter. As chairman of the commission, McCoy bore his share of responsibility for the FEC's failure. McCoy had hoped for a policy of genuine cooperation that would permit the FEC a meaningful role in formulating occupation policy. Yet, when MacArthur's ego demanded that the United States strip the FEC of any real authority, McCoy acted as his government's instrument in that effort. Too late, he sought to reverse course, arguing that the benefits of cooperation outweighed the short-term advantage of unilateralism. By that time, however, senior American officials had embraced the logic of the Cold War. Obsessed by their contest with the Soviet Union, they viewed Wilsonian ideals as naive and sentimental. Hence, they ignored McCoy's appeals and dismissed McCoy himself as an old man who failed to grasp the realities of the postwar world.

# 13

# The End of the Day

By 1949, the Far Eastern Commission had become moribund. Its chairman was a seventy-five-year-old man whose declining health interfered with his duties with growing regularity. These circumstances prompted McCoy to retire from public life once and for all. Effective the last day of November 1949—fully a half-century since he had joined Leonard Wood's staff in Cuba—McCoy resigned as FEC chairman and chief American delegate. In recognition of McCoy's service, the State Department presented him with its Superior Service Award.[1] Despite nagging medical problems, McCoy enjoyed an active and productive retirement. After leaving the FEC, he and Frances remained at 1633 31st Street N.W., in a house acquired when they had moved to Washington in 1945. It was the first house that McCoy's peripatetic career permitted them to own. The retired soldier and diplomat busied himself with a variety of projects. Membership in the Philippine Club of New York, of which he was a former president, offered opportunity for reminiscing about the days of empire with old cronies such as Cameron Forbes and Peter Bowditch. As honorary chairman of the American Leprosy Foundation, formerly the Leonard Wood Memorial, he took an active interest in the campaign to alleviate the effects of the disease that had been Wood's great personal cause. McCoy devoted most of his energies to the Theodore Roosevelt Memorial Association. After becoming the organization's president in 1951, he led the effort to purchase and donate to the people of the United States an island in the Potomac River to be maintained as a natural preserve in Roosevelt's memory. He also laid the groundwork for the purchase of Sagamore Hill, Roosevelt's home at Oyster Bay, as a memorial to him. McCoy followed with satisfaction the continuing success of younger comrades such as Matthew Ridgway, now a four-star general. He may even have felt a certain vindication when Ridgway became supreme commander in the Far East in April 1951, following MacArthur's relief by President Truman. (From Tokyo, Ridgway graciously wrote his old mentor: "Through all my efforts runs the unfailing inspiration of your guidance and leadership through the years."[2])

In 1953, McCoy made a final jaunt from home, spending a leisurely vacation in Honduras. By the end of the year, his health had deteriorated considerably. For several months, he was either hospitalized or confined to his home with what doctors had diagnosed as leukemia. Finally, on June 4, 1954, he died at Walter Reed Army Hospital. At funeral services conducted on June 8, George C. Marshall and Ridgway, now army chief of staff, led two squads of pallbearers from the post chapel at Fort Myer, Virginia, to nearby Arlington National Cemetery. There McCoy was laid to rest on a knoll overlooking the deceased veterans of the Spanish-American War—just a few feet from the gravesite of Leonard Wood.[3]

In an editorial published after his death, the *New York Times* praised McCoy as an "outstandingly brilliant" public servant who had been "one of the best soldiers this country has produced." Reviewing McCoy's career, the *Times* concluded that "military terms are far too restricted to describe his unusual service to his nation." What qualities earned McCoy such accolades? Despite the *Times*'s assertion of his brilliance, McCoy was not an exceptionally gifted man. Although able and intelligent, he possessed neither imagination nor critical insight, especially when it came to viewing with detachment the men and institutions to which he devoted his life. An appraisal by Sir George Sansom comes closer to the mark. "He was a man of no great intellect," the British diplomat and scholar remarked of McCoy, "but he had character—so much more important than intellect." Chief among the attributes of that character were a sense of duty, unimpeachable personal integrity, and loyalty to those whom he served. Although often partisan, he was no ideologue. His strongest attachments were to the army, the nation, and cherished associates such as Theodore Roosevelt, Wood, and Stimson rather than to any particular body of thought. McCoy's own views changed frequently, reflecting the temper of the day or the assumptions of the reigning political leadership. This remained the case whether those assumptions reflected turn-of-the-century Anglo-Saxonism, Wilsonian idealism, or the cautious collective security of Henry Stimson. Only after World War II did McCoy find himself out of step, espousing international cooperation while the Truman administration was girding itself for the Cold War.[4]

This malleability helps to explain McCoy's usefulness to divergent national administrations. To implement policy, political leaders want reliable agents, not free thinkers. To his masters, McCoy time and again demonstrated his ability to serve with competence, discretion, and self-effacing loyalty. This last quality deserves special emphasis. As a military professional, McCoy understood the need for discipline in any complex undertaking. Even when he disagreed with

American policy, as during his years with the FEC, he would not permit his own opinions to override his obligation to support his superiors. McCoy refused to engage in bureaucratic obstructionism, media leaks, or public protest. When pushed into the unfamiliar role of dissenter, he presented his objections quietly, respectfully, and hence, on the whole, ineffectively.

Given this country's tradition of civilian control of the military, McCoy's superiors had every reason to expect such obedience from a professional soldier. Rather than assuming, therefore, that McCoy made himself useful as an agent of American foreign policy *despite* being a soldier, we may well conclude that he did so *because* of that fact. McCoy understood authority and respected its pre-rogatives. However delicate, obscure, or ambiguous an assignment, McCoy's masters could depend on him to carry it out. He was free from the most common disabilities of public officials of our own day. He catered to no special interests. He entertained no ambitions for elective office and so felt no obsessive concern for his "image." He was no publicity monger—exposure in the press benefited his ego only slightly and his career not at all. And last, he did not view public service as a means to enrich himself.[5]

As a personality, McCoy displayed none of the flamboyance of MacArthur or Wood. Unlike Pershing or Marshall, he never exercised great wartime responsibilities. Lacking intellectual originality, he left no legacy comparable to Billy Mitchell's theory of air power. And so, despite the generous praise that marked his passing, McCoy was soon forgotten—even as his friends and associates were being elevated into the pantheon of American military heroes. This was to be expected. Theodore Roosevelt was supposed to have remarked once that "Frank McCoy is the best soldier I ever laid eyes on." One can agree with TR that McCoy was in many ways an extraordinary soldier. But weighing his achievements against his limitations, Frank McCoy was not a great man.[6]

Even if McCoy himself merits only a narrow place in history, the implications of his career deserve scholarly consideration. McCoy's ties to civilian elites and his frequent ventures outside the traditional military realm call into question commonly held assumptions about the fabric of American civil-military relations. The interaction of civilian and military elites that McCoy's career illustrates suggests a reality more complex than most scholars acknowledge in portraying the pre-1940 military establishment as isolated and alienated. Such a conclusion does not dispute the existence of popular suspicion of the military in McCoy's day. Nor does it take issue with the notion that the average soldier of the pre-1940 era felt neglected. Yet, if historians should not discount altogether the concept of an isolated military, neither should they overstate it. To be sure, throughout McCoy's life, many Americans, from religious leaders to intellectuals, arrayed themselves against the encroachments of militarism. At the same time, important segments of the governing elite found military views compatible with their own and came to see military men as useful instruments of policy. As far back as the Spanish-American War, the shrewdest and most talented members of the officer corps exploited this sympathy to great advantage. By aligning themselves with helpful civilian allies, they advanced their own careers and gained a chance to play a broader role in public life. By joining Leonard Wood's circle in Cuba, McCoy secured his entry into this select group. His subsequent career in colonial government and diplomacy testifies to the opportunities available to members of this military elite. His friendship with like-minded political leaders, diplomats, businessmen, and journalists illustrates the bonds linking the civilian elite to their military brethren.

McCoy's recurring participation in foreign policy challenges the contention that civilian leaders before 1940 neglected to consult military officers on diplomatic issues. Instead, lacking bureaucratic mechanisms for coordinating policy with the army and navy, civilian officials routinely sought the counsel of individual officers whom they held in high regard. Friendship, not position in the hierarchy, sustained this informal channel of civil-military coordination, as the relationship between McCoy and Stimson suggests. Thus, in the evolution of American civil-military coordination, McCoy stands as a transitional figure. With others, he bridged the gap between the negligible coordination that characterized nineteenth-century policy formulation and the elaborate apparatus and ritualized procedures that have piled up since World War II.[7]

The willingness with which McCoy embraced this role disproves the theory that soldiers believed that their military status precluded them from involvement in making national policy. Well-connected members of the military elite—building on the tradition of politicized soldiers such as Wood and responding to the encouragement of civilians such as Theodore Roosevelt—refused to accept officership as a bar to participation in the debate over broad national issues. Rather, they welcomed opportunities to contribute to the formulation and implementation of policy, thereby insuring that the military's perspective on a variety of issues received a hearing.

Called upon to act as a partner—albeit a junior one—in shaping and executing American foreign policy, Frank McCoy appeared repeatedly outside the narrow domain to which soldiers were ostensibly restricted, serving his country in causes great and small, admirable and unworthy. Combined with the careers of such military contemporaries as Leonard Wood, Tasker Bliss, and James G. Harbord, an appreciation of McCoy's life makes it impossible to confine the military strictly to the battlefields of the American past. A persuasive interpretation of the professional soldier's role in American history must concede him a place in both war and peace. If seldom genuinely popular or decisively influential, leading military professionals did operate comfortably within the main currents of national life, thereby leaving a small but distinctive imprint on the events of their time.

Tucked within the quiet of Memorial Church in Harvard Yard hangs a gilded tablet honoring a once renowned Harvard graduate. Among the chapel's tokens of remembrance, the tablet is neither prominent nor today much noticed. Yet it represents an unusual tribute: Apart from Leonard Wood, the other sons of Harvard commemorated in the chapel gave their lives in wartime service to their country. Installed in happy remembrance of Wood by McCoy and others of the general's aides, the tablet impresses the present-day visitor as unusual for other reasons as well. The very setting seems anachronistic. For a great secular university to concede to God real estate that might otherwise support a laboratory or lecture hall suggests a throwback to a departed era. Nor, one imagines, does Harvard any longer celebrate as especially exemplary the ideals that lead dutiful young men to die doing the bidding of the state.

Above all, the inscription on this small memorial renders it a curiosity. The words are quaint, and the values they signify seem naive and almost embarrassingly unsophisticated. Yet the words depict their subject as he would want to be remembered, honoring him as

Soldier
Saver of Lives
Lover of Manly Sport
Restorer of Provinces Abroad
Forger of Sword and Shield
at Home

One can imagine McCoy, to whom eloquence never came easily, laboring over these phrases, determined in this simple testimonial to capture the essence of the man whom he had served so long and loved so dearly. If, in the end, the inscription recalls the essential Wood, it evokes something of his era as well: its robust and expansive spirit; its presumptuous idealism somehow combining benevolence with paternalism; its confidence in American righteousness; its ill-concealed, even unabashed bellicosity.

The tumultuous events of more recent times have rendered obsolete many of the values that animated Wood and that McCoy shared. Our differing outlook would not surprise McCoy because his own life and experience encompassed profound changes. McCoy never claimed to be other than a man of his own time; he would insist, therefore, that later generations judge him by the standards to which he himself had subscribed. It would have pleased him to think that words written to honor Wood might also serve as his own epitaph.

# Notes

## PREFACE

1. Stephen E. Ambrose, "An Overview," in *The Military and American Society,* ed. by Stephen E. Ambrose and James A. Barber, Jr. (New York, 1972), p. 3; Richard C. Brown, "Social Attitudes of American Generals, 1898–1940" (Ph.D. dissertation, University of Wisconsin, 1951), p. 268; Samuel P. Huntington, *The Soldier and the State* (New York, 1957), pp. 226–228; William A. Ganoe, *The History of the United States Army* (reprint ed., Ashton, Md., 1964), passim; Walter Millis, Harvey C. Mansfield, and Harold Stein, *Arms and the State* (New York, 1958), p. 21; Burton M. Sapin and Richard C. Snyder, *The Role of the Military in American Foreign Policy* (Garden City, N.Y., 1954), pp. 2–3; Emory Upton, *The Military Policy of the United States* (reprint ed., Washington, D.C., 1917), passim. The quotation is from W. T. R. Fox, "The Military and United States Foreign Policy," *International Journal* 38 (Winter 1982–1983): 42.

2. See, for example, Richard D. Challener, *Admirals, Generals, and American Foreign Policy, 1898–1914* (Princeton, N.J., 1973); John Morgan Gates, "The Alleged Isolation of U.S. Army Officers in the Late 19th Century," *Parameters* 10 (September 1980): 32–45; Peter Karsten, "Armed Progressives: The Military Reorganizes for the American Century," *Building the Organizational Society,* ed. by Jerry Israel (New York, 1972), pp. 197–232; Richard H. Kohn, *Eagle and Sword: The Beginnings of the Military Establishment in America* (New York, 1975); Paul A. C. Koistinen, *The Military-Industrial Complex in Historical Perspective* (New York, 1980); Jack C. Lane, "American Military Past: The Need for New Approaches," *Military Affairs* 41 (October 1977): 109–113.

## CHAPTER 1
## THE ROAD TO KETTLE HILL

1. Graduation speech, June 1892, Box 9, Frank Ross McCoy Papers, Library of Congress; hereafter cited as McCoy Papers.

2. "My Friend McCoy," anonymous memoir, Box 100, McCoy Papers; William S. Biddle, *Major General Frank Ross McCoy: Soldier-Statesman-American* (Lewistown, Pa.: n.p., 1956); McCoy file, Association of Graduates, U.S. Military Academy, West Point, N.Y.

3. "Physical Record of Cadet Frank R. McCoy," March 4, 1893, 58071, U.S., War Department, "Records of the Adjutant General," Record Group 94, National Archives; hereafter cited as RG 94, NA.

4. Walter Scott Dillard, "The United States Military Academy, 1865-1900: The Uncertain Years" (Ph.D. dissertation, University of Washington, 1972), pp. vi-ix.

5. Prof. Samuel E. Tillman, quoted in Roger Hurless Nye, "The United States Military Academy in an Era of Educational Reform, 1900-1925" (Ph.D. dissertation, Columbia University, 1968), p. 33; Charles W. Larned, *Education from a Military Viewpoint* (Manlius, N.Y., 1908); idem, "The Genius of West Point," in *The Centennial of the United States Military Academy at West Point, New York* (Washington, D.C., 1904), p. 475. Also see Nye, "United States Military Academy," pp. 18-19.

6. Memorandum for the chief of staff, November 6, 1913, Box 13, McCoy Papers; *Official Register of the Officers and Cadets of the U.S. Military Academy* (West Point, N.Y., 1894-1897); U.S. Military Academy, Class of 1897, *The Howitzer* (Philadelphia, 1897), pp. 22, 66-67, 79-80, 107; idem, *Commemoration of the 25th Anniversary of Graduation* (West Point, N.Y., 1922), p. 256; Archives of the United States Military Academy, series 102 (Registers of Cadet Delinquencies), vol. 31, Class of 1897; scrapbook, Box 92, McCoy Papers.

7. Newspaper clippings, Box 92, McCoy Papers.

8. McCoy to family, August 27 and 30, 1893, Box 3, McCoy Papers.

9. "Physical Record of Cadet Frank R. McCoy," June 8, 1897, 58071, RG 94, NA.

10. McCoy to family, undated and May 9, 1898, Box 3, McCoy Papers. McCoy did not question the racist assumptions of his day. Unfortunately, his correspondence only hints at his feelings toward the black enlisted men with whom he served. Those feelings were probably ambivalent, combining a certainty of his men's racial inferiority with a respect owed them as brave and loyal soldiers. A white officer might feel affection for his black subordinates, but he also believed that their status as inferiors was unalterable. After the Spanish-American War had ended, McCoy accompanied the Buffalo Soldiers to a new station at Fort Clarke, Texas. Along the way, the regiment's train stopped in a small Texas town to permit the troops to eat. After the stop, McCoy reported, some of the town's "patriotic white citizens fired into our car as we were pulling out but our black troopers hugged the floor and never answered a word or a shot." He was obviously proud of their self-restraint. Even the regiment's officers "felt like turning them loose," he added, but did not. The behavior of the white Texans was outrageous; such were the indignities that black soldiers were expected to endure. McCoy to family, undated, Box 5, McCoy Papers.

11. John Bigelow, Jr., *Reminiscences of the Santiago Campaign* (New York, 1899), pp. 12, 24-25, 36-40, 50; McCoy to family, June 7, 1898, Box 3, McCoy Papers.

12. T. G. Steward, *The Colored Regulars* (Philadelphia, 1904), pp. 116-117.

13. McCoy to family, July 16, 1898, Box 5, McCoy Papers; Frank Freidel, *The Splendid Little War* (Boston, 1958), p. 83; "General McCoy's Graphic Story of Cuba Fight," *Chicago Sunday Tribune,* April 25, 1948, Box 101, McCoy Papers,

14. McCoy to family, June 24 and 30, 1898, Box 3, McCoy Papers; Herbert H. Sargent, *The Campaign of Santiago de Cuba,* 3 vols. (Chicago, 1907), 2: 56-63; Bigelow, *Reminiscences,* pp. 90-91; Edward L. N. Glass, ed., *The History of the Tenth Cavalry, 1866-1921* (reprint ed., Fort Collins, Colo., 1972), p. 33.

15. Bigelow, *Reminiscences,* pp. 93-102; McCoy to family, undated and June 30, 1898, Box 3, McCoy Papers.

16. Sargent, *Campaign of Santiago,* 2: 93-96.

17. Glass, *Tenth Cavalry*, pp. 33-34, 113; Steward, *Colored Regulars*, pp. 194, 264; *Chicago Sunday Tribune*, April 25, 1948, Box 101, McCoy Papers.

18. *Chicago Sunday Tribune*, April 25, 1948, Box 101, McCoy Papers; Hermann Hagedorn, *Leonard Wood: A Biography*, 2 vols. (New York, 1931), 1: 178.

19. *Chicago Sunday Tribune*, April 25, 1948, Box 101, McCoy Papers; McCoy to family, July 6, 1898, Box 3, McCoy Papers.

## CHAPTER 2
## IN CUBA WITH WOOD

1. Hagedorn to McCoy, October 23, 1928, Box 21, Frank Ross McCoy Papers, Library of Congress; hereafter cited as McCoy Papers. The references are to Leonard Wood, military governor of Cuba, 1899-1902; McCoy; Matthew Elting Hanna, who redesigned Cuba's school system under Wood's direction; and Frank Steinhart, Wood's chief clerk and later consul general in Havana.

2. McCoy to Maj. John A. Johnston, February 7, 1899, 221948, U.S., War Department, "Records of the Adjutant General," Record Group 94, National Archives [hereafter cited as RG 94, NA]; Johnston to McCoy, February 19, 1899, Box 9, McCoy Papers.

3. McCoy to family, May 30 and June 8, 1899, Box 3, McCoy Papers.

4. David F. Healy, *The United States in Cuba, 1898-1902* (Madison, Wis., 1963), pp. 87, 97, 106, 186-187; William Harding Carter, *The Life of Lieutenant General Chaffee* (Chicago, 1917), p. 172; Leonard Wood, "The Military Government of Cuba," *The Annals of the American Academy of Political and Social Sciences* 21 (January 1903): 182; Jack C. Lane, *Armed Progressive: General Leonard Wood* (San Rafael, Calif., 1978), pp. 102-108.

5. U.S., War Department, *Report of the Military Governor of Cuba on Civil Affairs, 1900* (Washington, D.C., 1901), pp. 8, 11-12, 16, 34-35, 78, 94-95 [hereafter cited as *Civil Report, 1900*].

6. Leonard Wood, "The Existing Conditions and Needs in Cuba," *North American Review* 168 (May 1899): 593.

7. John Kendrick Bangs, *Uncle Sam Trustee* (New York, 1902), p. 193; Hermann Hagedorn, *Leonard Wood: A Biography*, 2 vols. (New York, 1931), 1: 275-276.

8. McCoy's father had died in July 1899. McCoy went briefly to Lewistown to handle family affairs and returned to Cuba by August. McCoy to family, January 31, 1900, Box 3, McCoy Papers.

9. Hagedorn, *Wood*, 1: 276.

10. Hagedorn interviews with McCoy, May 19, 1929, and undated, Box 17, Hermann Hagedorn Papers, Library of Congress; hereafter cited as Hagedorn Papers.

11. McCoy to family, April 1901, Box 3, McCoy Papers. Wood assigned McCoy the responsibility of keeping Alice Roosevelt out of mischief during her visit to Cuba (see Alice Roosevelt Longworth, *Crowded Hours* [New York, 1933], p. 52).

12. "Report of Frank R. McCoy," appended to *Civil Report, 1900*, p. 163.

13. "Report of Frank R. McCoy," pp. 158, 163.

14. "Report of Frank R. McCoy," pp. 157, 160, 162.

15. Carlton Beals, *The Crime of Cuba* (Philadelphia, 1933), p. 172; Philip S. Foner, *The Spanish-Cuban-American War and the Birth of American Imperialism, 1895-1902*, 2 vols. (New York, 1972), 2: 458-459, 461, 466-483. To Foner and others, of course, the ultimate beneficiary that Wood had in mind for these improvements was not Cuba itself but the American businessman. Wood's purpose in fostering a stable, efficient order in Cuba, according to this view, was to service the needs of American capital so that the end of the military occupation would leave the island a well-run American dependency. For those

such as James Hitchman who view Wood more sympathetically, the true aim of the occupation was simply "to prepare Cuba for nationhood." Seen in this light, the reforms of the Wood era were "the necessary educational, judicial, governmental and economic means to perpetuate a republic." James H. Hitchman, *Leonard Wood and Cuban Independence, 1899-1902* (The Hague, 1971), p. 212.

16. Howard Gillette, Jr., "The Military Occupation of Cuba, 1899-1902: Workshop for American Progressivism," *American Quarterly* 25 (October 1973): 410-425.

17. Hagedorn interview with McCoy, October 10, 1929, Box 16, Hagedorn Papers.

18. "Report of Frank R. McCoy," p. 164.

19. Hagedorn interview with McCoy, May 19, 1929, Box 16, Hagedorn Papers; McCoy to John Kendrick Bangs, February 18, 1902, Box 9, McCoy Papers. Bangs was a journalist sympathetic to Wood whom McCoy assisted in preparing a favorable account of the occupation. His book, *Uncle Sam Trustee* (New York, 1902), is dedicated to Wood and McCoy.

20. McCoy to family, May 1902, Box 3, McCoy Papers.

21. Hagedorn, *Wood,* 1: 392; Hugh Lenox Scott, *Some Memories of a Soldier* (New York, 1928), p. 233; Hagedorn interview with McCoy, December 6, 1929, Box 16, Hagedorn Papers.

## CHAPTER 3
## PACIFYING THE MOROS

1. Hugh Lenox Scott, *Some Memories of a Soldier,* (New York, 1928), p. 273. For the events surrounding Wood's selection as a regular army brigadier general, see Jack C. Lane, *Armed Progressive: General Leonard Wood* (San Rafael, Calif., 1978), pp. 114-116.

2. McCoy to family, August 18 and 29, 1902, Box 3, Frank Ross McCoy Papers, Library of Congress; hereafter cited as McCoy Papers.

3. McCoy to family, September 7, September 21, and October 19, 1902, Box 3, McCoy Papers. For British views of Wood's Cuban service, see Hermann Hagedorn, *Leonard Wood: A Biography,* 2 vols. (New York, 1931), 1: 374-375, 400; Scott, *Memories,* p. 270.

4. McCoy to family, October 19, 1902, Box 3, McCoy Papers.

5. McCoy to family, September 7, 1902, Box 3, McCoy Papers.

6. McCoy to family, September 21, 1902, Box 3, McCoy Papers; Lawrence F. Abbott interview with McCoy, December 28, 1927, Box 192, Leonard Wood Diary and Papers, Library of Congress [hereafter cited as Wood Papers].

7. McCoy to family, September 21, 1902, Box 3, McCoy Papers.

8. McCoy, "Stories of Roosevelt," June 1919, Box 84, McCoy Papers; McCoy to family, undated [1903], Box 3, McCoy Papers; William S. Biddle, *Major General Frank Ross McCoy: Soldier-Statesman-American* (Lewistown, Pa.: n.p., 1956). For an account of Roosevelt's duels with Wood, see Hagedorn, *Wood,* 1: 401-403.

9. Hagedorn, *Wood,* 1: 404-406; Lane, *Armed Progressive,* p. 118; McCoy to family, undated [1903], Box 3, McCoy Papers; Wayne Wray Thompson, "Governors of the Moro Province: Wood, Bliss, and Pershing in the Southern Philippines, 1903-1913" (Ph.D. dissertation, University of California at San Diego, 1975), p. 7.

10. McCoy to family, April 1903, Box 3, McCoy Papers.

11. McCoy to family, April 6 and May 8, 1903, Box 3, McCoy Papers.

12. McCoy to family, May 28 and June 1, 1903, Box 3, McCoy Papers.

13. McCoy to family, undated [June 1903], Box 3, McCoy Papers.

14. McCoy to family, June 24, 1903, Box 3, McCoy Papers.

15. McCoy to family, June 28, 1903, Box 3, McCoy Papers.

16. McCoy to family, July 13, 1903, Box 4, McCoy Papers.

17. McCoy to family, undated [1903], Box 3, McCoy Papers; Thompson, "Governors," pp. 1-4; George William Jornacion, "The Time of the Eagles: United States Army Officers and the Pacification of the Philippine Moros, 1899-1913" (Ph.D. dissertation, University of Maine at Orono, 1973), pp. 37-44. The Moro Province did not include all of Mindanao. Northern portions of the island, predominantly inhabited by Christian Filipinos, had been organized as separate provinces under civil administration.

18. Jornacion, "Time of Eagles," p. 48. On the Philippine insurrection, see John Morgan Gates, Schoolbooks and Krags (Westport, Conn. 1973).

19. Jornacion, "Time of Eagles," pp. 48-50; Thompson, "Governors," p. 29; Hagedorn interview with McCoy, June 7, 1929, Box 18, Hermann Hagedorn Papers, Library of Congress; hereafter cited as Hagedorn Papers. The Bates Agreement is reprinted as U.S., Congress, Senate, Treaty with the Sultan of Sulu, S. Doc. 136, 56th Cong., 1st sess., pp. 26-27. Peter Gordon Gowing, Mandate in Moroland: The American Government of Muslim Filipinos, 1899-1920 (Quezon City, Philippines, 1977), p. 36, states that the Moros viewed the pact as "inviolable" unless dissolved by mutual agreement.

20. William H. Taft, "Report of the Civil Governor of the Philippines," U.S., War Department, Report of the Philippine Commission (1903), part 1 (Washington, D.C., 1903), pp. 76-79.

21. For a colorful description of the Moro, see Allan R. Millett, The General: Robert L. Bullard and Officership in the United States Army, 1881-1925 (Westport, Conn., 1975), p. 167; McCoy to Capt. E. L. Munson, October 17, 1903, Box 10, McCoy Papers; McCoy to Charles E. Magoon, October 17, 1903, Box 10, McCoy Papers; McCoy to Edward Carpenter, December 2, 1903, Box 10, McCoy Papers.

22. Jornacion, "Time of Eagles," pp. 56-57, 62; "Report of the Governor of the Moro Province," U.S., War Department, Report of the Philippine Commission (1906), part 1 (Washington, D.C., 1906), p. 351; McCoy to family, August 16, 1903, Box 3, McCoy Papers; McCoy to General John P. Taylor, September 25, 1903, Box 10, McCoy Papers.

23. McCoy to Margaret McKinley, September 8, 1952, Box 56, McCoy Papers. An example of McCoy's racial antipathy is a letter in which he describes his negative feelings toward the Chinese of Mindanao and the Syrian-born provincial superintendent of education by comparing them to Jews (McCoy to family, May 28, 1905, Box 4, McCoy Papers).

24. "Annual Report of the Governor of the Moro province (1903-1904)," Report of the Philippine Commission (1904), part 2 (Washington, D.C., 1904), pp. 578-579. McCoy's recognition of the primacy of restoring order is reflected in a letter to his family, October 15, 1903, Box 3, McCoy Papers.

25. Undated entry headed "Generalizations," in Notebook 3 (June 17, 1904-March 13, 1905), Box 1, McCoy Papers; Wood to Roosevelt, August 3, 1903, cited in Hagedorn, Wood, 2: 5.

26. "Annual Report of the Governor of the Moro Province (1903-1904)" pp. 577, 582; McCoy to family, October 15, 1903, Box 3, McCoy Papers.

27. Jornacion, "Time of Eagles," p. 58; "Annual Report of the Governor of the Moro Province (1903-1904)," p. 574. Act 8, outlawing slavery in the Moro Province, is reprinted in Report of the Philippine Commission (1903), part 1, exhibit S, p. 484. McCoy to family, October 15, 1903, Box 3, McCoy Papers.

28. Scott, Memories, p. 325; McCoy to Carpenter, December 2, 1903, Box 10, McCoy Papers.

29. Millett, The General, p. 178; Scott, Memories p. 327; McCoy to Carpenter, December 2, 1903, Box 10, McCoy Papers. Emphasis added.

30. Leonard Wood Diary, November 25, 1903, Box 3, Wood Papers; "Report of General Wood as to Abrogation of Bates Treaty," Report of the Philippine Commission (1903), part 1, exhibit T, pp. 489-490.

31. "Acts of the Moro Legislature, 1903-1906," Box 216, Wood Papers; Thompson, "Governors," p. 50.

32. McCoy to mother, May 25, 1905, cited in Hagedorn, *Wood*, 2: 55; Thompson, "Governors," pp. 40-44.

33. Hagedorn interview with McCoy, June 7, 1929, Box 18, Hagedorn Papers; Wood to J. St. Loe Strachey, January 6, 1904, cited in Hagedorn, *Wood*, 2: 14; "Report of the Governor of the Moro Province" (1906), pp. 351, 357.

34. McCoy to family, September 2, 1904, Box 3, McCoy Papers; "Report of the Governor of the Moro Province" (1906), pp. 340, 345.

35. Thompson, "Governors," pp. 77-80; Jornacion, "Time of Eagles," pp. 163-164; Gowing, *Mandate*, pp. 108, 143.

36. McCoy to family, November 30, 1903, Box 3, McCoy Papers; Scott, *Memories*, p. 376; "Report of the Governor of the Moro Province" (1906), p. 347; "Report of the Governor of the Moro Province," *Report of the Philippine Commission* (1905), part 1 (Washington, D.C., 1905), p. 345; *Report of the Philippine Commission* (1904), part 1, (Washington, D.C., 1905), p. 10.

37. Gowing, *Mandate*, p. 151.

38. McCoy to family, April 12, 1904, Box 4, McCoy Papers; Notebook 2 (December 11, 1903-June 17, 1904), Box 1, McCoy Papers.

39. McCoy to family, May 6, 1905, Box 1, McCoy Papers.

40. McCoy to family, January 5, 1905, Box 4, McCoy Papers; Wood Diary, April 4 and 7, 1904, Box 3, Wood Papers.

41. James H. Reeves to George T. Langhorne, March 1, 1906, Box 37, Wood Papers.

42. Ibid. The exchange between Wood and Langhorne is quoted by Thompson, "Governors," p. 83.

43. McCoy to family, March 10, 1906, Box 4, McCoy Papers; McCoy interview with Hagedorn, June 7, 1929, Box 22, Hagedorn Papers; see also Hagedorn interview with Stuart Heintzelman, April 2, 1930, Box 22, Hagedorn Papers. Heintzelman, another aide present at Dajo, recalled that "when [Wood] was mentally upset he would be subject to the attacks."

44. McCoy to family, March 10, 1906, Box 4, McCoy Papers; Wood to Andrews, March 9, 1906, Box 11, McCoy Papers.

45. For a summary of press comment on Jolo, see "Killing Women and Children in Jolo," *Literary Digest* 32 (March 24, 1906): 433-434.

46. Wood to War Department, March 13, 1906, Box 37, Wood Papers.

47. Wood to Roosevelt, May 14, 1906, Box 37, Wood Papers.

48. Scott's defense of Wood, solicited by Secretary of War Taft, with endorsements by Taft and Roosevelt is reprinted in U.S., Congress, Senate, *Attack by United States Troops on Mount Dajo*, S. Doc. 289, 59th Cong., 1st sess. For a highly colored account, see McCoy to Andrew Peters, September 4, 1914, Box 3, McCoy Papers. Suggestive of the fleeting interest in the incident is that the *Literary Digest* surveyed editorial opinion on the subject only once; the *Reader's Guide to Periodical Literature* contains only four citations on the Bud Dajo—and two are defenses of Wood.

49. McCoy to family, December 3, 1903, Box 3, and March 4, 1904, Box 4, McCoy Papers; John R. White, *Bullets and Bolos* (New York, 1928), pp. 215-217. Saranaya is described in "Annual Report of the Governor of the Moro Province" (1904), pp. 577-578.

50. McCoy to family, May 20 and July 11, 1904, Box 4, and July 17, 1904, Box 3, McCoy Papers.

51. Translation of letter, Ali to Wood, July 14, 1904, Box 4, McCoy Papers. A Filipino official translated the letter from Arabic to Spanish; McCoy further translated it into English (Dispatch Book 5 [June-July 1904], Box 1, McCoy Papers).

52. McCoy to family, December 12, 1904, Box 3, McCoy Papers. Langhorne's comments to Wood are cited by Gowing, *Mandate,* p. 153. Langhorne functioned as acting governor while Wood was in the United States on medical leave. For the importance that the Americans attributed to Ali's elimination, see "Report of the Governor of the Moro Province," *Report of the Philippine Commission* (1906), pp. 343, 352. In it, Wood asserts that in the Cotabato Valley "some 20,000 recognized Datto Ali's authority" and that "his resistance kept the whole valley stirred up."

53. McCoy to military secretary, Department of Mindanao, October 31, 1905, and Buchanan to Wood, May 9, 1906, Box 11, McCoy Papers.

54. McCoy to military secretary, October 31, 1905, Box 11, McCoy Papers.

55. Ibid.

56. Roosevelt to McCoy, January 3, 1906, Box 4, McCoy Papers; *New York Times* [hereafter cited as *NYT*], October 29, 1905; Richard Barry, "The End of Datto Ali," *Colliers,* June 9, 1906, p. 17. Nor was Bud Dajo the last such episode in the Moro pacification. As late as June 1913, Brig. Gen. John J. Pershing, then governor of the province, killed over 500 Moros in an assault on Bud Bagsak on Jolo (see Donald Smythe, *Guerrilla Warrior: The Early Life of John J. Pershing* [New York, 1973], pp. 186-204).

## CHAPTER 4
## AN AVAILABLE AGENT

1. For one testimonial on McCoy's reputation, see Horace Fletcher to McCoy, April 11, 1907, Box 12, Frank Ross McCoy Papers, Library of Congress; hereafter cited as McCoy Papers.

2. McCoy to family, November 21 and 28, 1905, Box 4, McCoy Papers.

3. For the origins of the boycott and diplomatic efforts to resolve it, see Delber L. McKee, *Chinese Exclusion versus the Open Door Policy, 1900-1906* (Detroit, 1977), Chapters 6-9. On Roosevelt's reaction to the Lienchow Massacre, see Howard K. Beale, *Theodore Roosevelt and the Rise of America to World Power* (Baltimore, 1956), pp. 238-242. On American military preparations, see Richard D. Challener, *Admirals, Generals, and American Foreign Policy, 1898-1914* (Princeton, N.J., 1973), pp. 215-218.

4. McCoy to family, December 26, 1905, Box 4, McCoy Papers. The results of McCoy's inspection are his "Notes on Canton," Box 11, McCoy Papers. McCoy recalled the mission in a conversation with Nelson T. Johnson, U.S. minister to China, August 2, 1932, vol. 52, Nelson T. Johnson Papers, Library of Congress.

5. Roosevelt is quoted by Beale, *Roosevelt,* p. 245.

6. McCoy to family, April 17, 1906, Box 4, McCoy Papers; McCoy to military secretary, War Department, Box 11, McCoy Papers; Wood to McCoy, August 22, 1906, Box 37, Leonard Wood Diary and Papers, Library of Congress; hereafter cited as Wood Papers.

7. On the Cuban insurrection, see Allan R. Millett, *The Politics of Intervention: The Military Occupation of Cuba, 1906-1909* (n.p., 1968), Chapters 1 and 2. Steinhart's reports from Havana are reprinted in "Report of William H. Taft, Secretary of War, and Robert Bacon, Assistant Secretary of State, of What Was Done Under the Instructions of the President in Restoring Peace in Cuba," U.S., War Department, *Annual Reports of the Secretary of War, 1906* (Washington, D.C., 1906), pp. 444-447; hereafter cited as Taft-Bacon Report.

8. Ralph Elden Minger, "William Howard Taft and the United States Intervention in Cuba in 1906," *Hispanic American Historical Review* 41 (February 1961): 79.

9. Millett, *Politics,* pp. 148, 151-153; Taft to McCoy, September 24, 1906, Box 12, McCoy Papers.

10. Millett, *Politics,* pp. 93-94.

11. McCoy to Wood, October 18, 1906, Box 37, Wood Papers. McCoy's correspondence with rebel commanders Faustino Guerra, E. Loynaz Del Castillo, and Orestes Ferrera is reprinted in the Taft-Bacon Report, pp. 502-504. On the disarmament of insurgents see Taft-Bacon Report, p. 525, and Taft to General Montero, October 5, 1906, Box 12, McCoy Papers.

12. McCoy to Wood, October 18, 1906, Box 37, Wood Papers. Historians have endorsed McCoy's view of the stakes in the 1906 revolt. Describing the disputing factions, for example, Dana Munro comments that "in general there was little difference in their programs or policies" (Munro, *Intervention and Dollar Diplomacy in the Caribbean, 1900-1921* [Princeton, N.J., 1964], pp. 125-126).

13. McCoy to Mrs. Wood, October 7, 1906, Box 37, Wood Papers; Taft-Bacon Report, pp. 450-451; see also Wood to Steinhart, December 28, 1906, Box 37, and McCoy to Wood, July 14, 1907, Box 39, Wood Papers.

14. McCoy to Wood, October 18, 1906, Box 37, Wood Papers. On Estrada Palma's resignation and the decision to establish a provisional government, see Millett, *Politics,* pp. 96-102.

15. See, for example, the list of participants from the first occupation, dated September 27, 1906, in Box 12, McCoy Papers. It describes the positions occupied by each and identifies those considered especially able. Allan Millett notes that the "striking common denominator" of officers in the provisional government was that "they had been effective administrators in Leonard Wood's Cuban government" (Millett, *Politics,* p. 152). See also the cable from Matthew E. Hanna to McCoy, October 26, 1906, Box 12, McCoy Papers.

16. McCoy to Mrs. Wood, October 7, 1906, Box 37, Wood Papers; Magoon to Taft, October 19, 1906, Box 12, McCoy Papers; McCoy to Wood, October 28, 1906, Box 37, McCoy Papers.

17. McCoy to Wood, November 16, 1906, Box 12, McCoy Papers; McCoy to Wood, July 14, 1907, Box 39, Wood Papers; Lester D. Langley, *The Banana Wars: An Inner History of American Empire, 1900-1934* (Lexington, Ky., 1983), pp. 44-45.

18. J. Franklin Bell to McCoy, November 22, 1906, Box 12, McCoy Papers.

19. McCoy to Magoon, November 28, 1906, Box 12, McCoy Papers.

20. William Phillips, *Ventures in Diplomacy* (Boston, 1952), p. 6.

21. Ibid., pp. 6, 45; see also Martin Weil, *A Pretty Good Club* (New York, 1978), pp. 17-18.

22. William Franklin Sands, *Our Jungle Diplomacy* (Chapel Hill, N.C., 1944), pp. 5-6. On Grew, see his memoir, *Turbulent Era: A Diplomatic Record of Forty Years,* 2 vols. (Boston, 1952), 1:12-13.

23. Waldo H. Heinrichs, Jr., "Bureaucracy and Professionalism in the Development of American Career Diplomacy," *Twentieth Century American Foreign Policy,* ed. by John Braeman, Robert H. Bremner, and David Brody (Columbus, Ohio, 1971), p. 152; Robert D. Schulzinger, *The Making of the Diplomatic Mind* (Middletown, Conn., 1975), p. 111. For examples of Family correspondence, see Boxes 5-7 of the Leland Harrison, Jr., Papers, Library of Congress, which contain numerous exchanges with Henry P. Fletcher, Joseph C. Grew, and James Logan. The Straight-Fletcher correspondence is found in Boxes 3 and 4 of the Henry P. Fletcher Papers, Library of Congress [hereafter cited as Fletcher Papers], and on reels 3-5 of the Willard Straight Papers, Cornell University Archives, Ithaca, New York.

24. While visiting the Roosevelt home at Oyster Bay, for example, McCoy reported a long ride in the morning, followed by chess with Theodore, Jr. Then, in midafternoon, "the President routed me out" for five sets of tennis in a "drizzly rain" (McCoy to family, undated, Box 7, McCoy Papers).

25. Mrs. J. Borden Harriman, *From Pinafores to Politics* (New York, 1923), p. 267; George V. Allen, "Notes on 'The Family,'" in "A History of DACOR," compiled by Richard Fyte Boyce, unpublished manuscript in the possession of the Diplomatic and Consular Officers, Retired (Washington, D.C., n.d.), pp. 98-99.

26. For a complete Family roster, see ibid., pp. 110-112.

27. Straight to Fletcher, March 10, 1916, Box 4, Fletcher Papers.

28. "The Reminiscences of James F. Curtis," Columbia Oral History Collection, Butler Library, Columbia University, New York, pp. 312-313. An early Family member, Curtis was assistant secretary of the Treasury from 1909 to 1913 and deputy governor, Federal Reserve Bank of New York, from 1914 to 1919. William Appleman Williams, *American-Russian Relations, 1781-1947* (reprint ed., New York, 1971), pp. 107, 108, 127.

29. Straight to Fletcher, April 6, April 18, and June 3, 1914, Box 3, Fletcher Papers. Family membership also earned free publicity. When Woodrow Wilson selected Fletcher as ambassador to Mexico, Family journalist George Marvin published an adulatory profile of the appointee, touting him as "a diplomatist of the new order" and claiming that "a better selection could not have been made" ["Henry P. Fletcher," *The World's Work* 31 (January 1916): 443, 450].

30. Untitled memorandum, July 2, 1919, Box 25, McCoy Papers; McCoy to James G. Harbord, January 11, 1923, Box 25, McCoy Papers; McCoy to Roosevelt, undated, Box 57, McCoy Papers; Wood to McCoy, December 13, 1907, Box 39, Wood Papers.

31. Charles E. Magoon, *Report of Provisional Administration, 1908* (Havana, 1909), pp. 135-137; Magoon to Taft, April 8, 1908, Box 12, McCoy Papers.

32. McCoy to family, May 8, 1908, Box 4, McCoy Papers; McCoy to Taft, May 9, 1908, Box 12, McCoy Papers.

33. McCoy to Taft, May 9, 1908, Box 12, McCoy Papers; McCoy to Brig. Gen. Clarence Edwards, Bureau of Insular Affairs, undated [May 1908], Box 10, McCoy Papers; McCoy to Wood, May 8, 1908, Box 43, Wood Papers.

34. Magoon, *Report,* pp. 137-138.

35. McCoy to family, January 1, 1909, January 13, [1909], April 2, 1910, April 10, 1910, Box 5, McCoy Papers; acting adjutant, 3d Cavalry, November 20, 1908, Box 12, McCoy Papers.

36. McCoy's 1909 efficiency report is at 58071, U.S., War Department, "Records of the Adjutant General," Record Group 94, National Archives; [hereafter cited as RG 94, NA].

37. Stimson Diary, "Trip to Arizona and New Mexico in September and October 1911," "Work of the War Department in the Autumn of 1911," "My Chicago Speech," "Army Appropriation Veto," Henry Lewis Stimson Diary and Papers, Yale University (hereafter cited as Stimson Papers); Stimson to McCoy, December 24, 1912, 1993336, RG 94, NA; McCoy to Stimson, December 25, 1912, Box 37, Stimson Papers; Stimson, *My Vacations* (privately printed, 1949), pp. 134-143.

38. James L. Abrahamson, *America Arms for a New Century: The Making of a Great Military Power* (New York, 1981); McCoy to Frankfurter, November 11, 1913, Box 13, McCoy Papers.

39. Ibid. For other views by McCoy on reform see his letter to another preparedness advocate, Theodore Roosevelt, April 19, 1913, Box 13, McCoy Papers. For a discussion of Wood's views see Russell F. Weigley, *Towards an American Army: Military Thought from Washington to Marshall* (New York, 1962), pp. 208-217.

40. Robert Stelark to McCoy, May 25, 1911, Box 13, McCoy Papers. Numerous letters in Box 13 indicate McCoy's role in covert intelligence activities.

41. Wood to Lindley M. Garrison, October 11, 1913, Box 74, McCoy Papers. This memorandum summarizes for the secretary of war the origins of the Atrato question and

Wood's subsequent actions. For background on the "Atrato routes," see Gerstle Mack, *The Land Divided: A History of the Panama Canal and Other Isthmian Canal Projects* (reprint ed., New York, 1974), Chapter 20.

42. Wood Diary, December 20, 1911, Box 6, Wood Papers.

43. Cheney, "Diary," Box 74, McCoy Papers, provides a narrative of the expedition.

44. Ibid.; Cheney to Wood, February 12, 1912, Box 74, McCoy Papers; Cheney to McCoy, "Supplementary Memorandum," February 12, 1912, Box 74, McCoy Papers.

45. Ibid.

## CHAPTER 5
## MEXICO AND THE APPROACH OF WAR

1. Arthur S. Link, *Wilson: The New Freedom* (Princeton, N.J., 1956), p. 347; see also Howard F. Cline, *The United States and Mexico*, rev. ed. (New York, 1976), p. 140.

2. Cline, *United States and Mexico*, pp. 126-128, 130-134.

3. Ibid., pp. 140-151, 155-160, 172-174.

4. McCoy to Borglum, October 2, 1913, Box 13, Frank Ross McCoy Papers, Library of Congress [hereafter cited as McCoy Papers]; McCoy to Scott, March 14, 1914, Box 13, McCoy Papers.

5. Charles H. Harris III and Louis R. Sadler, "The Plan of San Diego and the Mexican-United States War Crisis of 1916: A Reexamination," *Hispanic-American Historical Review* 58 (August 1978): 383-385.

6. McCoy to Stimson, April 1, 1915, Box 48, Henry Lewis Stimson Diary and Papers, Yale University [hereafter cited as Stimson Papers]; McCoy to family, March 15 and August 20, 1915, Box 5, McCoy Papers.

7. McCoy to family, April 1, 1915, Box 5, McCoy Papers.

8. McCoy to family, undated [May 1915], May 24, and June 4, 1915, Box 5, McCoy Papers. Arthur S. Link's comprehensive discussion of the *Lusitania* crisis is found in *Wilson: The Struggle for Neutrality* (Princeton, N.J., 1960), pp. 368-455.

9. McCoy to family, May 24, 1915, Box 5, McCoy Papers; Roosevelt to McCoy, June 22 and July 10, 1915, and July 9, 1916, McCoy to Roosevelt, July 1, 1915, Gordon Johnston to McCoy, June 17, 1915, and McCoy to Johnston, undated, Box 14, McCoy Papers; McCoy to family, August 4, 1916, Box 5, McCoy Papers; Stimson to McCoy, July 19, 1916, and McCoy to Stimson, August 2, 1916, Box 57, Stimson Papers. On Roosevelt's reaction to the *Lusitania*'s sinking, see William Henry Harbaugh, *Power and Responsibility: The Life and Times of Theodore Roosevelt* (New York, 1961), pp. 476-477.

10. McCoy to family, August 20, [1915], Box 15, McCoy Papers; Wood to McCoy, July 9 and October 28, 1915, Box 14, McCoy Papers; Johnston to McCoy, June 17, 1915, Box 14, McCoy Papers; Straight to McCoy, August 21 and 27, 1915, Box 14, McCoy Papers. Plattsburg widened the interaction between civilian and military elites. There, Straight befriended army captains Halstead Dorey and Gordon Johnston, both intimates of McCoy and members of the Wood circle. John Garry Clifford, *The Citizen Soldiers: The Plattsburg Training Camp Movement, 1913-1920* (Lexington, Ky., 1972), p. 67 (n46). In addition, see John Whiteclay Chambers II, *To Raise an Army: The Draft Comes to Modern America* (New York, 1987), pp. 73-101.

11. Straight to McCoy, June 30, 1915, Box 14, McCoy Papers.

12. Harris and Sadler, "Plan of San Diego," pp. 388-390.

13. Ibid., p. 389; McCoy to family, September 5, 1915, Box 5, McCoy Papers.

14. McCoy to family, September 5 and 30, 1915, and September [1915], Box 5, McCoy Papers; "Report of the Secretary of War," U.S., War Department, *Annual Reports of the Secretary of War, 1915*, Part 1 (Washington, D.C., 1916), p. 7. For press reaction to the border raids, see *Literary Digest* 51 (September 18, 1915): 576-578.

15. Croly to McCoy, September 8 and 24, 1915, Box 14, McCoy Papers; "On the Mexican Border," *The New Republic* 4 (October 9, 1915): 256-257. McCoy advocated recognition of Carranza's government as "for the moment the nearest thing to responsibility in Mexico" (McCoy to family, October 10, [1915], Box 5, McCoy Papers).

16. *New York Times*, October 22, 1915; McCoy to family, October 25, 1915, Box 5, McCoy Papers.

17. McCoy to Wood, November 10, 1915, Box 89, Leonard Wood Diary and Papers, Library of Congress [hereafter cited as Wood Papers]; McCoy to family, November 24, 1915, and January 23, March 26, and May 23, 1916, Box 5, McCoy Papers.

18. James Parker, *The Old Army: Memories, 1872-1918* (Philadelphia, 1929), pp. 424-427; McCoy to family, May 23, 1916, Box 5, McCoy Papers.

19. Harris and Sadler, "Plan of San Diego," pp. 399-400; Arthur S. Link, *Wilson: Confusions and Crises* (Princeton, N.J., 1964), pp. 299-301; McCoy to family, June 21, 1916, Box 5, McCoy Papers.

20. "Report of the Chief of Staff," U.S., War Department, *Annual Reports of the Secretary of War, 1915*, Part 1 (Washington, D.C., 1916), p. 190; Parker, *The Old Army*, p. 425.

21. McCoy to family, July 7, 1916, Box 5, McCoy Papers.

22. McCoy to family, July 11 and August 21, 1916, Box 5, McCoy Papers; McCoy to Wood, July 19, 1916, Box 89, Wood Papers; McCoy to Wood, November 3, 1916, Box 14, McCoy Papers.

23. McCoy, *Principles of Military Training* (New York, 1917), pp. 9, 95, 152-160, 175, 364.

24. McCoy to family, November 26, 1916, Box 5, McCoy Papers; Parker, *The Old Army*, p. 426.

25. On Hanna's role in Cuba, see James H. Hitchman, *Leonard Wood and Cuban Independence, 1899-1902* (The Hague, 1971), pp. 51-59. For evidence of Hanna's continued close relations with the Family, see Fletcher to McCoy, November 8, 1921, Box 16, McCoy Papers; Phillips to McCoy, October 25, 1915, Box 14, McCoy Papers; McCoy to family, June 9, 1917, Box 6, McCoy Papers. The Family's intimacy with some of Woodrow Wilson's most vocal opponents did not go unnoticed. As Phillips recorded privately on February 9, 1917: "There was considerable flurry to-day over Fletcher's staff and its Republican flavor. Frank McCoy, being General Wood's right hand man, is assumed by some to be anti-administration; Fletcher is also tainted some people think" (diary entry, William Phillips Papers, Houghton Library, Harvard University).

26. McCoy to family, February 22 and March 16, 1917, Box 6, McCoy Papers.

27. McCoy to Maj. Ralph H. Van Deman, March 14, 1917, 9700-87, U.S., War Department, "Records of the War Department General and Special Staffs," Record Group 165, National Archives; hereafter cited as RG 165, NA. Van Deman was the officer to whom McCoy reported at the War Department.

28. On the Zimmermann Telegram, see Arthur S. Link, *Wilson: Campaigns for Progressivism and Peace* (Princeton, N.J., 1965), pp. 342-346, 353-359, 433-436.

29. File 862.2012, U.S., Department of State, "General Records of the State Department," Record Group 59, National Archives [hereafter cited as RG 59, NA]. This file contains numerous reports of alleged Mexican aid to Germany. See especially Frank L.

Polk to Fletcher, April 24, 1917, 862.2012/332a, and Pershing to War Department, March 29, 1917, 862.2012/165, RG 59, NA; Lansing to Wilson, April 18, 1917, 711.12/43A, RG 59, NA (microfilm series M314, reel 2).

30. McCoy to family, March 27, 1917, Box 6, McCoy Papers; Friedrich Katz, *The Secret War in Mexico: Europe, the United States and the Mexican Revolution* (Chicago, 1981), p. 433.

31. McCoy to Van Deman, undated (received by War Department, April 19, 1917), 9700-93, RG 165, NA; McCoy to Van Deman, April 4, 1917, 9700-91, RG 165, NA.

32. "Memorandum for the Ambassador relative to German Activities in Mexico," May 3, 1917, 862.20212/331 (microfilm series M336, reel 55), RG 59, NA; McCoy to chief of the War College Division, General Staff, May 29, 1917, file 9944-G-1, RG 165, NA; Intelligence Section, War College Division, "Weekly Intelligence Summary," June 9, 1917, in Richard D. Challener, comp., *United States Military Intelligence: Weekly Summaries, June 2– October 13, 1917* (New York, 1978).

33. McCoy to family, May 10, 1917, Box 6, McCoy Papers; Fletcher to Polk, May 22, 1917, Box 4, McCoy Papers; McCoy to family, June 9, 1917, Box 6, McCoy Papers.


CHAPTER 6
WORLD WAR AND ITS AFTERMATH

1. McCoy to Cheney, September 15, 1920, Box 16, Frank Ross McCoy Papers, Library of Congress [hereafter cited as McCoy Papers]; see also McCoy to James G. Harbord, November 14, 1927, James G. Harbord Papers, New York Historical Society.

2. Dwight D. Eisenhower, *At Ease: Stories I Tell to Friends* (Garden City, N.Y., 1967), pp. 136, 147, 151, 155; Matthew B. Ridgway, *Soldier: The Memoirs of Matthew B. Ridgway* (New York, 1956), p. 34; McCoy to family, July 1, 1917, Box 6, McCoy Papers.

3. A full list of the members of the GHQ staff is found in *Order of Battle of the United States Land Forces in the World War: American Expeditionary Forces* (Washington, D.C., 1937), pp. 1–3. The role of the staff is discussed in Edward M. Coffman, *The War to End All Wars* (New York, 1968), pp. 124–127, and in Donald Smythe, *Pershing: General of the Armies* (Bloomington, Ind., 1986), pp. 33–38.

4. McCoy to family, June 21 and December 20, 1917, Box 6, McCoy Papers; Straight to Dorothy Straight, January 2, 1918, reel 6, Willard Straight Papers, Cornell University; Robert Bacon to wife, October 24, 1917, quoted in James Brown Scott, *Robert Bacon: Life and Letters* (Garden City, 1923), p. 308; McCoy to Mrs. Bacon, undated, ibid., pp. 311–312; Stimson Diary, February 15 and April 14, 1918, Henry Lewis Stimson Diary and Papers, Yale University [hereafter cited as Stimson Papers]; James G. Harbord, *Leaves from a War Diary* (New York, 1925), pp. 99, 129–133, 155–160; McCoy to family, September 3, 1917, Box 6, McCoy Papers.

5. McCoy to family, July 1 and October 10, 1917, Box 6, McCoy Papers.

6. Stimson Diary, January 4, 1918, Stimson Papers; McCoy to family, March 25, April 10, and April 12, 1918, Box 6, McCoy Papers.

7. Hugh J. Reilly, *Americans All: The Rainbow at War* (Columbus, Ohio, 1936), p. 208; McCoy to family, May 6, 1918, Box 6, McCoy Papers.

8. McCoy to Mrs. Wood, May 26, 1918, Box 193A, Leonard Wood Diary and Papers, Library of Congress; Reilly, *Americans All,* pp. 209, 213; McCoy to family, May 21 and June 4, 1918, Box 6, McCoy Papers; Francis P. Duffy, *Father Duffy's Story* (New York, 1919), pp. 92–93.

9. Duffy, *Father Duffy's Story,* pp. 96, 122; Reilly, *Americans All,* p. 212.

10. American Battle Monuments Commission , *42d Division: Summary of Operations in the World War* (Washington, D.C., 1944), pp. 6-12 [hereafter cited as ABMC with unit designation]; D. Clayton James, *The Years of MacArthur*, 3 vols. (Boston, 1970), 1: 173-177. This biography of Douglas MacArthur, chief of staff of the Forty-second Division, provides a thorough narrative of the Rainbow's battle history in World War I.

11. Reilly, *Americans All,* pp. 272-273, provides McCoy's account of the action at Champagne.

12. Ibid.; ABMC, *42d Division,* pp. 12-15; James, *MacArthur,* 176-180.

13. Coffman, *War to End All Wars,* pp. 234-245; ABMC, *42d Division,* pp. 17-18. On the significance of the Aisne-Marne counteroffensive, see Smythe, *Pershing,* pp. 152-158.

14. ABMC, *42d Division,* pp. 18-22; Reilly, *Americans All,* pp. 379-380; James, *Years of MacArthur,* 1: 182-185.

15. ABMC, *42d Division,* pp. 23-24; Reilly, *Americans All,* pp. 380-381; James, *Years of MacArthur,* 1: 185. According to Father Duffy, McCoy expressed vigorous opposition to the proposed attack *(Father Duffy's Story,* p. 163).

16. Reilly, *Americans All,* p. 382; James, *Years of MacArthur,* 1: 186-189. During World War II, Donovan headed the Office of Strategic Services (OSS).

17. Duffy, *Father Duffy's Story,* pp. 189-191; ABMC, *42d Division,* pp. 26-30.

18. Reilly, *Americans All,* pp. 382-383. Among the regiment's dead at the Ourcq was the poet Joyce Kilmer.

19. McCoy to family, August 6 and 20, 1918, Box 6, McCoy Papers; Edward Bowditch to W. Cameron Forbes, August 11, 1918, W. Cameron Forbes Papers, Houghton Library, Harvard University [hereafter cited as Forbes Papers].

20. McCoy to family, September 1, 1918, Box 6, McCoy Papers.

21. Joint War History Commissions of Michigan and Wisconsin, *The 32nd Division in the World War, 1917-1919* (Milwaukee, Wis., 1920), pp. 27, 81-85, 88-90, 149; ABMC, *32d Division: Summary of Operations in the World War* (Washington, D.C., 1943), pp. 25-30; Glenn W. Garlock, *Tales of the Thirty-Second* (West Salem, Wis., 1927), p. 231.

22. Joint War History, *The 32nd Division,* pp. 90-110; ABMC, *32d Division,* pp. 37-62, 68; Bowditch to Forbes, October 20, 1918, Forbes Papers.

23. Joint War History, *The 32nd Division,* pp. 121-124; ABMC, *32d Division,* pp. 65-68; McCoy to family, November 11, 1918, Box 6, McCoy Papers.

24. Harbord to McCoy, September 25, 1918, James G. Harbord Papers, Library of Congress [hereafter cited as Harbord Papers, LC]; McCoy to family, November 24, 1918, Box 6, McCoy Papers.

25. McCoy to family, November 24, 1918, Box 6, McCoy Papers; Harbord to McAndrew, January 31, 1919, Harbord Papers, LC.

26. Benedict Crowell and Robert Forrest Wilson, *Demobilization* (New Haven, Conn., 1921), pp. 39-40; Harbord to Wood, February 4, 1919, Harbord Papers, LC.

27. McCoy to family, January 14 and 21, 1919, Box 6, McCoy Papers; Duffy to McCoy, Thanksgiving Day 1918, Box 14, McCoy Papers.

28. McCoy to family, January 3, January 14, February 19, March 1, and March 2, 1919, Box 6, McCoy Papers.

29. Jack C. Lane, *Armed Progressive: General Leonard Wood* (San Rafael, Calif., 1978), pp. 203, 221-222, 224-225.

30. McCoy to Wood, March 19, 1919, Box 15, McCoy Papers.

31. James B. Gidney, *A Mandate for Armenia* (n.p., 1967), pp. 3, 5-6; Joseph L. Grabill, *Protestant Diplomacy and the Near East: Missionary Influence on American Policy, 1810-1927* (Minneapolis, Minn., 1971), p. 51.

32. Gidney, *Mandate,* pp. 12-23, 31-34, 42-45, 65; Grabill, *Protestant Diplomacy,* pp. 60-63, 68-79.

33. John A. DeNovo, *American Interests and Policies in the Middle East, 1900-1939* (Minneapolis, Minn., 1963), pp. 110-115.

34. Ibid., pp. 118, 223; Gidney, *Mandate,* p. 79; Grabill, *Protestant Diplomacy,* pp. 194-195.

35. Gidney, *Mandate,* pp. 106-115, 168-170; Hughes et al. to Wilson, June 22, 1919, 184.021/34, U.S., Department of State, "General Records of the American Mission to Negotiate Peace, 1918-1931," Record Group 256, National Archives [hereafter cited as RG 256, NA].

36. Thomas A. Bailey, *Woodrow Wilson and the Lost Peace* (reprint ed., Chicago, 1963), p. 206.

37. Morgenthau and Hoover to Wilson, July 5, 1919, 184.021/34, RG 256, NA; Robert Lansing to AMMISSION, Paris, August 1, 1919, 184.021/35, RG 256, NA; Frank Polk to Harbord, August 13, 1919, 184.021/142, RG 256, NA; John Philip Richardson, "The American Military Mission to Armenia" (M.A. thesis, George Washington University, 1964), pp. 33, 38-39, 109-110; Grabill, *Protestant Diplomacy,* pp. 208-210.

38. McCoy to family, August 2, 1919, Box 6, McCoy Papers. Morgenthau, head of the American Committee for the Relief of the Far East, was largely responsible for Harbord's selection, having decided earlier that the general would make a suitable governor of the American mandate that Morgenthau earnestly sought for Armenia (Morgenthau to Harbord, June 25, 1919, 184.021/28, RG 256, NA). An American contingent remained with the Allied occupation forces in the Rhineland, but it was not part of the Allied Expeditionary Force (AEF).

39. "Who's Who: Members of the Mission," August 16, 1919, 184.021/101, RG 256, NA; McCoy to Leland Harrison, August 16, 1919, 184.021/173, RG 256, NA; McCoy to family, August 26, 1919, Box 6, McCoy Papers.

40. "Armenian Narrative Notes," entries for August 3 and 5, 1919, 184.021/106, RG 256, NA.

41. W. H. Buckler to Harbord, August 7, 1919, 184.021/126, RG 256, NA.

42. Richardson, "American Military Mission," p. 43; James G. Harbord, "Investigating Turkey and Trans-Caucasia," *The World's Work* 40 (May 1920): 36; "The Reminiscences of William Wilson Cumberland," Columbia Oral History Collection, Butler Library, Columbia University, pp. 69-70; undated memorandum, 184.021/234, RG 256, NA.

43. "Military Mission to Armenia," Box 8, George Van Horn Mosely Papers, Library of Congress. For a description of the ambush see the radio message from the *Martha Washington* to Rear Adm. Mark L. Bristol, October 5, 1919, 184.021/305, RG 256, NA. Harbord, "Investigating Turkey and Trans-Caucasia," p. 36. Harbord published two other articles describing the mission's travels: "Mustapha Kemal Pasha and His Party," *The World's Work* 40 (June 1920): 176-193, and "The New Nations of Trans-Caucasia," ibid. (July 1920): 271-280.

44. Harbord, "Investigating Turkey and Trans-Caucasia," p. 36; McCoy to family, September 11, 1919, Box 6, McCoy Papers; Harbord to Bristol, September 21, 1919, 184.021/276, RG 256, NA. Harbord reiterated these views at the end of the mission's travels (see Harbord to Polk, October 6, 1919, 184.021/307, RG 256, NA).

45. "An Account of a Conversation between Mr. Hohler and Brigadier-General McCoy," October 14, 1919, in E. L. Woodward and Rohan Butler, comps., *Documents on British Foreign Policy, 1919-1939,* first series, vol. 4 (1919) (London, 1952), 4: 821; Harbord to Bristol, September 21, 1919, 184.021/276, RG 256, NA; Harbord to Polk, October 6, 1919, 184.021/307, RG 256, NA; Polk to Lansing, October 25, 1919,

184.02102/18, RG 256, NA. Harbord's account of the conversation with Kemal is in "Mustapha Kemal Pasha and His Party," pp. 184-188.

46. Gidney, *Mandate,* pp. 59, 96.

47. Harbord to Polk, October 6, 1919, 184.021/307, RG 256, NA; Polk to Lansing, October 25, 1919, 184.02102/18, RG 256, NA.

48. James G. Harbord, "Report of the American Military Mission to Armenia," Box 239, RG 165, NA, pp. 4, 8, 15 [hereafter cited as Harbord Report]; other copies of the report can be found at 184.02102/5, RG 256, NA, and in Box 69, McCoy Papers.

49. Harbord Report, pp. 20, 23.

50. Harbord Report, pp. 29-31; Hornbeck, "Political Factors and Problems," Appendix A, Harbord Report.

51. Hornbeck, "Political Factors and Problems," Harbord Report, pp. 35, 43; Mosely, "The Military Problem of a Mandatory," Appendix J, Harbord Report.

52. Harbord Report, p. 38; "The Reminiscences of William Wilson Cumberland," p. 72.

53. Harbord Report, pp. 38-43.

54. Mosely, "Military Problem"; "The Reminiscences of William Wilson Cumberland," p. 72; Harbord to McCoy, June 15 and August 18, 1920, Box 16, McCoy Papers.

55. *New York Times* [hereafter cited as *NYT*], August 15, 1919; Thomas A. Bailey, *Woodrow Wilson and the Great Betrayal* (reprint ed., Chicago, 1963), pp. 90-114, 132-143, 168-192.

56. Lansing to AMMISSION, Paris, October 9, 1919, 184.02102/3, RG 256, NA.

57. *NYT,* April 6, 1920; Paxton Hibben, "Arbitrating for Armenia," *New Republic* 23 (July 16, 1920): 87; Gidney, *Mandate,* p 189; "No American Mandate for Armenia," *Current History* 12 (July 1920): 710-713. For an account of the congressional debate, see also Richardson, "American Military Mission," pp. 105-107. The basic report was published as Senate Document 266, 66th Congress, 2d session; Mosely's appendix appeared separately as Senate Document 281, 66th Congress, 2d session. The Republican party found further political use for the Harbord Report, citing it in the 1920 party platform as evidence that Wilson's support of a mandate was a "striking illustration" of his "disregard of the lives of American boys or American interests" ("Text of the Republican Platform," *Current History* 12 [July 1920]: 562).

58. In addition to the series in *The World's Work,* Harbord published a feature article in the *New York Times* on February 22, 1920, calling for assistance for the "500,000 destitute people . . . left on our national doorstep." Harbord to McCoy, June 15 and August 18, 1920, Box 16, McCoy Papers.

59. McCoy to Barton, April 25, 1920, Box 16, McCoy Papers.

## CHAPTER 7
## RETURN TO THE PHILIPPINES

1. McCoy to Eliot Wadsworth, August 21, 1924, Box 19, Frank Ross McCoy Papers, Library of Congress [hereafter cited as McCoy Papers].

2. Edward M. Coffman, *The War to End All Wars* (New York, 1968), pp. 357-358; Donald Smythe, *Pershing: General of the Armies* (Bloomington, Ind., 1986), p. 265.

3. McCoy to family, February 5 and March 27, 1920, Box 6, McCoy Papers; McCoy to Stimson, April 20, 1920, Box 72, Henry Lewis Stimson Diary and Papers, Yale University [hereafter cited as Stimson Papers].

4. "Memorandum on the Mexican Problem" [June 1920], Box 16, McCoy Papers. McCoy believed that intervention in Mexico was "as sure to come as fate" (see McCoy to General William Crozier, June 17, 1920, Box 16, McCoy Papers). Stimson to McCoy, April 12, 1920, Box 72, Stimson Papers.

5. Wesley M. Bagby, *The Road to Normalcy: The Presidential Campaign and Election of 1920* (Baltimore, 1962), pp. 25-31, 84-96; Hagedorn interview with Johnston, February 1, 1929, Box 21, Hermann Hagedorn Papers, Library of Congress [hereafter cited as Hagedorn Papers]. For a detailed narrative of the Wood candidacy, see Jack C. Lane, *Armed Progressive: General Leonard Wood* (San Rafael, Calif., 1978), Chapters 18 and 19.

6. *New York Times,* October 26, 1920; Lane, *Armed Progressive,* p. 250.

7. McCoy to family, July 14, 1920, Box 6, McCoy Papers; Gibson to McCoy, September 14, 1920, and McCoy to Gibson, October 28, 1920, Box 16, McCoy Papers.

8. Lane, *Armed Progressive,* p. 251.

9. U.S., Congress, *Congressional Record,* 66th Cong., 3d sess., p. 26; Peter W. Stanley, *A Nation in the Making: The Philippines and the United States, 1899-1921* (Cambridge, Mass., 1974), pp. 202-208, 212-219; Michael Onorato, "The Jones Act and Filipino Participation in Government," in *A Brief Review of American Interest in Philippine Development and Other Essays* (Berkeley, Calif., 1968), pp. 27-34. McCoy refused an opportunity to serve as Harrison's aide (see Brig. Gen. Frank McIntyre to Harrison, September 3, 1913, Entry 2074848, U.S., War Department, "Records of the Adjutant General," Record Group 94, National Archives; hereafter cited as RG 94, NA).

10. Gerald E. Wheeler, "Republican Philippine Policy, 1921-1933," *Pacific Historical Review* 28 (November 1959): 378-379.

11. Lane, *Armed Progressive,* pp. 251-252; Hagedorn interview with Johnston, February 1, 1929, Box 21, and with McCoy, May 19, 1929, Box 22, Hagedorn Papers; Hagedorn, *Leonard Wood: A Biography,* 2 vols (New York, 1931), 2: 377; Frederic Gilman Hoyt, "The Wood-Forbes Mission to the Philippines, 1921" (Ph.D. dissertation, Claremont Graduate School, 1963), pp. 20, 26-28.

12. Hoyt, "Wood-Forbes Mission," pp. 10-11; Wheeler, "Republican Philippine Policy," pp. 378-379. For a roster of the mission, see U.S., War Department, *Report of the Special Mission on Investigation to the Philippine Islands* (Washington, D.C., 1921), p. 6; hereafter cited as Wood-Forbes Report. For a biographical sketch of Johnston, see H. Jordan Theis, "Colonel Gordon Johnston, " *The Cavalry Journal* 43 (November-December 1934): 48.

13. Wood Diary, March 27, 1921, Box 14, Leonard Wood Diary and Papers, Library of Congress [hereafter cited as Wood Papers]; Wood-Forbes Report, pp. 7-10.

14. Wood-Forbes Report, p. 13; Hoyt, "Wood-Forbes Mission," pp. 90-92, 96-98, 111-112, 114a; McCoy to family, May 15, 1921, and March 30, 1922, Box 6, McCoy Papers.

15. For views of the American community, see Hoyt, "Wood-Forbes Mission," pp. 88-89, 123-131, 134-140, 173-175, 198, 227-236, 369. On McCoy's questionnaire, see 22639-A-12, U.S., War Department, "Records of the Bureau of Insular Affairs," Record Group 350, National Archives; hereafter cited as RG 350, NA.

16. "The Political and Military Relations of the Philippine Islands to the United States," April 27, 1921, Box 82, McCoy Papers. This article consists of a series of memos provided Wood by the military staff in Manila. Rhodes, "The Problem of the Pacific," and Straus, untitled memorandum, April 28, 1921, Box 82, McCoy Papers.

17. McCoy to family, May 27, 1921, Box 6, McCoy Papers. For a descriptive narrative of the mission's investigation, see Hagedorn, *Wood,* 2: 383-393.

18. McCoy, "General Administration," undated [1921], Box 13, McCoy Papers.

19. The phrase "infection of politics" appears on page 23 of the Wood-Forbes Report. The ideas and phraseology of McCoy's memorandum on "General Administration" that appear in the final report suggest that he played a large role in drafting it.

20. Wood-Forbes Report, pp. 22–32. The allusion to morality was more than casual. Harrison's sexual preferences, especially his alleged proclivity for very young Filipino girls, greatly disturbed the strait-laced members of the mission. Privately, Wood described Harrison as "almost a degenerate" (Wood to Mrs. Wood, July 5, 1921, Box 192, Wood Papers). Forbes called Harrison a "degenerate renegade (Journal of W. Cameron Forbes [Wood-Forbes Mission], undated entry, p. 162, W. Cameron Forbes Papers, Houghton Library, Harvard University; hereafter cited as Forbes Papers). See also Hoyt, "Wood-Forbes Mission," pp. 155–157, 160–162.

21. Wood-Forbes Report, pp. 34, 38–40, 42. For details on the Philippines's economic plight, see the "Report of the Secretary of Finance," in U.S., War Department, *Report of the Governor General of the Philippine Islands, 1921* (Washington, D.C., 1922), pp. 109–111.

22. McCoy, "General Administration," Box 13, McCoy Papers; Wood-Forbes Report, p. 17.

23. *The Manila Times*, October 15, 1921, Box 283, Wood Papers. McCoy's suspicion of Japan was of long standing. In 1905, he favored Russia in its war against Japan, remarking: "I believe . . . in the yellow peril. As long as we hold the Philippines, and engage in the commercial war in China, there'll be the ever present danger of conflict with the Jap cock of the walk. They won't help hold the open door, but'll soon develop a doctrine of . . . protection for themselves and China" (see McCoy to family, May 28, 1905, Box 4, McCoy Papers).

24. McCoy, "General Administration," Box 13, and "Suggestions for Recommendations by Colonel McCoy," undated, Box 82, McCoy Papers.

25. McCoy, "General Administration," Box 13, McCoy Papers; Wood-Forbes Report, p. 46.

26. McCoy to family, September 7 and October 1, 14, and 20, 1921, Box 6, McCoy Papers.

27. Lane, *Armed Progressive,* pp. 255–256.

28. Wood to Mrs. Wood, July 29, 1921, Box 192, Wood Papers; Forbes to Secretary of War John L. Weeks, August 6, 1921, 22639-A-87-A, and Wood to Weeks, September 2, 1921, 22639-A-14, RG 350, NA; Weeks to Wood, September 19, 1921, Box 83, McCoy Papers; Forbes to Weeks, November 2, 1921, Box 16, McCoy Papers. As late as December 1922, Forbes was still importuning President Harding to name McCoy as Wood's successor and was lining up the votes needed for Senate approval (Forbes to McCoy, December 22, 1922, Box 16, McCoy Papers).

29. Onorato, "Leonard Wood and His Khaki Cabinet in the Philippines, 1921-1927," *A Brief Review,* p. 126; William Hart Anderson, *The Philippine Problem* (New York, 1939), p. 143; McCoy to family, November 12, 1921, and January 8, April 10, and April 30, 1922, Box 6, McCoy Papers; McCoy to Johnston, January 8, 1922, Box 16, McCoy Papers; Bowditch to Forbes, December 9, 1921, and February 2, 1922, Forbes Papers; Wood to Weeks, January 26, 1923, Box 82, McCoy Papers; Wood to McCoy, September 9, 1925, Box 197, Wood Papers; Marguerite Wolfson, "In the Spirit of Manila," *Asia* 24 (February 1924): 146 (this article reprints letters that Wolfson wrote early in 1922).

30. McCoy to Forbes, April 5, 1922, Forbes Papers.

31. The best studies of American rule in the Philippines are Stanley, *A Nation in the Making,* which covers the years 1899 to 1921, and Theodore Friend, *Between Two Empires: The Ordeal of the Philippines, 1929-1946* (New Haven, Conn., 1965), which

takes up the story after Wood's regime ended. The statistics are drawn from the *Report of the Governor General, 1921*, p. 13. On the lack of American interest in the Philippines, see Onorato, *A Brief Review*, pp. 5-7.

32. Wood's inaugural address is reprinted in *Report of the Governor General, 1921*, pp. 45-46.

33. For a useful review of progressive convictions—admittedly a complex issue—see Thomas K. McCraw, "The Progressive Legacy," *The Progressive Era*, ed. by Lewis L. Gould (Syracuse, N.Y., 1974), p. 182.

34. McCoy to family, November 12, 1921, Box 6, McCoy Papers; McCoy to Forbes, April 8, 1926, Forbes Papers.

35. Wiebe, *The Search for Order, 1877-1920* (New York, 1967), p. 160; Hays, *The Response to Industrialism, 1885-1914* (Chicago, 1957), pp. 152-153, 156-157.

36. McCraw, "Progressive Legacy," pp. 191-194.

37. Mayo interview with McCoy, March 26, 1924, Box 100, McCoy Papers.

38. McCoy to Mosely, February 18, 1922, vol. 10, George Van Horn Mosely Papers, Library of Congress [hereafter cited as Mosely Papers]; McCoy to family, January 1, February 18, and March 7, 1922, Box 6, McCoy Papers; U.S., War Department, *Report of the Governor General of the Philippine Islands, 1922* (Washington, D.C., 1924), pp. 2, 27, 31-32.

39. *Report of the Governor General, 1922*, pp. 5, 9, 11-13; Onorato, "Leonard Wood: His First Year as Governor General," *A Brief Review*, p. 70.

40. Ibid., pp. 68-69; *Report of the Governor General, 1922*, p. 15, 17, 25; Hagedorn, *Wood*, 2: 423-424.

41. Bowditch to Forbes, December 28, 1921, January 17, 1922, and December 9, [1922], Forbes Papers.

42. McCoy interview with Richard V. Oulahan of the *New York Times*, January 17, 1924, Box 19, McCoy Papers.

43. The Philippine case is presented in a series of documents reprinted in U.S., War Department, *Report of the Governor General of the Philippine Islands, 1923* (Washington, D.C., 1925), pp. 42-44, 49-56, 58-59. For indications that Philippine leaders arranged for the passage of defective bills to goad Wood into using the veto, see Onorato, "The Jones Act and Filipino Participation in Government," *A Brief Review*, pp. 30-31, and the interview with Mayo, March 24, 1924, Box 100, McCoy Papers.

44. *Report of the Governor General, 1923*, pp. 35-36. For an account of the Conley affair that brought on the cabinet crisis, see Michael Onorato, *Leonard Wood and the Philippine Cabinet Crisis of 1923* (Manila, Philippines, 1967), pp. 49-52.

45. Harbord to Mosely, October 30, 1923, vol. 10, Mosely Papers; McCoy to family, February 22, 1923, Box 6, McCoy Papers; Wood Diary, April 6, 1923, Box 18, Wood Papers.

46. McCoy to family, August 31 and September 5, 1923, Box 6, McCoy Papers; Noel F. Busch, *Two Minutes to Noon* (New York, 1962), p. 38.

47. McCoy, "Final Report of the American Relief Mission to Japan," November 9, 1923, Box 75, McCoy Papers; McCoy to James R. Garfield, September 29, 1923, Box 17, McCoy Papers; Busch, *Two Minutes*, pp. 75, 147, 149; Tokyo Municipal Office, *The Reconstruction of Tokyo* (Tokyo, 1933), p. 9.

48. McCoy to family, September 12, 1923, Box 6, McCoy Papers. On the need to avoid offending the Japanese, see an interview with McCoy published as "American Praise for Japan," *Far Eastern Review* 19 (October 1923): 646.

49. McCoy to family, October 3 and 24, 1923, Box 6, McCoy Papers; "Final Report of the American Relief Mission," Box 75, McCoy Papers.

50. McCoy to family, October 3, 1923, Box 6, McCoy Papers; "Substance of a Conversation," between McCoy and General Tanaka, "Final Report of the American Relief Mission," and unidentified newsclipping by B. W. Fleisher, Box 75, McCoy Papers.

51. McCoy to family, November 23, 1923, Box 6, McCoy Papers.

52. Oulahan interview with McCoy, Box 19, McCoy Papers. For Philippine criticism of the "khaki cabinet," see *Report of the Governor General, 1923*, p. 44.

53. Friend, *Between Two Empires*, pp. 4, 32, 39-42.

54. Mayo interview with McCoy, March 24 and 25, 1924, Box 100, McCoy Papers.

55. Ibid. Bowditch to McCoy, February 15, 1924, Box 18, McCoy Papers.

56. Wood to secretary of war, March 14, 1924, Box 19, McCoy Papers; McCoy to Arthur W. Page, December 18, 1923, Box 17, McCoy Papers. Wood, too, reported that Philippine leaders told him privately that the islands were not ready for independence (Wood to secretary of war, December 4, 1923, Box 17, McCoy Papers, and Wood interview with Katherine Mayo, March 28, 1924, Box 348, Wood Papers).

57. McCoy to Maj. Gen. Frank McIntyre, March 9, 1924, Box 19, McCoy Papers; Mayo interview with McCoy, March 24, 1924, Box 100, McCoy Papers; McCoy to Forbes, March 17, 1924, Forbes Papers.

58. McCoy to Forbes, March 17, 1924, Forbes Papers; U.S., War Department, *Report of the Governor General of the Philippine Islands, 1924* (Washington, D.C., 1926), pp. 4-5, 9-10, 11, 13; Harbord to McCoy, February 13 and December 4, 1924, and McCoy to Harbord, July 18, 1924, and January 9, 1925, James G. Harbord Papers, New York Historical Society; Col. Charles E. Kilbourne to McCoy, February 13, 1924, Box 19, and Bowditch to McCoy, February 15, 1924, Box 18, McCoy Papers.

59. Mayo interview with Wood, March 27, 1924, Box 348, Wood Papers; Lane, *Armed Progressive*, p. 274; Onorato, *Leonard Wood and Cabinet Crisis*, pp. 66-67.

60. McCoy to Carpenter, March 3, 1925, Box 20, McCoy Papers; Hagedorn interview with Johnston, February 1, 1929, Box 22, Hagedorn Papers.

61. McCoy to family, May 10 and June 1, 1924, and undated [April 1925], Box 7, McCoy Papers; McCoy to Forbes, May 21, 1924, Box 18, McCoy Papers.

62. Interview with Brig. Gen. Sherman V. Hasbrouk, Stone Bridge, New York, June 3, 1980; Hagedorn interview with Johnston, February 1, 1929, and McCoy, February 14, 1929, Box 22, Hagedorn Papers.

## CHAPTER 8
## MISSION TO NICARAGUA

1. Mrs. J. Borden Harriman, *From Pinafores to Politics* (New York, 1923), p. 256.

2. McCoy to family, July 1, 1922, Box 6, Frank Ross McCoy Papers, Library of Congress; hereafter cited as McCoy Papers.

3. McCoy to family, January 27 and February 1, 1924, Box 7, McCoy Papers; Wood Diary, January 26, 1924, Box 20, Leonard Wood Diary and Papers, Library of Congress [hereafter cited as Wood Papers]; *New York Times* [hereafter cited as *NYT*], January 27, 1924.

4. McCoy to family, February 1, 1924, Box 7, McCoy Papers.

5. McCoy to Forbes, March 1, 1924, W. Cameron Forbes Papers, Houghton Library, Harvard University [hereafter cited as Forbes Papers]; Michael Pearlman, *To Make Democracy Safe for America* (Urbana, Ill., 1984), p. 101.

6. McCoy to Harbord, May 21, 1925, James G. Harbord Papers, New York Historical Society; McCoy to family, May 26 and June 16, 1925, Box 7, McCoy Papers; McCoy to

Stimson, July 25, Box 88, Henry Lewis Stimson Diary and Papers, Yale University [hereafter cited as Stimson Papers]; McCoy to Wood, June 18 and July 18, 1925, Box 177, Wood Papers.

7. *NYT,* September 6, 1925.

8. McCoy to Mrs. Wood, November 14, 1925, Box 177, Wood Papers.

9. McCoy to Wood, September 30, 1925, Box 177, Wood Papers.

10. McCoy to Mrs. Wood, November 14, 1925, Box 177, Wood Papers; McCoy to Forbes, November 30, 1925, Folder 176, Forbes Papers.

11. McCoy to Wood, June 30, 1926, Box 181, Wood Papers; Burke Davis, *The Billy Mitchell Affair* (New York, 1967), pp. 240, 336, 342.

12. McCoy to family, May 17, June 15, and July 4, 1926, Box 7, McCoy Papers; "Value of Diversion," July 30, 1926, Box 63, McCoy Papers.

13. Jack C. Lane, *Armed Progressive; General Leonard Wood* (San Rafael, Calif., 1978), pp. 275-276; McCoy to Halstead Dorey, August 21, 1927, Box 21, McCoy Papers; McCoy to Mrs. Wood, August 30, 1928, Box 193A, Wood Papers.

14. *NYT,* August 9, 1927; *New York American,* October 17, 1927, and *Mindanao Herald,* September 10, 1927, Box 101, McCoy Papers; McCoy to family, October 20 and December 1, 1927, Box 8, McCoy Papers.

15. Standard accounts of U.S.-Nicaraguan relations are Dana G. Munro, *Intervention and Dollar Diplomacy in the Caribbean, 1900-1921* (Princeton, N.J., 1964), pp. 160-216, 388-425; idem, *The United States and the Caribbean Republics, 1921-1933* (Princeton, N.J., 1974), pp. 157-308; and William Kamman, *A Search for Stability: United States Diplomacy toward Nicaragua, 1925-1933* (Notre Dame, Ind., 1968).

16. *NYT,* February 22, 1927.

17. Robert Freeman Smith, *The United States and Revolutionary Nationalism in Mexico, 1916-1932* (Chicago, 1927), pp. x-xi.

18. "Department of State Memorandum on the Nicaraguan Situation," January 1927, 817.00/5854, U.S., Department of State, "General Records of the State Department," Record Group 59, National Archives [hereafter cited as RG 59, NA]. For press reports of Mexican aid to Sacasa, see *Literary Digest* 92 (January 1, 1927): 14, and (January 8, 1927): 5; James J. Horn, "U.S. Diplomacy and the 'Spector of Bolshevism' in Mexico (1924-1927)," *The Americas* 32 (July 1975): 31-45, assesses the overall impact of State Department fears of Mexican radicalism.

19. Elting Morison, *Turmoil and Tradition: A Study of the Life and Times of Henry L. Stimson* (Boston, Mass., 1960), pp. 271-278, describes Stimson's mission to Nicaragua.

20. Charles C. Eberhardt to Frank B. Kellogg, July 20, 1927, Box 211, Stimson Papers.

21. On the battle of Ocotal, see Neill Macaulay *The Sandino Affair* (Chicago, 1967), pp. 62-82.

22. For press reaction, see *Literary Digest* 94 (July 30, 1927): 5; for a survey of congressional opinion, *St. Louis Post-Dispatch,* August 2, 1927, scrapbook, Box 93, McCoy Papers.

23. "How to Get Out of Nicaragua," *New Republic* 53 (January 18, 1928): 234, assesses European editorial opinion.

24. McCoy to Forbes, August 17, 1927, Forbes Papers.

25. Kellogg to McCoy, June 26, 1927, Box 20, McCoy Papers.

26. McCoy to family, September 27, 1927, Box 8, McCoy Papers; McCoy to Kellogg, September 12, 1927, 817.00/5028, RG 59, NA.

27. McCoy to Sherwood Cheney, April 4, 1928, Box 21, McCoy Papers.

28. Kellogg to Munro, January 17, 1928, 817.00/5276, RG 59, NA; *NYT,* January 17, 1928.

29. Munro to Kellogg, October 4, 1927, 817.00/5054, RG 59, NA.

30. McCoy to Munro, undated, Box 79, McCoy Papers.

31. McCoy to Kellogg, April 3, 1928, Box 50, McCoy Papers; McCoy to family, January 29, 1928, Box 8, McCoy Papers; McCoy to Kellogg, February 2, 1928, 817.00/5361, RG 59, NA.

32. Draft letter, McCoy to Kellogg, February 15, 1928, Box 8, Francis Le Jau Parker Papers, Library of Congress; hereafter cited as Parker Papers.

33. *NYT,* March 13, 1928.

34. Munro to Francis White, February 18, 1928, Box 14, Francis White Papers, National Archives [hereafter cited as White Papers]; memo entitled "Nicaragua," March 2, 1928, 817.00/544 1/2, RG 59, NA.

35. *NYT,* March 14, 1928; "Deputies—14 March 1928," Box 1990, U.S., Department of State, "Records of International Conferences, Commissions, and Expositions," Record Group 43, National Archives (prepared by a Guardia Nacional stenographer, this memorandum describes events in the Chamber of Deputies; hereafter cited as RG 43, NA); "Legality versus Necessity," undated memo, Box 80, McCoy Papers; McCoy and Eberhardt to Kellogg, March 14, 1928, Box 80, McCoy Papers.

36. On March 26, 1928, McCoy wrote William Howard Taft: "It looked for a time here as though the government might follow President Palma's lead and throw full responsibility at me, and at one time I dug out of the Foreign Relations for 1906 the copy of your proclamation which inaugurated the provisional government" (Box 22, McCoy Papers).

37. Walter B. Howe, "Development of the Presidential Decree of March 21, 1928," Box 7, Parker Papers.

38. U.S., Department of State, *Papers Relating to the Foreign Relations of the United States* (1927), vol. 3 (Washington, D.C., 1942), pp. 482-485, reprints the decree; hereafter cited as *FRUS.*

39. *Washington Herald,* April 1, 1928, scrapbook, Box 93, McCoy Papers.

40. U.S., Congress, *Congressional Record,* 70th Cong., 1st Sess., April 16, 1928, p. 6523; see also the series of articles by Carlton Beals in *The Nation* from February through April 1928. According to Beals, "if Sandino had arms he could raise an army of ten thousand men by snapping his fingers; . . . if he marched into Managua, the capital, tomorrow, he would receive the greatest ovation in Nicaraguan history" ("This is War, Gentlemen!" *The Nation* 126 [April 11, 1928]: 406).

41. "Memo on Sandino," undated, Box 1953, RG 43, NA; undated memorandum, Box 79, McCoy Papers.

42. Kellogg to McCoy, March 3, 1928, Box 79, McCoy Papers.

43. McCoy to Kellogg, March 5, 1928, 817.00/5450, RG 59, NA. Rear Adm. David F. Sellers reported to the Navy Department that there was a "deep feeling of resentment" among the marines that any army officer had been appointed to the type of mission "that had always been done in the past by the Navy or Marine Corps" (Sellers to Admiral Charles F. Hughes, April 6, 1928, Box 3, David Foote Sellers Papers, Library of Congress; hereafter cited as Sellers Papers).

44. McCoy to Kellogg, March 5, 1928, 817.00/5450, RG 59, NA.

45. Sellers to Hughes, April 6, 1928, Box 3, Sellers Papers. Later Sellers commented: "Just why it was thought necessary to confer rank upon General McCoy which made him temporarily senior to the Squadron Commander while in Nicaragua and thus lower the prestige of the Navy, has never been clear or understood," but since "controversies about rank and precedence . . . generally brand those who engage in them as being captious or of small mental caliber," the admiral had been reluctant to complain too loudly (Sellers to Munro, January 4, 1929, Box 3, Sellers Papers).

46. McCoy to Stimson, April 16, 1928, Box 99, Stimson Papers; Feland to Sellers, April 19, 1928, Box 6, Sellers Papers.

47. *NYT,* March 1 and June 15, 1928; McCoy to Kellogg, August 2, 1928, Box 79, McCoy Papers.

48. Eberhardt to Kellogg, July 20, 1928, 817.00/5845, RG 59, NA; Munro to White, June 28, 1928, Box 14, White Papers; Summerlin to Kellogg, July 21, 1928, 817.00/5848, RG 59, NA.

49. Robert E. Olds to McCoy, April 13, 1928, Box 14, White Papers.

50. Richard Millett, *Guardians of the Dynasty* (Maryknoll, N.Y., 1977), p. 71; Feland to Sellers, March 22, 1928, Box 3, Sellers Papers; Eberhardt to White, January 31, 1929, Box 11, White Papers; "Executive Memorandum No. 22 of the American Electoral Mission in Nicaragua," November 22, 1928, Box 79, McCoy Papers; McCoy to Elias R. Beadle, August 30, 1928, Box 6, File 1, U.S. Marine Corps, "Records of Marine Units in Nicaragua," Federal Records Center, Suitland, Maryland.

51. Macaulay, *Sandino Affair,* p. 128; *NYT,* October 31, 1928.

52. McCoy reported that after dinner one evening, he became "the principal target . . . in a symposium on Nicaragua, being quizzed with interest by Senators Hiram Johnson and Walsh of Montana. Frances [his wife] thought I was too mild and lacking in belligerency. With intent, however, and you will be glad to know that I didn't raise my voice" (McCoy to family, June 7, 1928, Box 8, McCoy Papers).

53. McCoy to Blanton Winship, February 28, 1937, Box 60, McCoy Papers; Stimson to White, September 23, 1927, 817.00/5043 1/2, RG 59, NA; McCoy to Stimson, August 14, 1927, Box 95, Stimson Papers.

54. See Boxes 21 and 22, McCoy Papers, especially Felix Frankfurter to McCoy, October 11, 1928, and Newton D. Baker to McCoy, November 7, 1928, Box 21; also, McCoy to Stimson, October 24, 1928, Box 101, Stimson Papers.

55. "Summary of Events and Policy from Stimson Agreements to Date," undated, Box 79, McCoy Papers.

56. Kellogg to McCoy and Eberhardt, April 19, 1928, *FRUS* (1928), vol. 3, p. 534; McCoy to family, July 5, 1928, Box 8, McCoy Papers; Munro, *United States and Caribbean Republics,* p. 249.

57. Munro to McCoy, May 17, 1928, Box 21, McCoy Papers.

58. McCoy to Capt. Alfred W. Johnson, USN, June 13, 1930, Box 25, McCoy Papers; see also draft cable, Parker to McCoy, May 22, 1928, Box 8, Parker Papers.

59. Draft cable, Parker to McCoy, May 22, 1928, Box 8, Parker Papers.

60. Eberhardt to Kellogg, June 27, 1928, 817.00/5782, RG 59, NA; *NYT,* July 8, 1928; "Notes on Session of 23d July," Box 1977, RG 43, NA (these are handwritten minutes of the election board proceedings made by its secretary, Maj. Cary I. Crockett).

61. Eberhardt to Kellogg, July 27, 1928, 817.00/5913, RG 59, NA; *NYT,* September 8, 1928.

62. McCoy to family, September 15, 1928, Box 8, McCoy Papers.

63. *NYT,* October 13, 1928.

64. *NYT,* November 5, 1928.

65. *NYT,* November 10, 1928; Munro, *United States and Caribbean Republics,* p. 254.

66. *The Nation* 127 (November 7, 1928): 467; *NYT,* November 18, 1928; *New York Herald Tribune,* November 16, 1928, scrapbook, Box 93, McCoy Papers.

67. McCoy interview with Henry Cabot Lodge, Jr., undated, Box 89, McCoy Papers.

68. Undated memorandum, Box 79, McCoy Papers.

69. Sellers to Hughes, November 1928, Box 3, Sellers Papers.

70. Draft cable, McCoy to Kellogg, November 14, 1928, Box 79, McCoy Papers.

71. *NYT,* December 18, 1928, and February 7, 1929.

72. Kamman, *Search for Stability,* pp. 186, 194-208.

## CHAPTER 9
## TROUBLESHOOTING FOR STIMSON

1. William R. Garner, *The Chaco Dispute: A Study of Prestige Diplomacy* (Washington, D.C., 1966), pp. 21-51; David H. Zook, Jr., *The Conduct of the Chaco War* (n.p., 1960), pp. 49-52; Gordon Ireland, *Boundaries, Possessions, and Conflicts in South America* (Cambridge, Mass., 1938), pp. 66-72.

2. Garner, *Chaco Dispute,* pp. 57-58. For Kellogg's efforts to persuade Bolivia and Paraguay to consent to a commission of inquiry and conciliation and to recruit members, see U.S., Department of State, *Papers Relating to the Foreign Relations of the United States* (1929), vol. 1 (Washington, D.C., 1942), pp. 818-835; hereafter cited as *FRUS*.

3. The protocol establishing the commission is reprinted in *FRUS* (1929), vol. 1, pp. 835-836; McCoy, "Informal Memorandum on the Organization and Procedures of International Commissions and Conferences," undated, Box 90, Frank Ross McCoy Papers, Library of Congress [hereafter cited as McCoy Papers].

4. Bowditch to Forbes, January 7, 1929, W. Cameron Forbes Papers, Houghton Library, Harvard University; Frederick P. Hibbard (U.S. chargé in Bolivia) to Stimson, October 26, 1929, 724.3415/805, U.S., Department of State, "General Records of the State Department," Record Group 59, National Archives [hereafter cited as RG 59, NA]; McCoy, "Confidential Report of the American Commissioners, Commisson of Inquiry and Conciliation, Bolivia and Paraguay," Box 70, McCoy Papers, p. 87 [hereafter cited as "Confidential Report"].

5. Conversation between Stimson and Eduardo Diez de Medina (Bolivian minister), August 21, 1929, 724.3415/669, RG 59, NA; Garner, *Chaco Dispute,* p. 61; Bryce Wood, *The United States and Latin American Wars, 1932-1942* (New York, 1966), p. 21.

6. *Proceedings of the Commission of Inquiry and Conciliation, Bolivia and Paraguay* (Washington, D.C., 1929). This volume, which exceeds 1,200 pages, contains the minutes of all plenary sessions along with a variety of Bolivian and Paraguayan memorials, statements, maps, and appendices. McCoy to Munro, May 11, 1929, 724.3415/525, RG 59, NA; H. F. Arthur Schoenfeld to White, May 13, 1929, 724.3415/527, RG 59, NA; McCoy to family, May 22, 1929, Box 8, McCoy Papers. The commission's resolution on the exchange of prisoners is reprinted in *FRUS* (1929), vol. 1, pp. 852-853.

7. McCoy to family, June 24, 1929, Box 8, McCoy Papers; McCoy to Robert L. Bullard, August 12, 1933, Box 29, McCoy Papers; "Confidential Report," pp. 16-17, 30, 33, 49.

8. McCoy to family, undated, Box 8, McCoy Papers; "Confidential Report," pp. 48, 51, 57, 86.

9. Emerson B. Christie, "The Chaco Boreal," undated, 724.3415/652 1/2, RG 59, NA (this was a State Department study prepared at McCoy's request); McCoy to Malcolm Davis, May 7, 1934, Box 31, McCoy Papers; "Confidential Report," pp. 47, 52-55, 80-81, 82-84.

10. McCoy to Bolivian and Paraguayan delegations, August 31, 1929, 724.3415/688, RG 59, NA; "Confidential Report," pp. 61-62, 64-69. The text of the proposed convention of arbitration is reprinted in *FRUS* (1929), vol. 1, pp. 875-880.

11. Stimson to George L. Kreek (U.S. minister to Paraguay), September 7, 1929, 724.3415/686B, RG 59, NA; Stimson to Hibbard, September 7, 1929, 724.3415/686A, RG 59, NA; Bolivian delegation to McCoy, and Paraguayan delegation to McCoy, September 9, 1929, 724.3415/714 1/2, RG 59, NA.

12. McCoy to Bolivian and Paraguayan delegations, September 12, 1929, 724.3415/714 1/2, RG 59, NA; "Confidential Report," pp. 73-74.

13. "Confidential Report," pp. 40-42, 46. For the conciliation protocol, see *FRUS* (1929), vol. 1, pp. 860-861.

14. "Confidential Report," p. 108; McCoy to Stimson, September 16, 1929, 724.3415/713 1/2, RG 59, NA.

15. Stimson to Hibbard, September 16, 1929, 724.3415/704A, RG 59, NA; conversation between White and Diez de Medina, September 17, 1929, 724.3415/704 1/2, RG 59, NA; Hibbard to Stimson, October 9, 1929, 724.3415/774, RG 59, NA; Hibbard to Stimson, October 26, 1929, 724.3415/805, RG 59, NA. For assessments of McCoy's performance that suggest forbearance and impartiality on his part, see conversation between Stimson and General Guillermo Ruprecht (the Uruguayan delegate), undated, 724.3415/714, RG 59, NA, and "Supplementary Memorandum by the Secretary General and the Counsellor of the Commission," undated, Box 70, McCoy Papers.

16. McCoy to Kellogg, December 30, 1929, Box 13, Francis White Papers, National Archives; McCoy to Malcolm W. Davis, May 7, 1934, Box 31, McCoy Papers.

17. "Confidential Report," p. 102. Although not indicative of any unique prescience, McCoy's prediction on page 33 of his "Confidential Report"—that failure to resolve the territorial issue would lead to war—proved correct. For an account of the Bolivian-Paraguayan armed conflict of 1932-1935, see Zook, *Conduct of the Chaco War.*

18. Stimson Diary, February 14, 1931, Henry Lewis Stimson Diary and Papers, Yale University; hereafter cited as Stimson Papers. Stimson apparently overcame temptation; McCoy did not fill in for Cotton during the latter's illness.

19. On McCoy's continuing involvement with Nicaragua, see Stimson Diary, January 13, 29, and 30 and February 2, 5, and 20, 1931, Stimson Papers.

20. *New York Times* [hereafter cited as *NYT*], July 22, 30, and 31; August 5, 22, and 30; and September 1, 1930.

21. McCoy to Stimson, August 11, 1930, Box 107, Stimson Papers; *NYT,* September 25, 1930.

22. Grayson Kirk, *Philippine Independence* (New York, 1936), pp. 73-107.

23. For a comprehensive statement of the Hoover administration's position, see U.S., Congress, Senate, *Independence of the Philippine Islands,* S. Doc. 150, 71st Cong., 2d sess. Later, during the Manchurian crisis, Stimson remarked that "the whole trouble with Japan and her intransigence is based upon her belief that we are going to give up the Philippines and that we do not wish to remain a Far Eastern power"; were the United States to correct that misapprehension, "we should have no trouble with Japan" (Stimson Diary, February 3, 1932, Stimson Papers).

24. Stimson to McCoy, June 11, 1930, Box 106, Stimson Papers; Stimson Diary, October 1, 1930, Stimson Papers. According to William R. Castle, around the time of his inauguration, President Hoover "had practically decided" to appoint McCoy governor general but chose Dwight Davis at the last minute (William R. Castle Diaries, February 28 and May 18, 1929, Houghton Library, Harvard University).

25. Stimson Diary, October 3 and 4, 1930, Stimson Papers. McCoy's association with the unpopular regime of Leonard Wood did his candidacy little good in Philippine eyes.

26. Ibid., May 19, 1931.

27. Ibid., June 3, 10, and 14, 1931.

28. Memorandum prepared by McCoy and Quezon, June 18, 1931, Box 27, McCoy Papers. Emphasis added.

29. McCoy to Hurley, "Concerning relations between the United States and the Philippine Islands, summarizing considered views of all executive departments, with certain conclusions and recommendations," June 18, 1931, Box 83, McCoy Papers.

30. Stimson Diary, June 14, 1931, Stimson Papers; Theodore Friend, *Between Two Empires: The Ordeal of the Philippines* (New Haven, Conn., 1965), pp. 61-67; Henry L. Stimson and McGeorge Bundy, *On Active Service in Peace and War* (New York, 1948), pp. 147, 149. Reason exists to question the sincerity of Quezon's support for the plan from the

outset. Hoover and Stimson clearly had McCoy in mind as the last governor general to oversee the transition to dominion status. But in October 1931, before the demise of the dominion plan, Quezon and his colleagues succeeded in blocking another attempt to appoint McCoy as governor general (Stimson Diary, October 29, 1931, Stimson Papers).

31. For an adulatory account of Butler's career, see Lowell Thomas, *Old Gimlet Eye: The Adventures of Smedley D. Butler* (New York, 1933); more recent is Hans Schmidt, *Maverick Marine: General Smedley D. Butler and the Contradictions of American Military History* (Lexington, Ky., 1987).

32. Schmidt, *Maverick Marine*, p. 204.

33. Ibid., pp. 205-208.

34. *NYT*, January 27 and 30, 1931; Stimson Diary, January 27, 1931, Stimson Papers. For an account of the affair from Butler's point of view, see Robert B. Asprey, "The Court-Martial of Smedley Butler," *Marine Corps Gazette* 43 (December 1959): 28-34.

35. Thomas, *Gimlet Eye*, p. 307; *NYT*, January 30, January 31, and February 3, 1931; "Our Comic Opera Court-Martial," *Literary Digest* 108 (February 28, 1931): 10.

36. Stimson Diary, January 30 and February 4, 1931, Stimson Papers.

37. Ibid., February 4 and 6, 1931.

38. McCoy, "Memorandum to go with newspaper articles—Smedley Butler," October 30, 1931, Box 26, McCoy Papers; *NYT*, February 9 and 10, 1931.

39. Stimson Diary, January 30 and February 6, 1931, Stimson Papers.

## CHAPTER 10
## THE LYTTON COMMISSION

1. League of Nations, *Manchuria: Report of the Commission of Enquiry Appointed by the League of Nations* (Washington, D.C., 1932), pp. 67-72 [hereafter cited as Lytton Report]; Gary B. Ostrower, *Collective Insecurity: The United States and the League of Nations during the Early Thirties* (Lewisburg, Penn., 1979), p. 11.

2. Henry L. Stimson, *The Far Eastern Crisis: Recollections and Observations* (New York, 1936). Manchuria also received extensive treatment in Stimson's memoirs (see Stimson and McGeorge Bundy, *On Active Service in Peace and War* [New York, 1948], Chapter 9). The best study of Stimson's role in the crisis is Armin Rappaport, *Henry L. Stimson and Japan, 1931-1933* (Chicago, 1963). The best overall study is Christopher Thorne, *The Limits of Foreign Policy: The West, the League, and the Far Eastern Crisis of 1931-1933* (New York, 1973). For an extended treatment of McCoy's role, see Susan Bradshaw, "The United States and East Asia: Frank Ross McCoy and the Lytton Commission, 1931-1933," (Ph.D. dissertation, Georgetown University, 1974).

3. Akira Iriye, *Across the Pacific* (New York, 1967), pp. 182-186; Thorne, *Limits*, pp. 50-52, 56.

4. Thorne, *Limits*, pp. 50-52, 56; Rappaport, *Stimson*, p. 36.

5. Robert H. Ferrell, *American Diplomacy in the Great Depression* (New Haven, Conn., 1957), passim; Rappaport, *Stimson*, pp. 34-37; Stimson, *Far Eastern Crisis*, p. 56.

6. Stimson, *Far Eastern Crisis*, pp. xi, 34; Stimson Diary, September 22, October 9, and October 16, 1931, Henry Lewis Stimson Diary and Papers, Yale University [hereafter cited as Stimson Papers].

7. Stimson Diary, September 23 and 24, 1931, Stimson Papers.

8. Rappaport, *Stimson*, p. 30; Stimson Diary, October 16 and 19, 1931, Stimson Papers.

9. Stimson Diary, November 14, 1931, and April 27, 1932, Stimson Papers.

10. Ibid., November 20 and 21, 1931, February 21, 1932, and April 28, 1932; Stimson to Reed, August 11, 1932, 793.94 comm/334A, U.S., Department of State, "General

Records of the State Department," Record Group 59, National Archives [hereafter cited as RG 59, NA]; Stimson, *Far Eastern Crisis*, p. 188; Ostrower, *Collective Insecurity*, pp. 102, 125.

11. Stimson Diary, December 21 and 22, 1931, Stimson Papers; Maj. Gen. Frank Parker to McCoy, January 6, 1932, Box 28, Frank Ross McCoy Papers, Library of Congress [hereafter cited as McCoy Papers]. McCoy was actually the third candidate considered. The League itself suggested Walter D. Hines, a New York City lawyer, and Stimson proposed Henry P. Fletcher, McCoy's compatriot from 1718 H Street and a retired foreign service officer. When both Hines and Fletcher declined the appointment, Stimson recorded that he was "very much relieved . . . because I think McCoy is a better man than either of those two" (Stimson Diary, December 22, 1931, Stimson Papers).

12. Prentiss Gilbert to Stimson, December 23, 1931, 793.94 comm/13, RG 59, NA; Stimson Diary, December 26, 1931, Stimson Papers.

13. Stimson Diary, December 26, 1931, Stimson Papers.

14. Ibid., January 20, 1932, and February 1, 2, and 4, 1932. Because he was in Washington preparing for his mission at this time, McCoy also assisted Stimson and the State Department inner circle in drafting the secretary's well-known letter to Senator Borah (James C. Thompson, Jr., "The Role of the State Department," *Pearl Harbor as History*, ed. by Dorothy Borg and Shumpei Okamoto [New York, 1973], p. 93).

15. Biographical data on the commissioners is contained in Box 77, McCoy Papers.

16. Personal interview with Maj. Gen. William Biddle, USA, Ret., Alexandria, Virginia, July 7, 1978. Lieutenant Biddle accompanied McCoy in the capacity of military aide.

17. Biddle, "Military Narrative of the Travels and Work of the Far Eastern Commission of Inquiry," Box 76, McCoy Papers, p. 9; McCoy to family, March 4, 1932, Box 8, and McCoy to Sherman V. Hasbrouk, April 15, 1932, Box 28, McCoy Papers; *Japan Advertiser*, March 6 and 7, 1932, scrapbook, Box 95, McCoy Papers.

18. "Record of Interview with Lieut. General Araki—War Minister of Japan," March 5, 1932, Box 72, McCoy Papers.

19. "Record of Interviews with Mr. Yoshizawa, Foreign Minister of Japan," March 7, 1932, Box 76, McCoy Papers.

20. "Military Narrative," pp. 10–11; Nelson T. Johnson to Stimson, March 26, 1932, 793.94 comm/150, RG 59, NA.

21. "Military Narrative," p. 19; Lytton Report, pp. 84–88; Thorne, *Limits*, pp. 204–210; Stimson Diary, February 8, 1932, Stimson Papers.

22. Lytton Report, p. 84; Wilbur J. Carr (acting secretary of state) to American consul, Shanghai, March 18, 1932, 793.94 comm/146, RG 59, NA; McCoy to family, April 9, 1932, Box 8, McCoy Papers.

23. Lytton Report, p. 84; McCoy to family, April 9, 1932, Box 8, McCoy Papers.

24. McCoy to family, April 9, 1932, Box 8, McCoy Papers; Taylor to McCoy, March 18, 1932, Box 29, McCoy Papers.

25. McCoy to family, April 9, 1932, Box 8, McCoy Papers. For further evidence of McCoy's favorable opinion of the Kuomintang, see "Military Narrative," pp. 28, 34.

26. Lytton Report, p. 11. McCoy apparently found the layover in Peking discouraging. To a friend he wrote: "It is pretty hard to keep up the guise of hopeful peacemakers when we are wandering around in such dense oriental jungle" (McCoy to Col. T. A. Roberts, April 5, 1932, Box 29, McCoy Papers).

27. Blakeslee, "The Lytton Commission," speech delivered to the U.S. Army War College, December 7, 1932, Box 78, McCoy Papers; Joseph Grew, "Memorandum of Conversation between the Ambassador and General F. R. McCoy," July 14, 1932, 793.94 comm/310, RG 59, NA; Johnson to Stimson, June 16, 1932, 793.94 comm/316, RG 59, NA.

28. McCoy to family, May 19, 1932, Box 8, McCoy Papers; M. S. Myers (U.S. consul general in Mukden), undated memorandum, 793.94 comm/281, RG 59, NA; Blakeslee, "Lytton Commission"; "Military Narrative," p. 71. For a firsthand account of Japanese security measures, see Amleto Vespa, *Secret Agent of Japan* (Garden City, N.Y., 1938), pp. 147-159.

29. "Record of Interview with Lt. General Honjo, Commander in Chief, Kwantung Army," undated, and "Record of Interviews with Colonel Komatsubara, Chief of Special Service, Kwantung Army, Harbin," May 13, 1932, Box 76, McCoy Papers.

30. "Memorandum of Conversation between the Ambassador and General F. R. McCoy," July 14, 1932; Blakeslee, "Lytton Commission"; C. Walter Young, "An Interview with General Ma Cha Shan," October 4, 1933, Box 30, McCoy Papers. McCoy developed a high opinion of the Japanese forces in Manchuria. He told Henry Luce, the publishing magnate, in Peking that the Kwantung Army was "a magnificent war machine"; Japan had "soldiers that any officer would be proud to command," and they "were prepared to . . . settle the issue by combat" ("Conversation," June 10, 1932, 793.94 comm/297, RG 59, NA).

31. Lytton Report, p. 12.

32. "Memorandum of Conversation between the Ambassador and General F. R. McCoy," July 15, 1932, 793.94 comm/310, RG 59, NA; "Record of Interview of Count Uchida, Foreign Minister of Japan," July 14, 1932, Box 76, McCoy Papers.

33. "Memorandum of Conversation between the Ambassador and General F. R. McCoy," July 15, 1932. Emphasis in the original.

34. "Record of Interview of Count Uchida, Foreign Minister of Japan," July 14, 1932; "Memorandum of Conversation between the Ambassador and General F. R. McCoy," July 14 and 15, 1932; McCoy to Gordon Johnston, June 18, 1932, Box 28, McCoy Papers; McCoy to Mrs. Ogden Reid, June 17, 1932, Box 29, McCoy Papers.

35. "Record of Interview of Count Uchida, Foreign Minister of Japan," July 12 and 14, 1932.

36. Ibid.

37. "Memorandum of Conversation between the Ambassador and General F. R. McCoy," July 14 and 15, 1932; "Conversation," July 21, 1932, 793.94 comm/340, RG 59, NA.

38. McCoy to Stimson, July 22, 1932, Box 111, Stimson Papers.

39. McCoy to family, March 4, 1932, Box 8, McCoy Papers.

40. Blakeslee to Hornbeck, September 14, 1932, reprinted as an appendix to Rappaport, *Stimson*, pp. 207-231; McCoy to family, August 8, 1932, Box 8, McCoy Papers.

41. Blakeslee to Hornbeck, September 14, 1932, in Rappaport, *Stimson*, pp. 207-231; "Work of the Commission," June 13, 1932, vol. 52, Nelson T. Johnson Papers, Library of Congress [hereafter cited as Johnson Papers].

42. Blakeslee to Hornbeck, September 14, 1932, in Rappaport, *Stimson*, pp. 207-231.

43. Ibid.; Biddle interview, July 7, 1978.

44. McCoy to family, September 6, 1932, Box 8, McCoy Papers; Lytton Report, pp. 23, 29, 38, 71, 97, 126, 128.

45. Lytton Report, pp. 129-131, 133-138.

46. "Report of League Commission, etc.," September 1, 1932, vol. 52, Johnson Papers. McCoy told Johnson that the United States "did not appreciate the methods of the Japanese," especially that country's penchant for initiating hostilities by means of unannounced, preemptive attacks. McCoy and Johnson both agreed that the Japanese "would be quite capable . . . of attacking us."

47. Blakeslee to Hornbeck, September 14, 1932, in Rappaport, *Stimson*, pp. 207-231; Stimson Diary, September 26, 1932, Stimson Papers; see also Stimson to McCoy, October 5, 1932, Box 28, McCoy Papers.

48. "Summary of American Editorial Opinion on the Lytton Report," October 5, 1932, 793.94 comm/433, RG 59, NA; Rappaport, *Stimson*, p. 174.

49. Rappaport, *Stimson*, pp. 183-184, 188-191.

50. Ibid., pp. 185-188; Hugh Wilson to Stimson, November 25 and December 4, 1932, 793.94 comm/560 and 603, RG 59, NA.

51. Wilson to Stimson, December 4, 1932, 793.94 comm/604, RG 59, NA.

52. Stimson Diary, December 31, 1932, and January 4, 1933, Stimson Papers. Even before Stimson could meet with McCoy, Secretary of War Patrick Hurley drafted him to assist in writing Hoover's veto of a just-passed Philippine independence bill (see folder labeled "Philippine Islands 1932 [*sic*] Veto Message," Box 83, McCoy Papers).

53. Thorne, *Limits*, pp. 334-336; Rappaport, *Stimson*, pp. 198-199.

54. Cranford to Military Intelligence Division, War Department, July 13, 1932, 793.94 comm/318, RG 59, NA.

55. McCoy to Lytton, September 4, 1933, and Lytton to McCoy, October 3, 1933, Box 30, McCoy Papers.


CHAPTER 11
NEW DIRECTIONS

1. MacArthur to McCoy, August 2 and October 28, 1932, Boxes 8 and 28, Frank Ross McCoy Papers, Library of Congress; hereafter cited as McCoy Papers.

2. Stimson Diary, February 10 and March 2, 1933, Henry Lewis Stimson Diary and Papers, Yale University; hereafter cited as Stimson Papers.

3. Ibid., May 25, 1933; Stimson to McCoy, May 21, 1933, Box 30, McCoy Papers; McCoy to family, June 1, 1933, Box 8, McCoy Papers; McCoy to Blanton Winship, June 13, 1933, Box 31, McCoy Papers; McCoy to George Corcoran, September 6, 1933, Box 29, McCoy Papers.

4. McCoy to Corcoran, September 6, 1933, Box 29, McCoy Papers.

5. MacArthur to McCoy, April 11, 1934, Box 32, McCoy Papers.

6. McCoy to family, May 1, 1934, Box 8, McCoy Papers; McCoy to MacArthur, May 1, 1934, Box 32, McCoy Papers; "Notes on the question of the continuance of compulsory military training at the University of Minnesota," April 30, 1934, Box 32, McCoy Papers; Charles Chatfield, *For Peace and Justice: Pacifism in America, 1914-1941* (Knoxville, Tenn., 1971), pp. 152-158.

7. *The Kansas Industrialist*, February 21, 1934, Box 89, McCoy Papers; "The Army," April 4, 1934, Box 89, McCoy Papers; Stimson Diary, October 5, 1934, Stimson Papers; McCoy to H. Otley Beyer, November 8, 1934, Box 31, McCoy Papers.

8. McCoy to family, April 3, 1935, Box 8, McCoy Papers; Forrest C. Pogue, *George C. Marshall: Education of a General* (New York, 1963), pp. 288-289, 298-299. McCoy and Marshall remained close friends thereafter (see Larry I. Bland, ed., *The Papers of George Catlett Marshall: "The Soldierly Spirit," December 1880-June 1939*, 2 vols. [Baltimore, 1981- ], 1: 344, 406, 506, 615-616).

9. Col. Charles Burnett to McCoy, January 30, 1936, Box 33, McCoy Papers.

10. McCoy to family, March 11 and June 16, 1936, Box 8, McCoy Papers.

11. McCoy to family, July 1, 1936, Box 8, McCoy Papers; Stimson Diary, November 22, 1935, and January 14, 1936, Stimson Papers; McCoy to Walter H. Mallory (executive director of the Council on Foreign Relations), May 18 and October 29, 1936, Box 72, McCoy Papers; "A Conference for University Men on a Reassessment of the Traditional Bases of American Foreign Policy," Box 72, McCoy Papers; "Conference for University Men on 'Ways of Staying Out of War,'" Box 72, McCoy Papers; Edgar P. Dean to McCoy,

June 15, 1938, Box 72, McCoy Papers; on the history of the Council on Foreign Relations, see Robert D. Schulzinger, *The Wise Men of Foreign Affairs* (New York, 1984).

12. *New York Times* [hereafter cited as *NYT*], July 29, 1938, and October 9, 1939; for McCoy's honorary degrees, see Box 100, McCoy Papers.

13. McCoy to Forbes, August 20, 1938, W. Cameron Forbes Papers, Houghton Library, Harvard University [hereafter cited as Forbes Papers]; draft article for the *St. Louis Post-Dispatch,* November 29, 1938, Box 89, McCoy Papers; "Remarks to *Herald-Tribune* Forum," October 26, 1938, Box 89, McCoy Papers; "Broader Aspects of National Defense," January 31, 1939, Box 90, McCoy Papers; "A System for the Conduct of War by Our Democracy," *Proceedings of the Academy of Political Science* 18 (May 1939): 99-102 [typescript in Box 90, McCoy Papers]; see also *NYT,* May 4, 1939.

14. Russell F. Weigley, "The Role of the War Department and the Army," *Pearl Harbor as History,* ed. by Dorothy Borg and Shumpei Okamoto (New York, 1973), pp. 166, 188.

15. McCoy to Stimson, December 6, 1934, Box 118, Stimson Papers.

16. Laurence A. Shoup and William Minter, *Imperial Brain Trust: The Council on Foreign Relations and United States Foreign Policy* (New York, 1977), pp. 70-72. Although the Council on Foreign Relations and the Foreign Policy Association were on friendly terms, their relationship was not that of equals. As McCoy commented in 1942, "we have a very pleasant relationship with the personnel at the Council and we continue to talk over more or less parallel activities from time to time and we help each other out on occasion. The cooperation has been, however, mostly on our side, but we will continue to be Christian-like" (McCoy to Harvey N. Pike, December 22, 1942, Box 68, Foreign Policy Association Papers, State Historical Society of Wisconsin, Madison, Wisconsin; hereafter cited as FPA Papers, Madison).

17. Foreign Policy Association (FPA), *Fifty Years: The Story of the Foreign Policy Association, 1918-1968* (New York, n.d.), pp. 3-7; Frank Winchester Abbott, "From Versailles to Munich: The Foreign Policy Association and American Foreign Policy" (Ph.D. dissertation, Texas Tech University, 1972), pp. 10-30, 40-42.

18. FPA, *Fifty Years,* pp. 7-9; Abbott, "From Versailles to Munich," pp. 43-44, 54-55, 96-98.

19. Abbott, "From Versailles to Munich," p. 282; *NYT,* February 2, 1978.

20. *NYT,* July 10, 1939; "Democracy and Foreign Policy," October 29, 1939, Box 90, McCoy Papers. For a record of McCoy's speaking engagements, see the report of the FPA Speaker's Bureau, December 18, 1940, "FPA Office Reports," Foreign Policy Association Files, maintained at FPA headquarters, 345 E. 46th Street, New York; hereafter cited as FPA Files, New York. McCoy also contributed occasionally to FPA publications. For example, see his "Our Relations with the Far East," in *Foreign Policy Reports* 19 (October 15, 1943): 190-193 (copy in Box 91, FPA Papers, Madison). McCoy apparently harbored earlier doubts about the association. After accepting his new appointment, he wrote to a friend that "I've changed my mind since learning more about the work of the F.P.A. which interests me now very much" (McCoy to Harbord, June 29, 1939, James G. Harbord Papers, New York Historical Society).

21. "Draft for Notice in Bulletin," undated, Box 67, FPA Papers, Madison. At the end of World War II when Mrs. Dwight Morrow solicited McCoy's signature on a petition asking the president to distribute surplus food to war-ravaged areas, McCoy responded that the FPA policy of "not taking action on public issues" did not permit him to sign. He added: "I have made it a practice not to join committees having to do with such matters of a public nature" (McCoy to Mrs. Morrow, September 10, 1945, Box 68, FPA Papers, Madison).

22. On FPA activities and expansion, see "Informal Report of the President for the Year 1940" and similar documents for 1941-1945 in "FPA Office Reports," FPA Files,

New York; also, "Minutes of a Meeting of the Board of Directors of the Foreign Policy Association," October 25, 1939, "FPA Corporate Record, Jan. '39–Jan. '43," FPA Files, New York.

23. "The FPA in the War," *Foreign Policy Bulletin* 21 (December 26, 1941): 2–3 (copy in FPA Files, New York); "Minutes of a Meeting of the Board of Directors of the Foreign Policy Association," January 27, 1943, "FPA Corporate Record, Jan. '43–Jan. '45," FPA Files, New York.

24. Robert A. Divine, *Second Chance: The Triumph of Internationalism in America during World War II* (New York, 1967).

25. Shoup and Minter, *Imperial Brain Trust,* pp. 118–122; Schulzinger, *Wise Men,* p. 94.

26. *NYT,* March 6, 1941; "Report of Civil Air Mission of the Inter-American Escadrille to the American Republics," scrapbook, Box 97, McCoy Papers (this scrapbook contains a large number of press clippings from a variety of Latin American newspapers, indicative of the prominent foreign press coverage that the mission received); McCoy to W. Cameron Forbes, February 26, 1941, Folder 182, Forbes Papers; on U.S. concerns over Axis penetration into Latin America, see Stetson Conn and Byron Fairchild, *The Framework of Hemisphere Defense* (Washington, D.C., 1960), pp. 6–14.

27. Elting Morison, *Turmoil and Tradition: A Study of the Life and Times of Henry L. Stimson* (Boston, 1960), pp. 478–482; Henry L. Stimson and McGeorge Bundy, *On Active Service in Peace and War* (New York, 1948), pp. 350–351, 500, 530; Stimson Diary, September 12 and 21, 1940, January 31, 1943, and February 1, 1943, Stimson Papers; John Garry Clifford and Samuel R. Spencer, Jr., *The First Peacetime Draft* (Lawrence, Kansas, 1986), p. 97.

28. Stimson Diary, December 16, 1941, Stimson Papers; *NYT,* December 17, 1941; Martin V. Melosi, *The Shadow of Pearl Harbor: Political Controversy over the Surprise Attack, 1941–1946* (College Station, Tex., 1977), pp. 31–33.

29. William R. Castle Diaries, December 8, 1941, Houghton Library, Harvard University.

30. Melosi, *Shadow of Pearl Harbor,* pp. 38–44; "Report of the Roberts Commission," Joint Committee on the Investigation of Pearl Harbor Attack (79th Cong., 1st sess.), *Pearl Harbor Attack,* part 39 (Washington, D.C., 1946), pp. 1–18; Gordon W. Prange, *At Dawn We Slept: The Untold Story of Pearl Harbor* (New York, 1981), pp. 592–604.

31. Stimson Diary, January 25 and 26, 1942, Stimson Papers. The *Times* and *Sun* quotations, both from editions of January 26, 1942, are in Box 84, McCoy Papers, which contains other clippings pertaining to the Roberts Report.

32. The best scholarly analysis of the reasons for American unpreparedness on December 7 is Roberta Wohlstetter, *Pearl Harbor: Warning and Decision* (Stanford, Calif., 1962). Melosi, *Shadow of Pearl Harbor,* traces the course of the controversy stemming from the attack.

33. *NYT,* June 28 and July 3, 1942.

34. Undated press release [July 1942], Box 79, McCoy Papers; Stimson Diary, July 9, 1942, Stimson Papers.

35. Stimson Diary, July 1 and 6, 1942, Stimson Papers; press release, July 8, 1942, Box 79, McCoy Papers.

36. Stimson Diary, July 9, 1942, Stimson Papers; "Secret Saboteur Trial," unidentified newspaper clipping, Box 79, McCoy Papers.

37. Stimson to McCoy, August 11, 1942, Box 79, McCoy Papers; McCoy to McCormick, August 13, 1942, Box 79, McCoy Papers.

## CHAPTER 12
## THE FAR EASTERN COMMISSION

1. George F. Kennan, "The Sources of Soviet Conduct," *Foreign Affairs* 25 (July 1947): 582; Henry R. Luce, "The American Century," *Life* 10 (February 17, 1941): 61-65; on American public opinion in 1945, see John Lukacs, *1945: Year Zero* (Garden City, N.Y., 1978), Chapter 7.

2. "Establishment of a Far Eastern Advisory Commission," SWNCC 65/2, April 27, 1945, U.S., Executive Branch, "Records of the State-War-Navy Coordinating Committee," Record Group 353, National Archives; hereafter cited as SWNCC Records, RG 353, NA. This document, approved by the president on June 5, 1945, indicated that U.S. interest in an allied commission stemmed from the fear that the American people would support "only grudgingly" a situation in which the United States "would carry the sole burden" for the occupation. U.S., Department of State, *Occupation of Japan: Policy and Progress* (Washington, D.C., n.d.), pp. 7-8; for the terms of references of the FEAC, see ibid., pp. 67-68; George H. Blakeslee, *The Far Eastern Commission: A Study in International Cooperation, 1945 to 1952* (Washington, D.C., 1953), pp. 2-5.

3. McCoy's resignation as president of the Foreign Policy Association was effective April 1, 1946. Honoring McCoy's contributions to the FPA, Mrs. Thomas Lamont, a member of the association's board of directors, contributed $100,000 to the FPA to establish the Frank R. McCoy Fund (Florence Lamont to William W. Lancaster, July 20, 1946, "FPA Office Reports," Foreign Policy Association Files, FPA headquarters, 345 E. 46th Street, New York).

4. Blakeslee, *Far Eastern Commission*, pp. 5-7.

5. Ibid.

6. William R. Castle Diaries, November 15, 1945, Houghton Library, Harvard University; McCoy to Byrnes, October 26, 1945, Box 223, U.S., Department of State, "Records of the Far Eastern Commission," Record Group 43, National Archives [hereafter cited as FEC Records, RG 43, NA].

7. "Confidential Minutes for F.E.A.C. Meetings," November 7 and 16, 1945, Box 3, FEC Records, RG 43, NA.

8. Blakeslee, *Far Eastern Commission*, p. 12-13. On U.S. reluctance to revise the FEAC terms of reference and its determination to avoid any loss of authority in doing so, see SWNCC 65/12, October 18, 1945, SWNCC Records, RG 353, NA.

9. "Far Eastern Commission Terms of Reference," December 30, 1945, Box 3, FEC Records, RG 43, NA. This document contains the terms of reference of both the FEC and the Allied Council.

10. Ibid.

11. Ibid. All of the safeguards of U.S. authority with the exception of the veto were lifted directly from McCoy's October 26 memorandum to the secretary of state, cited above. These safeguards subsequently became the devices by which the United States disabled the FEC.

12. "Summary of Meeting of U.S. Delegation, Far Eastern Commission," January 13, 1947, Box 224, FEC Records, RG 43, NA.

13. The commission continued to call itself the FEAC throughout its trip to Japan. Once back in Washington, however, it assumed its new title and added a representative of the Soviet Union. The commission's secretariat, internal organization, and operating procedures remained unchanged; McCoy continued to serve as permanent chairman of the FEC.

14. "The Reminiscences of Sir George Sansom," Columbia Oral History Collection, Butler Library, Columbia University, p. 77. Sansom was a prominent Japanologist and a member of the British delegation to the FEC. Blakeslee, "Report on the Far Eastern Commission's Trip to Japan, December 26, 1945–February 13, 1946," George Hubbard Blakeslee Papers, Clark University; hereafter cited as Blakeslee Papers.

15. Nelson T. Johnson, "Memorandum of Interview with General of the Army Douglas MacArthur," January 30, 1946, Box 43, Nelson T. Johnson Papers, Library of Congress [hereafter cited as Johnson Papers]. MacArthur told the FEC that the Japanese emperor was the "most perfect example of a stooge or Charlie McCarthy that one could imagine," but he favored his retention. For McCoy's impressions of the trip to Japan, see "Memorandum by the Chairman of the Far Eastern Commission to the Secretary of State," March 4, 1946, U.S., Department of State, *Papers Relating to the Foreign Relations of the United States (1946)*, vol. 8 (Washington, D.C., 1942), pp. 159–160; hereafter cited as *FRUS*.

16. Transcript of first meeting, February 26, 1946, Box 7, FEC Records, RG 43, NA.

17. Johnson, "Memorandum by the Secretary General of the Far Eastern Commission," January 30, 1946, *FRUS* (1946), vol. 8, 124; *New York Times* [hereafter cited as *NYT*] March 13, 1946; Blakeslee, *Far Eastern Commission*, p. 55.

18. D. Clayton James, *The Years of MacArthur: Triumph and Disaster, 1945–1964* (Boston, 1985), pp. 126–128, 135; Blakeslee, *Far Eastern Commission*, pp. 45–47; for a revised version of the draft constitution, see Department of State, *Occupation of Japan*, pp. 117–132; MacArthur's public endorsement of the constitution is at ibid., pp. 132–133.

19. Transcripts of third and fourth meetings, March 14 and 20, 1946, Box 7, FEC Records, RG 43, NA; "Reminiscences of Sir George Sansom," p. 75.

20. Transcript of third meeting, March 14, 1946, Box 7, FEC Records, RG 43, NA.

21. Transcript of fourth meeting, March 20, 1946, Box 7, FEC Records, RG 43, NA; for the policy decision and consultation, see *FRUS* (1946), vol. 8, pp. 182–184.

22. "Reply by General MacArthur to Far Eastern Commission on Timing of Elections," March 29, 1946, Department of State, *Occupation of Japan*, pp. 138–140.

23. Transcript of sixth meeting, March 30, 1946, Box 7, FEC Records, RG 43, NA.

24. Transcript of fifth meeting, March 27, 1946, Box 7, FEC Records, RG 43, NA; on the FEC's surprise at SCAP's announcement of a draft constitution, see transcript of sixteenth meeting, June 20, 1946, Box 7, FEC Records, RG 43, NA.

25. "Far Eastern Commission Communication for General of the Army Douglas MacArthur," April 10, 1946, *FRUS* (1946), vol. 8, pp. 194–196; McCoy to MacArthur, undated [April 1946], Box 221, FEC Records, RG 43, NA.

26. MacArthur to McCoy, April 15, 1946, *FRUS* (1946), vol. 8, pp. 202–205.

27. Vincent to Byrnes, April 19, 1946, Box 237, FEC Records, RG 43, NA; McCoy to MacArthur, April 22, 1946, *FRUS* (1946), vol. 8, pp. 213–214 (original in Box 221, FEC Records, RG 43, NA).

28. "Summary of Meeting of American Group on the Far Eastern Commission," May 6, 1946, Box 224, FEC Records, RG 43, NA; Blakeslee, *Far Eastern Commission*, pp. 49–50.

29. Transcript of eleventh meeting, May 13, 1946, Box 7, FEC Records, RG 43, NA. Because McCoy placed great value on the appearance of consensus, he was reluctant to use the veto. When opposing a motion, McCoy simply recommended that it be referred back to a committee for further discussion. The other members, knowing that McCoy *could* veto a proposition if pushed into doing so, fell into the habit early on of acquiescing in his requests for deferral. Eventually, however, the practice greatly annoyed the allies, who resented McCoy's enjoying the benefits of a veto while priding himself in not having

employed it (see transcript of forty-second meeting, January 23, 1947, Box 7, FEC Records, RG 43, NA).

30. MacArthur to the Joint Chiefs of Staff, May 4, 1946, *FRUS* (1946), vol. 8, pp. 220-226.

31. Transcripts of thirteenth and fourteenth meetings, May 29 and June 5, 1946, Box 7, FEC Records, RG 43, NA.

32. Ibid. "Tactics to be employed in FEC Proceedings," March 2, 1946, Box 223, FEC Records, RG 43, NA (this memorandum went on to recommend that McCoy be informed "that the State Department desires him to pursue a policy of great generosity in meeting the desires of other nations . . . to participate responsibly and very actively in the FEC activities"); SWNCC 294/1, May 7, 1946, SWNCC Records, RG 353, NA.

33. Unsigned memorandum, "ESP and JK Views Regarding the Far Eastern Commission," undated [July 1946], Box 223, FEC Records, RG 43, NA.

34. Galbraith to John H. Hilldring (assistant secretary of state for occupied areas), July 15, 1946, Box 223, FEC Records, RG 43, NA. There was, of course, another view. Those who made the pilgrimage to Tokyo generally took the position, expressed by one observer, that the FEC was "out of touch with realities" and insufficiently appreciative of the job that SCAP was doing (see Kenneth Colegrove to McCoy, April 26 and June 15, 1946, Box 237, FEC Records, RG 43, NA; and C. Stanton Babcock to Nelson T. Johnson, July 11 and 26, 1946, Box 43, Johnson Papers).

35. FEC 031/19, "Basic Principles for a New Japanese Constitution," reprinted in *Activities of the Far Eastern Commission: Report by the Secretary General, February 26, 1946-July 10, 1947* (Washington, D.C., 1947), pp. 65-66; Byrnes to Johnson, July 12, 1946, *FRUS* (1946), vol. 8, pp. 266-267. On allied dissatisfaction with the draft, see Berendsen's remarks in transcript of twenty-first meeting, July 25, 1946, Box 7, FEC Records, RG 43, NA.

36. For correspondence pertaining to amending the constitution, see *FRUS* (1946), vol. 8, pp. 276-280, 289-291; summary of U.S. delegation meeting, August 19, 1946, Box 224, FEC Records, RG 43, NA.

37. Blakeslee to Dwight Lee, July 6, 1946, Box 9, Dwight E. Lee Papers, Clark University; hereafter cited as Lee Papers. In a policy statement drafted at McCoy's direction and approved by SWNCC, Blakeslee went so far as to argue that to permit the FEC to approve the constitution would violate the Potsdam declaration's promise to create a government "in accordance with the freely expressed will of the Japanese people" [SWCC 228/8, July 16, 1946, *FRUS* (1946), vol. 8, pp. 269-271].

38. Transcripts of twenty-fifth, twenty-sixth, and twenty-eighth meetings, September 12, 19, and 25, 1946, Box 7, FEC Records, RG 43, NA.

39. Daniel Fahey to McCoy, September 6, 1946, Box 221, FEC Records, RG 43, NA; transcripts of twenty-sixth and twenty-seventh meetings, September 19 and 21, 1946, Box 7, FEC Records, RG 43, NA.

40. FEC 031/40, *Activities of the Far Eastern Commission*, p. 67. MacArthur's response to the October 17 policy decision is reprinted in *FRUS* (1946), vol. 8, pp. 352-353.

41. Transcripts of thirty-second, thirty-third, and thirty-fifth meetings, October 31, November 1, and November 21, 1946, Box 7, FEC Records, RG 43, NA; summary of meetings of U.S. delegation, November 12, 1946, Box 224, FEC Records, RG 43, NA.

42. McCoy to acting secretary of state, September 24, 1946, *FRUS* (1946), vol. 8, pp. 317-318; summary of meeting of U.S. delegation, November 18, 1946, Box 224, FEC Records, RG 43, NA; McCoy to Hilldring, December 27, 1946, Box 238, FEC Records, RG 43, NA.

43. Transcript of thirtieth meeting, January 2, 1947, Box 7, FEC Records, RG 43, NA.

44. Ibid.

45. "The Question of Publication of the FEC Policy Decision on the Review of the New Japanese Constitution," undated, Box 221, FEC Records, RG 43, NA; MacArthur to State Department, January 22, 1949, Box 221, FEC Records, RG 43, NA; W. Walton Butterworth to Conrad Snow, March 21, 1949, Box 221, FEC Records, RG 43, NA; Howard C. Peterson to Hilldring, May 12, 1947, *FRUS* (1947), vol. 6, pp. 390-392; SWNCC 380, July 22, 1947, SWNCC Records, RG 353, NA.

46. Blakeslee, *Far Eastern Commission,* p. 194; transcript of fifty-ninth meeting, May 29, 1947, Box 8, FEC Records, RG 43, NA; Robert W. Barnett to Charles E. Saltzman, September 23, 1948, Box 223, FEC Records, RG 43, NA.

47. McCoy to Hilldring, August 11, 1947, *FRUS* (1947), vol. 6, pp. 271-273.

48. SANACC 380/2, October 24, 1947, Box 238, FEC Records, RG 43, NA; SANACC 389, December 5, 1947, "State-Army-Navy-Air Force Coordinating Committee Records," RG 353, NA (this committee, known by the acronym SANACC, was the successor to SWNCC).

49. Summary of meeting of U.S. delegation, September 8, 1947, Box 224, FEC Records, RG 43, NA; Blakeslee to Lee, June 16, 1946, Box 9, Lee Papers; "A Survey of the Attitudes of the States Composing the Far Eastern Commission," undated, Box 6, Blakeslee Papers; Samuel S. Stratton to McCoy, March 9, 1948, Box 223, FEC Records, RG 43, NA.

50. "The United States and the Far Eastern Commission," May 18, 1948, Box 224, FEC Records, RG 43, NA. This was the talking paper that McCoy used for his interview with Marshall.

51. Michael Schaller, "MacArthur's Japan: The View from Washington," *Diplomatic History* 10 (Winter 1986): 10-14.

52. Frank G. Wisner to William H. Draper, June 23, 1948, Box 223, FEC Records, RG 43, NA; "U.S. Responsibility for Delay in the FEC," November 23, 1948, Box 223, FEC Records, RG 43, NA; see also Michael Schaller, *The American Occupation of Japan* (New York, 1985), p. 123.

53. "The Far Eastern Commission: Accomplishments and Problems," January 24, 1949, Box 223, FEC Records, RG 43, NA.

54. Saltzman to Acheson, undated [January 1949], Box 223, FEC Records, RG 43, NA. Another State Department memorandum circulated at this time proposed that McCoy be instructed "to discontinue efforts to carry on the work of the Far Eastern Commission in a spirit of international harmony and accord" and to pay more attention to verbal sparring with the Soviets (Jack B. Tate to W. W. Butterworth, January 11, 1949, Box 223, FEC Records, RG 43 NA).


CHAPTER 13
THE END OF THE DAY

1. McCoy to Carolyn Martin, May 17, 1949, Box 73, Frank Ross McCoy Papers, Library of Congress [hereafter cited as McCoy Papers]; John H. Finlator to McCoy, October 6, 1950, Box 55, McCoy Papers.

2. For papers pertaining to McCoy's postretirement activities, see Boxes 83-85 and 88, McCoy Papers; Ridgway to McCoy, September 19, 1951, Box 56, McCoy Papers; see also Ridgway's memoir, *Soldier: The Memoirs of Matthew B. Ridgway* (New York, 1956), p. 37.

3. Blakeslee to McCoy, March 31, 1953, Box 56, McCoy Papers; McCoy to William A. Delano, November 7, 1953, Box 19, William A. Delano Papers, Yale University; *New York Times* [hereafter cited as *NYT*], June 6, 1954; personal interview with Brig. Gen. Sherman V. Hasbrouk, USA, Ret., Stone Bridge, New York, June 3, 1980. Section 21 of Arlington

National Cemetery, where Wood and McCoy are buried, is a VIP plot. Since 1954, only John Foster Dulles and Chief Justice Earl Warren have joined the two soldiers.

4. *NYT*, June 6, 1954; "The Reminiscences of Sir George Sansom," Columbia Oral History Collection, Butler Library, Columbia University, pp. 76–77.

5. After fifty years of public service, McCoy's estate was not even large enough to pay off the mortgage on his house. In a conversation with the author, Forrest Pogue recalled that after McCoy's death General Marshall raised sufficient funds from among McCoy's old friends to enable Mrs. McCoy to stay in her home.

6. "The Army's McCoy," *Literary Digest* 121 (April 25, 1936), scrapbook, Box 97, McCoy Papers.

7. Richard D. Challener has already pointed out the importance of this personalized civil-military consultation (see *Admirals, Generals, and American Foreign Policy, 1898-1914* [Princeton, N.J., 1973], pp. 402–412).

# Selected Bibliography

## PRIMARY SOURCES

*Personal Papers*

George Hubbard Blakeslee Papers, Clark University, Worcester, Mass.
William R. Castle Diaries, Harvard University, Cambridge, Mass.
William A. Delano Papers, Yale University, New Haven, Conn.
Henry P. Fletcher Papers, Library of Congress, Washington, D.C.
W. Cameron Forbes Papers, Harvard University, Cambridge, Mass.
Joseph C. Grew Diary and Papers, Harvard University, Cambridge, Mass.
Hermann Hagedorn Papers, Library of Congress, Washington, D.C.
James G. Harbord Papers, Library of Congress, Washington, D.C.
James G. Harbord Papers, New York Historical Society, New York, N.Y.
Leland Harrison, Jr., Papers, Library of Congress, Washington, D.C.
Nelson T. Johnson Papers, Library of Congress, Washington, D.C.
Dwight E. Lee Papers, Clark University, Worcester, Mass.
Frank Ross McCoy Papers, Library of Congress, Washington, D.C.
George Van Horn Mosely Papers, Library of Congress, Washington, D.C.
Francis Le Jau Parker Papers, Library of Congress, Washington, D.C.
William Phillips Papers, Harvard University, Cambridge, Mass.
Hugh Lenox Scott Papers, Library of Congress, Washington, D.C.
David Foote Sellers Papers, Library of Congress, Washington, D.C.
Henry Lewis Stimson Diary and Papers, Yale University, New Haven, Conn.
Willard Straight Papers, Cornell University, Ithaca, N.Y.
Francis White Papers, National Archives, Washington, D.C.
Leonard Wood Diary and Papers, Library of Congress, Washington, D.C.

*Unpublished Government Records*

U.S. Archives of the United States Military Academy. West Point, N.Y.
U.S. Department of State. "General Records of the State Department." Record Group 59, National Archives. Washington, D.C.

————. "Records of International Conferences, Commissions, and Expositions." Record Group 43, National Archives. Washington, D.C.

————. "General Records of the American Mission to Negotiate Peace, 1918-1931." Record Group 256, National Archives. Washington, D.C.

U.S. Executive Branch. "Records of the State-War-Navy Coordinating Committee." Record Group 353, National Archives. Washington, D.C.

U.S. Marine Corps. "Records of Marine Units in Nicaragua." Federal Records Center. Suitland, Md.

U.S. War Department. "Records of the Adjutant General." Record Group 94, National Archives. Washington, D.C.

————. "Records of the War Department General and Special Staffs." Record Group 165, National Archives. Washington, D.C.


*Published Government Reports and Documents*

*Activities of the Far Eastern Commission: Report by the Secretary General.* Washington, D.C.: Government Printing Office, 1947.

Challener, Richard D., comp. *United States Military Intelligence: Weekly Summaries, June 2-October 13, 1917.* New York: Garland Publishing Company, 1978.

*The Far Eastern Commission: Second Report by the Secretary General.* Washington, D.C.: Government Printing Office, 1949.

*The Far Eastern Commission: Third Report by the Secretary General.* Washington, D.C.: Government Printing Office, 1949.

Harbord, James G. *Report of the American Military Mission to Armenia,* 66th Cong., 2d sess. Senate Document 266. Washington, D.C.: Government Printing Office.

League of Nations. *Manchuria: Report of the Commission of Enquiry Appointed by the League of Nations.* Washington, D.C.: Government Printing Office, 1932.

Magoon, Charles E. *Report of Provisional Administration, 1908.* Havana: Rambla and Bouza, 1909.

Mosely, George Van Horn. *Mandatory Over Armenia,* 66th Cong., 2d sess., Senate Document 281. Washington, D.C.: Government Printing Office.

U.S. Congress. *Congressional Record.*

————. Joint Committee on the Investigation of the Pearl Harbor Attack. *Pearl Harbor Attack,* 79th Cong., 1st sess.

U.S. Department of State. *Papers Relating to the Foreign Relations of the United States* (1926-1932, 1945-1947). Washington, D.C.: Government Printing Office.

————. *Occupation of Japan: Policy and Progress.* Washington, D.C.: Government Printing office, n.d.

U.S. Senate. *Attack by United States Troops on Mount Dajo,* 59th Cong., 1st sess., Senate Document 289. Washington, D.C.: Government Printing Office.

————. *Independence of the Philippine Islands,* 71st Cong., 2d sess., Senate Document 150. Washington, D.C.: Government Printing Office.

————. *Treaty with the Sultan of Sulu,* 56th Cong., 1st sess., Senate Document 136. Washington, D.C.: Government Printing Office.

U.S. War Department. *Annual Reports of the Secretary of War* (1906, 1915-1916). Washington, D.C.: Government Printing Office.

————. *Civil Report of the Military Government of Cuba, January 1 to May 1, 1902.* Washington, D.C.: Government Printing Office, 1902.

————. *Report of the Governor General of the Philippine Islands* (1920-1925). Washington, D.C.: Government Printing Office.

———. *Report of the Military Governor of Cuba on Civil Affairs* (1900). Washington, D.C.: Government Printing Office, 1901.

———. *Report of the Philippines Commission* (1903-1906). Washington, D.C.: Government Printing Office.

———. *Report of the Special Mission on Investigation to the Philippine Islands.* Washington, D.C.: Government Printing Office, 1921.

Woodward, E. L., and Rohan Butler, comps. *Documents on British Foreign Policy, 1919-1939,* first series, vol. 4 (1919). London: Her Majesty's Stationary Office, 1952.


*Published Writings of Frank Ross McCoy*

McCoy, Frank Ross. "Mobilitate Vigemus." *Journal of the United States Cavalry Association* 23 (November 1912): 524-527.

———. "Mounted Push Ball." *Journal of the United States Cavalry Association* 20 (January 1910): 802-805.

———. "Notes on the German Maneuvers." *Journal of the United States Cavalry Association* 14 (July 1903): 21-33.

———. "The Passage of Streams by Cavalry." *Journal of the United States Cavalry Association* 18 (October 1907): 327-331.

———. *Principles of Military Training.* New York: P. F. Collier and Son, 1917.

———. "A System for the Conduct of War by Our Democracy." *Proceedings of the Academy of Political Science* 18 (May 1939): 99-102.

———. "The Taking of Havana by the British and Americans in 1762." *Journal of the United States Cavalry Association* 14 (October 1903): 228-260.


*Other Primary Sources*

Columbia Oral History Collection, Butler Library, Columbia University, New York:
"The Reminiscences of William Wilson Cumberland."
"The Reminiscences of James F. Curtis."
"The Reminiscences of Sir George Sansom."
Foreign Policy Association Files, 345 E. 46th Street, New York, N.Y.
Foreign Policy Association Papers, State Historical Society of Wisconsin, Madison, Wis.
Personal Interviews by the Author:
Maj. Gen. William S. Biddle, USA, Ret., July 7, 1978, Alexandria, Va.
Dr. Harold W. Dodds, June 21, 1977, Princeton, N.J.
Brig. Gen. Sherman V. Hasbrouk, USA, Ret., June 3, 1980, Stone Bridge, N. Y.
General Matthew B. Ridgway, USA, Ret., March 7, 1978, New York, N.Y.


## MEMOIRS

Bigelow, John, Jr. *Reminiscences of the Santiago Campaign.* New York: Harper and Brothers, 1899.

Bullard, Robert Lee. *Personalities and Reminiscences of the War.* New York: Doubleday, Page and Company, 1925.

Duffy, Francis P. *Father Duffy's Story.* New York: George H. Doran, Co., 1919.

Eisenhower, Dwight D. *At Ease: Stories I Tell to Friends.* Garden City, N.Y.: Doubleday and Company, 1967.

Grew, Joseph C. *Turbulent Era: A Diplomatic Record of Forty Years*. 2 vols. Boston: Houghton Mifflin, 1952.

Harbord, James G. *Leaves from a War Diary*. New York: Dodd, Mead, and Company, 1925.

Harriman, Mrs. J. Borden. *From Pinafores to Politics*. New York: Henry Holt and Company, 1923.

Heiser, Victor. *An American Doctor's Odyssey*. New York: W. W. Norton, 1936.

Hobbs, Horace P. *Kris and Krag: Adventures among the Moros of the Southern Philippines*. N.p., 1962.

Longworth, Alice Roosevelt. *Crowded Hours*. New York: Charles Scribner's Sons, 1933.

Parker, James. *The Old Army: Memories, 1872–1918*. Philadelphia: Dorrance and Company, 1929.

Phillips, William. *Ventures in Diplomacy*. Boston: Beacon Press, 1952.

Ridgway, Matthew B. *Soldier: The Memoirs of Matthew B. Ridgway*. New York: Harper and Brothers, 1956.

Scott, Hugh Lenox. *Some Memories of a Soldier*. New York: Century Company, 1928.

Stimson, Henry L. *My Vacations*. Privately printed, 1949.

Stimson, Henry L., and Bundy, McGeorge. *On Active Service in Peace and War*. New York: Harper and Brothers, 1948.

White, John R. *Bullets and Bolos*. New York: Century Company, 1928.

Wilson, Hugh R. *Diplomat between Wars*. New York: Longmans, Green, and Company, 1941.

## NEWSPAPERS AND PERIODICALS

*Current History*
*Literary Digest*
*The Nation*
*The New Republic*
*The New York Times*
*The Outlook*
*The World's Work*

## SECONDARY SOURCES

Abbott, Frank Winchester. "From Versailles to Munich: The Foreign Policy Association and American Foreign Policy." Ph.D. dissertation, Texas Tech University, 1972.

Abrahamson, James L. *America Arms for a New Century: The Making of a Great Military Power*. New York: Free Press, 1981.

Ambrose, Stephen E., and Barber, James A., Jr., eds. *The Military and American Society*. New York: Free Press, 1972.

American Battle Monuments Commission. *42d Division: Summary of Operations in the World War*. Washington, D.C.: Government Printing Office, 1944.

———. *32d Division: Summary of Operations in the World War*. Washington, D.C.: Government Printing Office, 1943.

"American Praise for Japan." *Far Eastern Review* 19 (October 1923): 646–647.

Anderson, William Hart. *The Philippine Problem*. New York: G. P. Putnam's Sons, 1939.

Asprey, Robert B. "The Court-Martial of Smedley Butler." *Marine Corps Gazette* 43 (December 1959): 28–34.

Bagby, Wesley M. *The Road to Normalcy: The Presidential Campaign and Election of 1920*. Baltimore: Johns Hopkins University Press, 1962.

Bailey, Thomas A. "Interest in a Nicaragua Canal, 1903-1931." *Hispanic American Historical Review* 16 (February 1936): 2-28.

————. *Woodrow Wilson and the Great Betrayal.* New York: MacMillan, 1945; reprint edition, Chicago: Quadrangle Books, 1963.

————. *Woodrow Wilson and the Lost Peace.* New York: Macmillan, 1944; reprint edition, Chicago: Quadrangle Books, 1963.

Bangs, John Kendrick. *Uncle Sam Trustee.* New York: Riggs Publishing Company, 1902.

Barry, Richard. "The End of Datto Ali." *Colliers,* June 9, 1906, pp. 17-19.

Beale, Howard K. *Theodore Roosevelt and the Rise of America to World Power.* Baltimore: Johns Hopkins University Press, 1956.

Beals, Carlton. *Banana Gold.* Philadelphia: J. B. Lippincott Company, 1932.

————. *The Crime of Cuba.* Philadelphia: J. B. Lippincott Company, 1933.

Biddle, William S. *Major General Frank Ross McCoy: Soldier-Statesman-American.* Lewistown, Pa.: n.p., 1956.

Blakeslee, George H. *The Far Eastern Commission: A Study in International Cooperation, 1945 to 1952.* Washington, D.C.: Government Printing Office, 1953.

Bland, Larry I., ed. *The Papers of George Catlett Marshall.* Vol. 1: *"The Soldierly Spirit," December 1880-June 1939.* Baltimore: Johns Hopkins University Press, 1981- .

Borg, Dorothy, and Okamoto, Shumpei, eds. *Pearl Harbor as History.* New York: Columbia University Press, 1973.

Bradshaw, Sister Susan, O.S.F. "The United States and East Asia: Frank Ross McCoy and the Lytton Commission, 1931-1933." Ph.D. dissertation, Georgetown University, 1974.

Braeman, John; Bremner, Robert H.; and Brody, David, eds. *Twentieth Century American Foreign Policy.* Columbus: Ohio State University Press, 1971.

Brown, Richard C. "Social Attitudes of American Generals, 1898-1940." Ph.D. dissertation, University of Wisconsin, 1951.

Busch, Noel F. *Two Minutes to Noon.* New York: Simon and Schuster, 1962.

Carter, William Harding. *The Life of Lieutenant General Chaffee.* Chicago: University of Chicago Press, 1917.

Cashin, Herschel V., and others. *Under Fire with the Tenth U.S. Cavalry.* New York: Arno Press, 1969.

Challener, Richard D. *Admirals, Generals, and American Foreign Policy, 1898-1914.* Princeton, N.J.: Princeton University Press, 1973.

Chambers, John Whiteclay, II. *To Raise an Army: The Draft Comes to Modern America.* New York: Free Press, 1987.

Chandler, Lester V. *Benjamin Strong, Central Banker.* Washington, D.C.: Brookings Institution, 1958.

Chatfield, Charles. *For Peace and Justice: Pacifism in America, 1914-1941.* Knoxville: University of Tennessee Press, 1971.

Clifford, John Garry. *The Citizen Soldiers: The Plattsburg Training Camp Movement, 1913-1920.* Lexington: University Press of Kentucky, 1972.

Clifford, John Garry, and Spencer, Samuel R., Jr. *The First Peacetime Draft.* Lawrence: University Press of Kansas, 1986.

Cline, Howard F. *The United States and Mexico.* Rev. ed. New York: Atheneum, 1976.

Coffman, Edward M. *The War to End All Wars.* New York: Oxford University Press, 1968.

Conn, Stetson, and Fairchild, Byron. *The Framework of Hemisphere Defense.* Washington, D.C.: Government Printing Office, 1960.

Crowell, Benedict, and Wilson, Robert Forrest. *Demobilization.* New Haven, Conn.: Yale University Press, 1921.

Cummins, LeJeune. *Quijote on a Burro.* Mexico City: La Impresora Azteca, 1958.

Cunliffe, Marcus. *Soldiers and Civilians.* Boston: Little, Brown, and Company, 1968.

Daniel, Robert L. "The Armenian Question and American-Turkish Relations, 1914–1927." *Mississippi Valley Historical Review* 46 (September 1959): 252–275.

Davis, Burke. *The Billy Mitchell Affair.* New York: Random House, 1967.

Dennett, Raymond, and Johnson, Joseph E., eds. *Negotiating with the Russians.* Boston: World Peace Foundation, 1951.

Denny, Harold Norman. *Dollars for Bullets.* New York: Dial Press, 1929.

DeNovo, John A. *American Interests and Policies in the Middle East, 1900–1939.* Minneapolis: University of Minnesota Press, 1963.

Dillard, Walter Scott. "The United States Military Academy, 1865–1900: The Uncertain Years." Ph.D. dissertation, University of Washington, 1972.

Divine, Robert A. *Second Chance: The Triumph of Internationalism in America during World War II.* New York: Atheneum, 1967.

Dodds, Harold W. "American Supervision of the Nicaraguan Election." *Foreign Affairs* 7 (April 1929): 488–496.

Ferrell, Robert H. *American Diplomacy in the Great Depression.* New Haven, Conn.: Yale University Press, 1957.

*Fifty Years: The Story of the Foreign Policy Association, 1918–1968.* New York: Foreign Policy Association, n.d.

Fitzgibbon, Russell H. *Cuba and the United States, 1900–1935.* Menasha, Wis.: George Banta Publishing Company, 1935.

Foner, Philip S. *The Spanish-Cuban-American War and the Birth of American Imperialism, 1895–1902.* 2 vols. New York: Monthly Review Press, 1972.

Fox, W. T. R. "The Military and United States Foreign Policy." *International Journal* 38 (Winter 1982–1983): 39–58,

Frederick, Olivia M. "Henry P. Fletcher and United States Latin American Policy, 1910–1930." Ph.D. dissertation, University of Kentucky, 1977.

Freidel, Frank. *The Splendid Little War.* Boston: Little, Brown, and Company, 1958.

Friend, Theodore. *Between Two Empires: The Ordeal of the Philippines, 1929–1946.* New Haven, Conn.: Yale University Press, 1965.

Ganoe, William A. *The History of the United States Army.* New York: Appleton-Century, 1936; reprint edition, Ashton, Md.: Archon, 1964.

Garlock, Glenn W. *Tales of the Thirty-Second.* West Salem, Wis.: Badger Publishing Company, 1927.

Garner, William R. *The Chaco Dispute: A Study of Prestige Diplomacy.* Washington, D.C.: Public Affairs Press, 1966.

Gates, John Morgan. "The Alleged Isolation of U.S. Army Officers in the Late 19th Century." *Parameters* 10 (September 1980): 32–45.

———. *Schoolbooks and Krags.* Westport, Conn.: Greenwood Press, 1973.

"George T. Summerlin." *Assembly* 7 (April 1948): 9–11.

Gidney, James B. *A Mandate for Armenia.* N.p.: Kent State University Press, 1967.

Gillette, Howard, Jr. "The Military Occupation of Cuba, 1899–1902: Workshop for American Progressivism." *American Quarterly* 25 (October 1973): 410–425.

Glass, Edward L. N., ed. *The History of the Tenth Cavalry, 1866–1921.* Fort Collins, Colo.: Old Army Press, 1972.

Gott, Camillus. "William Cameron Forbes and the Philippines, 1904–1946." Ph.D. dissertation, Indiana University, 1974.

Gould, Lewis L., ed. *The Progressive Era.* Syracuse, N.Y.: Syracuse University Press, 1974.

Gowing, Peter Gordon. *Mandate in Moroland: The American Government of Muslim Filipinos, 1899–1920.* Quezon City: Philippine Center for Advanced Studies, 1977.

Grabill, Joseph L. *Protestant Diplomacy and the Near East: Missionary Influence on American Policy, 1810-1927.* Minneapolis: University of Minnesota Press, 1971.

Greene, Fred. "The Military View of American National Policy." *American Historical Review* 66 (January 1961): 354-377.

Hagedorn, Hermann. *Leonard Wood: A Biography.* 2 vols. New York: Harper and Brothers, 1931.

Harbaugh, William Henry. *Power and Responsibility: The Life and Times of Theodore Roosevelt.* New York: Farrar, Straus, and Giroux, 1961.

Harper, James William. "Hugh Lenox Scott: Soldier-Diplomat, 1826-1917." Ph.D. dissertation, University of Virginia, 1968.

Harris, Charles H., III, and Sadler, Louis R. "The Plan of San Diego and the Mexican-United States War Crisis of 1916: A Reexamination." *Hispanic American Historical Review* 58 (August 1978): 383-408.

Hays, Samuel P. "The Politics of Reform in Municipal Government in the Progressive Era." *Pacific Northwest Quarterly* 55 (October 1964): 157-169.

————. *The Response to Industrialism, 1885-1914.* Chicago: University of Chicago Press, 1957.

Healy, David F. *The United States in Cuba, 1898-1902.* Madison: University of Wisconsin Press, 1963.

Hitchman, James H. "The American Touch in Imperial Administration." *The Americas* 24 (April 1968): 394-403.

————. *Leonard Wood and Cuban Independence, 1899-1902.* The Hague: Martinus Nijhoff, 1971.

Horn, James J. "U.S. Diplomacy and the 'Spector of Bolshevism' in Mexico (1924-1927)." *The Americas* 32 (July 1975): 31-45.

Hoyt, Frederic Gilman. "The Wood-Forbes Mission to the Philippines, 1921." Ph.D. dissertation, Claremont Graduate School, 1963.

Huntington, Samuel P. *The Soldier and the State.* New York: Vintage Books, 1957.

Hurley, Vic. *Swish of the Kris: The Story of the Moro.* New York: G. P. Dutton and Company, 1936.

Ireland, Gordon. *Boundaries, Possessions, and Conflicts in South America.* Cambridge, Mass.: Harvard University Press, 1938.

Iriye, Akira. *Across the Pacific.* New York: Harcourt, Brace, and World, 1967.

Israel, Jerry, ed. *Building the Organizational Society.* New York: Free Press, 1972.

James, D. Clayton. *The Years of MacArthur,* 3 vols. Boston: Houghton Mifflin Company, 1970-1985.

Joint War History Commissions of Michigan and Wisconsin. *The 32d Division in the World War, 1917-1919.* Milwaukee: Wisconsin Printing Company, 1920.

Jornacion, George William. "The Time of the Eagles: United States Army Officers and the Pacification of the Philippine Moros, 1899-1913." Ph.D. dissertation, University of Maine at Orono, 1973.

Kamman, William. *A Search for Stability: United States Diplomacy toward Nicaragua, 1925-1933.* Notre Dame, Ind.: University of Notre Dame Press, 1968.

Katz, Friedrich. *The Secret War in Mexico: Europe, the United States and the Mexican Revolution.* Chicago: University of Chicago Press, 1981.

Kennan, George F. "The Sources of Soviet Conduct." *Foreign Affairs* 25 (July 1947): 566-582.

Kirk, Grayson. *Philippine Independence.* New York: Farrar and Rinehart, 1936.

Kohn, Richard H. *Eagle and Sword: The Beginnings of the Military Establishment in America.* New York: Free Press, 1975.

Koistinen, Paul A. C. *The Military-Industrial Complex in Historical Perspective.* New York: Praeger, 1980.

Lane, Jack C. "American Military Past: The Need for New Approaches." *Military Affairs* 41 (October 1977): 109–113.

———. *Armed Progressive: General Leonard Wood.* San Rafael, Calif.: Presidio Press, 1978.

Langley, Lester D. *The Banana Wars: An Inner History of American Empire, 1900–1934.* Lexington: University Press of Kentucky, 1983.

Larned, Charles W. *Education from a Military Viewpoint.* Manlius, N.Y.: St. John's School, 1908.

———. "The Genius of West Point." *The Centennial of the United States Military Academy at West Point, New York.* Washington, D.C.: Government Printing Office, 1904.

Lea, Homer. *The Valor of Ignorance.* New York: Harper and Brothers, 1942.

Link, Arthur S. *Wilson: Campaigns for Progressivism and Peace.* Princeton, N.J.: Princeton University Press, 1965.

———. *Wilson: Confusions and Crises.* Princeton, N.J.: Princeton University Press, 1964.

———. *Wilson: The New Freedom.* Princeton, N.J.: Princeton University Press, 1956.

———. *Wilson: The Struggle for Neutrality.* Princeton, N.J.: Princeton University Press, 1960.

Lockmiller, David A. *Magoon in Cuba: A History of the Second Intervention, 1906–1909.* Chapel Hill: University of North Carolina Press, 1938.

Luce, Henry R. "The American Century." *Life* 10 (February 17, 1941): 61–65.

Lukacs, John. *1945: Year Zero.* Garden City, N.Y.: Doubleday, 1978.

Macaulay, Neill. *The Sandino Affair.* Chicago: Quadrangle Books, 1967.

McCoy, Donald R. *Calvin Coolidge: The Quiet President.* New York: Macmillan Company, 1967.

Mack, Gerstle. *The Land Divided: A History of the Panama Canal and Other Isthmian Canal Projects.* New York: Octagon Books, 1974.

McKee, Delber L. *Chinese Exclusion versus the Open Door Policy, 1900–1906.* Detroit: Wayne State University Press, 1977.

Melosi, Martin V. *The Shadow of Pearl Harbor: Political Controversy over the Surprise Attack, 1941–1946.* College Station: Texas A&M University Press, 1977.

Miller, William J. *Henry Cabot Lodge.* New York: James H. Heinerman, 1967.

Millett, Allan R. *The General: Robert L. Bullard and Officership in the United States Army, 1881–1925.* Westport, Conn.: Greenwood Press, 1975.

———. *The Politics of Intervention: The Military Occupation of Cuba, 1906–1909.* N.p.: Ohio State University Press, 1968.

Millett, Richard. *Guardians of the Dynasty.* Maryknoll, N.Y.: Orbis Books, 1977.

Millis, Walter. *Arms and Men.* New York: G. P. Putnam's Sons, 1956.

Millis, Walter; Mansfield, Harvey C.; and Stein, Harold. *Arms and the State.* New York: Twentieth Century Fund, 1958.

Minger, Ralph Elden. "William Howard Taft and the United States Intervention in Cuba in 1906." *Hispanic American Historical Review* 41 (February 1961): 75–89.

Mishler, Edward Charles. "Francis White and the Shaping of United States Latin American Policy, 1921–1933." Ph.D. dissertation, University of Maryland, 1975.

Morison, Elting. *Turmoil and Tradition: A Study of the Life and Times of Henry L. Stimson.* Boston: Houghton Mifflin Company, 1960.

Munro, Dana G. "The Establishment of Peace in Nicaragua." *Foreign Affairs* 11 (July 1933): 696–705.

————. *Intervention and Dollar Diplomacy in the Caribbean, 1900–1921*. Princeton, N.J.: Princeton University Press, 1964.

————. *The United States and the Caribbean Republics, 1921–1933*. Princeton, N.J.: Princeton University Press, 1974.

Norton, Nile Brown. "Frank R. McCoy and American Diplomacy, 1928–1932." Ph.D. dissertation, University of Denver, 1966.

Nye, Roger Hurless. "The United States Military Academy in an Era of Educational Reform, 1900–1925." Ph.D. dissertation, Columbia University, 1968.

Onorato, Michael. *A Brief Review of American Interest in Philippine Development and Other Essays*. Berkeley, Calif.: McCutchan Publishing Corporation, 1968.

————. *Leonard Wood and the Philippine Cabinet Crisis of 1923*. Manila, Philippines: University of Manila, 1967.

*Order of Battle of the United States Land Forces in the World War: American Expeditionary Forces*. Washington, D.C.: Government Printing Office, 1937.

Ostrower, Gary B. *Collective Insecurity: The United States and the League of Nations during the Early Thirties*. Lewisburg, Pa.: Bucknell University Press, 1979.

Palmer, Frederick. *Bliss, Peacemaker*. New York: Dodd, Mead and Company, 1934.

Pearlman, Michael. *To Make Democracy Safe for America*. Urbana: University of Illinois Press, 1984.

Pier, Arthur S. *American Apostles to the Philippines*. Boston: Beacon Press, 1950.

Pogue, Forrest C. *George C. Marshall: Education of a General*. New York: Viking Press, 1963.

Prange, Gordon W. *At Dawn We Slept: The Untold Story of Pearl Harbor*. New York: McGraw-Hill Book Company, 1981.

Rappaport, Armin. *Henry L. Stimson and Japan, 1931–1933*. Chicago: University of Chicago Press, 1963.

Reilly, Hugh J. *Americans All: The Rainbow At War*. Columbus, Ohio: F. J. Heer Company, 1936.

Richardson, John Philip. "The American Military Mission to Armenia." M.A. thesis, George Washington University, 1964.

Sands, William Franklin. "Basil Miles: An Appreciation." *American Foreign Service Journal* 7 (March 1930): 79–82.

————. *Our Jungle Diplomacy*. Chapel Hill: University of North Carolina Press, 1944.

Sapin, Burton M., and Snyder, Richard C. *The Role of the Military in American Foreign Policy*. Garden City, N.Y.: Doubleday and Company, 1954.

Sargent, Herbert H. *The Campaign of Santiago de Cuba*. 3 vols. Chicago: A. C. McClurg and Company, 1907.

Schaller, Michael. *The American Occupation of Japan*. New York: Oxford University Press, 1985.

————. "MacArthur's Japan: The View from Washington." *Diplomatic History* 10 (Winter 1986): 1–23.

Schmidt, Hans. *Maverick Marine: General Smedley D. Butler and the Contradictions of American Military History*. Lexington: University Press of Kentucky, 1987.

Schulzinger, Robert D. *The Making of the Diplomatic Mind*. Middletown, Conn.: Wesleyan University Press, 1975.

————. *The Wise Men of Foreign Affairs*. New York: Columbia University Press, 1984.

Scott, James Brown. *Robert Bacon: Life and Letters*. Garden City, N.Y.: Doubleday, Page and Company, 1923.

Shoup, Laurence A., and Minter, William. *Imperial Brain Trust: The Council on Foreign Relations and United States Foreign Policy*. New York: Monthly Review Press, 1977.

Smith, Robert Freeman. *The United States and Revolutionary Nationalism in Mexico, 1916–1932*. Chicago: University of Chicago Press, 1972.

Smythe, Donald. *Guerrilla Warrior: The Early Life of John J. Pershing*. New York: Charles Scribner's Sons, 1973.

———. *Pershing: General of the Armies*. Bloomington: Indiana University Press, 1986.

*Songs of the Class of '97*. Highland Falls, N.Y.: News of the Highlands Print, 1895.

Stanley, Peter W. *A Nation in the Making: The Philippines and the United States, 1899–1921*. Cambridge, Mass.: Harvard University Press, 1974.

Steward, T. G. *The Colored Regulars*. Philadelphia: A. M. E. Book Concern, 1904.

Stimson, Henry L. *The Far Eastern Crisis: Recollections and Observations*. New York: Harper and Brothers, 1936.

Theis, H. Jordan. "Colonel Gordon Johnston." *The Cavalry Journal* 43 (Nov.–Dec. 1934): 48.

Thomas, Lowell. *Old Gimlet Eye: The Adventures of Smedley D. Butler*. New York: Farrar and Rinehart, 1933.

Thompson, Wayne Wray. "Governors of the Moro Province: Wood, Bliss, and Pershing in the Southern Philippines, 1903–1913." Ph.D. dissertation, University of California at San Diego, 1975.

Thorne, Christopher. *The Limits of Foreign Policy: The West, the League, and the Far Eastern Crisis of 1931–1933*. New York: G. P. Putnam's Sons, 1973.

Tokyo Municipal Office. *The Reconstruction of Tokyo*. Tokyo: Kawaguchi Printing Works, 1933.

U.S. Military Academy, Class of 1897. *Commemoration of the 25th Anniversary of Graduation*. West Point, N.Y.: n.p., 1922.

———. *The Howitzer*. Philadelphia: n.p., 1897.

Upton, Emory. *The Military Policy of the United States*. Washington, D.C.: Government Printing Office, 1904; reprint ed., Washington, D.C.: Government Printing Office, 1917.

Vagts, Alfred. *Defense and Diplomacy: The Soldier and the Conduct of Foreign Relations*. New York: King's Crown Press, 1956.

Weigley, Russell F., ed. *The American Military*. Reading, Mass.: Addison, Wesley Publishing Company, 1969.

———. *Towards an American Army: Military Thought from Washington to Marshall*. New York: Columbia University Press, 1962.

Weil, Martin. *A Pretty Good Club*. New York: W. W. Norton & Company, 1978.

Wheeler, Gerald E. "Republican Philippine Policy, 1921–1933." *Pacific Historical Review* 28 (November 1959): 377–390.

Wiebe, Robert H. *The Search for Order, 1877–1920*. New York: Hill and Wang, 1967.

Wilgus, William J. *Transporting the A.E.F. in Western Europe, 1917–1919*. New York: Columbia University Press, 1931.

Williams, William Appleman. *American-Russian Relations, 1781–1947*. New York: Octagon Books, 1971.

———, ed. *From Colony to Empire: Essays in the History of American Foreign Relations*. New York: John Wiley and Sons, 1972.

Wohlstetter, Roberta. *Pearl Harbor: Warning and Decision*. Stanford, Calif.: Stanford University Press, 1962.

Wolfson, Marguerite. "In the Spirit of Manila." *Asia* 24 (February 1924): 96–101, 146–148.

Wood, Bryce. *The United States and Latin American Wars, 1932–1942*. New York: Columbia University Press, 1966.

Wood, Leonard. "The Existing Conditions and Needs in Cuba." *North American Review* 168 (May 1899): 593–601.

————. "The Military Government of Cuba." *The Annals of the American Academy of Political and Social Sciences* 21 (January 1903): 153–182.

Zook, David H., Jr. *The Conduct of the Chaco War.* N.p.: Bookman Associates, 1960.

# Index